MORE MOHAVE MYTHS

West of River			East of River
1	Hamulye-tɬieme		
2	Amaṭ-kuvataqanye		
A	Miakwa'orve		
4	Amaṭa-hotave		
5	Hanemo-'ara		
6	Aksam-kusaveve		
7	δokupita-toδompove		
B	Avi-kutaparve		
8	Avi-itɬierqe	←→ A	Iδo-kuva'ire
		1	KwilyeΘki
		2	Avi-tutara
		3	Nyamasave-kwahave
C	Avi-kwa-'ahwaṭa	6	Aqwer-tunyive
		7	Ahtɬye-'iksamata
		9	Amaṭ-kukyeta
		B	Qara'erve
		10	Hukeiyeme
10	Aha-kwaΘo'ilye	10x	Malyko-vetɬierqe
11	HukΘara-tɬimanive	C	Selye'aye-kumitɬe
12	Ahmo-ke-tɬimpape	D	Sukwily-'ihu
13	Muhunyake	12	Aha-havasu
		E	Aqwaq-iove
		14	Hanyo-kumasΘeve
		15	Kuya-k-aqwaΘa
		15x	Moδilye-halye-tapmeve
D	Mat-aqwaΘ-kutɬyepe	←→ F	Selye'aye-tumatɬ
		17	Amai-nye-qotase
		18	Aha-kevare
E	Hokusave	←→ G	Kamahnulye
16	Oyatɬ-ukyulyuve		
17	Akatai-vasalyve		
F	Hatɬioqvatveve	←→ H	(A)ha-ıoδape
		Hx	Aha-kumaΘe'e
		20	Vanyor-ivava
		20a	Kamus-huvutatɬe
		20b	Akyase-t-Θitɬive
		21	Aha-tɬepuve
		21a	Hia-tukoro
G	Amaṭ-kusayi	←→ I	Qav-kuvaha
		Ix	Hamka-vaδulve
20	Av'a-Θemulye	←→ 22	Tɬies-ivave
		23	Aha-'anya
H	Avi-haiy-kwa'ampa	←→ J	Amaṭ-tasilyke
		Jx	AΘ'i-kupome
		24	Sa'ontɬive, Seqwaltɬive
		24a	Ahahta
		25	Aha-kupinye, -kuminye
21	Selye'aye-itɬierqe	←→ 26	Aqaq-nyi-va
22	Amaṭ-kaputɬor-a, -ilyase		
22a	Kutɬes-ta'orve		
23	Θono-hiδauve		
24	Horrave-iδauve, Korrave-		
25	Ihne-va'uve		
J	Save-tɬivuta	←→ K	Ah'a-kwinyevai
		27	Aha-kukwinve
		28	Aha-kwa'a'i
		28x	Avi-nye-va
		28y	Hwat-imave
		L	Hivistive
		Lx	Asta-kwanakwe
K	Analy-ohwele	29	Av'a-ku-tanakwe,
			Akyas-ku-ΘaraΘara
27	Amaṭ-kwohoatɬe	30	Hatom-kwiδike
28	Tohopav-'ivave	31	Sate-hiraitɬive
29	Avi-kwe-satuve	N	Hoturveve
		34	Amaṭ-kunive
29a	KwamhaΘeve	O	Savet-toha
		Ox	Ahaṭ-haiy-'apmeve
		P	Apen-yi-va
		36	Aha-qwalinyo
		R	Honyave-hetɬqwantɬive
		38	Taiye-huyi
		S	Qaqauve
		Sx	Hamkye-nye-va
30	Akwanva-'averve	←→ 39	Hoskyive-yetukyere
30a	Ahtotahto	40	Nyahveve, Nyahweyeve
30b	Numika-vakirta	T	Va'orve
		U	Hanyo-hane
		43	Avi-tɬitɬe
		44	Nyitɬerqa-'ulyive
		44x	Ispany-kwiyu
		45	Ipaktem-vatɬutɬi-vavitɬe (J9)
31	Hatalompa	←→ V	KwiΘa'oqa
31a	Turise		
32	Ahpaly-kiv'ava		
32a	Avi-motohayi		
33	Kuhu'inye	X	Sampuly-k-uvare
L	Mepuk-tɬivauve	←→ Y	Atɬqaqa
		Z	Kwaparvete

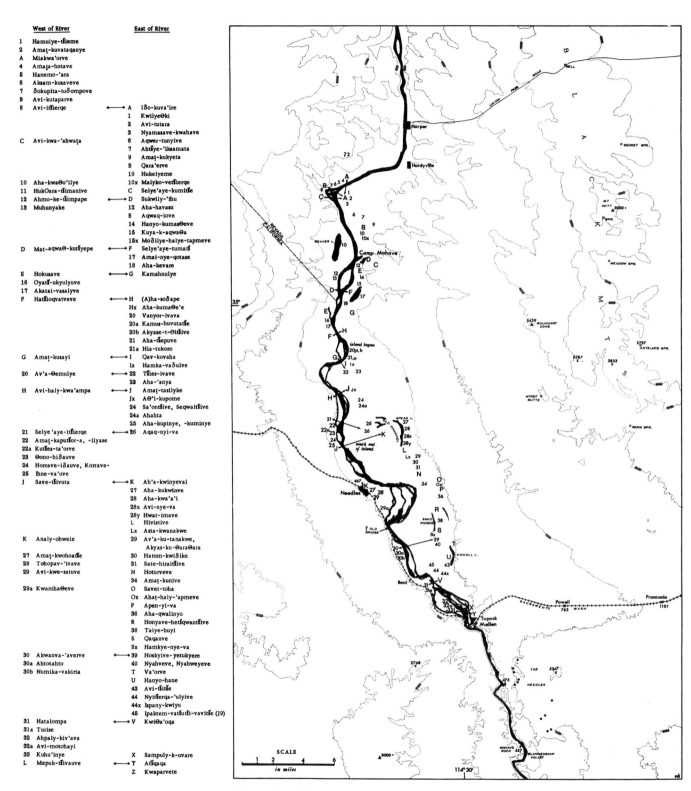

SCALE

1 2 3 4 5 6

in miles

SOURCE: UC-AR 11:2.   MAP 1—MOHAVE VALLEY

MORE MOHAVE MYTHS

BY

A. L. KROEBER

ANTHROPOLOGICAL RECORDS
Volume 27

UNIVERSITY OF CALIFORNIA PRESS
BERKELEY · LOS ANGELES · LONDON
1972

UNIVERSITY OF CALIFORNIA PUBLICATIONS

ANTHROPOLOGICAL RECORDS

Advisory Editors: J. B. Birdsell, D. J. Crowley, E. A. Hammel, R. F. Heizer,
Roger Keesing, C. W. Meighan, H. P. Phillips, A. C. Spaulding

Volume 27

Approved for publication June 11, 1970

Issued January 31, 1972

University of California Press
Berkeley and Los Angeles
California

University of California Press, Ltd.
London, England

PREFACE

The manuscript copy of this monograph was the last scholarly task to which Kroeber gave completed form. He finished it in August of 1960, three or four days before leaving for his conference in Burg Wartenstein, Austria, on Anthropological Horizons. Now, in the autumn of 1967, Professor Robert Heizer and I have only just read the manuscript. At long last it goes to complete the Mohave Myths Trilogy, as Kroeber wished it to do, becoming the third of the series, the first and second of which are Seven Mohave Myths and A Mohave Historical Epic (UC-AR 11:1, 2).

The reader will note that whereas most of the tales were collected by Kroeber in the early 1900s, the Satukhota and Tortoise narratives, Nos. 18 and 19, and the geographical data in this volume were not collected until the 1950s. This came about through Kroeber's going, in the Februarys of 1953 and 1954, to Parker, Arizona, on the Colorado River and more or less in the center of the Mohave Reservation, where he did some weeks of field work. He was accompanied by his wife and a graduate student and was joined in Parker by Mohaves who became his informants and guides and, when necessary, his interpreters.

These were his last field trips and they were immensely rewarding to him for a number of reasons, a principal one being his satisfaction in doing what he had always wanted to do but had felt until then he could not take time for: To spend the hours and days needed to retrace and identify as far as possible (and it is possible to an amazing degree) the routes, overnight stopping places, and sites mentioned in the song cycles—places that are the scaffolding of the dreamed tales Mohaves tell. Some of the tales are wholly grounded geographically; in others the literal accuracy of the geography fades as the dream carries the dreamer farther and farther from home. On the desert and on the river Kroeber and his companions followed the dreams, mapping them as minutely as they could. In a shallow-bottomed boat, which would not hang up on the shifting red-silt peaks that build up under water from the river bed, they even reached Avikwama, the place of origin of the Mohave people. There they beached their boat and took pictures of that old and sacred site where everything began.

We have re-placed Kroeber's Epilogue at the beginning of the volume as a Prologue, even though it is plain from its first sentence that it was written only after the manuscript was completed; it seemed lost, buried back behind the Appendices. When he wrote finis, in August of 1960, fifty-nine years after his first Mohave field trip in 1901, there must have been some at-the-back-of-the-mind sense that this might well be the last field report he would be making. And thus it was he wrote a few pages of summing-up, an almost intimate statement of how he felt toward the long task now done. Kroeber was little given to such declarations of faith in science and the scientist, that faith being left by him implicit in performance. The scientist Kroeber and more than a little of the artist Kroeber are palpable in the Prologue/Epilogue, and the man in both aspects may be followed by way of a delicate clue through the tales and what he says about them.

Theodora Kroeber
November 8, 1967

CONTENTS

PART II: DISCUSSION

TABLES

PROLOGUE/EPILOGUE

This has been a long undertaking, in time and in pages, and I want to consider in how far it may have been worth the expenditures.

Basically, it has been a "descriptive" job—the conveying to the intellectual world of an organized body of new information. That seems the main service which this volume renders; and I regard the service not deprecatingly but with satisfaction.

Intelligible description of course is not random itemization but an organized presentation with sufficient elucidation of background and context to make it meaningful in the culture to which it is presented. If the body of information conveyed has significance in the originating culture, it will have some significance in the receiving culture, though not an identical one. Some of the original values will be lost in the transfer; but new ones will be acquired within the incorporating culture, as it stores the information and values received—stores them mostly hidden away in its bone marrow, as it were. It is the task of the transmitter to keep the losses and malformations minimal, and to maximize the possible fidelity and value of what is transferred, by means of elucidation, comment, and initial comparisons. Full comparisons, in the sense of systematized ones, usually constitute a separate stage; but though often deferred, and sometimes long deferred, they can be provocatively suggested along with the original descriptive presentation. I have not done all that is possible in this respect, but I have done what time free of other claims permitted.

There are even matters of cross organization of content which I did not get around to developing, though they would have helped: thus, an ordered inventory of themes or motifs extracted from context association; also, an index of all native terms, which would be a special desideratum because Mohave is a language still without a grammar and therefore without standardized orthography, and my apperception, and therefore my spellings, varied somewhat between 1900 and 1954.

Preservation of the myths and tales rests essentially on my rendering of the Englishing of bilingual interpreters, with only proper names and places and occasional key words in the original tongue. It would undoubtedly have been more adequate to secure both the

Mohave and the English version, the former as a future check and authentication of the latter. This, however, would have involved analysis of the Mohave language to the point of working out the essentials of Mohave grammar, and would have manifolded, several times over, the years required to complete the present work. The question that confronted me in 1901 was whether to secure intensive documentation on a single group of languages and tribes in California, or a less intensive record of many. For better or worse, I chose the latter course; perhaps in part because it coincided with my personal curiosities, though it certainly also conformed with the program of responsibilities for research which brought me to the University of California at the beginning of my career. What I renounced doing with the Mohave language made possible perhaps most of what I did salvage and record on the Yurok, Yuki, Yokuts, Luiseño, and other tribes, and comparatively on native California as a whole.

I did record in writing some passages of myth in Mohave text, perhaps tolerable phonologically but only quite approximative in translation. These are listed in Appendix II, together with some additional passages recorded on phonograph cylinders, of which at least part were transferred, though with some loss of quality, to magnetic tape in recent years.

One obstacle that usually confronted me in the first decade or so of the century, when much of the languages and memories of native California still flourished, was that the Indians spoke only picked-up English. This was often fully adequate for conveying substantive information, but it made analysis of text into grammatical form, and any exact translating, difficult and time-consuming. By the time literate interpreters had grown up, the aged people who knew the substance of old narratives and rituals had pretty well died off. The languages as such mostly survived two or three decades, but now those who can even speak them fully and correctly have generally become very few.

In a partly completed manuscript of Yurok myths and tales, probably more bulky than this volume, I have recorded a comparison between versions of some narratives by the same narrator in text and in English. As regards content there is always some difference, but it is usually not great, and more often the English-told version is the fuller. This is because the slowness of the writing down of dictated native text elicited in informants a reaction toward compression and omission. I am speaking only of narrative substance. Style of course is inherently dependent on the language that is the medium.

While this volume, then, is a sort of truncated yet basic edition of Mohave formalized narrative, nearly all of which they themselves partly profess and partly believe to have acquired by personal dreaming—and in which I believe there reside some permanent values to the world at large—I have tried to fulfill also the ancillary duties of an editor. Versions of the Satukhota tale, which seems aesthetic rather than religious in motivation, having been published from two other tribes of Yuman stock, I have dissected all three intensively in order to compare them, since there can be no doubt that historically they are renderings of a single original tale. I have not brought together the comparable creation or origin myths of the Yuman tribes and those of southern California because they are so diverse as to need special and separate treatment. But I have in table 1 made an outline concordance of "creation" incidents that occur in my Mohave collection. I have also computed the frequency of expression in the corpus of several diverse features: human emotion, imagery of landscape or atmosphere, didacticism, and magic. This is a haphazard array, but it is a beginning of generalized characterization, which others may extend to corpuses from other tribes, or expand by compiling additional features in Mohave. The sections on tale itineraries and topographic detail I worked out at first because I felt compelled to know the geography which was so intimately interwoven with most of the narratives. I left it in the volume for others because it is an integral part of the native documentation. It can be ignored by those not interested; yet who so wishes can experience it, and more fully relive the Mohave stories, especially with a few free days in a car.

I see my job in this volume as one of scholarship in the old-fashioned sense. It is work which one probably cannot do properly unless one likes the doing,

and the doing can come close to becoming an obsessive addiction. It is work which one does in a sense humbly, yet with a pride of responsibility to certain standards, and to an elite to which one thereby belongs. As separate individuals, the larger world may treat scholars with some seeming negligence; but I have always found that in principle the world mostly respects and values scholarship, and passes a due measure of this respect on from our class to us as individuals. It may understand and want to understand only a small part of what we achieve; but it takes for granted that what we aim at is worthwhile and commendable.

In return, I believe we owe a respect to our materials, to the knowledge we control and try to extend. Knowledge is the basis of understanding; and all increase of knowledge leads potentially to increase of understanding and a truer living, for each of us and for all. We should content ourselves with the pleasure and satisfactions which new insights bring to their discoverer. Control of knowledge is more than an opportunity to display virtuosity and earn plaudits. While the continuing goal of all science is deeper insight and ever more new understanding, much of this follows almost inevitably from increase of properly organized knowledge. I do not deny originality nor genius; but without knowledge, even genius can do little. Almost always it is when ideas and theories are forced on us by phenomena that they become sound and important. The scientist who sheds his load of knowledge to rise to greater heights by superior intellection alone, is trying to enhance himself, not his work; and he may end up by doing tours de force or uttering jargon.

I have long pondered to whom we owe the saving of human religious and aesthetic achievements such as are recorded here. It is probably not to the group that produced them. Why should we preserve Mohave values when they themselves cannot preserve them, and their descendants will likely be indifferent? It is the future of our own world culture that preservation of these values can enrich, and our ultimate understandings grow wider as well as deeper thereby.

                                                    A.L.K.

MORE MOHAVE MYTHS

BY
A. L. KROEBER

INTRODUCTION

This monograph supplements two preceding ones that have appeared, namely "Seven Mohave Myths" of 1948 and "A Mohave Historical Epic" of 1951 (UC-AR 11:1, 2); and it completes the presentation of mythical and legendary material that I obtained from the Mohave. Since the two previous publications embodied 8 narratives, the newly presented ones are numbered in continuation, from 9 to 19.

There are included here two narratives (Nos. 9, 10) and a third incomplete one (No. 15) that I recorded in or around Needles in 1902 and 1903; a repeat of the published Cane story No. 1, as present No. 17, by the same informant, Bluebird, secured for comparison after a four years' interval in 1908; three recognized narratives (Nos. 11, 12, 13) and part of a doctor's dreaming (No. 16G), all told by an informant at the University of California in 1910; the Goose song-tale (No. 14), recorded at the University in 1905 by the same narrator who then also told Nyohaiva (No. 3), already published (UC-AR 11:1, pp. 27-36); and various fragments (Nos. 16A-G).

Finally, there are added two narratives, Nos. 18 and 19, which I wrote down at Parker in 1953 and 1954 as evidence that some of the older Mohave were still preserving their religious culture essentially intact more than fifty years after I first encountered it. I was pleased to note this preservation, not only because of interest in the culture, but also because the discovery

freed ethnologists of native California from the imputed onus of having had to go out of business because their Indians had completely lost knowledge of their aboriginal culture. If the budding anthropologists of today no longer collect local ethnography, it is because they have substituted new interests and because many of them would not know how to elicit ethnographical data, having learned about primitive culture chiefly in the abstract, not having absorbed into their minds the extant record of it for California.

The new data are presented here much as before: the English text of each tale, with or without a summarized outline, and preceded by an account of the narrator, the circumstances of his narrating, and statements by him or others as to the nature and function of the tale. Where it seemed feasible and advantageous, the song scheme of tales is discussed, or variant versions, or resemblances between distinct tales. For one story, No. 18, Satukhota, outlines are given of full versions of the same tale as preserved from two other Yuman tribes—Diegueño and Halchidhoma—and an endeavor is made to reconstruct its history.

Toward the end of the monograph, in Part II, there is a discussion of over-all features of Mohave mythology as regards certain features of content. And a final section in Part II summarizes, organizes, and corrects both previous and new data on the topography that underlies and permeates this highly localized body of mythology.

ABBREVIATIONS

These tales form a third installment of Mohave myths. The first installment, Seven Mohave Myths (UC-AR 11:1, 1948), contained the following:

1. Cane
2. Vinimulye-pātše
3. Nyohaiva
4. Raven
5. Deer
6. Coyote
7. Mastamho

The second installment was the following:

8. A Mohave Historical Epic (UC-AR 11:2, 1951)

PHONETIC SYMBOLS AND DIACRITICS

θ	English surd th, as in thick
δ	English voiced th, as in this
tš	English ch
ṭ	Palatal t, with effect nearly of English tr
q	Velar k
ny, ly	Palatalized n, l, as in onion, million; the y is not a vowel
ā, ī, ū	Long
ê, ô	Long, open

PART I

NARRATIVES

THE INFORMANT

This "creation tale" was secured in March 1902, from Nyavarup, near Needles. Jack Jones interpreted.

Nyavarup was an old man and a confessed doctor. This latter is in accord with his being willing to tell about first origins, which most Mohave are afraid to narrate—at least avowedly and systematically—and sometimes even fear to hear told, because this lore is associated with doctoring or being a doctor. I suppose the association and reluctance are because the central theme of the earlier part of the Origins myth is the illness and death of Matavilya, the great first god that died. Personally, however, Nyavarup, as an old man, had little to fear from practice as a curing doctor or from his avowal thereof. In fact, as will be seen, he spoke of his shamanistic power with a certain pride.

Nyavarup was also a historic character, though I did not know it at the time of our acquaintance. He is mentioned several times, as "Navarupe," in Möllhausen's 1860 account in German of the Ives ascent of the Colorado River in 1858 in the steamer "Explorer," as being a friendly young fellow who voluntarily attached himself to the expedition.[1] When the steamer had to turn back, a German cook volunteered to go on up with Nyavarupe on foot to see if they could reach the Virgin River upstream on the right bank. They left on March 14, 1858, and rejoined the steamer on March 18 with a successful report.[2] Next day, Navarupe was sent downriver ahead of the steamer with a message to chiefs Kairook and Mesikehota.[3]

In 1902, Nyavarup said this about himself:

I saw all that I am telling about Mastamho: I was there when it happened. Only some men were there, those who are doctors. I shall see it all again tonight, when I dream.

No, doctors do not learn from older doctors: they are born to be doctors; they learn only from Mastamho.

[1] Möllhausen, 1860, 1:395.
[2] Ibid., 2:408.
[3] Ibid., 2:409.

There are four sicknesses I can cure:
1. Pains in the back.
2. When a baby gets sick with a cough from its father or mother eating the black seeds called kovθo.
3. From getting hit with a stick.[4]
4. A small child sick from eating food cooked with the wood of kutšiêrse, a plant with hooked thorns [cholla cactus? catsclaw acacia?].
There are other sicknesses I can treat.[5]
5. A baby passing blood from its father having eaten the remnants of birds killed but only partly devoured by a "chicken hawk" [atšyôre, falcon, probably] or large hawk [sokwilye-akatai].
6. Sickness from eating birds, rabbits, or deer killed by oneself, or fish one has caught. This sickness is painless; one lies around, sleeps, does not feel right. A man may eat his own fish if the net in which he has caught them is old; but if it is new, he will go out of his mind and will work his hands as if making a net. He becomes sick because the ghosts (nyaveδi) of the fish he caught take away his shadow (matkwisa), and he becomes weak and sleepy. Then I bring back his shadow by singing what Mastamho told me to sing for this, and by blowing saliva on him.

These six illnesses I cure: I have a song for each. I learned the songs from Mastamho. He sang them to me as he stood by me, and told me for what to use it. I would not have known them if he had not taught them to me. He also said to me to blow my spittle white [frothy], not black [clear]. He told me to keep this in my heart. If Mastamho had told me to cure like the white people, with medicine, I would have known how to do that; but he did not tell me.

He also told me how to catch fish. He told me to take a pointed stick of arrowweed[6] and pierce the lower jaw of the fish as I took them from the net. He called this stick tinyam-esīrqa.[7] So I am good at fishing; I can always make a catch.

[4] Reference probably is not to a bruise or bone broken by a blow from another person, but to a branch or twig springing back against one and making him ill magically. Cf. UC-AR 11:1, p. 46, first paragraph, about a female doctor's powers.
[5] Sic by informant. Four is ritually and habitually so dominant in Mohave culture that he fell into the pattern, though he had immediately to expand it to the secondary pattern of six.
[6] Iθava, Pluchea sericea.
[7] Night-(?); a mythological-ritual or dream name.

I can go at any time to ask Mastamho whatever I want to know: I could go tonight. It does not take me long to reach him.

When a baby is still in the belly, and also after he is born and lies there looking up, that is when he goes to Mastamho at Avikwame, every night. When he is larger, he begins to understand; when he is so big [gesture] he knows; when he is an old man, he knows it fully.

Besides this semipersonal information, Nyavarup imparted to me the Alyha myth, here included as No. 10; an account of Mountain Lion's and Jaguar's (or Wolf's) institutings, No. 16A; and a brief Coyote tale, No. 16B.

THE TELLING

When I visited Needles in 1902, my knowledge of Mohave culture and my hearing of Mohave speech were still in a preliminary stage. My only previous visit, late in 1900, had lasted only about a week. The orthography of names is visibly imperfect in the tale that follows.

I was also somewhat unskilled in handling an informant as regards a lengthy narration, and Jack Jones was only in the stage of learning to be an ethnologist's aid and interpreter. These circumstances necessitate some statements as to what was done with the dictation and translation as written down.

This narrative is here presented with its parts arranged somewhat differently from the order in which they were dictated. The sequence followed in print is, as nearly as seems probable, the sequence of events in the story. The narrator, however, did not begin at the beginning, with the production of living beings— gods, men, and animals—by Heaven and Eart as primal parents. He began instead with Mastamho, when he succeeded the elder god Matavilya on the latter's death. This is just what informant Jo Nelson did when he told his version of Origins, to which I assigned the name Mastamho myth as it has been printed (UC-AR 11:1, pp. 50-68). Beginning thus is in accord with the general mythologic practice of the Mohave, to whom the causer of origins, physical and cultural, the institutor, is always Mastamho. Matavilya does not really institute, produce, or create anything of consequence, except to build a house at Ha'avulypo. His essential function in the myth is to die, after handing on leadership and direction to Mastamho. His slow death, including disposal of his remains, forms a sort of landscape or backdrop against which the beginnings of most Mohave myths are set, either by explicit recounting of particular episodes in Matavilya's death and funeral, or by allusion or implicit reference.

When Nyavarup on the second day had completed his consecutive narrative of "how the world began,"

and it was evident that it did not contain anything as to actual first origins, in our sense, I asked about these, and was given a series of episodes about Sky and Earth and Matavilya and his death, which I have put together as part A of the myth—the narrator's main story, as he told it first, being printed as part B. It was evident at once, however, that this Matavilya material did not form a consecutive, connected whole in the informant's mind, as did the Mastamho narrative. Earlier and later episodes of part A were mixed by him in random order; and before long there was a shift of interest back to Mastamho, and new (or revised) incidents about him were told. In part, but only in part, this confusion may have been caused by me injecting occasional questions.[8] Yet I would hardly have done this if the narrator had continued to follow a thread of his own initiative, as he had while dealing with Mastamho. But now he would tell an episode or two as if they were discrete, then either go on to something different that occurred to him, or wait for me to ask about a topic.[8] In any event, it is clear that what he had in his memory about Matavilya and the actual origin of the world was much less organized than what he knew about Mastamho and the instituting of things; it was more like a sketchy or broken background; and this difference is significant.

My rearrangement therefore does some violence to the full native patterning of the basic mythology, but I have thought the rearrangement necessary in order to save the content of the thought from seeming incoherently confused to us. The order in which the paragraphs of the story as it is given here were actually written down, is as follows:

March 10, 1902: 10-23

March 11, 1902: 24-41, 9, 42-44, 50, 1, 5, 3, 2, 6, 8, 7, 4; then material on curing and other matters; then 45-46, 49, 48, 47.

(March 12, 1902: The Alyha institutional myth, No. 10.)

It will be seen that the Mastamho part of the story, 10-50, is given as originally told, except that 9 has been taken out and transferred by me to the end of the Matavilya part; and except that 45-49, which were told separately later, have been inserted by me in the consecutive Mastamho story just before the end, where they would belong by the compulsion of our logic of clarity and order.[9]

The full presentation herewith has been preceded by an outline (pp. 314-316) in a comparative article by me in 1906 on southern California creations myths.[10]

---

[8] By modern technique, of course, one does not ask until one has to, and then is careful to note the question as well as the answer. The former rule I generally observed from a sort of tact, in 1902; the latter was not yet practiced in those more casual days.

[9] This last transposition no doubt partly accounts for the differences between the accounts of the sending away of the tribes in 9:43 and in 9:45-46; but only partly, since the "conflicting" paragraphs were told on the same day.

[10] "Two Myths of the Mission Indians," JAFL 19:309-321, 1906.

MORE MOHAVE MYTHS

Narrative 9
ORIGINS

THE ORIGIN MYTH

Part A: Matavilya

1. Ammaya, Sky, was a man, the father of all; Amaṭa, Earth, a woman; all beings were born from them in the same day—Matavilya, Mastamho, people, plants, and everything else. They were born far west across the ocean at Pi'in,[11] in darkness: there was no day then. Matavilya was the first to be born; the others followed. Now he came from there, from the west, leading the rest. He did not walk in coming here; he moved without stepping, turning to the right and left, to right and left, four times [like sliding]: in four motions he arrived here, and all the people followed. At Pi'in Sky and Earth are still having intercourse; Sky constantly comes down to Earth and rises again.

2. When Matavilya reached this land, he had no wife, but he said, "This is my daughter, (Blue-)green Flat, Havasum-kukelape." He was a young man, Mastamho a little boy, Frog a girl. Hiqo[12] came with them from the west. To the east the world is high; toward the west it is low. They had climbed up eastward until they came near the center of the earth. Now Matavilya was measuring with his hands outstretched: one of them did not reach to the end. Then he moved on a little, measured again, and each hand touched: so he knew that where he stood was the middle of the earth.[13] He said: "This is the middle: here I will stay and build a house." There he built it; at Ha'avulypo.[14]

3. When Matavilya built his house there, it was dark, but he had no wood for it: he made the timbers, out of nothing. Now he was lying near the center of the house; his daughter lay with her head to the south, just west of the door.[15] Matavilya went out to relieve himself, crawling on hands and knees, and in passing in the dark he put his hand on her privates. Outdoors, he turned west. Frog sank down into the ground and traveled along. After a time she came up and looked for Matavilya; sank again and traveled on until she came up under him. He did not see her: his feces dropped into her gaping mouth and she swallowed them.[16] Then she returned to the house and lay down. Soon Matavilya came back also. He was sick, and crying from pain: "Eh! eh! eh!" Frog said: "My father, what is the matter?" He said, "I am sick." He lay down

[11] Nothing further has been learned about Pi'in from other Mohave, and Pi'in does not sound like a Mohave word. Pimu is Catalina Island in Shoshonean, but I am negatively doubtful about any connection.

[12] Also Haiqo or Haiko; the ordinary name for whites. The name is used also in some neighboring languages, such as Chemehuevi (UC-PAAE, 4:107, 1907).

[13] Like Water-skate in Zuni mythology. Cushing, BAE-R, 13:428, 1896.

[14] Aha-'av-'ulypo, "Water-house-post," i.e., House-post-water, several pinnacles (plate 1, e) some two miles or so from the Colorado River in the flat-bottomed wash up Eldorado Canyon, a tributary arroyo from the west, perhaps 25 miles below Hoover Dam. After Matavilya's death, Mastamho made the river to wash away his house, ashes, and bones (below, 9:12, 14-18). Ha'av'ulypo is referred to also in 4:1; 5:1; 7:1-6, 11 (UC-AR 11:1, pp. 38, 52-53, 54); and below, 11:1, 12:3, 13:1, 17:1b, 19:1.

[15] Which is invariably on the south of the house.

[16] This is a widespread motive in the southern California dying-god myth, and of course is an exemplification of contagious-sympathetic magic; but the Mohave only laugh at the idea of its being a present-day technique of bewitching. "The witch would vomit," one of them said.

with his head to the east. Then he lay with his head to the north: he spat blood. Thereupon he lay with his head to the west: now he spat his white saliva. Hĩqo knew that the red which he spat was gold and that the white was silver; but the people did not know it. Then Matavilya lay with his head to the south[17] and sweated. His sweat is ore: it is mined in the mountains. He said: "I cannot endure this any longer. I am going where it is dark. I will be gone." Then he died.

4. As Matavilya had lain dying, he covered himself with a net, ihulye, and said: "I am content." He called the net uyatetonikwanyai. He called it also ihatškutšule. That is why people have nets now.[18]

5. When Matavilya became sick, he said to one who was sitting on the west side of the house: "Come here: sit close by." He was Hĩqo, but Matavilya called him Koro-koro-pa.[19] Now Frog, his daughter, put her hands on Matavilya's breast. She said to Koro-koro-pa: "Come, Matavilya is nearly dead"; but Koro-koro-pa, sitting there at the west of the house, said nothing. He made a hole, sank down out of the house, and went off westward,[20] making a loud noise. He went back to Pi'in where Matavilya and all of them had been born. He did not remain to see Matavilya and his house burned: that is why the whites do not burn the dead or their houses.

6. Matavilya did not speak loudly, and no on heard him. When he said: "Mastamho, come here," Mastamho paid no attention, for he was playing about. When Matavilya spoke to him again, he still did not listen. But when Matavilya was sick, he said once more in a low voice: "Come here! Listen. I want to give you my instructions." Then Mastamho came and stood by him and leaned toward him to listen with his right ear.[21]

[17]Antisunwise circuit, E, N, W, S.
[18]An obscure paragraph, both as to general purpose and the meaning of the terms.
[19]Meaning unknown.
[20]The direction usually assigned to whites. The Spaniards simultaneously came overland from Sonora, via the Yuma, and sailing up the coast, but their permanent missions and presidios were near the coast west of the Mohave. The Americans from the east of course arrived three-quarters of a century later, in the lifetime of men like the narrator.
[21]As in 9:10.

7. The sun, the moon, and the stars were made by Mastamho. Matavilya had told him to make them. He said to him: "Do what I am telling you now. These people are unable, but you can do it."

8. If Matavilya had lived, everyone would have lived forever; but because he died and was burned, everybody dies. The small lizard[22] said, "I wish people to die. If they all keep on growing, there will be no room. There will be no place to go to; if we defecate, the excrement will fall on someone's foot." So people began to die. If lizard had not said this, no one would die.

This same lizard was later sent eastward by Mastamho to see if the ma-selye'aye seeds were growing. Another lizard, Kwatulye, was sent westward by him to see how the kwaθepilye seeds were growing.[23]

9. Frog was afraid that she would be killed for having been the cause of Matavilya's death. So she sank back into the ground and fled from Ha'avulypo. She came up to the south, at Na'aikunyilaqa,[24] and opened her mouth wide to cool it. Then she sank down again and came up across the river at Hanyiko-itš-qwampa.[25] When she emerged there, she still heard the people crying for Matavilya and continued afraid. So she went back into the ground and traveled on. She came up again at another Hanyiko-itš-qwampa, to the south of the first. But she sank down once more, and finally emerged far southeast. She said: "I will not go farther. I will always stay here. This mountain will be called (H)Ikwe-nye-va."[26]

[22]Unfortunately, the native name was not recorded. The previous sentence makes this passage superfluous; but the theme of lizard and coyote, or meadowlark and coyote, determining human life and death occurs elsewhere in California, and it evidently drifted into the Mohave scheme of origins as an extra.
[23]For these desert seeds, see 9:22, 24, 47, and note 53, below; also, in 7:15 (UC-AR 11:1, p. 55), both are planted by Mastamho for the Chemehuevi. According to Castetter, kwaθepilya is sage, chia, Salvia columbariae. Ma-selye'aye is unidentified and may be the also unidentified sile' of Walapai, Havasupai, and Yavapai.
[24]A mountain northerly of Needles, W of the river, "still in California" (not Nevada).
[25]A conspicuous and large depression below the top of the mesa, a little north of east of Needles. It is above a white patch that is conspicuous on the slope of the mesa as seen from Needles. Hanyiko means frog; qwampa, emerge.
[26]"Clouds' home." Perhaps for Ikwe-nye-va, 8:102, note 90 (UC-AR 11:2, pp. 91, 161), and below, 19:55, a mountain near the confluence of Big Sandy and Santa Maria River. See also Part II, B, 4. Frog's fourth place of emergence is usually put in the general region of Phoenix, that is, Maricopa-Pima country.

Part B: Mastamho

DEATH

10. Mastamho was a little boy. His name was Ikinye-humas-kuvupare.[27] He was playing about where Matavilya was sick. Matavilya told him to listen and Mastamho turned his head and listened with his right ear.[28] Then Matavilya spoke to him. Other people were there, and Hĭqo; but Hĭqo did not remain, and did not see Mastamho, for it was night. Instead, he sank into the ground and went out under the house and traveled off westward still underground, making a noise like an earthquake. It was still constantly dark then, nor were there any stars. Frog was sitting on the western side of the house. Matavilya lay in the middle of the house, near her, somewhat toward the same side of the house. The boy Mastamho stood leaning with his right hand on his knee, listening to him. Matavilya said: "Call them Ikinye-humas-kwatθarve." He meant the people, but he did not say so. Matavilya could no longer speak loudly, but Mastamho nevertheless heard him. As Frog sat there, she said: "Matavilya is dead." All those in the house heard, but remained throwing sand at each other in play as if they had not heard. Then Mastamho said: "Stop! Do not do that," and he spread out his arms. Then they all stopped playing. All of them still were little boys, but Mastamho was a little taller than the rest. They were the Mohave.

MOURNING

11. When Matavilya died, his head was toward the west. Then Mastamho, without touching him, turned him around so that his head lay to the south. Matavilya had said: "Inye-kuksanam ("lift me up!"). The Mohave now would say: "Inye-kumanam."[29] Then Mastamho turned him back, so that his head was toward the west again. Then he turned him so that his head was to the north. Then he turned him with his head to the south.[30] Then he said: "Lift him up!" So all took him up and carried him to the door; there they laid him down. Then they took him up again and carried him outside. Then they carried him a little farther to the south, and put him down again. Then

they carried him once more and deposited him on the pyre. It was four times that they had laid him down. Ikinye-humas-kuvitšiбe and Ikinye-humas-kuvatšiбomo[31] stood by his body.

12. Now there was no fire. Then Hatšinye-humas-kupāma, who was also called Ikinye-humas-kupāma,[32] went west to get fire. Now Frog,[33] Blue-green-flat, who was also called Girl-Child-Flat,[34] stood up and wanted to make fire but said: "I do not know what to do." Then she rubbed her hands against the back of her thighs, under her willow-bark dress. Mastamho stood in front of her and said: "That will not make fire." She tried again, standing by the pyre. Letting no one see what she was doing, she broke off a strand of the bark and rolled that against her thigh. Then it began to burn. Then they took dry arrowweed[35] and placed it at the four corners of the pyre; Mastamho called it yatam'o-ku-tinyam-va. Frog [sic, error of notation] lit the pile at the northeast corner. Then Ikinye-humas-ku-tinyame[36] took the burning piece from her and hastened with it to the other corners and lit them. Now Ikinye-humas-kupāma, who had gone away to bring fire, was coming back with it. From the distance he saw the funeral pyre burning. So he put away his fire where he stood, in the west. When he arrived, the pyre had already burned down. Then he threw himself into the ashes and rolled about in them.[37]

13. Han'ava[38] sat with his hands in his lap looking down. No one cried; no one paid any attention to the dead one who had been burned. Then Han'ava raised

---

[27] "Boy-child-kuvupare," if humas is the ritual equivalent of humar, "child."

[28] Cf. 9:6, and just below.

[29] Kuksanam and kumanam suggest the distortions in myth 7:44-47 (UC-AR 11:1, p. 67).

[30] One feels there ought to be a circuit of four, but the order recorded is (W) S W N S.

[31] "Boy-child-ku-vitšiбe" and "-ku-vatšiбomo."

[32] "Girl-child-lie(?)" and "Boy-child-lie(?)"—which is certainly surprising for the same person. I suspect confusion with the Hatšinye—name of Frog in the next sentence. In all other versions, it is Coyote who leaves to get fire.

[33] In most versions, Mohave (7:3, UC-AR 11:1, p. 53) or other, it is Fly-woman that makes fire by "washing" her hands like a fire-drill twirler.

[34] Havasum-kukelape or Hatšinye-humas-kukelape.

[35] Iθava, Pluchea sericea, used by the Mohave for arrows, thatch, housewalls, granaries, kindling or torches, swimming floats, mush-stirrers, and other purposes.

[36] "Boy-child-night." Cf. the Yatam'o-night-va name for arrowweed just before.

[37] As Hame'ulye-kwitše-iбulye does in 7:5 (UC-AR 11:1, p. 53). The episode of Coyote leaping over Badger and Raccoon to snatch and steal Matavilya's unconsumed heart (7:4) is lacking here.

[38] Han'ava is a strident insect frequently mentioned by the Mohave; probably a locust or cicada. It was here described as harmless, a finger-joint long, winged, frequenting mesquite trees, and of four "kinds": white, yellow, brown, black. The larva lives underground; and the chrysalis, or its shell, is called mat-kanyeve. For the four colors, compare the mountain sheep in Salt, 12:2, and Chuhueche, 13:15, the coyotes in Tumanpa, 11:44 and note 80, and the successive colors of Tortoise's beard in 19:69a.

his head and made a loud noise. Four times he did
this. Then the people there all began to weep; it
was he who caused them to.

14. When Matavilya had burned all to ashes,
Mastamho was nearly a grown man. Now he said to
the people there: "Listen! I will look after you
because Matavilya told me to do so. What do you
think of these ashes? Are they good?" They all said:
"No, they are not good." So Mastamho said: "Somehow I will bring it about that no one will see them
or be reminded of them." He was standing facing the
northwest. Four times he spoke. Then a heavy wind
blew from the northwest: he wanted the wind to blow
sand on the ashes and to cover them up. But the
wind only blew the ashes away and left the bones
lying visible to all.

15. Mastamho asked: "What do you think about
this?" They said: "It is not good." He said: "I will
try again." Then he spoke four times, to make hail
come: then it hailed. He wanted the bones to sink
into the ground; but after it stopped hailing, the
bones were still there.

16. Then Mastamho said: "I will do something
else: I will have a heavy rain." Then there was a
heavy rain. It came down like water; but after it
was over, the bones were lying there as before.

THE RIVER

17. Then Mastamho said: "Let us go north; I will
do differently." So they all went north with him. After
a short distance, he stood. Then he said: "Let us go
on again." They went a little way and stopped. When
they had rested, he said: "Let us go on again." After
the fourth stop, they did not go farther. Mastamho
had taken four steps. After each of his steps, the
people rested. After his fourth step, they stayed there.
Then he said: "We are all here now. This is my land.
I am the one who has done this. I call myself Ikinye-
humas-kuveδi. I call myself also Ikinye-humas-ku-
vetšinalye. I can create from my breath and my
saliva: I can make anything."[39]

18. Now he wanted to make water come, so he
made a staff and put it into the ground and drew it
out toward the north, and water came and ran northward. But he stood in its way and so stopped it. Then
he made it come out again and it flowed to the east.
So he stood east of it and stopped it. Then he drew

out his stick, and the water came and flowed to the
west, but he stepped in front of it and stopped it
once more. Then he put the stick into the ground
again and, as he drew it out, held it in front of him
and stepped aside and watched the water run. This
time it ran to the south.[40] It made the river.[41] Now
the people stood behind him: he was stretching out
his arms to hold them back.

19. Then a boat[42] came out and floated on the river.
It was white. Mastamho saw it coming and took hold
of it. He put the Mohave into it, and the Yavapai, the
Yuma, the Maricopa, the Kamia, and the Kohoalche-
Paiute.[43] As they went in, he held the prow; then he
entered himself and let the boat float. It went south
with the river. The six tribes sat around the edge of
the boat. Then Mastamho played with them. He tipped
the boat, and those on the lower side left their places
and sat along the opposite edge. Then he made that
side dip, and they all went to the other side. He was
doing that when the boat came to this country here.
He said: "You do not know what I am doing. I make
the boat lean to one side because I want the country
to be wide there. I make it lean to the other side
because I want the land to be flat there too."[44] When
they came to the Needles Peaks, the boat went straight
along and the river became narrow. Wherever the boat
went straight, the river went straight; where the boat
turned, the river now bends. When they came farther
down, where the Parker reservation is now, Mastamho
wanted to make more valley, so he again tipped the
boat to each side and made flat land on both sides of
the river. So they arrived at Yuma. Here he tipped
the boat first to the right and then to the left; so that
there the flat land is very wide and there are no
mountains except in the distance. Then they came to
the sea.[45] Then Mastamho took the people out of the
boat and let it float away.[46] He also threw his spear[47]
into the sea. That is why there are many animals in the sea.

20. Now the people wanted to go upriver again; but
Mastamho said: "If I let you go as you wish, you will
drown. I will take you." He was so tall that he set the

[39]Mohave heroes and gods and doctors are quite childlike
in their boasting.

[40]N, E, W, S—another circuit missed.
[41]The Colorado, of course, which is in many ways the
Nile of the Valley Yuman tribes.
[42]The nearest thing to a boat the Mohave had was a
pointed rush raft or balsa. "Boat" may have been substituted
for "balsa" after the whites (hiqo) began to intrigue the
Mohave imagination: it becomes a "ship" below, note 46.
7:12 (UC-AR 11:1, p. 54) names the boat kasukye.
[43]Six tribes, three farming and three desert. They are
enumerated differently in 9:43 and 9:45-46. Cf. notes 88, 90.
[44]Cf. 7:12 (UC-AR 11:1, p. 54).
[45]Gulf of California.
[46]"After Mastamho let the boat drift away, Hĩqo took it
and made a large ship of it; so the whites have ships."
[47]Of breath and saliva; probably his river-drawing staff
or cane.

people on his outstretched arms and hands and shoulders. Thus he started to go upstream through the water. When it became too deep, he raised his arms. Soon the water came to his chin, and finally to his nose; so he snorted and blew it away. He came north to the mountain Akoke-humi.[48] On this was sitting Yellowhammer (redshafted flicker).[49] At that time it was called Ikinye-humas-towela. Its tail feathers were already wet at the ends.[50] Mastamho went up on the mountain. Four times he lowered his arms, each time farther down, and the fourth time set the people on the ground.

21. Now of the whole top of the mountain only a little island remained and there was not much room for the people, so that some of them stood partly in the water. Then Mastamho took four steps in the four directions.[51] and therewith made the land extend farther.

22. Then, standing there, he looked westward. He said: "I call it Yamaθam-leha. It will be my country. Those are my mountains." Then he faced east and said: "Those will be my mountains too. I call them Yamaθam-toyam."[52] He took four steps west and came to the mountains he had named there. Then he planted kwaθepilye sage (chia, Salvia) seeds there. He said: "It is a good dry place for them." Then he came back, took four steps to the east, to the mountains he had named, and planted ma-selye'aye[53] seeds there, because it was dry in that place also.

23. Then he made all the water go down, and the land became dry. If he had not done that, there would still be water everywhere. All the water that had flooded the land had come from the hole he had made in the ground for the river, and had kept on flowing and covering the world until he stopped it.

24. Now he stood and looked west and said: "What I planted has grown up." He looked east and said the same. As he did this, he had to look downward because

he was so tall; and he had long arms and legs. He was as large as a tree. Kwaθepilye, which he planted first, is our old food; ma-selye'aye is our younger food. So Mastamho said.

25. Then he went north four steps and stopped. Again he went north four steps, and once more stood. Then he went on and came to Avikwame,[54] taking the people with him. Then he said to them: "Now I will bring what I have planted for you. It will be food for people." He went west and gathered kwaθepilye seeds, but they were not yet ripe. Nevertheless he took a handful and, when he came back, he showed them to the people and said: "They are not yet ripe."

INSTITUTINGS

26. Thus he was providing for the people. Then he thought: "What shall I do for them?" Now at this time there was no wood and no pottery: people had nothing. Mastamho had a staff,[55] which he had made by drawing out his saliva and rolling it between his hands.[56] Then he told the people to listen, and went in front of them as they stood facing him looking up, for they were still all boys. He said: "Come toward me! Now step back, farther back! Listen to me! Hear what I say! I call you Patšumi-yamasam-kwatθarva.[57] If you listen to all that I say, you will dream well: you will be doctors; I will teach you everything." When he had finished, they all said "ê!" in assent, and sat down.

27. Tšinsents and Hatšin-kosente,[58] two Ants, were those who had first tried to make the water go down. As it sank (from Mastamho's efforts), they scratched, one here and one there, and so had helped to make the land dry. Now as Mastamho talked, he told these two also to stand back from him, but they did not hear what he said. Then they said: "We will build a little house for ourselves on top of the water." They do that now, making their houses on sticks and little islands in the water.[59]

28. Mastamho stood and said: "Listen to me! I want you to know! I am giving you words, so that you will know." Then he walked about. He went here and there.

[48]A bold, notable peak, 5102 feet high, downstream and southeast from Mohave Valley, fronting the mouth of Cheme-huevi Wash. It is the culmination of the Mohave mountain "range," which stretches across the river; and it lies oppo-site from modern Havasu Landing.
[49]Kukhó. Cf. tale 18, note 1.
[50]Hence no doubt the black tips of the orange feathers.
[51]"N, S, E, W"—but I suspect the interpreter was follow-ing the usual English order.
[52]I cannot safely translate Yamaθam (perhaps nyamaθam, white), -leha, and -toyam.
[53]Kwaθepilye and ma-selye'aye (selye'aye is sand) as above, 8, and below, 24, 25, 47, and in myth 7:15 (UC-AR 11:1, p. 55). Kwaθepilye, Salvia columbariae, must be the Walapai keθepile (Kniffen, AAA-M No. 42, pp. 18, 35, 55, 1935) which was there described not very accurately as sun-flowerlike, gone by July in the dry western Walapai districts (or, in the uplands, in August), and as being parched, ground, boiled, and drunk.

[54]From Akoke-humi to Avikwame, which is abreast of Davis Dam, is about 50 miles. See 11, note 1 for further discussion of Avikwame.
[55]Anya-sotata, sun-staff.
[56]He used the staff or cane to point with as he lectured the people.
[57]"Food-white(?)-kwatθarva."
[58]Both words seem garbled: they do not sound quite Mohave; the episode recurs in 7:21 (UC-AR 11:1, p. 56) and in 15:6 below, where the ants are called hanapuka.
[59]These floating houses suggest nonhymenopterous insects or army ants rather than ordinary ants.

At each of four places making a square he said: "Put
a post here!" All this happened on the summit of
Avikwame, but at that time there was no mountain
there and all the land was level. Ikinye-masam-kumirqe
said: "I will dig the hole for the posts." Mastamho
stood in the middle of the square. He said: "Yes, I
will let you dig. But before you do so, let us hear you
say something! We are all listening." Then Ikinye-
masam-kumirqe said: "Nnnn!" But Mastamho, as he
stood in the middle, listening, said: "You are a doctor:
go back! Stand farther away!" So Ikinye-masam-
kumirqe went back.

29. Then Hakemile[60] made the hole. He stood pushing
his hand down into the ground. He took out some of the
earth and stood up holding it out, and sang and danced.[61]
Then Mastamho said: "You are the man to dig the holes
for the post." Nimitša[62] was standing by with a post
ready and when Hakemile lifted his hand out of the hole,
Nimitša set the post in. Then Hakemile put the earth
back around the post. In this way they set up the four
posts.

30. Now Hateθilye,[63] who was called Ikinye-humas-
kokθame by Mastamho, was the one who put the horizontal beams in place. Mastamho spoke to him four
times. "Pick it up! Raise it up! Move it higher! Put
it in place!" he said.[64] Then Ikinye-humas-kokθame
put the beam in its place and Mastamho said: "It is
good." Mastamho called the beams uyatšem-suwinka,
while now we call them ikumnau. He called the posts
atšoqwar-imine, but we call them av'ulypo.[65]

31. Mastamho said: "I have built a house, but it is
dark. Now I will talk four times and make it day.
Come close to me! Now go back again! Is it not good,
what I have made? Listen to me! Now all shout!" Then
they shouted. Four times he said this to them: each
time they shouted. Then the fourth time it was day.
It was no longer dark: the sun was there. Mastamho
said: "I call it Ikinye-kutateδeve." We call it anya.
And we call the moon haly'a, but Mastamho called it
Hatšinye-anyai-kupāma.[66]

[60]Hakemile is a small bird, living in hollow cottonwoods,
and making a buzzing sound.
[61]The dancing consisted of raising both heels off the
ground and thumping them down.
[62]Nimitša is an insect, recorded as namitša in 7:22, 27
(UC-AR 11:1, pp. 56, 57); it may be a mud-dauber wasp; the
partner is amaṭ-kapisara in 7:22, 27.
[63]Hateθilye is a tree lizard. I suspect it runs on house
girders and hides in the thatch.
[64]"Kiaδauk, amailye koδauk, ami-ten koδauk, nikaorem."
This may be a song, or just the formal, jerky, shouting
style of utterance which the Mohave call "preaching."
[65]Naming of timbers also in 7:23, 25 (UC-AR 11:1, pp. 56,
57), and 15:10 below.
[66]Ikinye being boy and hatšinye girl, the sun is male, the
moon female.

32. After he had finished all this, he made doctors.
He said: "Now I will let you speak: I will listen." Then
one stood up and talked. But he did not speak right,
and Mastamho said "ê!" and stopped him. Then others
stood up and talked. To these Mastamho said: "That
is right! You are the ones! You have it right! Now let
me hear you talk again!" So these men spoke again,
and Mastamho once more told them: "Now you have
everything! You can tell them what to do. You are a
doctor." Then, as he stood and talked, all got up and
danced four times.[67] I danced also: I was there..

33. Mastamho said: "Now everything is done. But I
want to think of something else. It will not be best to
stand up all the time, lest you get tired. I think it will
be better to lie down when you are tired and to sleep."
Then he lay down with his head toward the door (southward) and spoke to them four times and the people all
said "ê!" and lay down too. Then he spoke once more,
making five times, and they all sat up again.

34. Mastamho stood up. He wished to bring the
people outdoors. Some of them stood behind him and
held on to his arms; others he encircled with his arms.
Thus he danced to the door and out through it with them,
saying: "I hold! I place! I sway back and forth! Up!"[68]
Then he said: "Plainly! I have it! I sway! It is pleasant!"[69]
When they were all outdoors, he said: "It is finished.
You know what I have said. You have all heard it. You
can do it yourselves. You have not failed to learn it.
You will do it right." Then he stood off to one side.

35. Now the people were in four divisions. The
leader of those to the northwest was Tinyam-kutšaqwora;
at the northeast was Hatšinye-hai-kutsaqwora; at the
southwest, Ikinye-humas-eremsa; at the southeast,[70]
Ikinye-humas-kuwetšinalye.[71] Mastamho spoke to these
four men, one after the other.

36. As he stood, he held in his hand a pipe,[72] which
he called ivatke-tšumine and ihatke-tšumine. He gave
it two names, but it was one pipe.[73] Now he gave each
of the four leaders a pipe. Those who saw him do this
now are prominent men, chiefs or doctors. Those who
did not see it have no luck.[74] If Mastamho had not
given these four pipes, there would now be no smoking.
In the same way, if Mastamho had not said that there

[67]Stamping their feet and saying "e!"
[68]"Istum, itšam, itšatš-kuvak, amai-m-tšiak." Cf. n. 64.
[69]"Atevim, istum, itšatš-onalk, waipayim."
[70]A missed or crossed-over sunwise half circuit: NW,
NE, SW, SE.
[71]Of the four names, the first lacks either "boy" or "girl,"
the second begins with "girl."
[72]Malyho.
[73]This again sounds like Mastamho's word-twistings in
7:44-47 (UC-AR 11:1, pp. 59-60).
[74]"Did not dream well." Similar episode in 7:57 (UC-AR
11:1, p. 61).

would be food and water and other things, these would
not now be.

SKY RATTLESNAKE

37. Now it was pretended among the people at
Avikwame that Tinyam-ereha was sick. Then Mastamho
sent a messenger to Humas-ereha,[75] whom we call
Kamaiavete,[76] who lived far to the south in the sea.[77]
He lived in a round roofless house or enclosure made
of hair. He was like a snake, with a long tail with
large rattles, and his head was as large as a house.
He was a great doctor. Mastamho said: "You, Hatšinye-
kutati-δompa, go south and tell Humas-ereha to come
to doctor Tinyam-ereha." The one he addressed thus
was Hal(y)toţa.[78] He went off downriver, but came
back without Humas-ereha.

38. Then Mastamho called Haθakwatai[79] and told him
the same, and Haθakwatai started. Now he came to
where Humas-ereha lived. He stood and blew towards
him and in this way made Kamaiavete follow him, he
himself leading the way. When they had gone some
distance, Kamaiavete said: "Let us stop and talk." But
Haθakwatai said: "You had better hurry: that man is
very sick." Then Kamaiavete began to be angry. He
raised his rattles and shook them, so that it sounded
like distant thunder. Mastamho, far in the north, heard
it. He said: "I hear him. He is coming. He is in my
country now, in Iny-amaţ-tinyam-kuvatše.[80] He is
coming: listen!" Haθakwatai said again: "Hurry! Let
us reach Avikwame before he dies. If we go slowly,
he will die before we arrive." So they went on fast.
They traveled so quickly that the earth was shaken
by earthquake, and roared, and houses shook.
Mastamho said again: "I hear him! He is coming!"

39. Then Kamaiavete said: "I call this mountain
Iny-amaţ-irive.[81] We will lie here for awhile." That
is the name of the mountain west of the town of
Needles.[82] Kamaiavete knew that they would kill him.

He thought: "No one is sick. They have sent for me
and when I reach Avikwame they will kill me. I know
it, but I will go. But I will do something before I die.
Soon a little hail and rain will fall on me, so that I
feel refreshed as I go." So as he lay there he blew
toward the northwest and made it hail and rain. Then
he said: "Now I will go on, but you, Haθakwatai, go
ahead and tell Mastamho that I will soon arrive. Say
that all the people are to leave the sick man. I do not
want anyone standing about when I doctor him." Then
Haθakwatai went ahead and reported to Mastamho. But
as Kamaiavete went, he made the wind blow and raise
the dust so that he might not be seen. Inside the dust,
he went on and no one saw him.

40. When he approached, all of the people left the
house. Now in the middle of the house some earth had
been heaped up and covered over, so that it looked like
a sick person, for they wanted to induce Kamaiavete
to enter. Inside the door Ikinye-humas-kutanyive, whom
Mastamho wanted to kill Kamaiavete, stood with an
"ax" in his hand, ready to cut off his head. Mastamho
was standing behind him. When Kamaiavete started to
enter, his head was too large. He tried to pry the door
apart and nearly tipped the house over. At last he got
his head in. Then Ikinye-humas-kutanyive chopped it off.

41. But the head was still alive, and rolled eastward,
down to the river. There it is now, a rock at the river.
Because Kamaiavete was killed then, doctors are now
killed; if he had not been killed, doctors would not be
killed.[83] He was so long that when his head was in the
house at Avikwame, his tail was still in the sea. A
red streak[84] in the mountain Iny-amaţ-irive is part of
his body. The sea is his blood. That is why the sea
is salty and not good to drink. Sometimes the waves
and foam are a little reddish from his blood.

42. After they had killed Kamaiavete in the house
that Mastamho had built at Avikwame, he said: "We
will go outside. We will burn the house[85] and cry. It
is not good for us to stay inside." They did not really
cry for Kamaiavete, but for Matavilya. They said:
"Kamaiavete was a doctor, and we are not sorry that
he is dead." But they were still sorry for Matavilya.
Mastamho went northward from the house four steps.
All stood there and cried. Then Mastamho told Ikinye-
humas-hiklatška[86] to set fire to the house. So he lit
it first at the southwest corner, then at the southeast,

---

[75]"Night-ereha" pretends to be sick to lure "Boy-ereha."
[76]K-ammai-ave-ta," "sky-rattlesnake-great," heard here as
Kumaiavete or Kamaiavete. He appears also in 1:1a (UC-AR
11:1, p. 4) and below, 11:29, 16G:11, 17-26.
[77]Ha-θo'i-lye, salt water, the Gulf of California.
[78]Haltoţa, halytoţa is spider, but it was here described as
like the water-skate or water-boatman.
[79]Haθakwatai is an insect, making a case or cocoon, sometimes found indoors. Cf. Yanaθa-kwe-'ataye of 3:4 (UC-AR
11:1, p. 29); Tonaθaqwataye of 5:6 (UC-AR 11:1, p. 43), and
θonoθakwe'atai of 1:35 (UC-AR 11:1, p. 9).
[80]"My-land-night-kuvatše." Still below Yuma; but Mastamho
is north of the Mohave country.
[81]"His-land-iriva."
[82]Probably Ohmo, Sacramento Mountain(s); cf. 7:14 (UC-AR
11:1, p. 55).

[83]Characteristic Mohave style; but the balance seems to
me to serve emphatic clarity rather than being sought as a
formal end in itself. The whole episode, 37-41, is motivated
by Mastamho's believing that Kamaiavete had bewitched Matavilya. Cf. note 75.
[84]A dark stratum near the top of the ridge.
[85]A house with a corpse in it would be destroyed.
[86]Unidentified.

then at the two northern corners,[87] and it burned
down completely.

TRIBES

43. Then Mastamho said: "Now you Chemehuevi
go to the northwest." So they went northwest soon
after. Then Ikinye-humas-uive, with a large crowd
of people, was standing at the northeast. Mastamho
told him: "Go northeast." So this man [later] went
off, and his people are the Walapai. At the southwest
stood a man called Ikinye-humas-erauve. Mastamho
said to him: "You are a leader. You are the one to
go southwest." Then he and his people went southwest
and became the Kamia. To the south stood Ikinye-
humas-ikinθka. To him Mastamho said: "Go south."
Then he went downriver with the Cocopa. Another
was standing to the south, Ikinye-humas-iθaminyaye.
Mastamho told him to go south also, to stand four
steps behind the other, to follow him slowly, and not
to go as far. This man led the Yuma. Then Mastamho
told Ikinye-humas-kuvatšióuka to go southeast. These
people were the Yavapai.[88]

44. So Mastamho sent them all away except the
Mohave, who were still with him. He said: "I do not
know where to send you Mohave. I think I will let you
you stay in this land. I will tell you what you will
do. Do you see willows and cottonwoods? You can
build houses of those. Do you understand? I have
told you everything." They said: "Yes, we know it
now. We can do it." So Mastamho said: "It is
finished."

45.[89] All the people were in the house with
Mastamho. At the northwest was Tinyam-erike: he
did not speak loudly. At the northeast was Ikinye-
humas-iarθa: he spoke loudly. At the southeast (to
the left of the door) was Umas-topokwinpa. At the
southwest was Tinyam-hiklatške-inyayi. Tinyam-erike

went out first, westward: he was the older, and his
people were the Vanyume. Ikinye-humas-iarθa went
out next, to the northwest: he was the younger, and
his people were the Koahaltše (Virgin River Paiute).
These two went first: that is why their language is
not understood. Then Umas-topokwinpa went out, east:
his people were the Walapai. Then tinyam-hiklatške-
inyayi went out, southeast: the people with him were
the Yavapai. These two went out last: that is why their
language is understood.[90]

46. Now the Mohave were still in the house. With
them were the Yuma and the Kamin and the Cocopa.
Then the Mohave stood on the east; the three other
tribes stood in a line on the west. Mastamho, standing
there, said to the Mohave: "Come here behind me!"
The Mohave went and stood behind him. He spread his
arms and they rested their heads against them. The
three others walked out of the house in a line, one
behind the other, the Yuma last. When they all came
to the Yuma country, the Yuma stopped and stayed
there. The Cocopa continued on to the south, and the
Kamia went westward into the mountains. The Mohave
were still little children; that is why they stayed with
Mastamho.[91]

FARMING LIFE

47. Now all the tribes had gone off to where they
would live: the Yuma were in their country, the Walapai
in theirs, and each tribe had its land. Nobody was left
but the Mohave. Mastamho was standing. With his arms
folded, he took two steps toward the west, thinking about

---

[87] Presumably antisunwise circuit, SW, SE, NE, NW.

[88] Here there are six tribes plus the Mohave, but different
from the six in the boat, in 19. Cf. notes 43, 90. The present
order is not geographical or a circuit. The correspondence
of tribes with the distinctive components of their leaders'
names is:

NW	Chemehuevi	?
NE	Walapai	nive
SW	Kamia	erauve
S	Cocopa	ikiaθka
S	Yuma	iθaminyaye
SE	Yavapai	kuvatšióuka

[89] Paragraphs 45-49 are not part of Nyavarup's continuous
Mastamho narrative. They are episodes told later, in supplement or in answer to my questions, and are inserted in this
place by me, because logically they would seem to belong
here.

[90] Here four desert tribes only are sent away (the farming
ones follow in 46) in sunwise order, but only half-completing
a circuit of the directions. The first two are Shoshonean and
their speech is therefore not understood.

NW	Vanyume	Night-erike
NE	Kohoalche	Boy-child iarθa
E	Walapai	Child-topokwinpa
SE	Yavapai	Night-hiklatške-day?

Even allowing for 43 and 45 being obtained in different context, we must admit considerable compartmenting in the
informant's mind if he held these two schemes side by side.
Or perhaps fluidity would be an apter term than compartmenting. Quite likely he had in mind not two near-parallel
rigid schemes, but one generic, hazy one, which he improvised into definite shapes, but somewhat varying ones, according to occasion or context—even to the names of the leaders.
If this view is correct, what a narrator like Nyavarup re-
members is chiefly a pattern and therewith a type of material,
and only secondarily particular episodes, names, and the
like. Thus Chemehuevi of 43 are replaced here by Vanyume
and Kohoalche. Compare also the listing in 19, where the
Maricopa are added, and Chemehuevi, Walapai, Vanyume,
and Cocopa are omitted.

[91] Par. 46 must of course be taken with 45; but it is
interesting that the desert tribe enumeration is the more
ritualized—directions, named leaders, number 4.

food. He went north two steps and stood with folded arms, thinking. He went east two steps, still thinking. Then he went south two steps and stood. Now he made a little hole and spat white [frothy] saliva into it. He thought he wanted to produce food. He thought: "I do not think the food in the east [namely, the ma-sel-ye'aye seeds] will be good." Then he looked west and thought of the food there, the kwaθepilye seeds. Of this also he thought that it was good food but not for the Mohave.[92] That is why there are no ma-selye'aye and no kwaθepilye seeds in this country. Soon something small grew up from the hole into which he had spat. Four men were standing by Mastamho. At the northwest was Ikinye-humas-kuvanalye; at the northeast, Ikinye-humas-tinyam-kuvaδi; at the southeast, Ikinye-humas-kuvakye. The man at the southwest[93] I do not know.[94] One of the two on the west said: "It is good. This will be good food for the Mohave." One of those on the east said the same. Then Mastamho said: "Listen to me. This is corn.[95] This is watermelons. This is squash. This is wheat. This is quail-beans.[96] They had all grown by this time. One of the men asked him: "How are we to plant them? With our fingers?" Mastamho said: "There is a place in the east: Hanoθe-kwilyemava. I will go there and bring four sticks, sharp at the end, to plant with." Now he continued to stand there. He did not go to Hanoθe-kwilyemava; but he was holding the four sticks.[97] Then he gave one to each of the four men.

48.[98] Mastamho had called his house on Avikwame Ava-ka-humara.[99] He was in the middle of it, the people around him along the sides. First he said: "Tinyam-kuvatse, come here! Stand before me! When you marry and have a daughter, her name will be

Kuts-hoalye."[100] Then he said: "Tinyam-kuvatski, come here and stand before me! When you marry and have a daughter, her name will be Maha.[101] Next he said: "Hatsinye-masam-kunoδoma,[102] come here! Stand before me! When you marry a woman and have a daughter, her name will be Owits."[103] So he told them all, one after the other. Tinyam-kuvatse sat nearest the door to the west, Tinyam-kuvatski next to him, Hatsinye-masam-kunoδoma, the next.[104] I was there, but I did not listen. Other old men know all this: I do not know it.[105]

49. Mastamho was singing.[106] He called a girl Hatsinye-masam-merîke.[107] He said to her: "Listen!" She said: "Yes, I hear." Mastamho said: "If you hear all that I sing, do you know it?" She said: "Yes." Then he said: "Let me hear you sing it." Then she sang: she sang to him: "Vanālye,[108] stand back!" She sang what he had sung. Then he said: "Yes, now you have it. It is good. You have not lost a word." She was the first Hwami.[109]

TRANSFORMATION

50. Now they had all gone and Mastamho was alone. He thought: "What shall I do? How shall I die?"[110] He lay down with his head to the west. But he thought: "It is not right," and sat up. Then he lay with his head towards the north. He sat up, and lay down towards the east, and sat up again. Then he lay down towards the south, but sat up again.[111] Then he stood and thought: "I wonder whether I shall go down?" Then he sank into the ground to the middle of his thighs. He thought: "No,

[92]Cf. 8, 22, 24, 25.
[93]Sunwise circuit: NW, NE, SE, SW.
[94]One wonders whether this covers a momentary lapse in improvised pattern filling, or whether the narrator went through the years aware of his not having dreamed the name and perhaps face of one of these four ritual attendants. It might be the latter: there are avowals elsewhere like: "X was there too but I did not listen" or "I did not dream about him." Cf. the end of 48.
[95]As in narrative 7 (UC-AR 11:1, pp. 50-68), farmed plants are dwelled on more lightly than spontaneously wild ones (or planted wild ones). In fact, the present paragraph was not included in Nyavarup's story, but evidently was told by him on my asking subsequently about the origins of agriculture. Note that there are _five_ plants enumerated.
[96]Marika-'ahma, because spotted like a quail: introduced black-eyed (cowpea) beans, Vigna sinensis. All other marika beans are teparies, Phaseolus acutifolius. See Spier, Vocabularies, 1946, p. 124, n. 11.
[97]Why is the place mentioned when he does not go to it?
[98]Paragraph 48 was evidently told in answer to my inquiry as to the origin of the patrilineal clans with distinctive names for their daughters. Cf. note 105, below.
[99]"House-ka-child," i.e., something like children's house.

[100]Kuts-hoalye does not occur in my list of Mohave clans as given in Handbook, p. 742. Hoalya is the female name of the clan whose totem is the moon, haly'a; and Kutkilya clan has an owl as totem. (See UC-AR 11:2, p. 116.)
[101]The implied totemic reference of Maha is a bird, perhaps the dove.
[102]Hatsinye means girl, but a woman's daughter is not of her clan. The everyday names of Mohave men often refer to women, especially when the names are ribald; but I do not believe that this habit extended to ritual names.
[103]The totem of the clan whose girls are called Owits is cloud.
[104]This looks like the beginning of a sunwise circuit beginning at SSW.
[105]Cf. n. 94. A detailed account of the taking of land in Mohave Valley by leaders of women-named clans occurs in the Epic, 8 (UC-AR 11:2, pp.174-176). In War, 15:11-12, clans are instituted much as here, but the list is longer, though also incomplete.
[106]This paragraph is certainly in answer to an inquiry about how transvestites came to be.
[107]Meaning of term unknown.
[108]Meaning unknown.
[109]Hwami are the rare women leading men's lives; the male alyha are not accounted for here.
[110]Viz., end, transform into ultimate condition. Cf. 7:82-84 (UC-AR 11:1, p. 64).
[111]Sunwise circuit: W, N, E, S.

that is not good," and he came out again. Then he
stretched his arms. When he saw feathers growing
out of them, he thought: "That is best: I will fly
away." He flapped his wings, trying to fly, but was
still too heavy. Four times he tried. Then he rose
and flew up. Then he tipped himself to each side
twice as he flew, four times altogether. He was high

up in the air. He called himself Saksak-atši-kutθa,
fish-eating bald eagle. Now when he wants to eat, he
comes from far off, drops into the river, and flies
off with a fish. He said: "Call me Saksak. You will
know that it is I."[112]

[112]This kind of eagle (or osprey) "is always lousy."
Answering me: "When we dream of Mastamho we see him
as a great man with a staff, not as a bird."

DISCUSSION

The first part of this origin legend, part A, on
Matavilya, paragraphs, 1-9, and the beginning of
part B, on his death and Mastamho's disposal of the
body, paragraphs 10-16, are told much alike by all
Yuman tribes as well as by the Shoshoneans of
southern California, as has long been recognized (for
instance, Kroeber, 1906, mentioned above).

The remainder of the tale, represented by two-
thirds of Nyavarup's narrative, is more specifically
Yuman and especially Mohave.

The beginnings of most Mohave song-myths refer
either to Matavilya's death at Ha'avulypo or to
Mastamho at Avikwame. Sometimes they linger a
while on one or another incident before setting out
on their own course. Such are Chuhueche, No. 13,
and Tortoise, No. 19.

Three other narratives, however, are also avowed
accounts of beginnings in general, like the present
one, though they abbreviate the very first beginnings
even more than Nyavarup's story and essentially deal
only with Mastamho's doings. These three are the
Mastamho story already printed, No. 7, and Tokwaθa's
so-called "Origin of War" (No. 15) and the doctor's
dreaming of Sky-Rattlesnake, No. 16G, below. These
three, like the present version, have been recorded
as straight narratives, without songs, though the "War"
version contains "preaching" or ceremonial oratory.
The only other narratives without songs that I obtained
among the Mohave were the long historical "epic" No.
8 (with its counterpart fragments discussed in UC-AR
11:2, 134-135), the Coyote stories No. 6, and the fragments, No. 16A, D, G.

Table 1 has been drawn up to show the resemblances
and differences between these four songless versions of
world origins by the Mohave, together with repeats of

episodes in Chuhueche, Tortoise, and occasionally in
other song-cycle narratives.

In keeping with the sacredness of creation, ritual
compound names are frequently used for persons,
objects, and acts in narrative 9. Most of these unfortunately are not fully translatable. The commonest
elements in the ritual designations for personages are:
humas (cf. humar, child); ikinye, boy; hatšinye, girl.
A record of occurrences of such compound ritual names
for personages, objects, or acts follows, listed according to their ordinary designation, and the paragraph
of mention.

Mastamho, 17
Hiqo, white man, 5
Human beings, 10, 26
Fly, 12
Pyre lighter, 12, house burner, 42
Flicker, 20
House-building assistants, 28, 30
Sun, moon, 31
Tribal leaders, 35, 43, 45
Sky-rattlesnake, 37
Night-ereha, 37
Halytota, 37
Killer of Sky-rattlesnake, 40
Planters, 47
Clan leaders, 48
Hwami singer, 49
Net, 4
Lands, places, 22, 38, 39, 47
Pipe, 36
House on Avikwame, 48
To lift up, 11
Place tinder, 12

TABLE 1

Outline and Comparison of Origin Versions

9:1-50 Origins	7:1-102 Mastamho	15:1-19 War	16G:1-28 Sky-Rattl.	Incidents (and Cross References)
1-9	. . .	1	1-3	Sky and Earth; Matavilya; Ha'avulypo, Frog, sickness, death. (13:1-6, 13, 82; 19:1)
6,10	. . .	. . .	. . .	Matavilya instructs Mastamho.
11-12	1-2	3	4-8	Fire made, body burned. (13:7-13; 19:2)
13	3	2	10	Mourning. (13:14, 31; 14:21; 19:4)
14	5,11	4	12	Ashes covered. (11:12)
15-16	. . .	. . .	. . .	Bones not obliterated.
17-18	10	4	12	River made in N. (14:1)
19	12	. . .	12	Boat, travel, valleys widened.
20	. . .	4	13-15	Flood, tribes carried, on mountain peak, flicker's tail wet.
20-23	. . .	5	14	Water made to recede.
22	14	. . .	15	Mountains made. (14:75)
22-25	15-16	5,7	. . .	Wild seeds made for desert tribes.
25	8, (13)	6	15	Avikwame reached (made).
26	7	. . .	16	Teaching of people begins.
27	21	6	. . .	Ants help dry world.
28-30	24-29	9,10	. . .	Mastamho teaches house building.
29-30	22,27	. . .	5	Insect helpers.
7,31	28,33	. . .	. . .	Day and night, luminaries.
32	(57)	. . .	27	Doctors taught.
33	30-32	. . .	. . .	Sleep instituted.
34-35	. . .	. . .	. . .	People led outdoors.
36	. . .	. . .	. . .	Pipes given to doctors.
37-41	. . .	. . .	11, 17-26	Sky-rattlesnake sent for, killed. (1:1a; 11:29)
42	. . .	. . .	. . .	Avikwame house burned; more wailing.
43-44	(51-55)	8	. . .	Tribes segregated, given leaders (names).
45	(56)	. . .	. . .	Four desert tribes go off.
46	(56)	. . .	. . .	Three southern farming tribes leave.
47	56,77	. . .	10	Mohave stay, given farmed foods.
48	. . .	11,12	. . .	Given clans.
49	. . .	. . .	. . .	Given transvestites.
50	82-84	. . .	. . .	Mastamho transforms to Fish-eagle. (14:82, sakwiθei)
. . .	2, 4, 6	. . .	. . .	Coyote steals Matavilya's heart.
. . .	19	10	. . .	Languages given.
. . .	20, 23	. . .	16	Shade built.
. . .	34,85,98	. . .	. . .	Playground. (11:13)
. . .	36-42	. . .	. . .	Wild seeds farmed.
. . .	44-47	. . .	. . .	Counting taught.
. . .	48	. . .	. . .	Human hand made.
. . .	49-50	. . .	. . .	Directions taught.
. . .	59-66,69	15-19	. . .	Hawks and War. (14:73)
. . .	67-68,70-72	. . .	. . .	Dreaming of Eagle, Crane, Gnat-catcher, etc.
. . .	58,73-75	6	. . .	Mastamho's other names. (14:31)
. . .	76	. . .	. . .	Pottery.
. . .	85-92	. . .	. . .	Courtship instituted.
. . .	93-97	. . .	. . .	Water and valley birds transformed at Hokusave. (14:31)
. . .	98-101	. . .	. . .	Mountain birds transformed.
. . .	102	. . .	. . .	Sick bird transformed.

Tribal grouping varies in narrative 9. There are three enumerations, two of six tribes, a double one of eight (four Shoshoneans and Arizona mountain Yumans, four river Yumans). Altogether, ten tribes are mentioned, but the two lists of six share only three names, though five from each recur in the list of eight. The order is reversed from first to second list, and the third varies from both. It is clear there is neither fixed ritual order nor sharply delimited content.

TABLE 2

Order of Mention of Tribes

9:19	9:43	9:45, 46
		*1, Vanyume
*6, Kohoalche-Paiute		*2, Kohoalche (Koahaltše)
	*1, Chemehuevi	
	2, Walapai	3, Walapai
5, Kamia	3, Kamia	5, Kamia
	4, Cocopa	6, Cocopa
**4, "Maricopa"		
3, Yuma	5, Yuma	7, Yuma
2, Yavapai	6, Yavapai	4, Yavapai
1, Mohave		8, Mohave

*Shoshonean in speech; all others are Yuman.
**The Halchidhoma are probably meant.

Narrative 10
THE FIRST ALYHA

CIRCUMSTANCES OF THE TELLING

The account that follows was given by Nyavarup on March 12, 1902, a day after he finished the preceding Origins story. It might have been included in that, except that its telling was wholly separate. It takes what would presumably have been a one- or two-paragraph episode in the Creation story and elaborates it. And it is the sort of a dream or myth that is essentially a direct reflection, or projection backward, of a ritual, and is therefore particularly pallid as a narrative. It is what I have elsewhere called an institutional myth, in that it is more concerned with an institution than with a story and that the plot is essentially a recital of the sequence of the rite, in the thin guise of how it was performed the first time—while the world was still formative.

In fact, the informant, having finished his tale, went right on to tell how he conducted the ceremony. In my notes the only indication of the transition is a line left blank except for a colophon dash. I have broken the presentation there, thus dividing the total account into: A, the Myth, and B, the Rite. The informant undoubtedly was as conscious as we would be of the difference between what he dreamed or remembered from hearing, on the one hand, and what he actually did or sang, on the other. The characteristic differentiation is that he did not emphasize the separation as we would. Note, too, in this connection the lapse from myth into ethnography in paragraph 22.

Part A: The Myth

1. It was inside the house at Avikwame.[1] Four women were sitting near Mastamho.[2] He said to the one at the southeast (center post), to Hatšinye-(nya)-masām-arĩtše: "You are the one who will be a doctor, I think."

2. Then he said to the one sitting at the northeast, to Hatšinye-(nya)masām-hiwāim: "You are the one who will not listen to what your kin say to you; you will be loose." And to Umas-erau, a man sitting to the southwest, he said: "And you are the one who will have intercourse with her." Umas-erau did not answer.

3. Now two other women were sitting there: Hatšinye-kwatpārve at the northwest, and Hatsinye-kwatš'iδe[3] at the southwest.[4] Hatsinye-kwatpārve was about to have a baby, and Hatsinye-kwats'iδe was going to receive it and held out her left hand. But Mastamho said: "No, take it with your right hand:[5] that will be good. Now lay the child's head to the north, not to the south![6]

[1]The scene is to be visualized as follows. It is in the great house at Avikwame, with four centerposts, and the door as always to the south (leeward). Mastamho is sitting just outside the square of centerposts, off the southwest one (right front, as one looks from inside toward the door). The four women sit inside the square, each by a post, their order of mention being SE, NE, NW, SW—a counterclockwise circuit. The baby when born is laid in the middle of the central square. This precision of visualization is characteristic of the Mohave, and among themselves they mostly seem to think it important enough to describe. My notes contain a diagram. Unfortunately I failed to set down whether the diagram was scratched in the sand for me by the narrator (or interpreter), or was constructed by myself from their verbal explanation. However, the omission bears only on the question of how far the Mohave have impulses to give their dream visualizations kinesthetic conversion; the spatial organization of the visual imaginings is evident.
[2]"Mastamho called himself Pahutšatš-yamasām-kyuvetškĩ. There was a woman there (beyond the four mentioned) whom he called Hatšinye-masām-kupāwa. She answered, 'Yes, that is my name.'" (She did and said nothing else.)

[3]Or -kuvatš'iδe.
[4]Completing the anti-sunwise circuit, begun at the SE.
[5]The left hand is for doctoring.
[6]The dead go S from Mohave land.

[17]

Then it will dream well; if it lies to the south, it will dream badly."[7]

4. Now the baby lay there, looking around. "Sit back from him there," Mastamho said. "That boy knows much—more than you all: he will be a leader." The baby was looking this way and that, its eyes winking. Then it said: "I want a name. What will you call me?" Mastamho said: "He is a boy, but I think we will give him not a boy's name, nor a man's, but a girl's. I call him Hatšinye-hai-kwatš'iδe."[8]

5. Mastamho picked up the baby, held it in his hands, "I will tell you all about him. I want you to learn what I will teach about this child." Then he sang, swaying his hands from side to side with the child on them, and the four women[9] danced to his motions.

6. When he laid the child down, the boy thought: "I am a boy; but shall I wear a breech-clout or not? Shall I wear girl's clothes or boy's?"

7. I[10] was there: I saw it; I heard Mastamho singing. I did not sing then, but I know how to.

8. Now the boy was old enough to play about. There was no iδo, black willow, yet in existence; so Mastamho created it, to make a bow from. Then he gave it to him. Carrying his bow, the boy went outdoors to where little girls were playing; but he did not keep the bow. First he held it behind his back; then, looking around to see if he was unobserved, he threw it away.

9. When the little girls came indoors, Mastamho asked them: "Did the boy keep his bow?" One of them answered: "He had no bow." He had been ashamed to tell them of it.

10. Then Mastamho made him another: "Perhaps he did not like that one; perhaps he will like a different one." He split black willow, made a bow, feathered arrows, and gave them to him. Then the boy went outdoors; he went into a group of girls. He walked four steps and let his bow fall to the ground. They said to him: "Pick up your bow and arrow," but he did not answer. Then one of them, Hatšinye-masām-kuvetškíe,[11] went over, picked it up, and held it out to him. But he only looked at it; he would not take it.

11. They came indoors from their playing and Mastamho asked. "How about the boy?" A girl said: "He threw it away; I have it." "Yes?" said Mastamho; "he did not keep it?" "Yes, he did not keep it," she said.

12. Mastamho thought: "I think it did not suit him. I will make him a different one. I will scrape it fine and white and put a feather on it, and another, and another." So he gave the boy a pretty bow and arrow.

13. The boy went outside, took four steps horthwest of the house, threw down his bow and arrow where a group of girls had sat down to make dolls.[12] They said to him: "We will make you a doll." They did not look him in the face but said softly to one another: "I think the boy is going to be girl: he wants a doll." He said: "I do not want a doll: I know how to make it for myself." He would not take the one they offered him. He held his hands in front of him and moved them slowly in jerks[13] sidewise and out and back, singing[14] softly inside of himself. The girls said to one another: "Don't look at him, don't look at him, or he will be ashamed and not play with dolls any more!"

14. When they had played, they started to go indoors again. "Here, take your bow," a girl said and handed it to him. He did not take hold of it right, by the grip in the middle, but dangling from the string, and followed them in, "Look at him!" they thought; "he is not doing the right way. He is going to become a girl."

15. Mastamho asked them: "How did he do this time? Has he his bow?" They said: "No, when he arrived, he threw it northwest.[15] He did not take care of it but got a doll and sat like a girl,[16] with the doll lying across his thighs." "Then what did he do?" "I don't know: he played with his doll, the same as we."

16. So Mastamho called the boy to him. "Give me your hand," he said. "First we called you Hatšinye-

[7] Be unlucky, die soon.
[8] The same name as the midwife's, except for the element -hai-.
[9] The doctor woman, the promiscuous woman, the mother, and the midwife.
[10] The narrator, Nyavarup.
[11] It is not clear why she should be singled out for mention by name.

[12] Dolls may be of rude pottery, or perhaps of bast or rags.
[13] Why the jerky motion? He is probably making his doll. —The narrator illustrated with gestures, keeping time to a song.
[14] The words of the alyha's song were given as: "Idauk ilyuvĭk," "I hold it, it is finished." These recur in the songs of paragraph 31: the range of vocabulary in most Mohave songs seems to be remarkably limited and monotonous. See the examples in Raven, 4, notes 4, 8, 11, 13, 24, 31 (UC-AR 11:1, pp. 38, 39, 40); Deer, 5 (UC-AR 11:1, p. 42); in Handbook, pp. 757, 758, 763, 776; and passim below.
[15] This type of specification is characteristic. It would not matter to us what the direction was, nor would it matter in the tales of most primitive peoples. But the Mohave insist on being ritual-mannered in their myths; perhaps because they have so little formal ritual. Or it might be better to say that their myths are rituals—narrated, unperformed ceremonies. Certainly song-series like theirs usually are part of rituals. (NW would be behind the house to the left, as one faces the door.)
[16] Mohave women about 1902 sat with their legs stretched out, perhaps crossed at the ankles; or with one leg doubled under, the other either stretched out on the ground or with the knee up; or with legs folded over, Turk or tailor fashion. Men on the contrary sat on their legs both turned on the same side; or with their heels directly under them, thighs straight forward; both these being usual women's positions in the Plains, Plateau, and California. This is according to my observations as noted down.

kwatpārve.[17] But that will not be your name any
longer. You will be called Hatšinye-tomeδike. Now
you may go with these girls."

17. Then Mastamho made a set of stave-dice[18]
out of his breath and spittle and handed them to the
boy: "I give you this." The boy seized them, held
them tight so as not to lose them, tucked them away.[19]
Mastamho said: "Come on outdoors. Let us try whether
this boy will play dice like a girl. But do not turn to
the east[20]—who goes that way will be a doctor. Go
by the right hand, then it will be well." So all stood
about to see whether the boy would play like a girl.
A woman was sitting at the southwest, laughing; the
boy sat on the northeast (facing her). He took the
dice to throw them with his left hand; she said, "No,
throw them with the right!" When he threw them up,
she was opposite, struck them in mid-air, and scattered
them.[21] Then everyone laughed and there was a big
noise. And the boy too laughed like a woman now,
and smiled like one. Then the woman threw the staves
up and he struck them down; and again all laughed.
As they started again to play (the third time), all the
girls who had been sitting rose to kneel to see better;
and the boy threw. When the woman was to throw for
the fourth play, Mastamho called: "Stand up, everybody!
Are you all standing?" When they said: "Yes," the
woman threw, the boy caught them in his hand, and
all laughed: one could hear it far off. Now the boy
had it: he knew all that the girls knew.

18. Mastamho said: "When I made these (dice), I
gave them to this boy, and now he has them. Now all
you women and girls[22] come close by me: I will tell
you. That boy will stand in front; he will be the head
one." Then Mastamho sang: "Histūm!" ("He has it!").
Then he said to him: "Now you have it. And your
name will be Hatšinye-tomeδike."

19. Two women were laughing: they wanted the boy
to laugh like themselves. Then he laughed like that.
"Now you laugh like a woman," they said.

20. Then Mastamho went over to all the girls to
sing, and stood to the southwest, the boy facing him

from the northeast[23] and listening to him. And after
Mastamho had said it four times, the boy sang: "A'avek"
("I hear it"). Then he danced, first to the west, then
to the south, north, east,[24] four times.

21. Now Mastamho made a dress out of his body[25]
and handed it to the boy. "Nyā'áim nyahvai," "I give
you the dress," he said. So the boy put it on, the thick
wide apron piece behind, the narrow one in front. "Now
walk," said Mastamho, "so we can see how you look
moving." So the boy took four steps, then turned and
faced him. Mastamho asked him: "Now you have heard
what I told the women about how to dress and behave.
Do you understand that?" The boy said, "Yes," nodding
his head.

22. The alyha can cure sexual disease. Alyha is
also the name for gonorrhea. That is why the Indians
had that sickness: Mastamho gave it to them, and these
alyha were to cure it. Syphilis and blue scrotum came
from the whites,[26] gonorrhea they had before.[27]

23. Mastamho said: "We will sing and see how you
dance." So he sang, and all the women danced on the
east, the boy standing dancing alone on the west.
Mastamho wanted to lead them outdoors;[28] he was
singing, they following him dancing. When they were
all out, Mastamho asked Hatšinye-tomeδike: "Do you
understand what I have taught you?" "Yes, I heard it,
I know it." "Well, let me see you do it then." So the
boy stood facing west, with Mastamho behind him, and
talked to all the women opposite. Then they all together
answered "ê" with a loud noise. Mastamho walked about
behind the boy, listening whether he said everything
right: he had said: "You can do it; you know how, I
will not tell you more." So the boy was telling the
women and girls what to do, and they took one another's
hands and listened to him. He said: "Hatšinye-masām-
kwatšárve kinneik," "All you girls (and people),[29]
approach!" Then he sang and danced and they danced
with him. Mastamho had told him: "When you dance,
walk backward and make them follow you (forward)."
So he walked backward toward Mastamho, singing, and
Mastamho backed too, and all the others followed them.
He sang loudly, and they all sang with him, and as
he sang he blew saliva on them, white spots, as if

[17] His mother's name in 3. There may have been an error
in understanding or translation.
[18] Otaha. Four staves or billets of willow or similar wood
(Handbook, p. 741). One side is painted red and blue, generally perhaps with three different designs on the four pieces;
but the variation of pattern does not enter into the scoring.
The count is: all four plain sides up, 2 points; all four
painted, 1; any mixed combination, 0.
[19] Presumably in the band of his shirt—which, however,
he did not yet have on.
[20] East is to the left, coming out the door.
[21] This is how the game is played: one throws them up
close together, the other beats them down to scatter.
[22] A girl, masahai, has not yet borne a child; she may be
virgin or married. A woman, θenya'āka, is a matron, however youthful.

[23] With his back to the house.
[24] Not a circuit this time: W, S, N, E.
[25] By reaching into it and taking out what he wanted.
[26] Wherever in California I have had statements from
Indians on the source of syphilis, it was credited to the
whites. The only statement I have recorded which is possible
indirect evidence of gonorrhea in native times is a northwest
California Karok tale in which the lecherous culture hero and
trickster blinds his grandson by rubbing semen over his eyes.
[27] This paragraph is a digression from the myth.
[28] They have got indoors again, without explicit mention in
the narrative.
[29] "Men and women"—although hatšinye refers to little girls.

they were painted.[30]

24. When they finished singing, Mastamho spoke again. "I ordain[31] that some women when married will be quiet, and good workers. And some will not stay with their husbands but be loose. And some will be doctors, but not marry." That is why there are few women doctors. "Well, we are all

here.[32] Let us go south. After four steps,[33] I will arrange a place; I will call it Miakwa'orve.[34] That is where we will stop and do something." So they all came to Miakwa'orve. There Mastamho said: "I call you all Hatšinye-masām-mitšovθe";[35] and all the women danced as he talked to them.

---

[30]Having saliva froth blown on them is something the Mohave accept with indifference: it is standard in the process of being cured by shamans. It is of a piece with other customs; such as ribaldry as regards sex; cooking fish into stew with scales, bones, and perhaps entrails left in; one person after another sucking the sugar out of the same mass of mesquite meal. They are not a squeamish people. And this in turn is part of their pride in enduring discomfort and hardship cheerfully.

[31]"We appoint it," the interpreter said.

[32]Men as well as women.

[33]These steps are magically long: the distance is a number of miles.

[34]For Miakwa'orve see "A," west side, on Map 1 and p. 140, UC-AR 11:2. In the early historic period it seems to have been the uppermost permanent large settlement in Mohave Valley. It is where Nyohaiva originated, in 3:1 (UC-AR 11:1, p. 28). Here, "Amiakwa'orve" was heard; once I wrote "Imiakwa'orve"; the initial vowel is slurred; the word accent is on the a before k, and again on the o.

[35]Again, men as well as women appear to be included, cf. fn. 32 above.

Part B: The Rite[36]

25. A [prospective] alyha sends for me. Four [of us] doctors come and stay the night. The boy, or young man, has dreamed he will be an alyha; he has seen it so with Mastamho; then he will be one, he cannot help himself, because what one dreams, that will be.

26. Now he lies in the middle of the house, covered up; and the doctors, all night long, sing, and tell what Mastamho did and said, and how it was all instituted in the beginning. Three of them work on the woman's dress of willow inner bark. One of them shreds and folds and trims the bark; one spins cord on his thing; the third binds it into the [bunches of shredded] bark. The fourth one—that is I—holds the finished dress on his right arm and sings with it. As each one works, there is a song for it. Thus, spinning the cord, one sings, with each motion: "That-nye-vuδí, ihat-nye-va'āma," "Roll it this way,[37] roll it that way." This is how the doctors heard and saw Mastamho doing in the beginning with the first alyha.

27. In the morning, the young man is waked. A woman is sitting at each side of him. The one to the east gives him the hip skirt part of his new dress, the one to the west the front apron part.[38] Then they help him to rise, the one on the east taking his left arm, the west one his right.[39] Then one of the doctors —myself[40]—puts an [old] woman's dress on himself and sings and dances; the alyha follows and imitates

him, with his hands on the doctor's shoulders. All the people present dance too.

28. Then they move to the river, dancing and stopping four times on the way; the fourth time they reach the bank. The doctor lets fall the dress he is wearing, enters the water, and bathes; and all follow him. When they come out, the alyha stands like a woman, covering privates and rectum.[41] Then two women hand him the newly made clean dress to put on. Then they[42] bite off and chew white paint and spit it over his face [and hair?]. Then they go home.

29. The new alyha is still ashamed. So after four days, the two women again paint him white. They paint a vertical stripe down from each eye and another down the nose to the mouth. Then he is known as an alyha and is not ashamed any longer.

30. Now he always wins at gambling. Sometimes a man will give him beads to go off with him somewhere and then many come and have intercourse with him in ano. And he dies young: that kind does not live long. At gatherings, they speak and laugh and dance like women.

31. Other songs, sung by Mastamho and when the ritual is made, are:

istūm	I have it,	āvírk	done,
itsām	put it (on)	ka'avik	listen!
ilyuvík	it is finished,	kiδauk	hold it![43]

When they spit white paint: alem, decorating.

As the new dress is slowly dragged over the sand: ilyuvík, it is finished.

Just before the dress is put on: iδauk, I have it.

---

[36]From here on is straight ethnography—description of ritual. A condensation is printed in Handbook, pp. 748-749.

[37]Toward the body, then away.

[38]The edges of the narrower front and larger back "aprons" more or less meet down the front of the thighs.

[39]Showing that he had been sleeping or lying with head to N.

[40]I have the impression that the narrator was not boasting of his importance so much as narrating a particular performance of the ritual.

[41]Mohave women seem to show equal shame at exposure of anus and genitalia. A passage in the Epic, 8:106 (UC-AR 11:2, p. 92), suggests this.

[42]The two assisting women, apparently.

[43]This song has been given in Handbook, p. 748.

Narrative 11
TUMANPA

RECOGNIZED FORMS OF THE STORY

The meaning of the word Tumánpa is not known. It seems to be a proper name. It is usually one of the first myth cycles to be mentioned by the Mohave when they begin to enumerate their singings—perhaps because it can be danced to for amusement.

It has been reported as sung, under the same name, also by the Cocopa, the Diegueño, and the Serrano-speaking Vanyumé or Beñemé of Mohave River. A Diegueño Tutomunp or Tomanp song, said to have Mohave words, and phonographically recorded by Constance Goddard DuBois (on her cylinders no. 1081, 1097, the Museum's 1237, 1241), was immediately recognized by my Mohave and identified as of their "Long" version.

There are three of these Mohave versions or variants:

1) Tumanpa Akyulya, "Long."

2) Tumanpa Uta'uta, "Short," or Atatuana or Taravika, "Crooked," or Halyaδompa, "Odd, peculiar." This is the version narrated here.

3) Tumanpa Vanyume, "of the Vanyumé." Some not too consistent information as to this variant will be given at the end of the main narrative.

My second interpreter, Leslie Wilbur, told me in 1908 that he had heard Tumanpa when it was told to James Mooney at Parker (presumably when Mooney was making field studies on the Ghost Dance). The story began at Ha'avulypo, with Matavilya's death. The characters are two, brother and sister. They traveled north to Oqalihu, then turned and went south. Leslie remembered no fighting, but shinny and dice games. Also there was mention of a pair of han'ava mourning insects, one going into the ground, the other flying up. The brother and sister went downriver to Bill Williams Fork (Hakutšyepe) and beyond to a river slough north of Parker, where they turned east inland, married, and changed into rock. The place is called Sam-kutšoive, "sister-marry." So far this is Wilbur's recollection of the Tumanpa version heard by him.

This outline lacks the westward side trip of the present version and the fighting encountered therein. On the other hand, my full version that follows lacks

the preliminary northern detour, and the han'ava, shinny, and dice episodes. The beginning at Ha'avulypo, and end at Tšimu-sem-kutšoive southeast of Hakutšyêpe, correspond, as well as the petrifaction; though my version avoids allusion to incest. Since my version was specified as being Short Tumanpa, it may be that the story Wilbur was summarizing was Long Tumanpa.

In 1954 I was told at Parker by Perry Dean, narrator of tale 19, that the Short Tumanpa took one and a half nights longer to sing than did the Long, namely four as against two and a half. It contained 385 songs. The Long Tumanpa is so called because its travel route is longer.

Dean's wife Su'ulye asked whether my version told of incest. When I said it had brother and sister traveling and transforming together, but that there was nothing about their marrying, she said: "But they do."

My version mentions 118 or 123 songs, of which 32 were recorded (cylinders 1198-1209, 1542-1561). The narrator-singer said it took him three nights to sing these and tell the narrative. This is as against the four nights and 385 songs referred to by Perry Dean.

I am not disturbed by these several discrepancies, which are about normal as between versions or accounts from different informants.

Tumanpa is classed by the Mohave as among those of their cycles related to war, but I believe that this statement means only that it is one of the kinds of singings danced to when there was a major celebration such as was likely to occur on the return of a successful war party bringing scalps and slaves, or at a social harvest feast. There is nothing whatever about war in the narrative, except for a definitely minor episode near the beginning (4-6), in which three birds are seen fighting three insects and Buzzard gets scalped. There is a definite contrast with Vinimulye-patše, Nyohaiva, and Raven (tales 2, 3, 4) in this virtual absence of reference to war.

Another thing that is lacking, and wholly so, at least in the version that follows, is erotic preoccupation. This is the more strange in that other Mohave all agreed that the theme of Tumanpa was brother-sister incest. The personages are brother and sister indeed; but they are old from the beginning, and there is no trace in the present version of even an allusion to anything erotic or perverse.

The distances involved in the tale are about as follows.

With the center of the world and point of origins Ha'avulypo identified as in lower Eldorado side canyon, this is about 25 miles downstream from Boulder or Hoover Dam.

From Eldorado it is about 25 miles downriver to the north end of the former Cottonwood Island, now submerged under Lake Mohave.

From there to Davis Dam, which impounds Lake Mohave, it is again about 25 miles.

About two-thirds of the way down this last stretch, Avikwame Mountain[1] is abreast the river and present lake.

From Davis Dam it is four miles to Bullhead City, the former Harper, and nine or ten to Miakwa'arve and Iδo-kuva'ire, the uppermost permanent and considerable Mohave former villages, or about thirteen miles from the site of Fort (or Camp) Mohave.

Mohave Valley, from Fort Mohave to the Topock bridges at the foot (formerly called Mellen), is about 25 miles long by air, 27 by river, Needles City being situated nearly two-thirds of the way down this stretch, 11 miles above Topock.

Adding the 13 miles from Fort Mohave up to Davis Dam, we have a total for Mohave Valley of 40 miles, Dam to Topock; of which 30 contain the Mohave settlements shown in UC-AR 11:2, Map 1 from Iδo-kuva'ire to Atsqáqa at Topock.

From Topock to Chemehuevi Valley about where Chemehuevi Wash comes into the river I make it about 19 to 20 miles. The total to here is around 110 miles

(50 above, 40 in, 20 below Mohave Valley). To this must be added the distance to Tšimu-sem-kutšoive, given as half a day's travel (from Chemehuevi Valley or from Aubrey in Arizona?).

Geographically, this Tumanpa tale is unusually straight line. The two Tumanpa, brother and sister, proceed downstream from Ha'avulypo in Eldorado Canyon to Tšimu-sem-kutšoive southeast of Chemehuevi Valley; south of Bill Williams Fork, somewhere in the region of Aubrey in Arizona, they transform into two rocks. For about the first 12 song stations they are north of Mohave Valley; for the next 20, in Mohave Valley; then for 16 in the Mohave Canyon gorge between that and Chemehuevi Valley; and for 5 in Chemehuevi Valley; plus two paragraphs of story without singing which carry them to their destination. The straight downstream order is broken only in sections 3-6, in which they take the side trip off the Colorado into Chemehuevi territory to the west, near the Providence Mountains; after which in 7 they go northeast, and in 9 are back on the river (which Mastamho has meanwhile made to flow), and in 10 are at Eldorado Canyon again. The whole journey is made in two days; at least, they are mentioned only once as sleeping, at Iδo-kuva'ire (Avi-totara), above former Fort Mohave (18-20); about midway in the total journey, in miles.

As regards configuration, the story is of the item-by-item order; it does not rise and fall in suspense, nor change in interest. The episodes are all typical Mohave narrative material; but they are not built up into a climax. There is no sense of an end to be achieved, nor of retribution, nor of doom, nor on the contrary, of surprise. The two characters just travel on and on and see something at each next place. They meet no enemies and run no dangers, so that it is hard to participate emotionally with or against them. When they finally transform, there is no motivation cited: it is just time to turn into something. The tale thus remains mainly an itinerary, with only such interest as its endless disparate little episodes command.

Achyora Hanyava sang his Tumanpa to gourd-rattle accompaniment. It took three nights to chant in full, presumably including narrative as well as song. The breaks, he said, came after paragraphs or stations 15 and 32.

[1]Avikwame, the summit of Dead Mountain, 5800 feet high, is something over 40 miles S of Eldorado Canyon. Its peak is an airline ten and a fraction miles from Davis Dam, between NW and NNW from this (8.5 miles due W from the Dam and then 6 miles N). A sharp side peak is Newberry Mountain, something over 3000 feet high and less than 3 miles from the river. On some maps the name Newberry is applied to the main peak. The Mohave apply Avikwame both to the total mountain mass and to the highest peak. See plate 1, a, b. It is roughly 40 miles S of Ha'avulypo.

THE NARRATIVE OF TUMANPA SHORT

1. When Matavilya died at Ha'avulypo, Tumanpa said, "I will go." There were two of them: Tumanpa, an old man, and Kwa'akuyi-savepone,[2] his younger sister. So they started from Ha'avulypo. (2 songs).

2. They were going to Avikwame. Then they came to a level place northwest of the mountain, a mat'āre.[3] They told of that. (2 songs).

3. They went to Aha-kuvilye.[4] There is a spring there, with a little mesa to the north. They stood there on top of the mesa. "Well, we have arrived here from where we started, far away. And we will keep going; I don't know which way." (2 songs).

4. They started and came to north of Avi-kwa-havasu, Providence Mountains,[5] and looked west to Hayekwire-nye-mat'āre.[6] There they saw fighting: six were fighting: Buzzard, Blackbird, Meadowlark,[7] against White Fly,[8] Gnat,[9] and Mosquito[10] —three birds against three insects. (2 songs).

5. Tumanpa saw that fighting. He saw that Buzzard was whipped by White Fly and scalped. "They will put the scalp on a long pole and dance around it. I know that: I didn't tell them to do it, but they will." Now one can see that Buzzard is scalped: there are no feathers on his head. (2 songs).

6. They still stood at that place. "By and by people will do like this: the Mohaves will do it. When they fight with a tribe, they will take scalps. When the Mohave fight the Maricopa and Halchidhoma and beat them, they will get scalps. When the Maricopa beat the Mohave, they will cut off scalps and take them to Phoenix and dance. And the Mohave will go there and whip the Maricopa and bring the scalps to their land." They learned that from what the birds [and insects] did then. (2 songs).

7. Tumanpa went northeast from there. They came to sand hills and they said they would name them. "We will call them Selye'aya-kwa-hawaye and Selye'aya-kwa-hatšāma."[11] (2 songs).

8. From there they went to Aha-kwoana.[12] Jaguar and Mountain Lion[13] were living there, killing and eating rabbits. Tumanpa did not see them but he smelled them. He said: "I know: at this place there are two great beasts that hold the earth and hold the sky. I am afraid." He said again: "I know this earth is big. Even if I keep on going far, that will not be its end. I want to go back." He stood and looked south and thought he would go south. (2 songs).

9. Now there had been no river at Ha'avulypo; but when they came to Aha-kwoana and stood there, they saw the Colorado River running. "When Matavilya died, Mastamho was here, and he was wise. I did not see him, but I know he made it. Mastamho was a doctor, and a wise man, and he made the river far in the north. Now I see this river: it is good for everyone: it makes a noise and it looks nice." That is what Tumanpa said while they stood there. (2 songs).

10. They went south to Havirepoke[14] and stood there. Now Isuna-tamkwerqa,[15] a male bird, lived at Providence Mountains. Qo'a, a female bird, lived at Avi-ny-iδo.[16] Giant cactus grew around there.[17] When they are ripe, Qo'a wants Isuna-tamkwerqa to come to her, to make a hole with his sharp nose in the fruit of the cactus, to eat that.[18] Now Qo'a went to Providence Mountains to fetch him. As they came back, she went ahead and he followed. Tumanpa saw them coming across the

[2]Kwa'akuyi means old woman; the meaning of savepone is unknown. Subsequently the informant said that they were both Tumanpa, and the old man had no special name of his own. For save-pone, see also fn. 77.

[3]"Playfield," any level river terrace, low mesa, or playa lake bed bare of vegetation. Subsequently, in listing songs, the informant said the second stop was at Avikwame-hipuk, or butt of Avikwame, where they "sang of a place about 5 miles NW called Kwiltatpahve," mentioned also below in Salt, 12:2. This would be the mat'āre, and would be in northern Piute Valley.

[4]Aha-kuvilye is Piute Spring, in Chemehuevi territory. It may be Aha-kuhulya'i, "stinking water," of 2:26, n. 35.

[5]Avi-kwa-havasu, "blue-green mountains," some 30 miles SW of the Piute range in which Piute Spring is situated.

[6]"Rattlesnake's playfield," Mohave or Rogers dry lake bed (renamed Muroc by the Air Force), a playa 15 or 20 miles east of Mohave R.R. station and town. Actually, it is probably out of sight from the Providence Mountains. Certainly people there would not be visible: the distance is about 130 miles. See also 7:98 (UC-AR 11:1, p. 66), and below 12:22.

[7]Asei, Aθ'ikwa, and Kwaθitško. The identification of the last as Meadowlark is unsure.

[8]Ivaθo. Spier, Vocabularies, 1946, 117, Maricopa ivaθó, a stinging insect, name of a song.

[9]Malykapaka, a small fly or gnat that pesters horses.

[10]Sampulyke.

[11]Selye'aya is sand. They may have gone NW along the Providence Mountains. Half a dozen miles W of the range begins a 35-mile-long stretch of sand dunes, from near Kelso to Baxter on the Union Pacific R.R., S of Soda Lake, the playa sink of Mohave River about 30 miles WNW of the Providence Range.

[12]Or Ha'kwoana. Also unplaced; though evidently on the river; and it should be farther north than where they started at Ha'avulypo; because in 10 they go south to Eldorado Canyon. See below, tale 12, fn. 36, and Part II, B, 3.

[13]Numeta and Hatekulya; but these terms may really denote Mountain Lion and Wolf; see tale 5, fn. 1 (UC-AR 11:1, p. 41). See also 16A, below.

[14]The informant said "in Eldorado Canyon," but Havirepoke seems to be the channel bordering Cottonwood Island on the W.

[15]Probably a bird of woodpecker type; isona is "woodpecker."

[16]Unplaced. "Mountain's eye" or "tooth"?

[17]Giant or "candelabra" cactus is a'a, but it does not grow so far north as Eldorado Canyon or Providence Mountains. In Arizona its northern limit is on the lower Big Sandy. "There" means where the female bird was.

[18]These are birds that nest in giant cactus <u>stems</u>.

river. Qo'a flew straight and Isuna-tamkwerqa flew up and down. Tumanpa said: "I know you two, and I am going to give you a name so all will know you. Everybody will call you that. Your names are Qo'a and Isuna-tamkwerqa." They did not come near but he saw them coming. Standing at Havirepoke, he saw them flying by and said that. (2 songs).

11. When they got to Ah'a-kwaθarve,[19] a little south of Eldorado Canyon, many Chemehuevi came down [to?] the river.[20] At the bank, Tumanpa saw them. "You are my brothers who left long ago. You went away before me. I know you. I will call you Pa-hamaθole-mat-kuwāma."[21] He talked to them but the Chemehuevi did not understand his language. They answered him, but he did not understand their talk either. Then they looked at each other and only smiled and laughed, that's all. Tumanpa said: "Well, you can go on[22] the river: I am going south along its edge; you can go and I can go too." (2 songs).

12. They arrived at Ashes-come.[23] Tumanpa said: "When Matavilya died and they burned him, the ashes came here." He thought the wind blew the ashes north. "That is what they did, those ashes: they came from where Matavilya died. I know that."[24] (2 songs).

13. He went south to Amaṭ-ku-vataqanye, near Mat'āre-mai-muya (Miakwa'orve).[25] "I am going to give this place a name, so that everyone who comes will know it, like the earth and sky. The name is Amaṭ-ku-vataqanye for all time." (2 songs).

14. From there they came to Red Rock, Avi-kwa-ahwaṭa.[26] As they stood there, the old woman said: "That river does not go on far." Tumanpa said: "The river does not run straight. It is narrow and bends and after awhile it runs straight again." But the old

woman thought it was the end of the river, and they quarreled about it.[27] (4 songs).

15. As they stood there, driftwood came floating by from the north and the river made a noise against it. "It said something! Maybe it knows. It doesn't come straight on. Hear what it says." The driftwood wasn't talking. It was the water, but they thought it was the wood: it was the first time they had seen any; nobody knew it then. "We will call it a'i-hannaye,"[28] he said. "Now it has a name." (2 songs).[29]

16. They wanted to cross the river. "I want to get on that drift log and cross on it," she said. "No, we don't use that," he said, "the Mohave use it." Arrow-weed[30] was growing by the river. They tied its dead arrow-stalks into two bundles on which to cross. Then they entered the river, each with a bundle under an arm. "We never crossed before: we may be drowned and die," they said and cried. They did not know how to swim, so they drifted with the river. They said: "If we keep on like this, we cannot reach land. Maybe the river will take us along to its end." (2 songs).

17. They drifted down a little to where the river swirled back. They got into the eddy close to the bank and landed. They said: "I thought we should be drowned: but now we are saved." They had swallowed water and were nearly dead. Then they named three places close together here, Amaṭa-nyamasava-kwahava, Avi-totara, and Nyamasava-hataya.[31] (2 songs).

18. They had not come to these three places yet, they were still by the river. It was nearly sundown, so they went up to the places to camp there. They cut brush and piled it around, without a roof.[32] "If I do this, some tribe will do the same"; he meant the Walapai. Now it was quite dark and they started a fire: the

[19]Ah'a is cottonwood. The place might be Cottonwood Island, whose N end is about 25 miles S of Eldorado Canyon (Tatum), where in the 1850's some Mohave lived, and later the Chemehuevi. But it is probably farther S; see Part II, B, 3; N13 in list.

[20]"Down the river" was recorded.

[21]Pa for ipa, person; hamaθole, buckskin shirt; mat-, perhaps self, body; k-uwāma, verb stem—wear?

[22]By, along.

[23]Ham'ulye-tšieme. Not located; but the journey is now consistently south, that is, downstream, unless otherwise mentioned.

[24]It is perhaps implied that his thought was wrong. The prevailing wind is from the north; and Matavilya's remains are usually described as having finally been washed out of sight.

[25]Amaṭ-ku-vataqanye is a little sharp peak opposite Hardyville (or Hardy) in upper Mohave Valley, about six miles N of Fort Mohave, No. 2, west side, on UC-AR 11:2, Map 1. Close to it is the well-known "playfield" here called Mat'are-mai-muya, but mostly known to the Mohave as Miakwa'orve, and so entered on UC-AR 11:2, Map 1, A, west side.

[26]A red rock or bank on the west side, about four miles N of Fort Mohave, where the river, after having turned nearly west at Hardy, bends sharply south in a right angle. UC-AR 11:2, Map 1, C, west.

[27]These disputes about facts by a pair of brothers or man and woman occur in many myth travels. What she saw was the steep curved bank at Ameke-huvike and Avi-kutaparve (UC-AR 11:2, Map 1, B, west), and in her innocence she thought the river ended there.

[28]A'i is wood. Ihne is the usual word for driftwood or snag.

[29]It takes a night to sing to here, the informant said, though he had listed only 32 songs. Even assuming that he elaborated improvisations to bring the number up to double that, these would hardly fill a night. It may therefore be inferred that he had in mind a night of alternate narration and singing. Cf. note 60.

[30]Iθava, _Pluchea sericea_. For crossing the river, the Mohave use bundles of dry arrowweed stalks, or driftwood, or shaped reed balsas, or large pottery bowls for infants or belongings.

[31]These three places are less than a quarter of a mile apart (the two first appear with slightly different spelling, as nos. 3, 2, east, on UC-AR 11:2, Map 1) and are within a half mile of the much more often mentioned Iōō-kuva'ire (UC-AR 11:2, Map 1, east, no. A), about three miles N of Fort Mohave.

[32]The circular camp is mentioned elsewhere, as below in Salt, 12:16. A roof is hardly needed in the desert, where if it does rain a brush cover would be inadequate anyhow. But one would expect a windbreak leaned up against the north, rather than a ring of vegetation.

two of them were camped there. Then rats jumped
over the fire, and sometimes on their faces and arms
and legs. Tumanpa said: "I know you. You wanted to
be alive like anybody else. But you could not. Only
when Matavilya died you came to life from his body.
Now you have no names, but I will give them to you.
You are Ave, Uqale, and Ohulye."[33] So now each of
them had its name. (2 songs).

19. When darkness came, the stars came out too,
the seven stars and the three stars.[34] Tumanpa told
of them and of the dark. (2 songs).

20. After awhile, he saw the morning star, that big
star, coming up. Tumanpa was thinking about its being
the head of all the stars. It sent the little stars to
come first. "You go and I will come too," he thought
that big star said. There is no other star like it. He
called it the star that walks in the daytime.[35] (2 songs).

21. Then they started from the three places near
Iδo-kuva'ire and came to Amaṭa-kukyeta.[36] A great
bird Humaθe[37] came from the south. Tumanpa said:
"When you went away, you did not see Matavilya. When
he died, everybody stood around, but you did not come
and stand there, you went away. But I know you." He
said: "This Humaθe left first. I don't know how far he
went, but I know he went south to the sea,[38] and took
shells. He made a bracelet on his wrist and on his
ankle, and a belt. He got an armful of shells and made
beads and put them on his shoulder and his neck. I
know that, and I am going to give him a name: Humaθe.
I give him that." Then they saw a Beaver[39] coming
toward them. He lived in the river and ate willows
and cottonwoods. Now he wanted to come up on the
mesa, Tumanpa saw him, eating, a little way off. The
woman said: "What is that over there?" The old man
said: "I know him. He became alive from Matavilya's
ashes, or maybe from his bones. He does not know
that: he only thinks it; but I know. I am going to give
him a name: it is Apêna." The beaver turned back and
jumped into the river. (2 songs).

22. Now Humaθe came there to Qara'erva[40] where
the two were still standing. As he was flying, he saw
his shadow on the ground and thought it was another
bird, wanted to catch it to eat, and tried to catch his
shadow. But he fell down, then jumped up and seized
something else, a rock, as if he were getting himself
something to eat, a rabbit or a bird. He thought he
would make Tumanpa believe he had caught something;
but Tumanpa did not believe it. Humanθe made a noise
to make Tumanpa believe he had caught a bird and it
was crying; but he was doing it himself. Tumanpa said:
"I don't think you will catch anything. You cannot catch
it that way. Perhaps you will starve and die." That
kind of bird cannot catch things; sometimes he dies of
hunger;[41] he catches live brush rats, Ammilya. (2 songs).

23. From there the two went on to Selye'āya-kumítše.[42]
Then Tumanpa said: "When we began to come south,
we named birds and animals and places, but we did
not tell about our bodies. Now that we have come to
Selye'āye-kumítše, I am going to tell about my body.
I am going to show how I walk and how I do. When I
walk, I swing my hands. Anyone can see how I walk
and how I look around. I have not told that; nobody
knows it; but now I will tell it, and all will know the
way we walk, and the way we look around: and perhaps
people living here, by and by, will be like that."[43]
(2 songs).

24. They went on and came to Aqwāqa-(h)iova,[44] to
a level place on the mesa. A little thing grew there;
one of its thorns stuck in the old woman's foot. "Oh,
that hurts!" Then she said: "I will give a name to this
that stuck me. It is Akgulye-nya-haminyo."[45] (2 songs).

25. They went south to Hanyo-kumasθeve,[46] at the
edge of the mesa overlooking the valley. They gave
that name to the place. (2 songs).

26. Standing there and looking south they saw Kwiyak-
aqwāθa a little way off,[47] a rock and a hole and something yellow. Tumanpa said: "That shining comes to
my body and makes marks on it. When I came, my

[33]Rodents, at any rate. Ave is probably a field mouse or
small rat. Another "rat" is mentioned in section 22, below.

[34]The Hatša-Pleiades and Ammo-Mountain Sheep-Orion's
Belt, which the Mohave never tire of talking and singing
about.

[35]Hamuse-'anyam-kuva, star-day-travel, the morning star,
of course.

[36]Kukyeta is in the valley, but at the foot of the first
"mesa" or river terrace. It is Amaṭ-kukyeta, no. 9, east,
UC-AR 11:2, Map 1. It is near Qara'erve of note 40, no. B,
east, Map 1.

[37]I wrote "California Condor" in my notes on the basis of
the informant's description. I do not know whether this species
ranged regularly to the Colorado; but even rare individuals
would likely be remembered by the river Yumans, if their
interest in jaguar, bear, and wolf is an indication. In 18:36,
below, humaθe is described as a large slow "hawk."

[38]"Sea" without qualification means to the Mohave the
Gulf of California.

[39]Apêna.

[40]Frequently mentioned, as in 1:39 (UC-AR 11:1, p. 10),
and as B, east, UC-AR 11:2, Map 1. The action is still N
of Fort Mohave in the upper end of Mohave Valley.

[41]The antics of this bird seem exaggerated, whatever
species it may be; but he is ashamed and pretending.

[42]Selye'āya-kumítše is another much-mentioned place in
the vicinity of Fort Mohave, inland from it: C, east, UC-AR
11:2, Map 1; cf. 1:40 (UC-AR 11:1, p. 10).

[43]This narcissistic dwelling on how one looks walking
recurs in 3:31 (UC-AR 11:1, p. 33) and elsewhere.

[44]Aqwaq(a-h)iova is E, east, UC-AR 11:2, Map 1. They
are now past Fort Mohave: a quarter of a mile beyond it.

[45]"Long-its-sandal." It is only two or three inches high,
a spherical cactus with long spines. Cf. the incident in
Nyohaiva, 3:26 (UC-AR 11:1, p. 33).

[46]UC-AR 11:2, Map 1, no. 14, east; cf. 1:41 (UC-AR 11:1,
p. 10). Hanyo means slough.

[47]Kwiyak-aqwaθa (Kuya-k-aqwaθa), UC-AR 11:2, Map 1,
no. 15, east, a quarter mile S of where they are standing at
Hanyo-kumasθeve.

body was right, but now I am different. So I will give a name to that place: Kwiyak-aqwāθa. That name is what the people who live here will call it." They did not reach Kwiyak-aqwāθa, but saw it as they went by. (2 songs).

27. They went on south along the edge of the mesa to Kamahnuly-ve. Below, there was a lake. They stood there and named that low place. "I will name this place here. All the people who will live in this valley will remember that name: Kamahnulye-va."[48] (2 songs).

28. Starting from there, they came to Aha-ku-kwin-ve.[49] They stood there and saw Walapai coming from the east. People were living all along, on both sides of the river, and the Walapai were visiting them. Tumanpa saw them coming from Tomkutapeṭ-ve,[50] up on the mesa. He said: "I know them. They left before all the others, going first and east. Now they are coming back from the east. I know what they think: they are thinking about these people here and want to visit them." Then he said: "I will make a gourd rattle."[51] He made [took] one out of his body, and shook it with his left hand. He said: "This gourd is a doctor's:[52] I will give it to the Walapai." He made another, which he shook with his right hand; that one he gave to the Mohave. That is the reason why the doctors everywhere, when a man is sick, use their rattle in the left hand; but when people just sing, they shake the rattle in the right. And a doctor spits in his left hand when he cures.[53] (2 songs).

29. They started and went south to Nyahweye-ve.[54] Then they heard a rattlesnake and stood. Tumanpa said: "I know you, Kammai-ave-ta.[55] You were killed and your head was cut off, and your blood and shadow and sweat came to be alive.[56] But you can not be alive like a man: you have no legs; you are not like me; you turned into something else. I will call you, so

everyone will know you: Ave (rattlesnake). (2 songs).

30. From there they went up on a high mesa, stood on it and looked around. He said: "We have climbed up to this high place here and look around. I will give it a name: Va'orve.[57] (2 songs).

31. Starting again they went on south, still on the mesa. Our Mohave Valley country on both sides of the Colorado River ends here; a little beyond, it goes up into mountains. "Now I will tell about the places on both sides. I name this place Hatša-to'āma, Sampulye-kuvāre, and Atšqāqa:[58] three names for one place; so that everyone will know the names." (2 songs).

32. From there they went on to where the Topock bridge is now.[59] On a mesa, a high place close to the river, they stood and said: "Well, I will look back north to where Matavilya died. When he died, they burned the house to ashes, and there is no house there now. But when you dream, you see things. A man dies and becomes a ghost, you burn his house and his clothes, and dream and see that, and you think: 'I thought this house and all were burned up: I saw the ashes.' So when you dream and see your kin, your father and your mother, you think they have not died. When I die, you will dream and see me, and I will look like alive. I will tell that to all men. When they dream, they will see shadow people looking as if they were alive again." He said that as he stood there, at the place called Kwaparvete.[60] (2 songs).

33. Starting from there, they went south some four miles below where the bridge is. There they saw soft white paint rock, amaṭ-ehê.[61] No one knew about that then, but when he saw it, Tumanpa said: "That is good: for me and for everybody." The old man stood east of the place, the old woman stood west of it. Tumanpa took some of the white rock, crushed it between his hands, and rubbed it on his body and made it white. "That is pretty: that looks nice." Both of them did that. They said: "That is it, to paint the body like a dress,

[48]Kamahnuly-ve (Kamahnulye) is UC-AR 11:2, Map 1, G, east. Cf. 1:42, 3:5 (UC-AR 11:1, pp. 10, 29).

[49]Aha-kukwinve, UC-AR 11:2, Map 1, no. 27, east, was put "at Old Gus Slough" (is this Spears Lake?), across the river (northeast) from Needles City. This is a longer jump downstream.

[50]Tomkutapeṭ-ve is unplaced, but probably on one of the higher river terraces, or on the talus of the Black range, which the Walapai would cross in visiting the Mohave (unless like the railroad they came down Sacramento Wash to the south end of the valley).

[51]Ahnalya means both gourd and rattle.

[52]Doctors' singing and other singing are quite different: the former can take life.

[53]Doctors spray and rub their saliva on patients.

[54]They are now opposite Needles, more than halfway to the foot of Mohave Valley, UC-AR 11:2, Map 1, no. 40, east.

[55]Kammaiaveta, "great sky rattlesnake," as in 1:1a (UC-AR 11:1, p. 4) and below, 9:37-42 and 16G.

[56]The informant had power to cure the bites of rattlesnake, scorpion, spider, and ant, who got their venom through originating from the blood, sweat, etc., of Kammaiaveta. See Handbook, 775.

[57]Va'orve is T, east, UC-AR 11:2, Map 1, "straight east of the old Santa Fe R.R. bridge, which was about 3 miles S of Needles." [The later and present bridge at Topock is about 8 miles farther S than the old.] Va'orve is four miles [S] from Apenyiva (P) and [4 N from] Atsqāqa (Y). A slough Hanyo-hane (U, Powell Lake?) lies at the foot of the Va'orve mesa."

[58]Atsqāqa, UC-AR 11:2, Map 1, Y, east, is frequently mentioned as near Topock and at the foot of Mohave Valley. Here: "about a mile N of the bridge." Sampuly(e)-k(-)uvāre, UC-AR 11:2, Map 1, X, east, means "mosquito cannot reach it"—it is on a hill.

[59]As of 1910.

[60]Kwaparvete, UC-AR, 11:2, Map 1, Z, east, is close to the Topock bridge. They are nearing the river, preparatory to following the 8-mile gorge called Mohave Canyon below the bridge.—To here, the informant said, it took two nights to sing. Cf. note 29.

[61]Ehê-earth. It is a white earth or soft rock much used for painting the body. This site in the canyon is frequently mentioned.

like something we wear. And we will name this place: we call it Amaṭ-ehê-stūtšive, Take-white-paint."[62] (2 songs).

34. Going on, they came to the Needles Peaks (Hokiampeve).[63] Then they both said they were doctors. They did not walk straight and went every way and made a noise. "This earth shoots my feet: it pains here," the woman said. She could not walk, and sat down, and cried, and said to the old man: "You said you were a doctor: now cure me." But the old man said: "You said you were a doctor too. That's what you said: a great doctor, ahead of me. You can cure yourself." He was laughing and would not treat her. Then the old woman cried. So Tumanpa turned back and said: "Well, I will cure you, though you said you were a doctor like me. But you are no doctor, so now I will cure you." In a little while the woman got up and had no more pain. (2 songs).

35. From there they started to climb up the two peaks, The Needles. They stood on top and named the place Avi-kwa-tšohai,[64] right on the peak. From there they looked south and saw mesquite beans.[65] The old man said: "Those mesquite beans are ripe." The old woman said: "No, they are not ripe yet: it is too early. Mesquite beans and leaves dry when they are ripe." Tumanpa said: "About this season they are ripe. All people know that at this time mesquite beans are ripe."[66] (2 songs).

36. They still stood there. The mesquite beans were ripe and falling off. (2 songs).

37. They went on south to Selye'āya-mukyeṭa.[67] There Tumanpa saw two lizards striped with red. He said: "I know you: you are my brothers. You went off and I did not see you, but you are my brothers, and you turned to be lizards." The lizards just stuck their heads out of the sand and showed only their faces. He saw their faces and said: "I call you Selye'aya-mitši and Ave-

munyove."[68] Both these lizards live in the sand; that is why he gave them those names, because they own that place in the sand. (2 songs).

38. From there, they came to Hatuṭva,[69] still going south, and looked across the river. The old woman said: "Who is that over there? I see two men." She thought she saw men with long hair, tied like mine.[70] It looked like persons, but there was nobody. Tumanpa said: "I know that is my brother. He went off, long before Matavilya died, and came this way, and turned into rock. It looks like a man, but there is no one, just a rock." So the old man told the old woman. One can see it there, like two men. They called it Kwasu-kuly-ve.[71] (2 songs).

39. Going on, they came half way to where the bats live, telling how they had come, both talking, so that the bats heard them coming. The bats listened, and then all flew up out of their holes in the mountain. Tumanpa arrived and saw them flying. He said: "I know you: you came here when Matavilya died: you were like me [in shape], but here you turned into bats. I will call you Qampanyqa." The name of the place is Qampanyq-nyi-va.[72] (4 songs).

40. They went on south a little. As Tumanpa stood, mountain sheep came down from the mountains to drink at the river, but seeing Tumanpa, they ran back. They did not know him, but he knew them. "I know you: you live in the mountains. And the Chemehuevi live in the mountains: they eat you for meat. As you come to this river to drink, you make a road: so I will name this place Mountain-sheep's-road."[73] (6 songs).

41. They went on south[74] and saw a wash from the mountains. They stood and said: "We will give names to this wash so everyone will know it. The names are Tšimukwily-kwa-hakyê-ve and Humθavinye-tšanaly-ve."[75] (2 songs).

[62]Amaṭ-ehê-stūtšive, UC-AR 11:2, Map 2, no. 1, east, and p. 141.
[63]Hokiampeve, also Mukiampeve, often referred to, as in 1:104 (UC-AR 11:1, p. 19), and below, 6:B, 14-II:36; see UC-AR 11:2, p. 141 and Map 2, no. 2, east. Strictly, however, Hokiampeve does not denote the two spirelike peaks, which would be of little concern to the Mohave except as a landmark, but refers to a spot at their foot on the Colorado, where the river trail passed. This spot is about a mile from the white-earth-paint locus.
[64]Avi-kwa-tšohai is the summit of one of the pair of "Needles," UC-AR 11:2, Map 2, no. 3, east, and p. 141.
[65]Analya is the mesquite tree, aya the bean.
[66]"They ripen about the fifth month" [sc. after the winter solstice, presumably]; but the time usually stated is July. Castetter and Bell, 1951, p. 182: in Mohave territory, begin to ripen end of June, plentiful in July.
[67]Selye'āya-mukyeta is a sand (selye'āya) hill about two miles S of the Needles peaks, UC-AR 11:2, Map 2, no. 4a, east, and p. 141.
[68]The name of one lizard refers to sand, the other to rattlesnake.

[69]Hatuṭva is "about half a mile downstream from where they saw the lizards. They are traveling along the east edge of the river." It is UC-AR 11:2, Map 2, no. 5, east, and p. 141, mentioned also in 2:12 (UC-AR 11:1, p. 25).
[70]Gathered at the nape, from which there fall full-length rolled and plastered pencils of hair: standard man's coiffure.
[71]These manlike rocks are at the river, opposite Hatuṭva.
[72]Qampanyka is the usual name for bats, and Qampanyk-nyi-va is "Bats' Houses," UC-AR 11:2, p. 141, Map 2, no. 6, east; mentioned also below, in 8:C, note 6 and 14:II:40 (Sanquvanye).
[73]Ammo-ny-unye, "Mountain Sheep its Road," UC-AR 11:2, Map 2, no. 7, east, and p. 141. About one-half mile beyond Bats' Houses.
[74]Another half-mile downstream.
[75]Otherwise unidentified. Tšimukwily- may possibly have some etymological relation to Tšimuveve, the Chemehuevi, cf. note 107; but Tšimukwily-avi is Yucca, at the S end of Black Mountains, on Sacramento Wash, F9 and J4 on UC-AR 11:2, Map 2.—Humθaviny seems to denote the wearer of a nose ornament: 8:79, fn. 32 (UC-AR 11:2, p. 158).—The two places, with variant spelling, are 8 and 8a on UC-AR 11:2, Map 2, and p. 141.

42. From there they went on to Avi-rrove-hiδauve.[76]
They saw nothing there but tracks: tracks going everywhere. They looked around and old man said: "Somebody has been here. I know that old woman: she is a
doctor; she is my sister. I know that she made these
mountains. Where she goes, the mountain opens and
makes a wash. Sometimes she goes right through the
rock and makes a hole to the other side of the mountain. Her name is Kwa'aku-sava-teve."[77] (2 songs).

43. They started on and came to where coyotes had
a hole. They came from there down to the river to
drink and went back up into the mountain. Tumanpa
did not see the coyotes, but he saw their tracks. "I
know these two. They haven't feet like me. When first
they came this way, they were like other persons: now
they have changed. I will name them Hukθara, Coyote."
The place is Hamu-tšompa-kuya.[78] (2 songs).

44. From there they went on to Ivθe-kwa-'akyulye.[79]
Two Coyotes were crying in the sand hills. Tumanpa
heard them and said: "That Coyote said: 'I am Coyote,
but I know everything. I know when I am hungry, to go
eat. I know when I am thirsty, to go get a drink of
water. But I have no home: I just run around across
the desert; and I have no road. Yet I live all right.'
That's what Coyote said: I understand him: I didn't see
him but I heard him. There are four colors of Coyote.
Some are red, some white, some yellow, some real
Coyote color.[80] But this Coyote that I hear crying is
not one of these. His name is Coyote-owns-the-morn-
ing.[81] He is the kind that makes a noise in the morning, because he owns it: that is why I name him that."
(2 songs).

45. They went on and when they got to the top of
the sand hills at Selye'āya-'ita,[82] they saw Chemehuevi
Valley down below. They stood and could hear tribes[83]
of people to the south. All danced and sang and laughed
and made a noise, so they could hear them having a
good time from far off; but he could see them too.
"We will go down there. All those tribes are my
brothers: I want to see them. Let us go. I know those
who live there, those that dance and sing. Their names
are Cock,[84] Turkey,[85] Masohwaṭa,[86] Nighthawk,[87] Kuta,
and Tšamaδulye."[88] (4 songs).

46. From there they started to go to ghosts-their-
houses.[89] Tumanpa said: "When we first traveled we
cried all the way along. Now we come here and hear
them sing and dance and having fun. When we arrive
below, we shall not cry any more, but will take a swim,
and wash." The old woman said: "Yes, we will quit crying; and I think we had better wash." Tumanpa said:
"I don't know how to swim: I will jump in and lie on
my back." He wanted to find out how to swim. "Lie
over that way, and that way," she said. Tumanpa said:
"All right: when we get into the river we will know
how one swims." He was thinking about it. (2 songs).

47. They started south and then toward the river.
"When we get to the river we will bathe and dive under
four times," the old woman said. When they came to
the bank, she had things to paint with: black, white,
and red paint, and fat to mix it with. She had them
hidden where nobody could see it: Tumanpa did not
know where she kept them. She said: "When we have
bathed and come out again on the bank, don't look at
me. Look the other way and I can paint. I will reach
out and take four colors, red, black, white, and fat,
and we will paint with that."[90] Then the old woman
handed the paint to Tumanpa. He painted her, his sister.
Then he handed the paint back to her and she painted
him. They painted each other all over, white and black
and red. "Now we are right. We are using these paints

---

[76] About a mile below the last, no. 9 on UC-AR 11:2, Map
2, and p. 141.
    [77] This old woman who rends and bores the mountains is
evidently taken over from some other part of Mohave myth
stock. She is Tumanpa's "sister" perhaps in the sense
in which she calls many of the animals he meets his "brothers."
However, compare the similar names: Kwa'aku-sava-teve for
her, and Kwa'akuyi-save-pone for his actual sister and travel
companion.
    [78] UC-AR 11:2, Map 2, no. 10, east, and p. 141; see also
UC-AR 11:2, p. 101 (no. 159), "Hami-tsompa." Kuya is a den
or cave.
    [79] "Tall greasewood" or creosote bush, Larrea. The place
is no. 11 on UC-AR 11:2, Map 2, and p. 141; see also UC-
AR 11:2, p. 101 (no. 159).
    [80] Hukθara-tahank, "coyote true," like Spanish "legitimo."
For the four colors of coyotes, cf. the narrator's mountain
sheep of four colors below, in 13:15.
    [81] Hukθara-yaθe'a.
    [82] "Big-sand," viz., sand hills, one of several places so
called, here no. 12, east, on UC-AR 11:2, Map 2, and p. 142.
It is "not far" below Ivθe-kwa-'akyulye.—But I doubt whether
Chemehuevi Valley itself, on the west side of the river,
would be visible; possibly the opposite shore of the present
dammed Havasu Lake would be.
    [83] Kinds of birds; cf. notes 84-88.

[84] Qoluyauve or Qwaluyauve.
    [85] Orro-ta, which would mean "great nighthawk"—I don't
know why. Both chickens and turkeys of course were introduced by or from the Spaniards, along with wheat (although
wild turkeys may have been known from the eastern Walapai
country).
    [86] Masohwat(a) is a large red bird, perhaps imaginary,
certainly legendary; most Mohave say it did not live in their
country. It may be a macaw, known from repute or from
feathers or skins traded in, as they were traded to the
Pueblos. The Yavapai told Gifford it was a macaw.—The
Mohave of 1953-54 sometimes translate it as "parrot"; but
one of them called it a bird with a crest, smaller than a
robin, something like a cardinal.
    [87] Orro (also a Cocopa woman's name).
    [88] Kūta and Tšamaδulye are unidentified; according to 11:54,
note 102, below, the latter at least is a piss-ant, not a bird.
Spier, Vocabularies, 1946, 118, gives Maricopa tcimaculya,
red ant.
    [89] Nyaveδi-nye-vatše, "Ghosts-their houses," no. 13, east,
UC-AR 11:2, Map 2, and p. 142. It is to this region of sandhills below Needles Peaks, nos. 12, 13, 14 (Ha-tše-kupilyka),
east, of this map, that the souls of the dead are generally
said to go. See 2:11a (UC-AR 11:1, p. 25), and below, 8:159,
13:12.
    [90] This is about her only contribution to their careers.

and give them names so that hereafter everybody will use them." He stood there and gave names to the paints: Akwere, red paint; kwanyehilye, black paint; amaṭ-ehê, white paint; ammo-saye, mountain-sheep fat or marrow.[91] While they stood here they names the place where they were Hatšekupilyke.[92] (4 songs).

48. They went on south by edge of the river, to Avi-'pa:[93] a little way from there is Humar-otare. Tumanpa stood there and saw birds flying up and down and going into the bushes and trees. He stood and looked at them, and said: "I will give you a name: then everyone will know you. I call you Sakumaha."[94] (2 songs).

49. They went south a little way and reached Tinyam-kosama.[95] Not far away they saw a man wearing feathers. a bird with tall white feathers upright on his head and back. Tumanpa said: "You wear those feathers but they do not last long. You think that that is right, that it is funny, but you cannot be like that. When we were in the north we were like you; but we turned into moun-tains or something."[96] (2 songs).

50. They went on to Omaka.[97] Tumanpa said: "We stand here at the end of settlement. We will tell about it, will let them know that we have come, so that every-body will hear us." A man Numkumuhava went to meet Tumanpa there. Numkumuhava said: "You are my bro-ther. I wanted to see you. You went off, I don't know where. Now you have come this way and we are glad." Tumanpa said: "Well, you will see us forever. We have come to stay among these people here. The road I made, the road by which we came, that has been there always: it leads into your house: you will see me there." (2 songs).

51. So they went south together to Ahmo-kwe-'ataye, Many-mortars, and Akatu-'uvere,[98] which lie close

together. When they arrived, Tumanpa said: "This is as far as we will go: this is where we wanted to come. Now we are home." (2 songs).

52. He stood at Akatu-'uvere, north from a large shade.[99] Numkumuhava said to the old woman: "My sister, come into the center of this shade. I have a metate here; I have maize." Nobody knew it, but he had got that maize. At first we had only maize—no beans, no wheat, no pumpkin seeds: that was all we had. "Grind that maize," he said to the old woman; "Come and grind it." Two men stood on each side of her, and he wanted one man [at a time] to put a hand-ful of corn on the metate, so the old woman could grind more quickly. "Do that, and then cook mush and bread, so everyone can eat," Numkumuhava said. "We don't grind. We don't know how. All we have is mesquite beans."[100] He had a big [wooden] mortar and a long pestle, nearly a fathom's length, a wooden pestle. "We only use that [mesquite meal] in the big dishes, and put in water, and stir it up. And everybody sucks [the juice] and does not get hungry, and dances and has a good time. That is the way we do. Now when you grind maize, it is well. But, sister, I don't think you know how to grind."[101.] She did not say a word, but went ahead and ground and ground. (2 songs).

53. Numkumuhava called all the six birds by name. He said: "Come and stand around." Then he told Cock and Turkey to go east. To Masohwaṭa he gave a voice, so he could make a noise, and told him to go far west. Nighthawk was not to go anywhere, but to stay there and turn into a bird. Kūta and Tšamaδulye were to stay around there also. Tšamaδulye would live in the ground. We do not see Chickens or Turkeys or Masohwaṭa about here: we see only Nighthawk, Kūta, and Tšamaδulye. Then Numkumuhava said: "Well, they are all finished; some are birds, some ants."[102] [First said <u>no songs</u>, then <u>7 songs</u>].

54. Numkumuhava said he too wanted to become something: he wanted to be a desert. "I shall be a mountain, or sand; I don't know which." Then he said: "But if I am a rock, or a mountain, or sand, no one will know that. I think I shall be something like a grasshopper.[103] I will be that." He named himself Aya-kukitpute.[104] Now he used to shake his head while he was a man; and when he transformed, he said: "Now I will have my name from the way I do:[105] then every-

[91] I do not know why sheep rather than deer marrow. Per-haps because the rocky gorge had no deer; perhaps because the valley they are now entering had been occupied about 1850 by Chemehuevi.

[92] K-upilyk is to give for a funeral, destroy for a death; the place is no. 14, east, UC-AR 11:2, Map 2, and p. 142.

[93] Avi-'pa probably means "person-rock." It may be "Mohave Rock," now standing in Lake Havasu. It was said to be 5 miles from Hatšekupilyk and not yet in Chemehuevi Valley. No. 15, east, UC-AR 11:2, Map 2, and p. 142. Tinyam-kosama of the next paragraph is only a short way beyond but is already in the "Valley." Humar-otare, UC-AR 11:2, Map 2, no. 15a, east, and p. 142.

[94] Probably Oriole; cf. 7:90, fn. 141 (UC-AR 11:1, p. 65).

[95] Night-kosama, UC-AR 11:2, Map 2, no. 16, east, and p. 142.

[96] Not clear.

[97] Omaka or Umaka is "3-4 miles" downstream from Tinyam-kosama, and is no. 18, east, UC-AR 11:2, Map 2, and p. 142. It is mentioned in 8:159 (UC-AR 11:2, p. 101), and below, 14:40.

[98] Ahmo-kwe-'ataya is "many mortars," no doubt from the mortars in which the people there pounded mesquite beans, as in 11:52, above. The two places are on the river 3-4 miles S beyond Omaka (nos. 19, 19a, east, UC-AR 11:2, Map 2, and p. 142) and 8-10 miles S of the steamboat land-ing that used to stand opposite Chemehuevi Valley, where an American had a "ranch" (or mine?) in 1910.

[99] Ramada, brush roof without sides.

[100] Chemehuevi Valley seems to be richer in mesquite than in farm land. It does not flood very far back.

[101] Mesquite is pounded in the ahmo mortar, maize ground on the ahpe metate-quern.

[102] Tšamaδulye (Kūta also?) of note 88, are piss-ants (the previous "birds" of 45 being loosely inclusive); hence their living "in the ground."

[103] "White stripe down the back, a finger long, flies slowly, settles on trees." This might be almost any large insect.

[104] "Mesquite beans-pound."

[105] The insect wags its head, seemingly.

body will know me. I will live in Ha'avulypo[106] and everybody will call me Aya-kukitpute. As a mountain, nobody would know me; but when they see me flying around they will know me." [No songs].

55. Tumanpa stood there. He said: "When we arrived, we saw all these: now they are all turned into birds. There is nobody here, only you and I, only the two of us." He was a doctor. He said: "What are we going to be? Sky, or earth, or mountains? Shall we go up to heaven half way and live there forever?" The old man was thinking about that. "I don't think we will go up to the sky and stay: there is no place to sit on, no place to stand. Well, let us go up, anyway," he said to his sister. He held out his hand to her: "We are going to the sky." Then they went up in the clouds. But they came back from there and did not travel farther. They only went southeast to Tšimu-sem-kutšoive.[107] There they sat down together,

the old woman on the west, and Tumanpa on the east. They are the two rocks sticking up there now, near Aubrey: it takes about half a day to get there (from the river).[108] There is a rock, coming to a point, shaped like a man; he still holds his sister's hand.[109] [No songs].

The Mohave are the only ones who sing of Tumanpa.[110]

[106] Why back there?!

[107] Does Tšimu-sem-kutšoive have any connection with Tšimuveve, Chemehuevi? (Cf. note 75.) More likely with Sam-kutšoive, "Sister marry," given by Leslie Wilbur, see above.

[108] "Half a day" from Aubrey? Aubrey was said to be in Arizona somewhere near Lower Bill Williams Fork. There is an Aubrey peak in Arizona, about 10-12 miles N of the middle course of Williams Fork and 10-12 miles E of longitude 114°. It is some 4 miles S of McCracken Peak, which is a 4000+ foot ridge continuing the Walapai Mountains massif southward toward the NW end of Rawhide Range. It either is Avi-ku-nyamasave ("white mountain," UC-AR 11:2, Map 2, J7, L5, M3) or is very near it; see also 8:116, 148, and 154 (UC-AR 11:2, pp. 93, 99, 100). This mountain is 22 airline miles ENE of the mouth of Bill Williams Fork, and 15 NW or NNW of Kutpama (UC-AR 11:2, Map 2, I7) at the confluence of Big Sandy and Santa Maria rivers to form the Williams Fork. "Half a day" from there might mean within a radius of 10 miles.

[109] This is about as far as their incest seems to have gone—at any rate in this informant's version.

[110] This—evidently in answer to a question from me—is an error, as see the Introduction to Tumanpa.

OUTLINE AND SONG SCHEME

The Tumanpa Short song scheme is simple. There are 53 stages or stations, at 47 of which a pair of songs is normally sung. At stations no. 14, 39, 45, 47, there are four songs instead of two; at no. 40, six; and at 53, seven. This makes a total of 123. By the narrator's subsequent correction, station no. 14 has only two songs, the four first mentioned actually applying to both 14 and 15 as a double station, or two each; and no. 53 having four instead of seven songs. This would reduce the total to 118. It must be understood that all enumerations like this are only guides, not a ritually fixed scheme. If the narrator, or his audience, is in the mood, he is free to expand songs at any point. The list may well be thought of as a proper minimum. In fact, the informant said that he might sing tañai, but in the next song vary it to kañai—or hoseñia, howeñia; and similarly, he might sing more songs at any one station than shown by his listing. For each song, he said, he makes a knot, and by morning the string is a fathom long.

More songs do not mean that an episode has greater story importance. They do mean either that what is experienced at certain stations lends itself, by convention or by subject matter, to being sung of; or, that there is some tendency toward climactic piling up

songs as the story approaches its end. Thus, in the 118 total, all stations with more than two songs are in the last quarter of the narrative, nos. 39-53.

As usual, the final paragraphs describing the transformation are songless. One might infer that all Tumanpa songs are supposed to be as sung by Tumanpa on the journey leading up to his transformation; and correspondingly for the heroes of other cycles. They cannot however very well sing as they are turning into a rock or insect or bird; so this episode remains mere narration.

No. of Songs	Station	Place and Subject
2	1	Ha'avulypo
2	2	Avikwame
2	3	Aha-kuvilye
2	4	Providence Mountains, see fighting at Rattlesnake's Playfield
2	5	Same; see Buzzard scalped
2	6	Same; tribes will scalp
2	7	Selye'aya-kwa-hawa (ye); sandhills
2	8	Aha-kwoana; Jaguar and Mountain Lion
2	9	Same; river is running
2	10	Havirepoke; giant-cactus birds

No. of Songs	Station	Place and Subject
2	11	Ah'a-kwaθarve; Chemehuevi in skin shirts
2	12	Ashes-come; from Matavilya?
2	13	Amaṭ-ku-vataqanye (Miakwa'orve); playfield named
*4	14	Red Rock; sister thinks end of river. (*Later statement: 2 songs)
2	15	Same; see driftwood. (To here, one night of singing and telling)
2	16	Crossing the river on driftwood
2	17	Near Iδo-kuva'ire; reach east bank
2	18	Same; camp; rats come. It is night.
2	10	Same; stars; Pleiades, Orion
2	20	Same; morning star
2	21	Amaṭa-kukyeta, Humaθe and Beaver
2	22	Qara'erva; Humaθe pretends to catch
2	23	Selye'āya-kumitše; own body and walking
2	24	Aqwāqa-(h)iova; cactus spine in sister's foot
2	25	Hanyo-kumasθeve; place named
2	26	Same; see Kwiyak-aqwāθa, yellow shining
2	27	Kamahnuly-ve; place named
2	28	Aha-ku-kwin-ve; Walapai visit, rattle with left hand
2	29	Nyahweye-ve; rattlesnake
2	30	Va'orve; place named
2	31	Atšqāqa; place named
2	32	Kwaparvete; dreaming of the dead. (To here, two nights of singing)
2	33	Amaṭ-ehê- stūtšive; white paint
2	34	Hokiampeve; sister cured of foot pains

No. of Songs	Station	Place and Subject
2	35	The Needles Peaks; dispute over mesquite beans
2	36	Same; the mesquite is ripe
2	37	Selye'āya-mukyeṭa; sand lizards
2	38	Hatuṭva; see petrified men at Kwasukuly-ve
4	39	Bats'-house; see bats
6	40	Mountain-sheep's-road
2	41	Tšimukwily-kwa-hakyê-ve; name wash
2	42	Avi-rrove-hiδauve; mountains opened by Kwa'aku-sava-teve
2	43	Hamu-tšompa-kuya; Coyote tracks
2	44	Ivθe-kwa-'akyulye; Coyote who owns the morning
4	45	Selye'āya-'ita; hear people to south in Chemehuevi Valley
2	46	Ghost-houses; will bathe
4	47	Hatšekupilyke; do bathe; sister obtains paint
2	48	Avi-'pa; see Oriole
2	49	Tinyam-kosama; see man with feathers
2	50	Omaka; reach settlement; to house
2	51	Many-mortars; their destination
2	52	Same; Numkumuhava gives sister maize to grind; they pound mesquite
*7	53	Same; Numkumuhava disposes of birds. (*First statement, no songs; later, 4)
--	54	Numkumuhava turns into insect
--	55	Tumanpa and sister turn into two rocks
123 (118)		

WORDS OF TUMANPA SONGS

(Numbers in parentheses refer to stations, or paragraphs)

1. First song of the series, at Ha'avulypo (1):

nyuviuya	aya	hame
hanyok	hiemk	
dead	gone	(expletive)

2. Second, at Ha'avulypo (1):

kuma	hate	hive	hilye	(as sung)
ma-	te-	vi-	lya	(spoken syllables)
hima	hata	hapo	huikum	
ma-	te-	pu-	ik	
haθi	hinya	haδa	haukum	
i-	-	δa	uke	
aɲi	valam	ose	iya	(expletives)

Viz., ipuik viδauke, he died.

The manner of breaking words up into open syllables, irrespective of the etymology, and singing them with a ha-, hi-, hu- syllable preposed, is a bit reminiscent of the word plays on number, direction, and tribal names in 7 (UC-AR 11:2, p. 67).

3. At Avikwame(-hipuk), about Kwiltatpahve (2), first song:

Tiɲiyam huŋo kiɲinye.

This was said to be "Matavilya's language" for kuvetayam, several going (vs. iyem-k, one goes).

4. Second song there (2):

Tibimi	ŋavaŋa	(as sung)
Himim	kavavek	(spoken)
Cry	tell	

5. At Aha-kuvilye (3), first song:

Sewiŋiu	haya	huma
(Owiŋiu	waya)	
Kwanak	vatayemk	
Desert	cross	

Yaŋaima
Vetoyemka
Arrive

6. Second song there (3):

Kuŋuvi	hiyo	umaŋa

7. At Avi-kwa-havasu (4):

(Ti)waŋati	yaŋamani
	(yuŋomene)
Hiwa	Mathak
Heart	North

It is evident that the words of all of these are unrecognizably disturbed while sung—at least unrecognizable to us.

TUMANPA VANYUME

In March 1908 at Needles I heard of a man who knew Tumanpa Vanyumé. He was William Mellon, who answered also to the self-given obscene name of Hispanye-mehevik. He sang for me ten of the songs (cylinders nos. 924-933), apparently all but one from the early part of the story; but he was confused in his statements. He claimed that a Tejon or Tehachapi Indian named Távasqan (Sebastian?), who spoke Mohave, was the first to sing this kind of Tumanpa. If he was from Tejon, he would have been a Kitanemuk Serrano; if from Tehachapi, he was a Kawaiisu, a sort of aberrant Chemehuevi-speaking tribe; but if he was a Vanyumé, he belonged to the Serrano whom Garcés called Beñemé and found on Mohave River. Mellon varied in attributing the words of his songs to the Vanyumé or Mohave languages; and since he was one of the many singers who have great difficulty in reducing the distorted sung words to their spoken equivalents, he was hard to check on.

He had the action begin at Avikwame, which is certainly an error for Ha'avulypo, for in most of the songs Matavilya is still alive. This is my record:

Song 1. Sung about sunset; then we go on singing until midnight. This is by Matavilya:

    hapeaŋela (for hapĭli = ku-tinyam, "night")
    kumarenayumeka (for hiwak tšaman)
    amai .... (for isvare viv'aum)
    "The words are Vanyume"

Song 2. About darkness.

Song 3. I heard tiyaŋ-hinuyaŋ-hama. Sung slowly, this sounded like ikuševat iyav henuya.

Song 4. (missing or what?)

Song 5. I heard tinyam, "night."

Song 6. I heard oa-hoyomiyaŋ-karaŋ, or more slowly: oa yumi kaaŋ kavakuyum iakam, which Mellon again declared to be Vanyume.

Song 7. About the stars: tíyakayámi katšái kayáŋama-nuivaram, viz. tayámk hatšá kiyúk, which is certainly Mohave: "moving Pleiades see." (Handbook, p. 757.)

Song 8. Also about the stars: yáwe xatšám (ka)yóami kúmaríva kyóami, viz. hatšá kiyúk kumarév kiyúk: "Pleiades see name-them see."

Song 9. About Matavilya's being sick: tiyukam hiyam katiyuvam hiyam kuvasiyak šuvam iyam.

Song 10 was said to tell about Matavilya's being brought into the house, feeling bad, being laid near the door.

Song 11, the last recorded, was said to be the final one of the cycle. It refers to Amai-ku'úye, Sky-old woman (?), a man, wriggling into the ground at Avi-veskwi kaveik, "a little south of Boundary Cone," northeast across the river from Needles City. [This suggests what Wilbur said about the han'ava insect in the version heard by him. But if this was really the end of the journey, the route of this version is much shorter than any other.]

Mellon also said that Tumanpa Vanyume was danced to by people standing in a circle, hanging their heads, and jerking their chests. When I expressed surprise, he said that at any rate this is what was done at Kingman in 1904. This sounds like a sporadic attempt at diffusion to the Walapai, something like the Salt Singing recorded from the Walapai and discussed below, part II, C.

Later, when my old interpreter Jack Jones was available, I asked him about Tumanpa Vanyume. He said it was learned not from Tavasqan but from Tavasqan's Mohave-speaking kinsmen. The songs have Mohave words and he can understand them; in fact, he himself could "help in the singing," that is, sing along, if there was a leader. The story, however, was not told in Mohave but in Vanyume [if at all]. He knew that the songs began at Ha'avulypo, went as far west as Matavily-vove near Mohave River east (upstream) of Barstow, [then turned back to the Colorado River], and ended as Mellon said near Boundary Cone.

He added that analogously to this he had heard still another Tumanpa variety, Tumanpa ahwe, "foreign Tumanpa," originally belonging to the Cocopa, sung with Mohave words which he could understand, but not the story.

This, incidentally, again fits in with the Walapai singing a Mohave-Chemehuevi cycle like Salt (Tale 12, below) without having more than glimpses of the story, and the main thread of continuity being the places.

As to the Vanyumé Serrano, the presumption has been that the Franciscans drained these from Mohave River to the missions and that few if any returned to their original homeland. But again, an old Vanyume woman named Moha whom I talked with among the Mohave in the first years of the century had been brought to the Mohave as a girl or child about the time most of her people were massacred—allegedly by Mexicans; or according to two Chemehuevi accounts, by the Mohave themselves. At any rate in 1844, ten years after secularization, Fremont found no Indians on Mohave River except a party of armed Mohave Indians traveling through, who claimed the Mohave River as having once been theirs; they said that the Indian who interpreted into Spanish for them was originally a native of the region (that is, a Vanyumé), but finding no one in his ancestral country when he returned from the missions, he attached himself to them and now lived on the Colorado. He may indeed have been the very Tavasqan of Mohave memory; at any rate, Tavasqan was probably some one more or less in his situation, or a descendant.

Narrative 12
SALT

CHARACTER OF THE NARRATIVE

The Salt story was obtained from the same informant (Achyora Hanyava) who narrated Tumanpa, and on the same occasion, namely his visit to the University, along with Jack Jones to interpret, in 1910.

The tale is somewhat disappointingly unimaginative. Four people leave Ha'avulypo on Matavilya's death and cremation to wander until they transform into Salt. The two older manage to do this by sinking into the ground to the east, in Walapai land, but blow back the two younger when these try to follow them. These then travel west to the far end of the Mohave desert, in supposed sight of San Joaquin Valley tribes, then turn back with a southerly trend, and finally transform into Rock Salt well west of the Colorado River somewhere in the latitude of Parker. They meet, see, hear, or name various places, animals, or tribes; but nothing at all eventful happens, not even in their minds. Further, most of the incident-fillings recur in other narratives: the burnt house, Avikwame, swallows, wondering about their end, grasshoppers, owls, night, Pleiades and Orion, meteors, lake, people playing, rat. The sole

original item is the tobacco worms of four colors—and this seems not very relevant or clear.

The total journey east, north, west, southeast must aggregate several hundred miles, but appears to be covered in two days. At any rate, only one night in camp is mentioned—for which there is parallel in most Mohave tales. Perhaps we have here a pattern: a second night with nothing to sing about but the Pleiades and other stars might be unduly repetitive even to the Mohave. They are forever coming close to repeating, but not quite identically, at least not in the same story. Their imaginative range being narrower and more decorative than ours, this satisfies them. Their lack of deliberate, precise narrative repetition, with lack also of formal balance of expression, is interesting in this connection: it appears to be due to the lack in Mohave and other Yumans of ritual sense as it is exemplified for instance among Zuni, Navaho, and even Apache. Subjective, epic in breadth, decorative in treatment, nonritualized—these are four characterizations that can be applied to Mohave narratives.

SONG SCHEME

The song scheme shows 25 journey stages. To these there correspond 117 songs, or not quite five—from one to twelve—per station. More than a fourth of the total 117 are sung at the last three stations. After the fifteenth station, the informant said that here he had not yet sung through the night; or, since the whole took a night and the next day, not yet quite half. With this, his listing of song numbers is in accord: 54 songs in these first fifteen stages, 63 in the remaining ten.

Songs	Station	Event
2	1	Four Salt leave Ha'avulypo
2	2	Mountain sheep go west to Kwiltatpahve
2	3	Salt go east to Avikwa'me-ta

Songs	Station	Event
1	4	Traveling east to Tu'kuva, in Walapai desert
4	5	See Swallows at Hoalye-puke
4	6	Lost at Kwa'orve, north of Hackberry
6	7	Continue north, thinking of what they will become
4	8	Stamp as approach Ati'siara
6	9	At Ati'siara, two oldest sink in ground
6	10	Two younger weep salt of four colors
4	11	Two younger take names
4	12	Traveling north, they meet Grasshopper
5	13	See Atíse
2	14	Far northwest, see tobacco with four colors of worms

Songs	Station	Event	Songs	Station	Event
2	15	See Owls at ðokupíta-aha-soqîre	5	22	West to Rattlesnake's Field, hear western tribes
2	16	Camp there	9	23	Turn east to Haramaθeve-kutš-ia-va
8	17	Night and stars appear	11	24	East to large sandhills, see rat tracks
6	18	Shooting stars	12	25	On east to (Hi)me-kuvauve, turn to rock salt
4	19	Pleiades and Orion setting			
2	20	Daylight, go west to Uqaliho			
4	21	To Providence Mts., see lake to west	117		

THE SALT TALE

1. When Matavilya died and they fired the house, then Salt[1] had no home because it had been burned. There were four of them there. They went a little way east, stood, and two gave names to themselves. The oldest said: "My name is Aθ'i-meka-'ere." The next gave himself the name of Aθ'i-meka-to.[2] The two youngest did not yet take names. (2 songs.)

2. Four mountain sheep[3] started out first. West from Fort Mohave, halfway up the mountain, there is a little peak named Kwiltatpahve.[4] The four sheep were there. One was black, one white, one yellow, one was Amo-nyohaṭa.[5] They cut their hair with a knife.[6] "I am not going to stay here, I am going west," they said. "Perhaps somebody will use my hair and make something of me." That's what the mountain sheep said. (2 songs.)

3. The two Salt men who had taken names went east while the sheep were going west. The two came to a mountain east of Ha'avulypo, to Avikwa'me-ta.[7] They stood there and said: "I am going to think about my brothers, the sheep." They were not their brothers but they called them so. The two thought: "The sheep, my brothers, are going west. I don't know how far they will go, nor whether east or west or north or south." They stood there and thought of that. (2 songs.)

4. They went on again, across the desert west of Hackberry.[8] They were traveling east and in the middle of the valley came to Tu'kuva.[9] They said: "Well, I will tell of where we started, of where we came, downhill and up, and along the valley here. I am telling that. Bye and bye someone will hear me tell the way, and will tell it too." They kept going and telling while they walked along. (1 song.)

5. About the middle of the valley they saw birds flying up and making a noise. The two said: "Those are my brothers. You are my brothers. You went away[10] early, before everyone else went off. Nobody knows you, because nobody saw you leaving; but you are like me, like my own body. You went away to turn into something. I know you are my brothers, (though) you turned into birds." The birds had no name: so the two men said: "I will name you. I will give you this name: Swallow;[11] all will call you Swallow." The place there was Hoalye-puke.[12] (4 songs.)

6. They crossed the desert and climbed the mountain Kwa'orve, north of Hackberry.[13] They stood there and said: "We stand here, looking everywhere to see if we like a place to go to. Perhaps we shall go this way or that way. As we look around, if we like a place, we will go to it; if we don't like it, we will not go there." They saw that everywhere it was far to go; they could see no mountains. They said: "Now we are lost. That is what Matavilya said: 'When I die, you will not know where to go.' Now we really don't know which way to go: we stand here." (4 songs.)

[1]Aθ'í, singular and plural the same.
[2]Untranslated, except for the first element, "salt."
[3]Ammo, or amo, but the informant here said amo-nyohaṭa, which suggests ahaṭa, dog, tame animal, and hence domestic sheep. See below, note 5.
[4] This would be across the river from Fort Mohave but Kwiltatpahve seems otherwise unidentified.
[5]"Domestic-sheep-color"? See note 3.
[6]Ahkwe-tš-aθ'i-lye, "salt knife"?
[7]Suggests "great" or "real Avikwame," whose precise form is probably Avi-kwa'me.
[8]This is in Walapai country, in the level desert valley between the Cerbat Range at whose southern end lies Kingman, and the plateau edge at which Hackberry lies in a canyon.

[9]"A mountain in the middle of this desert about 6 miles from Walapai (Hualpai) R.R. station." I do not recall such a peak, nor the station.
[10]From the scene of Matavilya's death.
[11]Hamkye.
[12]"The farther end of the mountain stretching east from Kingman." The Hualpai Mountains begin east of Kingman and extend southward. They are named after their yellow pines, hoālye; and pūke occurs in a Cane tale hero's name with the apparent meaning of butt or root.
[13]This would be an escarpment rather than a peak. Kwa'orve suggests Miakwa'orve, at the north end of Mohave Valley.

7. From there they started north, to another valley, a big desert.[14] When they got into that, the older one was thinking of turning into something. "What will I be? A big hill of sand, a mountain, a large rock,[15] or a bird? When I have gone far, perhaps I can turn into something there, maybe into a big rock, here or somewhere. Perhaps I shall not want to go farther: I don't know yet. Matavilya said: 'Well when you know how you want to be, you can be something.' That is what Matavilya said. He didn't tell me to be like this or that, but: 'You can go where you want, and perhaps you will know something and can become like that, a rock, or water, or a bird, or sand, or whatever you wish.' That is what Matavilya said." He was thinking of that, while they were walking along. (6 songs.)

8. They kept going on, toward Ati'siara and Yava'awi,[16] but they had not reached there yet. The four of them were together, two with names and two without. Then the oldest one began to pound the ground with his feet as he walked; he was trying to make a hole and go down it. "When I get there, I will go inside; perhaps in a gulch. Maybe I shall be a big rock,"[17] he said. As he walked, he stamped,[18] trying to make a hole to get into. (4 songs.)

9. Then the two oldest went into a hole. The two younger wanted to get in too. But both of those who had entered were doctors,[19] and their breath blew the others back. Four times they tried to follow but were blown back each time. Then they learned they were not strong enough; so they stayed outside. (6 songs.)

10. The two outside cried. They looked east, toward the sun. "My tears, one drop of them, will be salt, red salt, far east." He turned northward; one teardrop to the north made black salt. To the west, one tear dropped on the earth and made white salt: white men use that. Then he looked south, and a teardrop made earthy salt,[20] such as the Mohave used to use for salt.[21] (6 songs.)

[14] North of Hackberry, there is high plateau all the way to the Colorado River, nothing that could be called a valley or true desert. To the northeast, however, toward dry Red Lake, is the northerly end of the flat desert valley which they had previously crossed going eastward toward Hackberry. But this does not agree with the localization in note 16.

[15] Mountain and rock are both avi.

[16] "One place with two names, in Walapai country, about a day's walk north from Peach Springs on the railroad." Peach Springs is less than 20 miles in an air line from the great southward bend of the Colorado as it flows around Shiwits Plateau, about halfway between Grand Canyon and Hoover Dam.

[17] Or mountain.

[18] "As the Mohave stamp when they sing Salt," said the narrator.

[19] Had supernatural power.

[20] Aθ'ī-amaṭ.

[21] Counterclockwise circuit beginning east, and with the color-direction association: E-red, N-black, W-white, S-earthy. Contrast the association in note 27.

11. The two youngest stayed there and thought of going north. They said: "My older brothers got a name and went into a hole. But I have no name. I want to get one so everyone will know me. Nobody knows me now. We will give ourselves names and all will know where we went. But I am still thinking: I am not ready to go yet." They were sitting there. Then the older of the two took the name Haseyaṭa. The other took the name Hiwaly-hayota.[22] (4 songs.)

12. Now the two[23] started north from there. As they walked, a little thing like a grasshopper came in front of them and sat there. Whenever they reached him, the grasshopper flew up and settled ahead of them. "If you keep doing that, I am going to give you a name, so everybody will know you," they said. "I call you Hunye-kampute-avunye-kwekatšinatše."[24] (4 songs.)

13. They kept going north and saw Atīse.[25] When he saw the two boys coming, he went back into his hole. They said: "I know you: you came out alive from Matavilya's pulse. We will give you a name. We will call you Atīse." (5 songs.)

14. They kept going north, but looked west. Then, from far off, they saw a place, A'u'vivave, northwest of Eldorado Canyon.[26] They said: "I see tobacco growing there. One vine goes north, one west, one south, and one east. And I see Hamesukwempe worms on every vine: they lie on it and hold to it. A yellow worm is on the east vine. A light gray (nyamaθave) worm is on the north vine. A blue worm lies on the west vine. The worm to the south is black on the back, with a mark down it; that is the tobacco the Mohave use, in the south. The yellow tobacco, the Walapai use. The northern white, the Kohoalche Paiute. The white man uses the blue in the west.[27] (2 songs.)

15. Then the two boys saw the place ðokupíta-aha-soqíre.[28] They came near it but did not get to it. Then they said that they were smart and had dreamed: Matavilya did not know much. He made the sun and moon and stars; he made Pleiades, and Orion too; he made them to shine so you can see to walk. And he made a

[22] Names unexplained.

[23] "Boys," here and often thereafter.

[24] "Black, about an inch long" (which would suggest a cricket, except for the flying). "This is the everyday name now" (for which it seems unduly long).

[25] Prairie dog? "Sticks his head out of his hole in the ground; like a rat; body light in color, tail "long"; Walapai eat, Mohave do not. Perhaps a rat or spermophile.

[26] A'uva is tobacco. They are looking a mighty long way, from where they are, across the Colorado where it flows south below Hoover Dam. But these are myth times: next they even see the worms on the tobacco plants there.

[27] Again counterclockwise circuit but beginning this time in the north, and with the color and ethnic association (given in reverse order!) as follows: N-light gray (white)-Kohoalche Paiute, W-blue-Americans, S-black-marked Mohave, E-yellow-Walapai. There is no correspondence whatever with the circuit of note 21.

[28] "Owl-water-soqíre"; not placed.

house out of darkness. But Matavilya died in the night; and he didn't know which way was east, south, north. After he died, Mastamho knew which way east, south, and north were. And the two boys said: "I know it too." Then they heard the owl, ðokupíta, making a loud noise, and they said: "I know you: you are my brother; I know you came to life from Matavilya's pulse.[29] You were like a man, but you turned to be a bird. I hear your voice and know you. So I am going to give you a name: I call you Owl, ðokupíta. Now you are ðokupíta." They said: "I know you: you live here. You don't live like anyone else: you live in holes and make nests there." Then the two boys gave names to six kinds of owls: Setšyaka, Kaθuweka, Turruirruive, Amaṭ-kunyeviye, Takoke, and ðokupíta. The last is head of the others, the leader. Amaṭ-kunyevive lives in holes in the ground, Turruirruive and Takoke in logs. (2 songs.)[30]

16. They arrived at ðokupíta-aha-soqíre. There is brush there, and small trees,[31] and grass. They pulled them up and laid them around and made a camp.[32] It was nearly sundown, and they saw darkness coming;[33] they told about that. (2 songs.)

17. Then dark was everywhere. Now came the big stars and the little stars, Orion and Pleiades. They told about that as they saw them coming. Matavilya had made the stars; they told of that. (8 songs.)

18. At midnight they saw some stars flying fast. The boys said: "Matavilya made these unlike the others. When he died, maybe these stars died too. They do not sit still but travel quickly. Perhaps they are turning into something. These stars that go fast have a name: Hamuse-lulim."[34] (6 songs about the shooting stars.)

19. They saw Pleiades and Orion moving west. They said: "The seven stars and the three stars are going down." They had not set yet, but they were halfway down. "I will tell of that so persons will know about it, about the three stars and the seven stars going down. When daylight comes, they have set, and it will be morning.[35] So everybody will know that." (4 songs.)

20. Soon it was daylight. Then they started from ðokupita-aha-soqíre to go to Aha-kwoana, Hosive, and Aqāq-tšuama. They stood at Aha-kwoana and didn't know which way to go. Then they went west, and came to Uqaliho. (2 songs.)[36]

21. From Uqaliho they went to Avi-kwa-havasu, the Providence Mountains. They stood there and looked west and saw a big lake. The older said: "As soon as we come down to the sea we will get shells." He wanted to wear them. The younger said: "No, that is no sea. That is a lake. When we get there we shall see tule reeds, and little shells, of two kinds, Hamuse-t-kwaθrava and Tannaha, and we shall see hasime, something like rags or leaves, in the water."[37] The boys were standing there and looking to where the Tule River Indians (Yokuts) live.[38] "That is no sea: it is only a big lake. We shall not find shells there, only four;[39] you will see." Now they quarreled. The older one said: "That is the sea. We shall find something you have never seen." (2 songs by each.)

22. Now they started from Providence Mountains, and came to Hayekwire-nye-mat'āre.[40] There they saw the lake.[41] People were living around it. The two heard the noise of voices and saw the smoke of fires. "I know that is my brothers who went off this way; I know it is they. I am going to give them a name. I will call these tribes Hamakhava-kwiahta[42] and Kwahalimo.[43] (5 songs.)

---

[29]"Heart."

[30]"Here I have not yet sung through the night. The whole of Salt takes all night and the next day to sing."

[31]Ivθe, Larrea.

[32]Ahutšye is the "grass." For the circular, roofless camp, see above, Tumanpa 11:18, and below, Chuhueche 13:67.

[33]To the Mohave, night does not "fall" or "come on" but it always "comes from the east," traveling like the sun. The idea is frequent in Housman's poetic imagery.

[34]Hamuse, star; lulim?

[35]If the Pleiades set by dawn, they rise at dusk. This is, I suppose, about December. To test whether the informant really knew his star times, I asked whether this was summer or winter. He repeated the passage and said the story did not tell what time of year it was. My experience among

various tribes points to two conclusions. (1) Most old Indians, in describing fixed star positions, are talking about the end of the night, before daylight, not about pre-bedtime evening like ourselves; although they rarely specify this fact. (2) At some time or other, they note the early-morning place of a constellation in the sky, and then tend to get this set in their memory, as if the place were fixed the year round. It is only by asking where a given constellation is now, this night, that they are likely to give its actual position.

[36]All essentially unlocalized, except that Aha-kwoana is mentioned above in Tumanpa Short, 11:8 as N of Ha'avulypo, and Uqaliho (Oqalihu) in the Wilbur outline of Tumanpa Long also as N of Ha'avulypo. They evidently cross the Colorado at (A)ha-kwoana, which Tumanpa mentions as on the river. The Providence Mountains mentioned next are west of the river, northwest of Needles City.

[37]Tule reeds: Scirpus lacustris, kwalinyo. I have no other references to either of the two kinds of shells, nor to the hasime trash. Hamuse means star.

[38]The Yokuts in the San Joaquin Valley are of course invisible from the Providence Mountains. Not only the Tehachapis but several ranges across the Mohave Desert intervene.

[39]Not clear.

[40]Hayekwire-nye-mat'āre, "Rattlesnake's field," is a flat or playa, Rogers or Muroc dry lake some 12 miles E of Mohave Station, SE of Tehachapi. The place recurs in 7:98 (UC-AR 11:1, p. 66) and above in Tumanpa, 11, fn. 6.

[41]Tulare Lake is meant: it is invisible from Rogers dry lake.

[42]"Like-Mohave." Discussed in Handbook, p. 612.

[43]Unidentified.

(We Mohave do not use these names; we call them Kwalinyo-kosmatši[44] and Vanyume.[45] I understand Matavilya's words and Salt's words, but others do not understand them. I understand because I heard it.)

23. The boys said: "I know they are our brothers who went away long ago.[46] Their words are different and they live differently. They don't understand me and I don't understand them. We will not go to those tribes: we will turn back." So they went east from Hayekwire-nye-mat'āre to Haramaθeve-kutš-ia-va and Haramaθeve-kutš-upai-va.[47] (9 songs.)

24. Then they came to Selye'aya-kuvataye.[48] They saw a big rat running around there, and told about its tracks. (11 songs.)[49]

25. They went on east and came to (Hi)me-kuvauve.[50] As they stood there, they said they wanted to go back to where Matavilya died. They did not go there: they just thought about it. "When I cry and my tears drop on the ground they will be salt." There was no mountain then, no rock, only sand. As they stood there, they said: "I think I will become rock and the rock will be salt." They said: "Now there will be rock here at (Hi)me-kuvauve. You will see a high mountain, all salt. (12 songs.)

When the Paiute (Chemehuevi) sing Salt, they dream from this place.[51] Maybe their story travels another way. I do not know where it goes, but they sing Salt too[52] and go on from here.

The Colorado River was not yet made at this time.

INFORMANT'S STATEMENT

"I sing Salt: I know where they started and where they ended. There are two men who can help me sing it: Mohan-kurrauve and θuwine-kwavkiove; but they don't know the order, and get mixed. I am the only one who can tell it all; and when I die, no one will know Salt.[53] As for Chuhueche, three men and a woman know it beside myself: Itšiere-θuwine, Mokwiθta, Avi-ahaku-haye, and the woman Kumeθi. All four of them dreamed it[54] and know it, and will be able to sing it after I am gone; but for Salt I am the only one."

After the long tale was ended, the informant said the following, without apparent sense of contradiction to the foregoing:

"Only three men and a woman, besides myself, know this Chuhueche. Long ago, old people knew it, taught me, and I learned and took their place. Now the three younger men know it and can tell it as I do."

---

[44] "Tule-sleep," the usual name for the Tulare Lake Yokuts (and neighboring Shoshoneans). See Handbook, 488. But the Tule-sleepers are not the Like-Mohaves, who are the Kitanemuk or Alliklik or some Serrano division: Handbook, 612.

[45] The name suggests Panamint (where the inhabitants spoke Shoshone proper; but I have interpreted my Mohave information on the Vanyume as referring to the Serrano-speaking residents along Mohave River whom Garcés called Beñemé, and this usage has become more or less standardized. See Shoshonean Dialects of California, UC-PAAE, 4:135, 1907, and Handbook, 614.

[46] The whole business of Matavilya's sickness, death, funeral, and obliteration, and of Mastamho's institutings, and the various beings wandering off and transforming into their final shapes, are usually described in the stories as occupying a matter of days only—two or four or six for the events of any one story. Yet the same myths also contain expressions like the present one, about "long before." Such "contradictions" evidently do not worry the Mohave, who are able to make themselves believe that they project their souls back and forth between the present and the time of world origins.

[47] "SE across one desert from Amboy" on the Santa Fe R.R. There is a level desert extending 40 miles SE from Amboy to the Iron Mountains. It is about 160 miles from Muroc Lake. Cf. a Haramaθeve-kwayumpa below in Chuhueche, 13:38, n. 58.

[48] "Sandhills S of Amboy, two deserts away to the W from the Colorado River at Parker." The name Selye'aya-kuvataye means great sand. This appears to be a somewhat winding stretch of sand desert beginning about 15 miles SE of the Iron Mountains and extending ESE 20 miles to within 3 or 4 miles of the Colorado River, S of the Turtle and then of the Riverside Mountains. But the dunes are SE, not S, of Amboy, and they are not two deserts W of the Colorado.

[49] A lot of songs to devote to rat's tracks.

[50] (Hi)me-kuvauve is "a day's (Mohave foot) travel west of Parker Reservation. The Chemehuevi come there for salt." Allowing 20 miles for such a day's foot travel, we would have Hime-kuvauve placed somewhere near the western part

of the sand dunes. Salt has been mined by Americans in Bristol dry lake just S of Amboy, and at Saltmarsh on the Santa Fe branch R.R. on Danby dry lake between Iron and Turtle Mountains.

[51] May mean that their tale begins here.

[52] This is confirmed by Handbook, 599.

[53] Among the Mohave. Chemehuevi and Walapai also sing Salt.

[54] The interpreter here commented that he had thought women did not dream. He may have been referring to their not shaking a rattle, and hence presumably not having themselves "dreamed" a song-myth cycle. The Coyote Tale, no. 6 (UC-AR 11:1, 46-48), I recorded from Lahoka's mother, who insisted she had dreamed it—though bystanders asserted she had dreamed it wrong; and it was unaccompanied by singing.

TRIBAL ORIGIN OF THE SALT MYTH

The Chemehuevi claim to sing Salt, and other Mohave besides Achyora Hanyava confirm that they do. The Walapai say that they have sung it since they learned it from the Chemehuevi when they were put on the Parker reservation for some years in the 1860's. The internal evidence on the Walapai version is analyzed below. The question remains whether the Mohave gave the story and songs to the Chemehuevi or the reverse. The geography of the tale bears on this problem.

The Mohave probably claimed Ha'avulypo in Eldorado Canyon (station 1), but have not lived there since Chemehuevi began to settle on Cottonwood Island soon after the Ives expedition of 1858. For stations 3-13 the Salt heroes are clearly in northern Walapai territory. From 14 to 20 the places named cannot be put on a map, but if east of the Colorado they were in historic Walapai territory, if west in Chemehuevi. The Tobacco Mt. which they look to far northwest of Eldorado

Canyon is certainly in the homeland of the Chemehuevi if not of the Las Vegas band of Southern Paiute of whom the "Chemehuevi" of the historic period are nothing but an emigrant offshoot and a culturally intergrading one. Station 21, the Providence Mts., is indisputable historic Chemehuevi territory; Muroc dry lake of 22 more liekly belonged to the Kanaiisu of Tehachapi —but these are also ethnically Southern Paiute, merely having diverged from the main stock a few centuries earlier than the Chemehuevi and penetrated somewhat farther northwestward. Stations 23-25 are in the nearer desert west of the Colorado which the Chemehuevi have undisputedly occupied since Americans knew them and probably since Garcés in 1776. If we could locate (Hi)me-kuvauve more precisely, where the Mohave tale ends, and about which the Chemehuevi are said to dream, we might understand better how to assign the myth as between Mohave and Chemehuevi.

ANALYSIS OF THE WALAPAI VERSION OF SALT

In 1929 one old Walapai, Blind Tom, was said to know the 106 songs of the Salt cycle.[55] He had learned them from two older Walapai, who in turn learned them from the Chemehuevi living near Parker[56] during the several years in the 1860's when the Walapai had been removed by troops from their homeland and were living at "Halapasa opposite Parker" (actually La Paz south of it). Blind Tom said that he did not know the story; by which he evidently meant that he had not learned the myth as a formal narrative. He had however been told enough about the words which he learned to sing in each song to be able to tell something of the situation to which they referred. When such comments on the separate songs are put together, they provide a rather hazy outline of plot. The singer's comments on the first 61 of the 106 songs were recorded; external circumstances prevented completion of the list.

With one exception, the recognizable words in the songs or comment on them are Yuman, not Shoshonean.

[55] F. Kniffen et al., Walapai Ethnography, ed. A. L. Kroeber, American Anthropological Association Memoir 42, 1935; see pp. 195-198.

[56] Halapasa is where the Walapai say they were kept on the Colorado Reservation, and one statement puts it "across the river" from Parker. Halapasa obviously is the former La Paz, near the southern end of the Reservation, west of the river. But the present-day Mohave at Parker say that the Walapai lived scattered among themselves.

Thus:

Hero, leader: Kwadaga'eva (Mohave, kwora'ak, old man, o'evitš, used in address to each other by brothers).

Song 2: tinyaim, night (Moh. tinyam).

5: koko, bird (Moh. kukho, yellowhammer).

6: Hakutšiepa (Moh. Hakutšyepa, mouth of Williams R.).

36: ipa, arrow (Moh. ipa).

41: hatsa, Pleiades (Moh. hatša).

47: ya-nako, bear (Wal. neqo).

52: matahai-sun, high wind (Moh. matha, wind).

58: kwaluyawa, fowl, chicken (Moh. qwaluyauve, cock).

61: smalkato, jimsonweed, Datura (Moh. smalykato).

The only Shoshonean word is mani, jimsonweed, in mane-yelo in this same song 61.

It is therefore clear that if the Walapai really learned their Salt songs from the Chemehuevi they either learned them with Yuman words; or else, having been told the meaning of each song, they reworded it into Walapai.

Salt, Deer, Mountain sheep, and Doctoring are the four singings which a Chemehuevi in Mohave Valley once told me his people had;[57] and presumably each

[57] Handbook, p. 599; based on JAFL 21:240-242, 1908.

—or at least the three first—was accompanied by a narrative. It is possible that the Chemehuevi took over Salt from the Mohave; or the reverse. The Walapai information does not illuminate this point.

The Walapai data suffice to outline the geography of the first half of the narrative. It begins at Mohave Ikwé-nye-vá "cloud home," Walapai Kwinyua,[58] somewhere "beyond Big Sandy, North of Phoenix;" that is, in Western Yavapai or Tolkepaya territory. See Part II, B, 4, on this peak. These are the references:

1, Kwinyuá. Although used by Walapai shamans, this mountain seems to have been just within Western Yavapai territory.

7, Hakutšiepa, mouth of Bill Williams R. into Colorado.

8, [back on] Big Sandy, N. affluent of Bill Williams R.

[58]This "Kwinyua" may be the same as Kwinyawa, Akwinyawa, Kwinyuvan (Kniffen et al., 1935, pp. 186, 189), the mountain from which Walapai shamans principally got their powers. It was variously said by the Walapai to refer to caves in the hills E of Signal, or to be Artillery Peak near Signal. Although "used" by the Walapai shamans, the mountain seems to have been just within Western Yavapai territory. The name is probably the same as Mohave Ikwé-nye-vá, "Clouds their house," mentioned along with Kutpama in 8:102, 108, 111, 148, 153, 156 (UC-AR 11:2, pp. 91, 92, 93, 99, 100), and shown together (as I 7-8) on UC-AR 11:2, Map 2 as near the confluence of the Big Sandy and the Santa Maria River to form Bill Williams Fork, not far from Signal. Presumably Kutpama was to the narrator of the Historical Epic, 8 (UC-AR 11:2), a habitation site, Ikwe-nye-va a mountain in the vicinity. There is also another Ikwe-nye-va in Gila drainage: see above, 9:9, note 26. In Tortoise, 19:55, below, Ikwe-nye-va is a great mountain in Arizona, of very vague situation. It is reached in the story from Bill Williams Fork, but hearsay of the other Ikwe-nye-va much farther off may have confused informant and interpreter. Resumé of the identifications in Part II, B, 4.

12, on Big Sandy, near Hapuk, which was the main settlement of the Walapai band owning the drainage of that stream. Hapuk is on the Sandy, 15-16 m. below the mouth of Trout Cr., 10-12 m. above the mouth of Burro Cr., 27-28 m. above the mouth of the Santa Maria.

23, Wenyaniat near Kwadigio, both unlocated.

29, below Yucca, on Sacramento Wash, on opposite side of the Hualpai range from Hapuk and Big Sandy.

30, when they come to the [Colorado] river they will see cottonwoods and willows.

33, 34, they will not drown in the river.

35, 36, they will see a new brush there, and make arrows [reference to arrowweed, Pluchea].

37-50, they spend the night in the open.

57, they shoot arrows into Wi-kiqidaqid, "Needles Mt.," (the Pinnacles?), Chickenhawk's future home.

58, at big mt. W of Colorado R.

62-106, unrecorded.

This is a wholly different itinerary from that of the present Mohave Salt version: it moves from east of the Colorado to west of it. From 8 to 29, the narrative progresses on southwestern Walapai soil. It does not begin at Ha'avulupo or Avikwame. All this suggests that the plot, at least in its present form as received by the Walapai, is not of direct Mohave origin, or at least not wholly so: the Yavapai-Walapai locale of the beginning would be contrary to Mohave precedent.

In short, the Walapai Salt cycle is much more likely to have been derived by them from the Chemehuevi than from the Mohave, as indeed stated by themselves, but the Walapai perhaps added some Walapai geography at the beginning.

Narrative 13
CHUHUECHE

CIRCUMSTANCES AND CHARACTER OF THE STORY

Chúhueche is the third song-myth told by Achyora Hanyava in December of 1910, the others being 11, Tumanpa, and 12, Salt. It is the longest of the three. Most of it is told in the same dry manner of an itinerary with only brief entry of happenings. But the last part of Chuhueche finally warms up into a human-interest story; though most of its plot in this portion recurs in 1, Cane, or in 6A, Coyote (UC-AR 11:1, 4-23, 46-47), or in 18, Satukhota, below; and these others are narrated with greater liveliness than Achyora Hanyava was able to muster. These correspondences of content are detailed below; as are some correspondences or near-repetitions in this informant's own three tales.

I have neither translation nor etymology for the name Chuhueche by which this singing is known among the Mohave. The hero-brothers are insects called Hayunyé, who live in house thatch and whose chirp or call reminds the Mohave of mourning wails. Like the Han'avá insects of other tales, they are said to have been the first to bewail the dead god Matavilya. Whether Hayunye and Han'ava are the same or different species of insects, I do not know: Mohave descriptions of such small fry of animal life—or even of larger forms—usually select traits which to us are so random and arbitrary as to make identification very difficult. The Hayunye might well be crickets; the Han'ava, cicadas.

As for the insect-heroes having one name and the song-tale another, there is parallel in the cycle uni-

versally referred to as Nyoháiva, whose heroine is the red-spotted insect Yanaθa-kwe-'atáye; and in Satukhóta, whose common name, as a bird, is kukhó, the yellowhammer. In these cases, also, no etymology could be obtained for the designation of the song cycle.

However, the present tale adds an unusual concept to its conventional beginning with the death of Matavilya. Six-song-cycles, personified, sit about the dying god, and later take him outdoors to his cremation pyre. Three of these six are the tales which Achyora Hanyava recited: Salt and Chuhueche, "the two oldest" of the six, and Tumanpa Short. The repeated specification of "six" shows that it is personified abstractions of the song-cycles that are referred to, not their heroes, for these aggregate more than six: a pair each in Chuhueche and Salt, four at least in the beginning of Salt, besides those in the three other singings.

This being a long narrative, it may be helpful to present its itinerary and outline before the full text. For convenience, I have organized the 85 song stations and "paragraphs" into six sections. Two of these deal with the first world-events at Ha'avulypo and Avikwame; two more with the hero brothers' journey west into the Chemehuevi desert and then return east and travel far south; and the last two with their adventures and end at Melyehweke mountain in historic Western Yavapai land, and the deeds of a posthumous son.

CHUHUECHE ITINERARY AND EVENTS

A. 1-13. Matavilya's Death at Ha'avulypo

1, 2. At Ha'avulypo. Matavilya sick.

3, 4. Same. Six song cycles are with him.

5, 6. Same. Badger and Raccoon fail to cure him.

7, 8. Same. Takse (Gopher) brings cremation wood from W.

9. Same. Mud-dauber wasp (Kapisara) digs cremation trench.

10-12. Same. The Six carry M. out, lay him on pyre.

13. Same. Coyote goes W for fire, but Fly makes fire, M. is burned.

B. 14-18. Hayunye-Chuhueche Mourn,
Go to Avikwame

14. At Ha'avulypo. Two Hayunye mourn M.

15. Same. Four Mountain Sheep go W.

16-18. S to Avikwame. Two Hayunye name playfields and Avi-kwa'ame.

C. 19-39. Hayunyes' Journey West
to New York Mts.

19. A little "W," to between fields. Older and younger Hayunye take names.

20. W to Tšimuweve-samire. They name a mountain.

21. W to Nyamaθave-tavave. Name it.

22. W to Kunalya-kuvatatše. Tell of way.

23. W, in desert. See Piss-ants and Horned Toad.

24. (W) to Kwanakwa-tšaθkine desert.

25. W to Kwesoqirve. Crackling leaves.

26-28. W to mountain grapes and mirage.

29. W to Piute Spring. Walking on sand.

30, 31. NW to Kwikam-tšotka. Dispute: then cry for Matavilya.

32. W to Ohuere-imave. Woodpecker.

33, 34. W to Aqāq-e'ara. See New York Mts., hold firebrands, make bow.

35. W to near N.Y. Mts. Make rain.

36. At N.Y. Mts. Stop rain.

37-39. W to Analya-kaθa. Rattlesnake, Haramaθeve sand, Like-Mohaves.

D. 40-67. Hayunyes' Journey East and
South to Kofa Mt.

40. At Analya-kaθa. Their hearts turn E.

41. (E) to Big Sand Hills.

42. To Oh'ara-'unuve. They are thin.

43. To Mokwiθta's field. Name it.

44. E to Ground squirrels' Houses. Name it.

45. E to Otah-kunuve, "Dice-gambling." Gamble with women's dice; older wins younger.

46-48. S to Screwbean Spring. See Kohore Mt., Coyote's spring.

49-50. S. See tracks of Deer, then of Mountain Lion and Wolf.

51-53. S to Aqwaqa-munyo. Make fire; forbidden to younger; spend the night; sing of stars; see Kuhu'inye and Sotulku peaks.

54. S to Ivθe-koskilye. Sore feet of younger cured.

55. S to Koskilye, Monument Range crossed. Sun's rays.

56. S to Kwiya-selye'aye. See mountains.

57-60. On (S) to Aha-talompa on river. See Frog; drink; make arrowweed floats.

61-62. Cross river to E.

63. Land at Mortar-rocks. Saved from drowning.

64. SE to Aqwāqa-have. Thin and dry.

65. SE to S end of Screwbean Mt. See Avi-melyehwéke, Kofa (?) Mt.

66. On way to Kofa Mt.

67. At Kofa Mt. Make house of darkness.

E. 68-76. At Kofa Mt., Younger Brother
Gets Wife, Power, Wins over
Elder, Transforms Both

68. Y. br. alone, goes far S to Tokwiyo Mt., finds Alakwisa tribe.

69. Returns with Alakwisa wife. Boasts, lying.

70, 71. N to house and o. br. O. br. who has mourned, now abuses wife.

72. Y. br. NE to Harquahala Mts. Kills much game.

73, 74. Y. br. W across river to Amohta. Cane speaks, he breaks it off.

75. Returns to Kofa. Brings cane; brothers quarrel.

76. At Kofa. Y. br. makes dice, plays, wins o. br.'s body, cuts, empties, makes him into flute, throws S. Turns self into rock at Kofa.

F. 77-85. Few Songs. Son's Power
and Transformation

77. Y. br.'s wife goes E to Gila Bend. Bears son.

78-80. At Gila Bend. Boy bitten by Horsefly, flips pellets and kills birds, then quail and rabbits.

81. Boy E to Avilyha. Blackbirds.

82. On E to Avi-hanye. Sees Frog, Matavilya's bewitcher.

83. S to ocean. Waves.

84. At ocean. Transforms into Small Cane.

85. Mother follows E, then S, to ocean. Turns into Snipe.

As usual, the number of songs per "station" tends to decrease as the story progresses, but the length of narrative per section tends to increase as the songs become fewer.

TABLE 3

Percentage of Songs and Narrative

Sec.	Par.	Percent Length	No. of Stations	No. of Songs	Song-Station Ratio
A,B	1-18	19	18	43	2.40
C	19-39	19	21	45	2.14
D	40-67	26	28	57	2.04
E	68-76	19	9	16	1.78
F	77-85	17	9	8	.89
Total	1-85	100	85	169	1.99

GEOGRAPHICAL ORIENTATION

In broader geographical terms, the route is this: At Ha'avulypo, Eldorado Canyon, 1-15. South to Avikwame, Dead (Newberry) Mt., 16-18. Thence westward for 21 stations (19-39) through historic Chemehuevi territory, via Piute Spring (29) to New York Mts. (36) and somewhat to the southwest thereof (37-39), from where they see the end of the sandhills to their west and far beyond these the "Like-Mohave" people of the Tejon region (actually invisible). From here they turn back "eastward" (40) to the "Big Sand Hills" (41), which I construe as the dunes below Riverside Mts., downstream and across the river from Parker, and reaching to within a few miles of the Colorado. This may not be the correct identification: it is 70 miles from their farthest west and definitely southeast of it, not east as stated. It also lies considerably to the south of the next place at which we can pick up their trail on the map, namely Dice-gamble (45), which is more or less west of Needles City on Sacramento Mts. in the desert, and well north of the "Big Sand Hills." From there they then proceed south. A "Big Sand Hills" situated somewhere between the New York Mts. and Sacramento Mts. would accordingly give a shorter and more consistent route than via the Riverside Mt. sandhills; but I know of no large stretch of sand in that area, farther north and near the Colorado River. The intervening stations 42-44 are named but not placed, so they are no help. It is possible that the informant did not really know where his Big Sand Hills lay.

At any rate, from Dice-gamble in Sacramento Mts. (45)—where we get the first tremble of true plot when the older brother wins the younger's body—they go south through the broken desert past Screwbean Spring (46-48) and Aqwaqa-munyo (51-53)—where they sleep or at least watch the stars—cross the Monument or Whipple range at Koskilye (55) near its western or inland end, and reach the Colorado River at Water-container (Aha-talompa, 57) and prepare to cross it (60). They reach the left bank at Mortar-rocks (63)

and go on southward through Aqwaqa-have (64) by
Bouse Wash to the southern end of Screwbean Mt.
(65), from which they see their goal, Avi-melyehweke
(67), which is Kofa or possibly Castle Dome Peak.
These peaks are 45 (or 60) miles distant, and historically they harbored a small band of Western Yavapai.
The brothers reach their mountain and build themselves a magic house of darkness (67).

From here on there is real plot, but the geography
goes wild. The younger brother goes off alone, far
south to an unlocated Tokwiyo Mt. (68), where he
finds the Alakwisa living—that mythical people who
later all died off at once in the midst of their
activity—and gets himself a wife and brings her
back (71). Next day he goes on a hunting trip some
40 miles northeast ("east" by the tale) to the Harquahala Mts. (72) and returns loaded with game.
Next he travels west across the Colorado to Amohta

(73, unlocated) and gets cane. Returning to Avi-melyehweke, he makes dice from the cane, gambles once
more with his brother, wins this time, cuts him up,
and throws his blown-out body far south to Cotton-
woods-their-makwoama (presumably in the Colorado
delta, 76) to become tall cane, and turns himself into
a rock on Avi-melyeheweke.

The wife goes east up the Gila to Gila Bend, Koaka-
'amaṭa (77), in historic Kavelchadhom territory, famous
as the home of Umase'aka in the Historical Epic, 8:14
(UC-AR 11:2, p. 78). There she bears a son, who
grows up miraculously (78-80), then goes east to
Avilyha and Frog Mountain in Maricopa and Pima
land (81, 82), then south through what would be Papago
territory to the ocean (Gulf of California, 83), where
he transforms into Small Cane (84). His mother tries
to follow him, also reaches the sea (85), and turns
into Snipe.

THE CHUHUECHE TALE

A. 1-13. Matavilya's Death at Ha'avulypo

1. At Ha'avulypo Matavilya had made a house out
of darkness and lived there. He told of the house,
calling by name the posts, the girders, all its parts,
the darkness, and saying that it was finished. So he
told. But Frog, Hanyiko, was a doctor and made him
sick without his knowing it.[1] Matavilya said: "There
is sickness on me, but I do not know from what it
comes. Perhaps I am sick from this house; perhaps
from telling about it; perhaps from that which I have
lain on (the ground).[2] My head is sick and heavy. All
of you listen to me! You know everything now, and
when I have died you will tell it in the same way as
I tell it." (2 songs.)

2. Matavilya said again: "I am very ill. My head
hurts and all my body is sick." (4 songs.)

3. At first Salt, Chuhueche, Long Tumanpa, Short
Tumanpa, Nyavaδôqa, and Avaly'unú[3] had not sat close
by Matavilya. Now, when he became sick, they said:

"Matavilya is sick and will die.[4] Let us sit near him
and hear what he says. Then we will know what he has
told." So they sat close by him while he was ill. Now
there was no water and no fire there. But Matavilya
said: "People will learn and will do the same as for
me." These six who were sitting close to him said:
"Let us get water and warm it for him. Let some
nurse him by driving the flies away. When the Mohave
are ill, they will do the same. And when a person has
died, everyone will leave the place." (2 songs.)

4. The six said: "Matavilya took over his word from
night. We will take over his words from him." They
said that to the other people there, who were sitting
in the corners of the house. (2 songs.)

5. There was a door at Ha'avulypo, but Matavilya
was lying in the middle of the house. He thought:
"When I die, what will they do? They know nothing as
yet." Now Badger, Máhoa,[5] and Raccoon, Námmaθa,[6]
were sitting at the east side of the house,[7] along the
middle of the wall, at the foot of the post on which
the beam from the center posts rests. Both were

---

[1]Cf. 7:1-4 (UC-AR 11:1, pp. 52-53) and 9:3, 10-13 above,
for a general parallel to present paragraphs 2-14. Cf. also
19:1-3, below, and allusions elsewhere.

[2]The Mohave fear sickness from contact with strange
foods and strange women. Matavilya seems here to think
that his new experiences—a house, sleep, telling about them
—may have been the cause of his sickness.

[3]The six singings are here personified. One might think
that the "heroes" of the six stories were meant. But these
would number more than six: four Salt brothers, two Chuhueche, Tumanpa and his sister, etc. The informant knew
and sang Salt and Short Tumanpa as well as Chuhueche. He

did not know Long Tumanpa. It goes west too, but follows a
different journey, he said. Very little is known about Nya-
vaδôka or Avaly'unu. And Avaly'unu the narrator attributed
to the Yuma.

[4]This is one of the prosaic recognitions of doom of which
the Mohave are so fond.

[5]Or Mahwa.

[6]Badger and Raccoon also figure as two short men in the
ring of people over whom Coyote leaped to snatch Matavilya's
heart. Cf. 7:4 (UC-AR 11:1, p. 53).

[7]The door is always south, so we would say "the left of
the house" (viewed from inside).

doctors. Then they made two pipes, from out of their bodies.[8] One pipe was red, the other blue. The six— Salt, Chuhueche, Long Tumanpa, Short Tumanpa, Nyavaδôqa, and Avaly'unu—said: "You two say you are doctors. Come therefore and treat Matavilya. He is very sick, so cure him, you two sitting to the east." So Badger and Raccoon came up and doctored Matavilya. (2 songs.)

6. Matavilya's body had been like that of a sick man. But now when Badger and Raccoon treated him, he began to feel cooler. Only his feet and hands were still hot. Then the two said: "He is well," and went back to the east wall of the house and sat down. But soon Matavilya said: "I am the same again: the sickness is in my body once more: I shall die." (2 songs.)

7. Then the six said: "Well, Matavilya will die. What shall we do with his body? It is best that we burn it: then all tribes will know how to do and will act that way. But there is no wood: we must have someone bring wood. Then Takse, Gopher,[9] who was sitting west of the door, said: "I will bring wood." They said: "Good! Bring it." (2 songs.)

8. So Takse went out of the house, stood in front of the door, and dug a hole. He entered this and traveled westward underground, for he was a great doctor. Arriving (in the west), he made four logs from his saliva, each a fathom long, and brought them back. Then he said: "Here is firewood with which to burn him: I have brought it. While I was still inside the house, I was named Takse. Now that I have brought wood, I shall be called Takse-kwinyamaθe."[10] Thus he gave himself that name. (2 songs.)

9. Now the wood was there. But the six thought: "We want someone to dig a hole (trench), so that we may lay the wood over it, put the body on top, lay on more wood, and burn it. That will be the best way. But who will do this?" Then Amaṭa-kapis'ara[11] said: "I will dig the hole." He went outside, dug with his hands, and threw the soil to the south. Then he threw it east, north, and west,[12] and the hole (trench) was deep. He said: "I have finished: I will take another

name. Now I am Ikĩnye-umas-utšye'm-kwa-amĩtše, Boy-child-throw-far." (2 songs.)

10. Now everything was ready: Matavilya died. Then the six said: "He is dead." All those in the house said: "He has died?" "Yes, he is dead." Then all stood up or rose to their knees, for they wanted to see. They walked about, not knowing what to do. Some asked: "Has he died?" and others said: "Yes." All were speaking of that, but no one cried. (2 songs.)

11. Now the six wanted to take Matavilya's body outdoors, but they did not know how, for the house was dark and they did not know on which side the door was. Then they thought: "Matavilya is lying with his head to the south. I think the door is to the south, and the firewood and the hole also. People will do the same way." (2 songs.)

12. Then the six put their hands under his body and carried it out of the door. They laid it on the ground, for they had never burned anyone before and did not know what to do next. They thought: "Shall we lay him on the wood or close by it? Shall we lay him on the ends of the wood or in the middle?[13] We do not know." Two timbers were lying over the hole. Salt and Chuhueche were the oldest of the six, and said: "Lay him lengthwise." The others asked: "Which way shall we put his head, to the east, or the west, or the north?" Salt and Chuhueche said again: "Put his head to the south, his feet to the north. When we burn him, his shadow (maṭkwesa) will go there (south). The way Matavilya goes is the road to Selye'aya-'ita and Hatša-kupilyka.[14] When people die, their shadows will go by the same road to where Matavilya will live." (2 songs.)

13. They laid the body on the two logs over the hole and placed the two other pieces of wood on it. But they had no fire. Then Coyote, θarra-veyo, said: "I will bring fire. There is Avi-'a'auva, Fire-mountain. It is far there, but I will go and bring fire from it. And I call myself Tinyãm-koθãma.[15] I am light and can run without tiring and will come back soon." So he went off west.[16] Now a woman, θily'ahmo,[17] stood at the side and thought: "Matavilya said, 'When I die they will not know anything: they will be foolish.' Now all the people are standing about, but I do not believe that Matavilya is dead. When he feels the fire I think he

---

[8]Favorite magic: One reaches into his body, or into space, and seizes what one wants. There are many such psychological infantilisms in this mythology.

[9]I am not altogether sure Takse is the Gopher. He is important in the climax of the Cane tale, 1:99, 100 (UC-AR 11:1, p. 18), but was there described (n. 94) more as a ground-squirrel or rat. And compare 18:2, n. 10, below.

[10]Meaning? Perhaps "White-Gopher" because of making firewood from his white spittle.

[11]Mud-dauber? Probably a wasp. Cf. 7:22-27 (UC-AR 11:1, pp. 56-57).

[12]Antisunwise circuit beginning S and ending W. He finishes his digging to the W. Gopher goes W to get his firewood, and in B (and other versions) Coyote goes W on a false errand to "Fire Mountain" to fetch fire for the cremation.

[13]This theme of childlike inexperience and ignorance is dwelt on endlessly by the Mohave. It emphasizes the incipience of the world.

[14]Selye'aya-'ita and Hatša-kupily-ka are 12 and 14, west side, UC-AR 11:2, Map 2, between Mohave and Chemehuevi valleys.

[15]"Hiθãwa, swift, light; tinyãm, night," was given as etymology.

[16]Fire Mountain to west also in 7:2 (UC-AR 11:1, pp. 52-53).

[17]Cf. 7:3 (UC-AR 11:1, p. 53). Described as large, gray, spotted.

will jump up from the wood." Then, while Coyote was
still on his way for fire, she rubbed strands of her
dress between her hands and thus made fire.[18] So Salt
and Chuhueche took dead arrowweeds[19] that were lying
about, lit them, laid two bundles on each side of the
body, and it burned. All the people looked on, and
when they saw that Matavilya did not come out of the
fire, they said: "He has really died. He has felt the
fire and not come out of it." (2 songs.)

B. 14-18. Hayunye-Chuhueche Brothers
Mourn—Go South to Avikwame

14. Now Matavilya was entirely burned to ashes.
While he was burning, they had set fire to the house
and it also was nothing but ashes. Now two persons,
Hayunye, had been in the arrowweed thatch along the
front of the house. When it burned, they moved out a
little way to the southwest and sat down. They thought:
"It is too bad that our house is all gone. The timbers,
the arrowweed, even the soil, are burned: nothing is
left; we are sorry."[20] As they sat and thought that,
they cried. Then they gave themselves the name
Hutšātš-moθnyunye.[21] (2 songs.)

15. The people were still standing about where
Matavilya had been. Now Mountain sheep, Ammo,
were of four kinds: black, yellow, white, and domestic
(Ammo-ny-ahaṭa).[22] These four said: "We are sorry
that Matavilya is dead: we will cut our hair. When
people die, they will do the same for them. We will
go to the west; then someone will use our hair."[23]
The two Hayunye who were sitting near by heard them.
(2 songs.)

16. Then the Hayunye went southwest to Avikwame.[24]
When they reached there and stopped, they saw the

people still standing at Ha'avulypo. Then the older
Hayunye said to his brother: "I will tell about their
all standing there; but we are going west. I do not
know what we shall be: perhaps rocks, or something
else. The people there are all thinking about us, and
if we tell nothing they will not know about us, but if
we speak they will know us." (4 songs.)

17. They were still standing there: they had not yet
named the mountain. To the south was a level place,
Amiakwa'orve,[25] to the north another, Mat'āre-amai-
muya.[26] The older Hayunye said: "I will name these
places, so that all will know and never forget them."
(2 songs.)

18. Still standing there, he said: "This mountain
here has clouds and wind and is pretty. It is pleasant
on top, a good place, so I will give it a name. I call
it Avi-kwa'ame,[27] so all will know it. People will come
and will see it; they will die and be born, and know
that name." (4 songs.)

C. 19-39. Hayunyes' Journey West to
New York Mountains

19. The Hayunye went a short distance[28] west. Now
the two level playfields were close by,[29] and they stood
in the middle between them. They said: "When we left
Ha'avulypo, all knew our names. Now we will have
other names for all to know. We went off to become
something; perhaps, they thought, to die or turn into
rocks. But now we have new names: Kutšyé-kutšye and
Kwaθpily-vata.[30] (1 song.)

20. They went westward a short distance to Tšimuweve-samire.[31] Standing there, they said: We stand here
to name the little mountain to the north: we call it
Tšohotave." (2 songs)

[18]She twirled the strands between her palms like a fire-
drill operator, and like a fly cleaning its forelegs. Her
motive here, apparently, was not to cremate Matavilya's
body but to make him leap up when he felt the fire.
[19]Iθava-'vi, "stone (hard) arrowweeds."
[20]They are crying not for dead Matavilya but for the
house whose walls they have inhabited. They mourn for
Matavilya—pro forma—later, in 31.
[21]The Hayunye are yellowish insects which frequent the
brush covers and walls of Mohave houses; evidently something like crickets. The name they gave themselves was
said to refer to their habit of "singing" by moving their
wings back and forth; "they do not sing with their mouths."
At the end of the story, the narrator answered a question
as to the relation of Hayunye and Chuhueche by saying that
these names "are the same." Hayunye, the insects, is what
the brothers were; "Chuhueche is what they sing when they
work their arms." Hutšātš-moθnyunye is their ritual name.
[22]Also in Salt, 12:2, above, and of the same four colors.
Ahaṭa means dog, domestic animal.
[23]Mohaves cut their hair in mourning; white people shear
the wool of their sheep to use; which parallel evidently in-
trigued the Mohave when they learned of it.
[24]Dead or Newberry Mountain, near the river but west
of it, and thus nearly due S of Ha'avulypo. It is perhaps 40

miles distant. Seeing the people standing on Ha'avulypo thus
is a feat impossible in reality, and not meant to be real in
our sense; for these myths happen in a dream world which
logically is supernatural and aesthetically surrealistic. Space
is stretched or condensed as is time. People are seen (or
heard) at a great distance also in section 39, below, and in
Salt 12:21-22, above.
[25]This is Miakwa'orve, UC-AR 11:2, Map 1, A, west.
[26]"Playfield-up-muya." Sometimes they seem to be two
names for one place.
[27]Or Avi-kwa'me, perhaps the full form of Avi-kwame.
It is associated with Mastamho as Ha'avulypo is with Matavilya. The Mohave are afraid to climb it, and have a legend
that one of them who did so came back deaf and dumb and
soon died.
[28]"A quarter of a mile."
[29]This seems hardly possible if they moved only a quarter-
mile from the peak of the mountain.
[30]Kutšyé-kutšye (accent on second syllable) was the older.
Asked for the meaning of the names, the informant replied:
"That is how people would sing their names when they sang
Chuhueche." Kwaθ(a)pilye are edible sage seeds (chia) in the
desert. Cf. 7:15 (UC-AR 11:1, p. 55), 9:22, above.
[31]"Chemehuevi-samire." They are actually in Chemehuevi
country, but I know neither the etymology nor the precise
location.

21. Starting westward again, they went a little way and stood again, looking south (or southwest) to a small mountain. "I call it Nyamaθave-tavave," said the elder. (1 song.)

22. Going on west, they came to Avi-halykoyowa and Kunalya-kuvatatše[32] and stood there. Kutšye-kutšye said to his brother: "I will tell of how we started, and of our way so far, so that people will know about it and will tell of it. As we traveled along, some places were high and we climbed them. Others were low, some washes, some rocky, some level. The land was not always the same. I will tell all that, and after a time people will say the same words."[33] (1 song.)

23. Going on west over the desert, of which they had not yet reached the middle, they saw many Tšama-δulya Piss-ants and stood and looked at them. They also saw a Horned Toad lying there: he swallowed the ants, but they walked through his body, came out of his rectum, and crawled off; they saw this as they stood there.[34] Then they said to the Horned Toad: "We give you a name: Amaṭa-kokwiθka." (1 song.)[35]

24. They went on a little way again and stood. "We have traveled until we have come into the desert, and will tell of that. In the middle is the white streak Kwesoqīrve.[36] People will call it that. And we give this desert the name Kwanakwa. A man who travels will say those two words as we have spoken them. And where we stand, we call it Kwanakwa-tšaθkine. (2 songs.)

25. They went on across the desert valley. When they reached Kwesoqīrve in the middle, they saw a plant whose leaves looked like those of kamtšulyke, and which had large sour grapes. The leaves were dry and as they walked over them broke and crackled. Kutšye-kutšye said to the plant: "You think I do not know you. You think I am afraid of you. But I do not fear you: I know you. I will name you, for I give a name to everything that I see. I will call you qwam-kupaka."[37] (2 songs.)

26. Now they were halfway across the valley. They were still going west. When they came where mountain

"grapes"[38] were growing, something small among them was making a noise with its legs. "What is this?" they thought. They looked but could not see it. They tried hard to find it, but the insect hid behind the vine, and though they tried to follow it they could not see it. So Kutšye-kutšye said: "I cannot see you but I will give you a name, since you make a sound. Your name is Memepūka-kutetšinye."[39] (2 songs.)

27. They went on west again. Now they had nearly crossed the desert valley and were approaching the mountains. They stood and looked north. Sometimes a small mountain looks high: sometimes a rock looks like a man, or it appears as if there were a person.[40] They saw that. Then Kutšye-kutšye said: "I know that: it is my brother who went away without telling anyone. No one knew of it, but he came this way. That is the shadow of Matavilya when he died. He knows everything. He can make something like a house of clouds or smoke. I know him and will give him a name. I will call him Hunyavere-katš-humeik." (2 songs.)

28. They stood in the same place and Kutšye-kutšye continued to talk. "I have given him a name. The one we have seen, Hunyavere, will do that on every desert." (3 songs.)

29. Then they went on west again and approached Aha-kuvilye.[41] When it rains, water runs down from the spring there into the valley, and the little stream flows through the sand. They were walking up this sand. As they went, Kutšye-kutšye told his brother: "We did not walk like this on our way here. This is sand and we cannot walk fast; it is soft and tiring. I will tell of this, because people will become tired when they walk on sand." (1 song.)

30. They turned to the northwest and came to Kwikam-tšotka,[42] northwest of Ana-kuvilye. There they stood, and Kwaθpily-vata, the younger, said: "We saw Matavilya die. We did not stand up and cry for him. Now we have arrived here. Matavilya said that we would not know which way to go. Now we are in the west and I see pine trees." But Kutšye-kutšye, his older brother, said: "No, they are something else: they are not pine trees. I see Spanish bayonet,[43] and ho'ulye, and tree yucca

[32]Both spots are unidentified, as are Tšohotave and Nyamaθave-tavave of 20 and 21.
[33]"As in describing the way to each other."
[34]It is not clear whether this is an exotic bit of actual or of folk natural history.
[35]For once "the place had no name, except Tšamaδulya-ny-eva, Piss-ant his house."
[36]Kwesoqīrve may be a common noun, not a proper name. The place is streaked from an occasional rush of water down it. It is in Piute Valley abreast of Highway 95 about where that crosses the California-Nevada state line and 1 mile S of where Highway 77 branches off E to Davis Dam.
[37]The qwam-kupaka only look like grapes and are inedible. The kamtšulyka which they resemble grow in Mohave land and are edible but not very good.

[38]"Ahtoṭa-'avi." According to Castetter and Bell (1951), pp. 204-205, ahtot-avi is Lycium exsertum (andersoni), and ahto-tahan is L. fremontii, both called wolfberry or desert thorn.
[39]Memepūka means knee. The insect is described as yellowish, the size of a large grasshopper, without wings, feathery on its back.
[40]The mirage.
[41]"Stinking water," Piute Spring, a large spring. A mountain stretches northeastward from this place. It was this mountain at which they saw the mirage as they approached it.
[42]The distance of Kwikam-tšotka from Piute Spring was not recorded. I would put it in the Piute Range.
[43]Vannata. Castetter and Bell (1951), p. 204, vuh not, "Mohave yucca."

(Joshua tree).[44] Those are not tall trees, but the mirage makes them look high, like pines. I told you that he would do such things. The place where those trees are is far away, across two deserts, and is called Aha-kwa-'ahtši, Aha-kwi-'ihore, and Aqāq-e'ara."[45] (2 songs.)

31. Then Kutšye-kutšye went on: "When Matavilya died we did not cry for him.[46] But we started to go away and have come here. Now we think of him again and will cry; but we will not cry very long, only a little while. Now we are sorry for Matavilya, and because we think of him we cry." That is why the Chemehuevi also cry in mourning for the dead, but less than the Mohave.[47] (4 songs.)

32. After they had cried they went on westward again and came to Ohuere-imave.[48] There was a dead tree yucca there. Woodpeckers,[49] a male and a female, lived in a hole of this dead tree. Kwaθpily-vata, the younger brother, said: "Who is this living in the hole?" Kutšye-kutšye said: "I know my brother who came and turned into a bird and lived here; but I did not know what kind of a bird he was. Now before we go on, I will give him a name. I call him Is'ona, so that people will always know the name." (2 songs.)

33. Still going west, they came to Aqāq-e'ara. From there they saw the mountain Avi-waθa[50] to the west. "It is a good mountain, a pretty place. It is foggy and wet there and the mountain is green. We will give it a name before we reach it. We will call it Avi-waθa." (2 songs.)

34. They were standing there, holding in their hands, before their breasts, their malyekwitšk, the glowing sticks used for warmth in traveling.[51] Each of them had taken one of these brands from the fire when Matavilya was burned. If the stick of one went out, he lit it again from that of his brother. Thus they had kept warm. Now Kutšye-kutšye said: "As we traveled carrying this fire, when we saw any kinds of lizards,

we took a rock and struck them. Then we held the lizards against the glowing end of the stick. They did not cook, but they roasted a little. We cut off the cooked spot, divided and ate it. We have arrived here doing that way. But now I think it will be better if we make a bow. Then we can shoot rabbits or antelope or deer, and eat them and have enough. So we shall be well and strong and can travel better. We will make a bow and arrows here." So they made a bow, and that is how Chemehuevi learned to hunt. (4 songs.)

35. Going on again, they came near Avi-waθa, but before they reached it, Kutšye-kutšye thought: "Now we are near. In this place there are clouds and wind and rain. Rattlesnake used to make that; but I have never done it yet.[52] Then he kicked earth to the north, east, west, and south,[53] without letting his younger brother know what he was doing. He said: "I do not know this place. I have never been here before, but I think it will rain. I think they will grind (food) for us."[54] He was really trying to make it rain by kicking the dust, but would not admit it and laid it to rattlesnake.[55] Then the rain came, and the younger brother stood leaning over his bow to keep it dry. (4 songs.)

36. Then they went on again until they reached Avi-waθa.[56] Now Kutšye-kutšye said: "I am the man to talk about wind and rain. If I did not tell about it, if I did not know about it before, there would be no rain. No one has told me, but I can look up into the sky and stop it." Then he looked up, and the rain and wind and dust that were coming stopped. Kutšye-kutšye did that because he was a doctor. (2 songs.)

37. Then they went on west to Analya-kaθa.[57] As they approached a mesquite tree they saw two rattle-

[44] Huêlye.
[45] Aha-kwi-'ihore means sandbar willow water. Aqāq-e'ara is reached in 33.
[46] True, they cried for their burned house (14).
[47] They are in Chemehuevi land. In general, the Chemehuevi practice "less" of any formalized institution than the Mohave —perhaps basically because of ecological situation.
[48] Ohuere is the name of a song-cycle referring to the golden eagle, Aspa; the story of this is said to begin at the same New York Mountains, Avi-waθa, which are reached in 36. The place Ohuere-imave was described as perhaps two, three, or four miles from the last, viz., Kwikam-tšotka of 30, n. 42.
[49] Issona; also recorded as is'ona; I do not know which species of woodpecker.
[50] Avi-waθa is the New York Mountains, a northern extension of Providence Mountains. See n. 56. Aqāq-e'ara has been mentioned in 30 as "across two deserts" from Kwikam-tšotka, which would mean at least one intervening range. I would put it into Lanfair Valley, E of New York Mountains.

[51] The River Yuman tribes and the Chemehuevi carry glowing brands before their bodies for warmth as they travel. The Colorado got its first European name, Rio de los Tizones, from this practice as Alarcón observed it in 1540.
[52] There is a connection between rattlesnake and making wind and rain. Cf. the Kamaiaveta episode above in 9:39; also Handbook, p. 776 (from the same informant as the present myth), and p. 777, bottom.
[53] Not a circuit.
[54] I.e., will feed us. Tawam-k, grind on the metate, also means to offer food; nyitonai-k, also meaning to grind, is said when one first encounters rain in a new place: the rain is "treating" one.
[55] "So doctors do now: they make rain but refuse to admit it."
[56] Avi-waθa, generically New York Mountains, here probably a spot in them, presumably the pass or break midway in their length that is below the 5000-ft. contour. The place was described as being 2-3 miles W of Vanderbilt on a former branch of the Santa Fe Railroad; and this last would seem to be the Ivanpah station on the present Union Pacific line.
[57] Analya is mesquite. Analya-kaθa was said to be not far from the last, still in the valley NW of the New York and Providence Mountains through which the Union Pacific runs. The itinerary that follows makes me think that it may have been 25 or 35 miles distant SW, about opposite the N end of Providence Mountains, facing Kelso. It is their farthest west.

snakes under it and stepped back. Kutšye-kutšye said: "You thought I did not know you, but I do. You are my brother who went away long ago. Now you have become a rattlesnake and have no legs, no arms. Now you are Avé. I call you that; all people will call you that." (2 songs.)

38. They continued to stand there. To the west they saw a high mesa of sand. Kutšye-kutšye said: "I do not know that place; but I own it. It is far away, but I will name it. I call it Haramaθeve-kwayumpa."[58] (4 songs.)

39. They continued to stand there. Far to the northwest was a desert valley. In the middle of it there was a village of the people living in that country. They saw the smoke of their fires and heard them talking to one another. Kutšye-kutšye said: "I see their smoke and I hear them talk. No one saw them and no one knows that they have come to live here, but I will give them a name. I will call them Hamak-hava-kwiahta,[59] and they will live in that place." (1 song.)

D. 40-67. Hayunyes' Journey East and South to Avi-melyehwêke

40. Now they had finished here. Then they turned their hearts to the east and told of that. (1 song.)

41. Then Kutšye-kutšye said: "If we go back as we came there will be only one road: but if we go back by another road there will be two." So they started east in a different direction. When they came to Selye'aye-ku-vataye,[60] Kutšye-kutšye said: "This is Selye'aye-ku-vataye. While we were coming here we did not tell about the way. But now as we stand here we will tell about our journey, about our road across the desert. And people will always keep our road and travel it." (3 songs.)[61]

[58]Haramaθeve-kwayumpa "was across the desert which they were facing." In Salt, 12:23, Haramaθeve-kutŏ ia-va and Haramaθeve-kutš-upai-va are an unspecified (but apparently long) distance "E" of Rogers or Muroc playa lake near Mohave station and junction, and again SE of Amboy. The present Haramaθeve being a "high mesa of sand" may well be the E end of a long belt of dunes stretching from a few miles beyond Providence Mountains nearly 40 miles W along the Union Pacific R.R. to Baxter. These same dunes appear above under another name in Tumanpa, 11:7, note 11.

[59]"Like-Mohave, Resembling Mohaves." In Handbook, p. 612, they are the Serrano-related Shoshonean Kitanemuk or the Alliklik of the far-away region of Tejon Creek, Antelope Valley, Piru, and Castac Creek. They are of course completely beyond visibility. Most of the Mohave desert intervenes, and then rugged mountains. Cf. above, Salt, 12:21-23.

[60]"Much sand," or "great sand" or "sand hills." Mentioned (as Selye-aya-Kuvataye) also in Salt, 12:24, note 48, where the location is cited. This is about 70 miles SE of the sandy tract of note 58 above.

[61]Subsequently, four songs were specified. One runs: matšam heyi'i, which was said to be song distortion for av'unye tšamím, "making a road."

42. They started again. After a time Kutšye-kutšye said: "We have not had enough to eat. We have come here without eating. Both of us are thin: we are only bones and skin. I will call this place from that. I name it Oh'ara-'unuve.[62] (2 songs.)

43. They went on east again, and in the middle of the desert they saw Mokwiθta.[63] They saw him climb up a cactus, run inside it, and stay there. "What is that?" said Kwaθpily-vata. "I know," said Kutšye-kutšye. It is my brother, and I will name him before we start again. I call him Mokwiθta. And the place where we stand I will call after him, Mokwiθta-nya-mat'āre."[64] (4 songs.)

44. They went on east again until they saw Ground-Squirrel.[65] That was his place. They saw him running and climbing up into a thorny bush. Kutšye-kutšye did not know him, but he said he knew him. "You are my brother. You left long ago and have become something. Before we go farther I will name you. I call you Hum'ire. And the place where we stand I will call Hum'ire-nye-vatše." (2 songs.)

45. Still going on east, they came to Otah-kunuve.[66] Now Kutšye-kutšye wanted to gamble. Kwaθpily-vata did not know how. Kutšye-kutšye took cane[67] out of his body and split it and made four dice. "My younger brother, sit on the north side," he said. But Kwaθpily-vata refused. "Do what I say," said Kutšye-kutšye, "for I am the older, and the younger follows the older." Then Kwaθpily-vata agreed and sat to the north, and they began to play. They threw up the dice, hit them with their hands,[68] and saw how they fell. Four times they did that. Then Kutšye-kutšye said: "Well, you have lost. I have won your body, all of you. What I say, you must do. If I tell you to run, you must run fast. I have won that. Then there is the fire. I do not

[62]"Thin-be there." It may be an imaginary place name or a real one with a folk etymology.

[63]Mokwiθta was described as "something like a fox" (marho), also like a house cat, long-tailed, gray with small spots, abundant at Kingman, Arizona. This sounds like a carnivore, probably the swift fox, perhaps the ringtail or civet cat, though its running up a cactus is like a rodent; and the Walapai-Havasupai cognate probably denotes a tree squirrel. But what would a tree squirrel be doing in the open desert? The narrator may have known the animal's name but not its ecology.

[64]"Mokwiθta his playfield." If they really went E from the sand dunes, they would be close to the Colorado River.

[65]Hum'ire is the ground squirrel or spermophile. The place Hum'ire-nye-vatše means ground squirrel's homes (holes).

[66]Where they gamble with women's dice. Otah-kunuve is in Ohmo (Sacramento) Mountain SW of Needles City. This is far N of where we have them located last; but in 47 they are near Ohmo. In this paragraph there occurs the first stir of plot; so far there have been only itinerary and sights and thoughts.

[67]Mohave dice are billets of willow played with by women; myth dice are of cane and used by men.

[68]One tosses the dice, the other scatters them with a blow in mid-air.

want you to come near that, for I won that from you also. And then I will not let you drink, for I won that also. And I won your food, so I will not let you eat. For I won from you four times."[69] (2 songs.)

46. From there they turned south. Kutšye-kutšye said to his younger brother: "Go ahead of me! Walk fast! You lost everything and I won your body. So what I tell you to do you must do." (2 songs.)

47..They continued to go south, in the valley east of Ohmo,[70] until they came to Aha-kwa-'a'īse.[71] Then far south, below Parker and west of the river, they saw a mountain. Kutšye-kutšye said: "I see a good place, happy looking, with little peaks standing up sharply. I will give it a name. I call it Amaṭa-kohore.[72] (2 songs.)

48. Now there was the spring there, and as they walked to it, birds flew off from it down the valley. Kutšye-kutšye said: "The birds were drinking, but when they saw us they were afraid and flew away." Now they themselves wanted to drink, but when they looked at the spring there was a coyote in the water.[73] So Kutšye-kutšye said: "Coyote knows nothing. He drops his hairs into the water and it is no longer good to drink." As he spoke, the coyote came out. He went eastward a little way and climbed up a small hill and sat on top. Kutšye-kutšye said: "I know you. You know nothing, you have no house, nothing to eat, and you run about; that is how you live. I call you Hukθara. Everybody will call you that." (1 song.)

49. Now two deer had drunk there. Then they had gone west, turned south, and then gone east again. Now as Kutšye-kutšye and Kwaθpilya-vata went on south from the spring, they crossed the tracks of the deer. They saw they had traveled in long jumps. Kutšye-kutšye said: "I know you, my brothers. You used to be men, but you turned into something else. I have not seen you, but I know you by your tracks. I will call you Aqwāqa." They were standing on the desert when he said this. (1 song.)

50. Then they went on south a little way. Now Jaguar and Mountain Lion[74] had followed the deer,

and Kutšye-kutšye and Kwaθpilye-vata saw their tracks also. Then Kutšye-kutšye said: "This Jaguar has nothing (no weapon) to kill with, but he goes where the deer stepped. In that way he makes them sleepy; they walk slowly and do not go far. Soon perhaps he finds them asleep, and when they wake up he eats them alive. That is what he does. I have not seen him, but I know that that is what he will do." (1 song.)

51. Going on south, they came to Aqwāqa-munyo.[75] Then Kutšye-kutšye said: "Now it is sunset. My younger brother, go and get wood. For I won your body." Kwaθpily-vata said: "It is good," and went off eastward. There he dragged out a dead astaka tree. When he pulled it out of the ground he saw a tarantula come out of the hole left by the roots. Then he said: "I will give you a name: I call you Kwatš-haminyo-'ipa."[76] (1 song.)

52. Then he brought back the wood and made a little fire. The sun had set and it was beginning to be dark. Kutšye-kutšye sat down close to the fire on the north side. Kwaθpily-vata tried to approach the fire to warm himself, but his older brother said: "No; I have told you that you lost your body. I said, 'When I build a fire I do not want you near it'; and now I want you to sit over there." Then Kwaθpily-vata sat a little distance off to the south. Soon he stretched out his hands to warm them; but Kutšye-kutšye forbade him. Then the younger brother said: "Very well, I lost. It is well."[77] Soon darkness came, and the stars, and Kutšye-kutšye spoke their names. "I call them ammo (Orion), hatša (Pleiades),[78] hamuse-nye-viltaye (the large morning-star), hamuse-itšauwa (small bright stars), hamuse-ku-viltaye-anyayik (large bright stars), and hamuse-θameik (small-dull stars). Ammo is three stars and hatša is seven stars.[79] When they rise people will see

[69]Therefore he owns his body, fire, drink, and food.

[70]Ohmo is Sacramento Mountain W to SW of Needles City and is across the river from Sacramento Wash. Kutšuvave is a peak in the "Mohave Mountains" of our maps which stretch, S of Needles City, both E and W of the Colorado and include the Needles pinnacles, and, S of these, the peak Akoke-humi opposite Chemehuevi Valley. The highest peak of Ohmo is Mevukha, 3750 ft. high.

[71]Aha-kwa-'a'īse, "Screwbean Spring," is near the S end of Ohmo, according to the informant; probably at or near the head of Chemehuevi Wash.

[72]Unidentified. The sharp crests suggest Big Maria Mountains; the position permits it.

[73]"In" or "at" the spring? Bathing in or drinking from it? The informant used a similar incident above in Tumanpa, 11:43.

[74]Our old friends Nume-ta and Hatekulya of the Deer cycle, 5, note 1 (UC-AR 11:1, p. 41). They may really be Puma and Wolf. See also 16A, below.

[75]Aqwāqa-munyo means Deer-munyo. The informant said that this place was 2 to 3 miles W of the "old" railroad bridge which used to cross the river about 3 miles S of Needles. This Aqwāqa-munyo would therefore be in Mohave Valley—not in the bottomland but on the barren peneplain looking down on it. They would have come N from Screw-bean Spring. I think the informant had his geography mixed or there were two Aqwāqa-munyo's. In 1953 I had it placed definitely between Hatalômpa (Ha-talompa of 57, note 86) and Atši-ará peak at SW end of Whipple Range. This has it looking down on Parker Valley instead of Mohave Valley. This Aqwāqa-munyo is mentioned in 3:27 (UC-AR 11:1, p. 33) and is G, west side, of UC-AR 11:2, Map 2, though it is entered much too far S, below Big Maria instead of above Riverside Mountains. Or were there three places of this name?

[76]"Kwatš-sandal-person"?

[77]Here again there is a touch of human-interest plot, dormant since 45; but it gets dispossessed by the inveterate Mohave propensity to sing about the stars.

[78]The three stars of Orion's belt are ammo, mountain sheep. The Pleiades are hatšá, of unknown meaning, but with both vowels short, and therefore to be distinguished from Hatšá (or Hātšá), the name of two harvest festival songs.

[79]The narrator seemed to think there was a correspondence between the number of kinds of stars he mentioned here (6) and the number of songs sung about them (8); but he could not make the count tally. It was apparently with this in mind that he said that ammo was 3 stars and hatša

them and will call them by these names." (8 songs.)

53. When it was daylight, Kutše-kutše looked south and saw a mountain. He said: "Well, day is come and I can see. I see a place and will give it a name, for I know that. I call it Kuhu'inye. And another place I call Sotulku."[80] (2 songs.)

54. They started again and went south. When they reached Ivθe-koskilye,[81] as they walked over the rocks the younger brother's feet became sore and he cried. Then Kutše-kutše said: "You are not old enough to be a man. You cry because your feet hurt. I will tell about that." So as they walked on he spoke of his younger brother's feet in order to cure them.[82] (1 song.)

55. Farther south they came to Koskilye.[83] Then the sun rose. Kwaθpily-vata said: "Now my body is different. It was not like this until I came here. Now my body is striped and yours is striped too." But Kutše-kutše said: "I know what that is. The sun is rising and his eyelashes mark your body and make it look striped. But your body is not really marked." His younger brother had not know that.[84] (2 songs.)

56. Going on south, they came to Kwiya-selye'aya.[85] There they stood and looked southeast. Kutše-kutše said: "I see mountains, five, six mountains. But I will not go to every mountain; I will go only to the place that I like. When I see the mountain I wish to go to, I will not go farther." (3 songs.)

57. Going on they reached the river at Aha-talompa[86] and stood on the bank. There was an eddy, in which

driftwood lay and stood up. On the driftwood they saw a kind of frog. Kwaθpily-vata said: "What is that in the water, sitting on the driftwood?" Kutše-kutše said: "I know him. When we went west, we did not yet see this water. Then it was made and ran south. As it ran south, these came out with it. They own the water, for they are doctors. I know them, and now I will name them. You sitting here, I will call you Aha-nye-mitsqurqe."[87] Then the frogs all jumped into the water. (4 songs.)

58. Now the two brothers stepped into the river, drank of it, and came back onto the sand. They stood there, and the older said: "We have not eaten. We are hungry and thin. We did not wish to drink, but we drank. Now one can look through into our bodies, can look in and see the water there, because we are so thin."[88] (3 songs.)

59. He said again: "Well, let us cross. It will be best if we take driftwood and ride across on it. You bring the driftwood." But his younger brother did not know how to get it. Kutše-kutše meant that when people were to cross the river they would use driftwood.[89] (2 songs.)

60. Then Kutše-kutše said: "Well, gather dead arrowweeds and make them into bundles, one for each of us." They had never crossed the river before and did not know whether they could do it. Then each grasped his bundle and said: "Now we will start across." (1 song.)

61. When they were out in the river, Kutše-kutše said: "As we are doing, people will do. But if we continue to drift we will float down with the river. If we move our arms and legs we will travel across and reach the other side. That is how people will do." Then they swam (on their bundles).[90] (1 song.)

62. As they went on they swallowed much water. "My brother, we shall die," they said, and both cried. (1 song.)

63. Then they drifted to Avi-ahmo[91] and past it, but an eddy carried them back and they came to land there. Kutše-kutše said: "We have reached the land and are saved. I thought we should die, but we are doctors and have dreamed well." (2 songs.)

64. From there they went southeast to Aqwāqa-have, in the edge of the hills where a wash runs down.[92] They stood in this gully. Kutše-kutše said: "I drank

---

7 (hatša-ntšemaik-havik-nyitš). I suspect the Mohave no more see 7 Pleiades than we do with the naked eye, but that they have become confused from the Americans or Mexicans around them, and that like ourselves they now apply the name "Seven Stars" somewhat vacillatingly to both Ursa Major and Pleiades. It is only the latter that they were interested in aboriginally.

[80]Kuhu'inye is in the lowest part of Mohave Valley, UC-AR 11:2, Map 1, no. 33, W. Sotulku, also recorded as Setulyku, I take to be a few miles S or SW of Kuhu'inye, a peak, perhaps the one 2768 feet high in the NW end of the Mohave Mountains, west of the Colorado.

[81]Ivθe-koskilye the narrator placed W of Chemehuevi Valley about 15 miles from the river. Ivθe is "greasewood," more properly creosote bush, Larrea; Koskilye recurs as a place name below in 55, note 83.

[82]Here he seems to change to sympathy for his younger brother; or is it only derisive?

[83]Koskilye or Kwoskilye is "at the middle" of the crest of the Monument or Whipple Range stretching from opposite the mouth of Bill Williams Fork eastward; or, according to another account, at the summit of the trail crossing the W end of the range; or, by another informant, where the old Needles-Parker wagon road crossed it.

[84]Anya-δo-sunya, "sun eyelashes," are the visible rays. In spite of being on the verge of developing great supernatural power, the younger brother continues to be portrayed as inexperienced and ignorant.

[85]Unidentified. Selye'aya is sand.

[86]Or Ha-talompa; by the river; "on the Parker Reservation, about 7 miles SW of the Indian School and across the river from it." I recorded it also as Hatalômpa or Aha-telômve, "water basin" or "drip fast," on the west side of the river about a mile N of Vidal Wash, which flows SE between Whipple and Riverside Mountains.

[87]It is a long-legged leaping frog.

[88]Cf. 42.

[89]Ihne; light, dry driftlogs are used, not the water-logged ones, of course.

[90]With a dog-paddle stroke.

[91]The current had carried them about 3 miles from Hatalompa to Avi-ahmo ("mortar-mountain" or "mortar-rock").

[92]Aqwāqa-have, "Deer went through." On Bouse Wash, 9 miles from Parker. UC-AR 11:2, Map 2, no. 35, E, but placed there too far downstream.

water, but I do not know where it has gone. My skin
is all dry again and there is no water in me. I am
only bones. I can see my bones, I am so thin
(oharek)." (1 song.)

65. To the east was a mountain, Avi-a'ĩsa.[93] Going
southeast, they came near the south end of the range.
Then Kutšye-kutšye said: "Before this, when we saw
mountains to the east, we did not name them. Now I
will give them a name. I know that that [over there
ahead] is a good place. It looks good, and when we
are there we shall be happy. Therefore I will name
that place before we reach it. I will call it Avi-
melyehwêke."[94] (2 songs.)

66. Then they went on, a long way, across the
desert. Kutšye-kutšye said: "I see Avi-melyehwêke.
I see clouds and wind and rain there. It is cool and
a good place.[95] I have not arrived there yet, but I
am glad, for we shall reach it." (2 songs.)

67. Then they went on until they reached Avi-
melyehwêke. "Well, we have arrived. This is the
place I have wanted, the only place. There are mountains all about, but this is the one I have wished for.
I was born of Matavilya. I saw him make his house
of darkness. I came out of that, and I can do the
same thing. I will make a house of darkness so that
we can live in it." Thus spoke Kutšye-kutšye, and
made a house there out of darkness. Then he made
his bed on the east side, but his younger brother
made it on the west, and near the door. Kutšye-kutšye
said: "We will do that so that the Yavapai[96] will learn
it and will be able to do the same way." But they did
not do as Matavilya had told them when he told them
how to make a house. Their house was without a roof;
there were only walls of brush, like the shelters that
the Yavapai make when they travel. When they reached
this place it became night. (No songs.)[97]

[93]"Screwbean Mountain." A'ĩsa is the mesquite Prosopis
pubescens, the pods of which on drying curl into a tightly
wound screw. Avi-a'ĩsa begins near Aqwāqa-have; it is no.
38, E, on UC-AR 11:2, Map 2, but is placed too far S there;
it seems to be nearer Bouse Wash than to Moon Mountain.

[94]Avi-melyehwêke is a mountain famous among the Mohave,
but they have difficulty identifying it. It is in Arizona, downstream from Parker Reservation, toward Yuma, in Western
Yavapai territory; and is probably either Kofa Mountain,
4828 feet high, or Castle Dome Peak, 3793. These are something like 45 and 60 miles respectively from "Screwbean
Mountain," by map.

[95]Pleasant at least in the desert. Cf. the similar senti-
ments in 18 and 33 about Mt. Newberry and New York
Mountains.

[96]The range is in Western Yavapai territory.

[97]As if to mark that the itinerary ended and the plot part
of his tale began here, the narrator made a pause, and I
entered a paragraph; but there were no songs, he replied
when asked.

E. 68-76. Younger Brother Gets Wife,
Power—Overcomes Elder, Trans-
forms Both

68. In the morning Kwaθpily-vata went out and ran
to the south. He caused many mice to walk over his
tracks and thus efface them, so that his brother would
not see where he had gone. When he had gone far
across the desert, he went straight on, without having
the mice any longer go over his tracks. He ran far to
the south, to Avi-tokwiyo, in the country of the Alakwisa,[98] upstream from the Yuma but far east of the
river. He reached the end of the village of these
people. He said to them: "I heard your voices and
your talking, but I did not know what tribe you were.
My name is Kwaθpily-vata; my house is at Avi-melyehwêke; it was there that I heard your voices. Now I
know you: you are my brothers. You are Alakwisa: I
call you by that name." (2 songs, one containing his
name, and one theirs.)

69. Now Kwaθpily-vata was good looking and talked
well. Two girls were listening to him, one standing on
each side of him. The younger of them stood on the
north and held his hand.[99] Now it was afternoon, and
when he started to return, she went with him.[100] When
they had gone part way back to Avi-melyehwêke, they
stood at the mountain Hoθampeve.[101] Then Kwaθpily-vata
said: "I have told you that I had a house. When we
arrive, we shall have much meat, dried and fresh: you
will have much food. When we hunt, I and my brother,
we always kill. Every day we go east from where we
live. We have been everywhere about and our tracks
are there." He was only saying that; he was lying.[102]
(1 song.)

70. Then they went on. Kutšye-kutšye was sitting
outside the house, at its southeast corner, making
arrowpoints and putting them on the end of his arrows.

[98]This is the extinct and possibly fabulous tribe whose
legendary auto-catastrophic end is recounted in Handbook,
pp. 797-798. There, they are put near the river between
Cocopa and Kamia; here, the narrator said Avi-tokwiyo was
north of the latitude of Yuma but far east of the river.

[99]The Mohave type of idyll, and apparently realistic as to
behavior. Also characteristic is the preoccupation with how
people stand, and in what direction from one another.

[100]This manner of marrying was not unusual.

[101]Hoθampeve: "there is another mountain of this name
south of the Santa Fe Railroad bridge at Topock, but this
one is far south, beyond Avi-melyehwêke." The one near
Topock is actually Hokiampeve or Mukiampeve; see UC-AR
11:2, p.141, no. 2, E of River.

[102]Why he should boastfully lie is not clear; especially
as three paragraphs farther on he does suddenly kill quanti-
ties of game. The case seems another of the kind that makes
us feel the Mohave myth personages lack coherent motivation.
I suspect the psychology to be more or less like this: the
hero has great supernatural power; but he is so young and
inexperienced that he does not yet know it; hence he lies
like a small child.

He was crying, for he was thinking of his brother.
"My younger brother knows as much as I do. When
he went out I did not see which way he went; he
made mice walk over his steps. Now I am thinking
of war which there may be in all places. When he
arrives somewhere, perhaps they will kill him, put
him into a mortar, crush his flesh and bones, and
eat him."[103] As he thought this and cried, his younger
brother arrived, stood at the southwest corner of the
house, and said: "Why do you cry? I am well. I have
brought a good-looking girl. Now we shall not have to
work. We shall not bring wood or water or cook.[104]
She will work, for I have her here. Kutšye-kutšye
heard him but did not turn to look. (1 song.)

71. The older brother kept his face turned away.
But he said: "My younger brother, you say that you
are married to a good girl. I do not think so. That
is no virgin; she is a loose woman. I do not believe
what you say."[105] (1 song.)

72. At sunset the older brother went into the house
and lay down. The younger brother and his wife also
lay down. When it was day, the girl looked around her
and thought: "My husband said that when we came here
we should have much meat, but there is no meat here."
Soon Kwaθpily-vata got up and went out, taking his
curved tukoro throwing club. He went straight east to
Aha-kwa-hela.[106] There he stood, and sucking his lips,
in the way called hatšíθk,[107] he made rabbits and birds
and deer and mountain sheep come to him. As he
stood and called them thus, he saw the dust of their
coming. When they were close, he laid his stick over
their necks, bore down on it, and killed them. He
killed many animals of different kinds. Then he thought:
"It is enough: I cannot carry them all." He had a small
carrying net.[108] Into this he put them and took them on
his back: others he hung in his belt, or carried in his
hand. Before he returned to the house, the older brother said to the young woman: "My younger brother
has gone to hunt. I think he has killed much. It is
nearly sunset now: I think you had better go out and

bring in wood and water." "Good. I will bring wood
and water," said the woman. Then they saw him coming. When he arrived the fire was all ready. Hot charcoal was spread on the sand.[109] Then the older brother
took the birds, threw them on the fire to burn their
feathers, burnt the legs, broke them, and gave them
to the woman to eat hot. He opened their bodies, took
out the insides and the seeds and gravel in them, and
gave them to her.[110] Then Kwaθpily-vata said: "I will
tell you how I killed. When I arrived at the place, I
called. When I called, they all came to me. That is
how I did." (3 songs.)

73. Then it was night again and they went indoors
and slept. In the morning, the younger brother went
out again. He went west to the river, crossed it, and
went on to Amohta.[111] "I know that the first time that
cane grew, it grew here. Then it made a loud noise,
and thunder and lightning entered the roots:[112] that is
the speech of the cane. It is talking to me. It is
pleasant and pretty." (2 songs.)

74. He still stood there, for he wanted to break off
a piece of cane. Then he broke it. "Now I have a cane
with long joints, and I also have one of the tassels of
seeds." (2 songs, one about the cane stems and one
about the tassels.)

75. Now he had a piece of cane a fathom long. Then
he returned as he had come. When he had nearly reached
the house, he hid his cane in the brush. When he came
to the house, the sun was nearly set. Then they ate
meat; and when it was dark, they all entered the house.[113]
After a time he came out again to bring in his cane.
He took it into the house and slid it into the sand on
which he was sleeping. He was lying with his head to
the south[114] and stuck the cane towards the north. In
the morning he moved his hand (in the sand) and picked
up a grain of corn: Now there was no one with them
there to use corn or plant food; there was no one but
the three of them. But he continued, and found pumpkin
seeds, and beans; and cooked them on the charcoal
fire.[115] After a time he drew out his cane and said:
"Here is cane I have found." But his older brother said:
"No, you did not find it; I put it here in the house. It

[103]One of the last things in the world any Mohave would
do, but a concept that intrigues them. Cf. 1:75, 82b; 3:15d;
6B (UC-AR 11:1, pp. 12-13, 15-16, 31, 48), and 15:14 below.
[104]Strictly, there has been no reference to any of this
work except once to bringing firewood in 51.
[105]The motivation here seems to be envy. The interpreter
added: "Himepuik is what they call the abusing of relatives
in order to make husband and wife fall out." Cf. below Satukhota, 18:40.
[106]Aha-kwa-hela is the Harquahala Mountains, the focus of
life of a band of Western Yavapai. See 8:93, UC-AR 11:2, p.
88, and Map 2, H5, p. 148. However, to reach Harquahala
from Kofa or Castle Dome Peak, he would go NE, not
"straight E."
[107]Smacking or sucking the lips to attract rabbits; but his
power here is plainly magical.
[108]Mayu.

[109]The usual way of cooking small game.
[110]As a friendly treat? Or as an inferior portion? For
breaking the legs, cf. note 138 below.
[111]Amohta was said to be one day's foot travel upstream
from Yuma, west of the Colorado.
[112]Cane and lightning are associated: cf. 1:91, 102 (UC-AR
11:1, pp. 17, 18).
[113]They had eaten outdoors, in front of the door, perhaps
under the shade.
[114]Sometimes there is avoidance of laying the head to the
S since the dead go S; cf. Matavilya's position when he died,
above 9:3, 13:11.
[115]The motivation is not clear. Perhaps there is none,
beyond his now being in the full stride of displaying his
magic power.

is mine." But Kwaθpilye-vata said: "No, I found it.
You have been all over the house and did not find it.
I found this and it is mine." "Yes, it is yours," said
Kutšye-kutšye, "but I put it there. So I want you to
cut it in half. You can have the tip end, but I want
the butt end."[116] "No," said the younger brother, "you
take the upper end. I want the butt." But Kutšye-
kutšye continued to claim the butt and finally his
younger brother let him have what he wanted. He
himself took the upper end. They were in front of
the house as they quarreled over the cane. (2 songs.)

76. When he was about to split the cane, Kwaθpily-
vata thought: "How shall I cut it? With fire or with
my finger nail?" Then he split four pieces with his
nail. Each time as he split it, lightning flashed out
of the joint and his older brother fell down dead
(unconscious). Each time Kwaθpily-vata took him by
the arm, stood him up, and said to him: "I did not
do that; it came from inside the cane. That is how I
mark my dice." Four times he did that, marking each
of the dice.[117] Then he said: "Now we will play. When
we played before, you knew how to do. At that time I
sat to the north and you to the south." Now they played
again, sitting the same way. "That is one for me,"
said the younger brother. Each time they threw the
dice, he won. When he had won four times he said to
his older brother: "Now you have lost your body: I
have won it from you. When you beat me, you said
that I had lost drink, fire, and food as well as myself,
and you forbade me to use those. But I will not do
that. I will take only your body." "Well, you can do
with me as you like now," said his older brother. Then
Kwaθpily-vata told him to lie down on some dead
brush: "Older brother, lie here." Kutšye-kutšye lay
down. Kwaθpily-vata took his knife.[118] As he was about
to cut his throat, the older brother wept. Then Kwaθpily-vata said: "I see you looking as if you were crying. Do not do that!" He took up his knife again and
was about to cut open his body when the elder brother
cried again. "I do not want you to cry like that," said
Kwaθpily-vata. But Kutšye-kutšye said: "No, I am not
crying. You can do with me what you like." Kwaθpily-
vata said: "Now I will tell of your body, of the four
joints in it, the ankle, the knee, the hip, and the neck."
He wanted to make three holes in his older brother's
body, one in the chest, one at the base of the ster-
num, and one in the belly. When he had done that he
wished to turn him into cane.[119] Then he cut him and

blew into his head. He blew out his older brother's
internal organs until he was hollow and light. Then
he picked him up and threw him far south to Ah'a-
nye-makwoama,[120] far below the country of the Cocopa.
He said: "When I throw you to the south you will turn
into cane. You will grow there with long joints. You
will be tall cane. The Cocopa, the Yuma, and the
Kamia will break you off and make flutes[121] of you."
That is why cane grows there far in the south, and
why the Indians of that region use it for flutes. Then
Kwaθpily-vata thought: "When I came back here I
gambled with my brother, beat him, and turned him
into cane. Now he is gone but I am still here, and
my wife too. I am sorry I changed my brother: I will
cry for him. And I too want to become something. I
will turn into a rock." He was saying that to himself:
not to his wife. Then he climbed halfway up Avi-
melyehwêke. There he turned himself to stone. Now
he is a small rock about so[122] high. He thought: "Now
I will become stone. My name will be Avi-melyehwêke:
everyone will always know me." (2 songs, one on the
metamorphosis of each brother.)[123]

F. 77-85. Son's Miraculous Power
and Transformation

77. Now the woman was alone.[124] She thought: "My
mother and father and sisters and brothers are at
Avi-tokwiyo. If I go there and my baby is born, my
relatives will eat it; because my people would have
fought with these two men on account of my living
with one of them. So I will not go back to them; I
will go east." Then she went far east, to Koaka-
'amãtša.[125] When she arrived, the Halchidhoma and
Kuhwana[126] had houses there, but no one was in them:
only the houses stood there. She entered one of the
houses and lived in it. From there she went out north

---

[116]Closely reminiscent of the Cane brothers in 1:20 (UC-
AR 11:1, p. 7).
[117]Splitting his cane into dice, or marking one side of
them. Again, cf. 1:91 (UC-AR 11:1, p. 17).
[118]Ahkweṭ-kwa-hatšaqware.
[119]A cane flute.

[120]Unidentified; either mythical or more likely in the
Colorado delta. Ah'a are cottonwoods.
[121]Talytalye.
[122]Pointing: about 4 feet.
[123]This paragraph contains the climax of the entire narrative; but it has only two songs, and those on what the brothers
transformed to.
[124]The main story is over; from here on there is an epilogue demonstrating that the hero's son also is possessed of
great magic.
[125]"West of Phoenix, near 'Hildebrand' (sic for Gila Bend),
on the Southern Pacific Railroad." It is Gila Bend. See koaka-
matše 8:14, 81 (UC-AR 11:2, pp. 78, 87) and UC-AR 11:2,
p. 146. According to Spier it was the historic home of the
Kavelchaδom.
[126]Both tribes moved from the Colorado to the Gila within
the memory of Mohaves living in 1900; yet they are put on
the Gila in this period when the world was young. The
Halchidhoma left the Palo Verde or Blythe region about
1828 and settled on the Gila soon after 1833; the Kuhwana
left the Colorado a few years later.

to gather inyá'inya seeds. After she returned, she
went south, looking for corn where the people had
planted. Sometimes she would find a short ear that
someone had dropped; then she picked it up and put
it away. She wanted to keep the corn and the seeds
to eat when her baby was born so as to have milk
for it. She lived there like that four nights;[127] then the
child, a boy, was born in the morning, at sunrise. She
warmed water and washed him clean. Then she made
a cradle, laid the child on the bark dressing, and tied
him on. (1 song.)

78. Then she hung the cradle from the roof of the
shade in front of the house[128] and went away to gather
more seeds. While she was gone, a horsefly[129] came,
bit the child, and sucked its blood. The baby cried,
for he was wise.[130] He thought of the horsefly and said
to himself: "It takes away my blood and goes off east
with it."[131] That is why he cried. (1 song.)

79. Again the woman went off to gather seeds. Now
the baby's father had been a doctor; and he was a
doctor[132] too. Then, as he hung in his cradle high up
on the roof beam of the shade, he saw birds coming
about—one called otur-kepaye,[133] the other qamtoska.[134]
Then he spat on his hand[135] and rolled a little pellet.
This he flipped[136] from between his two index fingers.
The pellet struck one of the birds and broke its wing.
The boy was trying to make the birds approach the
fire. Then he struck the other in the same way. Both
birds, their wings broken, jumped and rolled about
until they were near the fire. When the woman returned, before sunset, she saw the two dead birds
lying there. She said: "Here are these birds! It is as
if someone were living with me. Who killed them?"
She wanted to know who had done it, and looked about
for persons' tracks. But no one had come there. Then
she said: "I think my baby boy has killed them. His
father was a doctor: perhaps he is a doctor too." Then
she was angry and cursed,[137] and her baby heard that

[127]Four days of pregnancy, and soon four of boy being in
the cradle.
[128]Where he was out of harm's way.
[129]Ho'au.
[130]With magic power, like his father.
[131]There is no ulterior meaning to east here, probably—
just a habit of mentioning directions.
[132]Shaman.
[133]A small bird with longitudinally striped top of the head
from carrying his gambling poles there: the name means
gambling poles (oture) carry on head (kepaye). See tale 16C,
below.
[134]Qamtoska is an unidentified bird, though mentioned
several times; possibly the common robin, as Devereux
alleges.
[135]This is a form of magic by production out of one's
body—or at any rate, creation from one's saliva, epidermis,
or dirt.
[136]Harremk.
[137]Presumably by referring to his dead ancestors; but
presumably she named no one, just mentioned "his" grand-
parents.

and cried. So she knew that he had done it. Then she
took the birds, put them on the fire, burned off the
feathers, broke off the legs,[138] and ate them. She saw
her baby looking on and smiling; and again she said:
"It is as I thought: my boy did it." (1 song.)

80. When she went out again, the boy did the same
thing; and when she returned this time, she saw quail
and rabbits lying about. She cooked and ate them. This
was twice. When she came back again she saw large
birds of all kinds lying dead; and she ate these. Now
it had happened three times, on three days. When she
went off again, the boy thought: "What kind of a boy
am I? This woman is here, but how did I come to be
here? There is a bird, kupa'-ya'ore;[139] he is wise and
knows everything. I will get him to tell me how I came
to be here." Then he spat into his hand, made a ball
as before, threw it, struck the bird, and broke its wing,
so that it lay on the ground unable to fly. Then the
boy came out of his cradle and took hold of the bird.
"I will not kill you: I will only ask you something and
you must tell me." The bird answered: "I am a bird,
but I will speak if you tell me to." The boy asked him:
"Here is my mother. Now how do I, a boy, come to
be here?" The bird said: "You are a real child,[140] for
your father was a doctor. Both he and his brother
were doctors. Your mother and her father, her mother,
her sisters, and her brothers live far away in the
west, at Avi-tokwiyo.[141] All your relatives are there."
The boy said: "It is good. That is what I wanted to
know. I said that I would not kill you." So he set the
bone of his wing: the bird was well again, and he let
him fly. Then he went back to his cradle. When it was
nearly sunset, the woman returned. Now the boy was
crying because he had heard that his father and his
father's brother were dead: he was mourning for them.
At night the woman took the child and tried to give it
her breast,[142] but he would not take it, only cried. She
thought: "Perhaps he has heard something and cries
for that." Then she wept also. So both of them wept
that night. (1 song.)

81. Now in the morning it was four days, and the
boy was grown up so high that he could run about and
play. Then he said: "My mother, do not go away to
gather seeds, but stay at home and make me a little
bow and an arrow without feathers,[143] so I can go about

[138]Cf. note 110.
[139]Kupa-ya'ore is unidentified.
[140]"A gentleman baby"; humare ma-tahanek, a very child
indeed.
[141]In 68, Avi-tokwiyo is E of the Colorado, but the boy
and his mother are now still farther E up the Gila in Maricopa country, so Avi-tokwiyo is W of them. I cannot place
it more precisely.
[142]He is only 4 days old.
[143]Otise (bow) hipa-kasa'eta (arrow unfeathered).

a little and shoot rabbits. Then when I come back, you can eat them." So she stayed in the house (a while) and made that and gave it to him. Then she went after seeds, and the boy also went off. He went eastward. But he thought: "I will not hunt: I will go on. I will go east. I am sorry for my father and his brother. I grieve for what I have heard: so I will not go back. I do not know where I will go. Perhaps I will turn into something." Then he went east to Avilyha.[144] There he saw blackbirds. When they saw him, they flew up. He said: "I could shoot you if I wished to, but I have not come here to kill birds. I am traveling east. But I will give you a name: Aθ'ikwa.[145] Everyone will call you that." (1 song.)

82. He continued to go east and came to Avi-hanye.[146] Then he said: "You frog, I know you. You came from Ha'avulypo when you made Matavilya sick. When he died and all the people cried, you traveled underground. When you came to Hanyiko-'itš-kw-ampeve,[147] you raised up your head. But hearing all the people still crying, you went on underground again. You went up on the mesa; and when you were close to the mountains, near Yucca,[148] you raised your head once more. But still hearing the noise from Ha'avulypo, you went underground again. Then farther on you again emerged, but sank down once more; and from there you traveled here to Avi-hanye. Here you no longer heard them crying: it was too far away. Then, you frog, you turned into a rock. But I know you; and I call this mountain Avi-hanye, Frog Mountain. The Maricopa[149] and Halchid-

homa and Kuhuana will call it the same way." (1 song.)

83. From there the boy went south between the country of the Papago[150] and that of the Pima and Maricopa and Kuhuana, until he reached the ocean. When he saw the waves, he told about them. (1 song.)

84. There he stood and thought of what he would be. "I can jump into the sea and become something there. I have come straight here, going southeastward.[151] Now I stand here. I think I will turn to be cane; not tall cane, but short, like grass.[152] I will be that; and I will be called Ahta-kaθiwu."[153] Then he turned into that; and the cane there now is short and low. (1 song.)

85. In the afternoon the woman returned to the house, thinking of her son. But the boy was not there. She looked all about: she did not find him. Then she searched for his tracks about the house, but could see none. Then she went the same way he had gone, though without seeing his tracks. She went as far as Avilyha, traveling the same way, but without seeing his traces. But from there she went southward.[154] She ran until she reached the sea. She did not stop at the edge but jumped in and dived down. When she came up back on shore and stood there, she was a bird, Snipe, Min-turisturis.[155] She thought: "I wanted to follow my son; but I came the wrong way: I did not go his road; now I have become a bird. I wanted to be where my son is, but I do not know where he is. Perhaps he has turned into something else."[156] (No songs.)[157]

[144]Avilyha I cannot place. It may be for Aví'alyha, "berdache mountain," cited by Spier, 1933, p. 23, as the Maricopa name, Vialyka, of Sierra Estrella, S of the Gila-Salt confluence.

[145]The point of the blackbird episode is not clear. At any rate they are something concrete to sing about. Blackbird appears also in 11:4, above.

[146]Avi-hanye, "frog-mountain," was said to be beyond Phoenix but before Tucson, that is, in Pima country. It is (H)Ikwe-nye-va in 9:9, above.

[147]Hanyiko-'itš-kw-ampeve (Hamyiko-itš-qwampa), or rather two places of that name, are mentioned also in 9:9, above.

[148]Yucca is up Sacramento Wash, farther from the Colorado than the first emergence. But the emergence crater was pointed out to me as visible from Mohave Valley, and as on the river side of the Black Mountains, at whose southern end lies Yucca.

[149]Hatpa-tahan, "real Maricopa," perhaps as distinct from later accretions like the Halchidhoma.

[150]Hatpa-'amai, "upper Pima," the Papago; the Pima are the Hatpa; the Maricopa, the Hatpa-'inya or "eastern Pima," although they lived downstream and west of the Pima. Thus my record; I do not know where the confusion lies. A line to the sea between the Papago and the other tribes would run nearly W, not S.

[151]It would be SW rather than SE.

[152]Pointing, 2-3 feet high.

[153]Ahta is cane; kaθiwu ?

[154]Whereas his course had been E (or from Avilyha to Avi-hanye rather SE).

[155]Snipe. "Has a white band on its neck, nods its head as it walks, runs along river as well as ocean." Cf. 1:103 (UC-AR 11:1), and below, 14:65, 17 II-77. All of them final transformations.

[156]Characteristic matter-of-fact, fatalistic, low-toned ending favored in Mohave narrative.

[157]I asked about names. "The boy had none: he was too young." And the woman? "She was just an Alakwisa at first. Then her husband gave her the name Makwakwaθ(a)."

INTERRELATIONS OF TUMANPA,
SALT, AND CHUHUECHE

These three tales having been recorded from the same informant, it seems worth comparing them.

As regards quality and manner, they are alike in a certain aridity and thinness of plot—even of incident. The characters' feelings are very little dwelled on. The paired personages sometimes squabble a little, but there are no strong clashes. Sex matters are prudishly not referred to, not even in Tumanpa which is supposed to be a tale of incest. There is some magic performed, but it is fairly tame and comes randomly rather than as evoked by crisis.

Itinerary and comments on what is seen at each spot take the place of stirring events; but the geography tends to become fuzzy when it gets far from Mohave territory—namely, beyond Mohave, Cheme-huevi, and Parker valleys.

The only strand of human interest plot in any of the three tales is in the last two sections of Chu-hueche, 13:68-85. Much of the content of 68-75 is found also in Cane: bringing home a wife, traveling to get cane, lightning cane (1:91, UC-AR 11:1, p. 17), quarrel of the brothers, gambling contest in which body is bet and lost, one brother kills the other. In both, the younger brother's wife also bears a posthu-mous son. But the Cane incidents are told with much more fullness and vividness; and with somewhat more motivation.

The final section of Chuchueche, 13:77-85, about the son, has fainter parallels with Cane (1:29-36, UC-AR 11:1, pp. 8-9), but strong ones with Coyote (6A, UC-AR 11:1, pp. 46-47), even to happening in Gila country; and with the Halchidhoma and Diegueño (but not Mohave) versions of Satukhôta, 18, below.

It is evident that when Achyora Hanyava used plot at all, he dealt with it half-heartedly and in reduction.

All three of his tales begin briefly with Ha'avulypo and then go on to Avikwame; except that Chuhueche lingers over the illness and death of Matavilya for a dozen or more paragraphs. Many Mohave do not like to hear about this, fatal illness, considering it doctors' stuff, preoccupation with which is likely to make them ill, or perhaps to speed them on a witching doctor's road; but this informant was a professed curing doctor.

From Avikwame, the route of Tumanpa turns briefly west, returns east, and then follows the river down without further detour.

Salt turns east into Walapai country, but most of the route cannot be traced because neither the Walapai nor the English equivalents of many of the Mohave place names are known. The informant may have really known the area, or just have juggled place names like counters. Thereafter the two Salt brothers recross the Colorado, and in three long jumps reach Muroc dry lake near Mohave city at the foot of Tehachapi pass that leads into the central California valley. There they face around, and in two stages to the southeast reach the spot where they turn into rock salt, appar-ently most of the way back to the Colorado. Through-out, the stages are long and much of the localization is fuzzy.

Chuhueche, after having dallied much longer at Ha'avulypo, also moves west from Avikwame, but by many slow stages to spots which the narrator seems to have visually in mind, to about as far into Cheme-huevi territory as Tumanpa, and much less far west than Salt. The return however is by long stages to unidentified places, and when the route is once more picked up, the heroes are in the first mountains short of the Colorado about abreast of lower Mohave Valley. From there they travel south, well west of the river, cross it below Parker, continue south sidling away from the river through Yavapai territory—most of this part of the route traceable on the map—to Kofa or Castle Dome Peak north-inland from the Yuma habitat. With them established at this peak, adventures and magic begin and the geography again becomes sketchy or imaginary.

It will be seen that in all three tales there is a westward trip followed by a return to the river. The western excursus is briefly dwelled on in Tumanpa, detailed in the two others. In all three there is either an overall drift southward or—in Tumanpa—a step-by-step progression south. Tumanpa is alone in that its route hugs the river, once the brief initial side trip west is disposed of. The two others, on the contrary, only cross the river (Chuhueche also parallels it), but nowhere follow it.

A consequence is that Tumanpa operates mostly in Mohave territory and nearly half of it in Mohave Valley proper; but the two other stories move largely in Chemehuevi, Walapai, and Yavapai territory, plus farther afield to the south in the plot portion of Chuhueche.

There are a number of more specific near-repetitions or parallels of content, indicative of a lack of vigor of originality. Such are:

The Like-Mohave etc. tribes seen (impossibly, in fact) from the farthest point west. 12:21, 22; 13:39.

Sand deserts or hills seen from the same places, or reached soon after. 12:23, 24; 13:38.

Mountain-sheep of four colors going off. 12:2; 13:15; (see also 11:40 for mountain-sheep; and for four colors of coyote, 11:44).

Driftwood or snags in the river make sound. 11:15; 13:57.

Crossing river, thinking they will drown. 11:17; 13:62.

Roofless circle of brush as camp for the night. 11:18; 12:16; 13:67.

Curing of companion whose feet hurt. 11:34; 13:54.

Woodpecker in hollow cactus. 11:10; 13:32.

Coyote homeless. 11:44; 13:48.

Main characters transform. 11:55; 12:25; 13:76.

In total number of songs the three cycles are not notably far apart (123, 117, 169). They do vary considerably in narrative length and in number of song stations—as one to three or four—in the order Salt, Tumanpa, Chuhueche (longest). The number of songs per station varies in inverse order: not quite so drastically, but still of the magnitude of two and a half to one.

11, Tumanpa: 55 stages, 47 with songs, number of songs 123 (118), number of songs per stage with songs, 2.6.

12, Salt: 25 stages, 117 songs, per stage, 4.7.

13, Chuhueche: 85 stages, 84 with songs, total 169 songs, per stage, 2.0.

Narrative 14
YELLAK: GOOSE

INTRODUCTION

I give both the Mohave and English name for this cycle because while the translation is very probable, it is not quite certain, and in fact is open as regards species. The fullest form of the word heard was Yellaka, the shortest, Yelak.

The informant was Aspá-sakám, "Eagle-sell," given English form as "Space," who was around forty years old in November 1905, when he came to the University with Jack Jones and told—and partly sang—both Yellak and Nyohaiva, as already told in the introduction to narrative 3, Nyohaiva (UC-AR 11:1, p. 27).

Goose is a long story and has many songs. Aspa-sakam's listing mentioned 427 songs in 65 clusters. This makes the average number of songs per station between 6 and 7—higher than found in any other cycle. The distribution is:

Songs in group: 2 3 4 5 6 8 10 13 14 15 18
Stations: 3 2 17 9 12 5 13 1 1 1 1

The Yellak story is long and monotonous. It tells how when Mastamho made the Colorado River by plunging his staff, Goose was the first to issue with the water, and was followed by the other water birds. They then swam down the river to its mouth, by which time they had assumed their full bird shape. However, their leader was no longer with them: he died when they reached Ha'avulypo (station 20 out of 65), and was succeeded by Halykūpa, probably Grebe; though parts of Goose's body sank into the river and were later encountered, transformed into invertebrates, by the birds as they neared the mouth. There follow two sections, 66-77 and 78-82, unaccompanied by songs. The first of these tells of Grebe's return, with two companions, to Mohave Valley, and their full transformation there by Mastamho; the second, Mastamho's own transformation.

The story has perhaps the fewest events or active incidents per page or hour of any Mohave narrative recorded. It consists in large part of statements of what will be, or may be, what someone is thinking, who is to be listened to or knows something and who not. This gives a subjective character that makes for dullness but which the Mohave do not seem to mind.

At stations 14-16 three land birds leave the party. In 34, Gnatcatcher and three other land birds take up land in Mohave Valley to "become Mohaves." In 43, 44 Woodpecker goes off to the east and Quail to the west; in 45-47, Oriole, Night-hawk, and Mockingbird waken the rest as they sleep. Otherwise, the water birds just journey on through to the sea, with only such divertisements as shifts from swimming in file to abreast, wondering about Yellak's condition, mourning for his death, hearing sounds from the transforming parts of his dead body, sleeping three times, being instructed how to lay eggs, being told their feathers will grow larger and they will fly, trying to walk and tiring, being refreshed by rain, leaving foot tracks as they vainly try to rise in flight, hearing strange sounds ahead, wondering how they will look when finished, and finally plunging into the ocean.

The songs end here; but there are in Eagle-sell's rendition the two additional sections of story about Grebe's return northward (with two companions), of his misadventures there, and his and then Mastamho's own final transformation—both of them into birds.

There is a subdominant theme running alongside the formally primary one of river journey by water birds. This theme is a relation of hostility—or at least avoidance, escape, or jealousy—toward Mastamho. Nine groups of songs, paragraphs 23-31, immediately following Yellak's death, tell how Grebe leads his following past Avikwame, warning them not to listen to the sounds from there. This long passage ends when they have finally got beyond Avikwame and Grebe at last tells them Mastamho's four ritual names. He also says that it is Mastamho who wants them because he claims all power; but Grebe urges them nevertheless to refuse and come with him to the ocean (31). In short, Goose and Grebe lead a sort of rebellion of fallen angels. Goose dies when they come abreast Ha'avulypo where Mastamho's father Matavilya died; and he is mourned for by Han'ava as Matavilya was mourned for. Why he dies is never made clear, nor even alluded to. Was it because he cut loose from Mastamho? I am uncertain. At any rate, Grebe tells his band that there is one of great power who went off to Avikwame and may prove stronger and

not let them pass, and who may draw them to him
and do something to them that may give them power
—but if they do not listen to him they will be happy
(29). It sounds a bit like the belief of the present
Mohave that as doctors grow old they bewitch people
to keep their "shadows" in captivity. Or perhaps
Mastamho is merely offering doctoring power to those
that come to him, and Grebe warns them against it,
for, to the nonshaman layman, doctor's power is fearful and at best ambivalent. The Mohave do sometimes
definitely class Yellak as being close to doctor's singings, as I have said in the Handbook, page 766. It is
not outrightly shamanism, for that the ordinary Mohave
does not want to hear sung or told of, and may walk
away from, on account of its suggestion of sickness,
witchcraft, and death. Yellak is not quite in this category, as Wellaka, Hikupk, and Beaver are; it is listened
to without reluctance, and it is not used for curing; but
it evidently has implications of shamanism—perhaps
only because of this very section 23-31.

Arrived at the ocean, the birds enter on it; but the
leader Grebe with two companions wants to return
north. They fly up until they see the oceans on four
sides of the earth, then head for—Avikwame itself!
They miss it, however, falling short, and an episode
follows of Grebe's claiming farmland which his follower
Gnatcatcher—a land bird—has taken, and of Grebe's

being undignifiedly worsted. He then goes to Hokusave
nearby on the river's bank where Mastamho has come
down from his mountain and is transforming and naming
other birds—especially the Hawks that give bravery
and power in war. He also transforms and names Grebe
and his two partners; and therewith the story ends; except for Mastamho's completing some items of his
creation, like fish and mountains; and then turning himself into a bird.

It will be seen that the whole long Goose-Grebe story
is encapsulated between a slim beginning and end about
Mastamho, with a side theme of opposition between them
developed in 23-31.

The second version, given below as Yellak II, has
at least an allusion to the rejection of Mastamho (II:59,
60), though transiently and in another part of the story;
the motif is thus at least not a purely individual idio-
syncracy of Eagle-sell's.

Yellak is so simple in general plot, and so minor
in incident, that in spite of its length a formal outline
does not seem requisite, and, apart from half-a-dozen
heads for main divisions, I have merely prefixed a
sidehead to each paragraph. The essence of the itinerary traversed will be found at the end, in the comparison of versions I and II, and geographical detail
in the notes.

THE YELLAK MYTH

A. Yellak First Leader of the Birds (1-20)

1. Mastamho makes river, Yellak, and birds:—Yellak[1]
came into being.[2] He did not grow from an egg like a
bird but came to life in water. There were no mountains then. The earth was level, wet, and soft. There
was no one but one person, no one but Pahutšatš.[3] He
was alone. No one but he stood there. He had a cane
as long as this.[4] He plunged it into the ground four

times. Then water came out of the ground. The first
one that came with the water was Yellak. After him
came all kinds of birds. That water was our water,
our river; it was what we Mohave use and drink.
(8 songs).

2. Yellak goes east to San Francisco Mountains.—
When he stood on the ground, Yellak said: "I give a
name to this place. I call it Nyaháim-kwiðík."[5] He
gave this place four names. He called it also Nyaháim-
tšumítše, Vaθáim-kwiyume, and Kwaθáim-hoá'pma.[6]
Four, five, six, seven, eight, nine[7] birds had come out

---

[1]Yellak or Yellaka was described as a wild goose or
possibly duck: broad bill, short legs, long neck, body brown-
ish, back bluish, blue and white on throat, rear top of head
bluish. Allowing for peculiarities of Mohave perception, and
the species distributions, it is most likely to be the small
Black Brant, Branta nigritans, or the large Canada Goose,
B. canadensis.

[2]Hípŭk, hípŭk, were the narrator's first words. Hípŭk
means root, butt, origin.

[3]Pa-hutšatš, in slow pronunciation Ipá-hutšátše, is Mastamho. The name is said to refer to food: he made food for
us. In 7:58 (UC-AR 11:1, p. 61) Mastamho names himself
Pahutšatš-yamasam-kwakirve.

[4]A fathom long. The magic cane or rod is referred to
again at the end of the story, in 78, 81. Cf. also Origins,
9:18 above; and 7:9 (UC-AR 11:1, p. 54), where the stick is
of sandbar willow but only a cubit long; and below 15:4,
without specification.

[5]Wet- ?

[6]Nyaháim, aháim means wet, moist, soft (ahá, water);
ny- might be "his, its." The places are beyond Mohave ken,
supposedly near the source of the Colorado. The names are
"ritualistic," that is, fabricated for the story according to a
pattern; and they jingle or rhyme on the accented syllable-
haim of the first member. Kw-iyume means "see." It recurs
(as -kiyume) in the beginning of the second Yellak version
outlined below.

[7]Mohave idiom. A large number is meant: they stand in
four rows.

with him, but they were not yet alive. Yellak said:
"I will give you names; but not yet; not here. Now
all stand in four rows!" Then he started eastward
with them. They went far east to Avi-kwa-hanapatše.[8]
When they arrived there, he thought about which one
might be oldest. He thought: "The oldest one, he who
emerged first, has taken this place already, I think."[9]
When he had thought thus, he prepared to return. He
said: "I will go back, but I will give a name to this
place here. I will call it Nyahaim-kuvare."[10] When he
had given it this name, he returned. (6 songs).

3. Goes southwest to San Bernadino Mountains.—
Now they came back to the first place, to Nyahaim-
kwiδik. He thought which way they should go. "I am
thinking about going north or south or west. There
are three more ways to go, and I do not yet know
which to take. Well, I will start. I will go southwest.
I will go to Kwaθakupaye.[11] Then he went,[12] and
arrived at Kwaθakupaye. (4 songs).

4. Returns to Nyahaim-kwiδik.—He said: "I have
come here, but I think I will return." Then he went
back to Nyahaim-kwiδik. He said: "Everything is made
and provided now.[13] I will not talk about it more. But
there is something else that I will teach you." The
others all looked at him. They wanted to learn what
he would do. Then he walked four steps. He said:
"Look at me. Can you do this? I want you to do the
same. Follow me. I want you to do it right." The
others looked at him. Then he also moved his wings.
"I want you to do that also," he said. "I will not give
you names here. After we have gone away I will give
you names." (10 songs).

5. – 8. Downriver to four places in four steps
each.

5. Yellak said: "Now we will leave this place: we
are going." Then he walked four steps on the water.[14]

The others saw him do it, then followed him. So they
went south. When he had taken four steps, he stood
and gave a name to the place which he had reached.
He said: "I call it Nyahaim-koreme. I will stand here
and sing four times." (4 songs).

6. Then he started again and walked four steps
more to the south. When he stopped, he said: "I name
this place Nyahaim-kumáike." (4 songs).

7. All the others had followed him but said no word.
He said: "We will go on again." He started and walked
four steps. When he stopped, he said: "I will give this
place also a name so that you will know it. I name
this place Nyahaim-kutšepáive."[15] (8 songs).

8. He went four steps south again. All the birds
followed him and then stood about listening. They
wanted to hear what he would say. He said: "I give
this place the name Nyahaim-kwatθárve."[16] (10 songs).

9. Swimming downstream.—Yellak said: "I have
given names to four places. That will be all." Then
he started to go. He went in the middle of the river,[17]
ahead, the others following. They were thinking about
his leaving them.[18] They thought: "Even if you make
a mistake, I shall be able to do something." They
thought they had dreamed and knew something and had
supernatural power. That is how they thought about
him. (8 songs).

10. Right and left distinguished, and west from east.
—Then, as they were in the middle of the river, Yellak
said: "This is the right arm, the right leg. They are
good. If you enter the water with them, it will be well.
This is the left leg, the left arm. If you enter the
water with them, you will be drowned.[19] If you do not
learn that, you will not be able to go on the water.
Now you know it. As we go down the river, the middle
is south. On the right hand is the west. On the left
hand is the east. Now you know that also. I want you
all to know it." (5 songs).

11. Foam of drift log talks.—As they went down on
the water, a log was floating[20] to the east of them.
Foam[21] traveled with it. Then the foam spoke: it said
something. Yellak said: "Do not listen to what it says.
We shall go on the right of it. We shall follow it on

[8] "Near Flagstaff." Probably the San Francisco Mountains.
[9] Older than himself, born from heaven and earth (?), or oldest of those that emerged with the river (?). The "very first" would be Matavilya; but Mastamho-Pahutšatš is probably meant here.
[10] Said to mean "wet-cold." Cf. note 6. I have hatšork for "winter."
[11] Two peaks east of San Bernardino, perhaps San Jacinto and San Gorgonio, flanking Cabezon Pass, the two highest peaks in southern California; or possibly San Gorgonio and San Antonio west of San Bernardino, between which Cajon Pass emerges to the north, through which the Mohave, after following up Mohave River, most often entered the plain of southern California.
[12] Followed by his train of birds, or alone?
[13] In the physical world? But even in that the mountains do not yet stand up (40), and rocks and desert remain to be made (79).
[14] The Mohave tend to translate "go" as "walk" in English. To walk four steps is a stereotyped phrase. "He walked four steps on the water" may mean that the narrator visualized just that, with him stepping on the surface of the river; or that he strode in shallow water.

[15] "The present Indians say Avi-ketšupaive" (viz., -ketšu- for -kutše-). "When I think much about a place, I sing eight songs; for others only one or two; for some, no songs."
[16] Making all told four sets of four steps, all southward or downstream. All these "Nyahaim-" names of course refer to mythological places, not geographical ones.
[17] This may mean that now he went into deep water and swam.
[18] The presaging of which the Mohave are so fond. First one thinks of a thing, then it happens; or one talks, then does it. Yellak does die in 20.
[19] The left hand is associated with doctoring, shamanism, and evil.
[20] Ihne, driftwood; also snags.
[21] (A)ha-kemalye, foam.

its right side. That side of it is good and we shall take it.[22] What you hear speaking there,[23] what it tells, is a lie. What I tell you I know: it is true." (10 songs).

12. Yellak hints at his death.—As they went on, he said: "If I dream bad,[24] I will become sick and die. No one may know of it, but I will become sick. I do not know who will take my place then. But take my words and do as I do. Listen to what I say. Hear me." Those who were following him thought about him: "I think he will not live long. I think he will become sick and die. He feels that; he knows it; but he will not say it."[25] Then they came to a place and he called it Nyahaim-kwatšáve.[26] (4 songs).

13. He promises to give names to some.—As they began to go on from that place, Yellak said: "Now I will give you names. I will not give them to all of you, only to three." Then those three said: "It is good. We want you to give us names." It was Raven,[27] Roadrunner,[28] and Gold-eye[29] who wanted names. But Yellak said: "I will give you names when we arrive farther down. I will not name you now as we start. When we reach Nyahaim-ko'óive[30] I will give you names." (2 songs).

14-16. Raven, Roadrunner, and Gold-eye named and go off.

14. But when they arrived at Nyahaim-ko'óive he still did not give them names; he went on. When they came to Hatekulye-nyi-kuyá,[31] he gave them names. First he gave a name to Raven: he called him Nyahaim-tunyíve.[32] Then Raven said: "I have a name: it has been given to me. Now I will go away: I will go into the mountains and live there. When I am there, I also will give myself a name. I will call myself Aqāqa and all will know me. When they see me and hear my cry they will know me, for I will say 'aqāqa, aqāqa.' All will know me even in the dark." (5 songs).

15. They continued to go on. Yellak said to the next one: "I will give you a name too." But he did not stop.

He continued to go on with them all. When they came to Hátevilye-kutšehwérve,[33] he gave Roadrunner a name. He called him Nyahaim-kurrêve. When Roadrunner had been given this name, he left the water and ran back and forth over the ground four times. Then he said: "I have a name now, but I want to give myself a name too. My name will be Talypo: everyone will call me that." So Roadrunner said. (4 songs).

16. Yellak said to Gold-eye: "I will give you a name also." Gold-eye said: "What am I to do?" Yellak said: "I will tell you. Jump four times." "On the ground?" "No, in the water. Dive four times. Now you are not yet completed; but then your neck, your legs, and your feathers will be finished." Then, when Gold-eye had dived, he gave him a name. "Your name will be Nya-hai-yuvīsma."[34] Then Gold-eye said: "I will call myself Kasunyo. I will give myself that name. Everyone will call me that." (5 songs).

17. Yellak blocks river: but feels sick.—When Gold-eye had called himself by that name, he no longer went with the others but followed them at a distance. He thought: "Now I am finished. I have given myself a name. I will do something." He was thinking about what he would eat, about the little fish and the worms in the river; and he also eats mud. Yellak said to the other birds: "Gold-eye is provided for: he can do as he wishes. He can think about something: it will be well." Then they came to Amaṭ-hamak.[35] There Yellak opened his wings and stretched them out so that the other birds could not pass. He wanted them to stay back. When he stopped stretching his wings, they tried to pass on. Then again he would not let them go by but stretched his wings in front of them.[36] He did that four times. So they all remained where they were. He thought: "I think I am sick, but I do not know of what I am sick. I do not know what it is that made me sick. Perhaps it is the clouds, or the sky, or the wind, or the earth, or the water. I do not know. I have no pain, but I can hardly walk. My legs are tired so that I cannot lift them. All my body has become sick." (15 songs).

18. The birds wonder about Yellak.—All the birds stood about him. They did not say a word. They listened to him, but they did not ask him anything. Then they all went on again. When they came to θáweve,[37] Yellak

[22]Again the right side is good.
[23]"The foam's talk was plain, that of the driftwood confused, like an echo from the bank." The slight murmur of the ripples against the log is alluded to, apparently.
[24]Have bad luck.
[25]More presage.
[26]Untranslated. But all these places are mythological only, fabricated for the story.
[27]Aqāqa.
[28]Talypo. Have these two landbirds been swimming down the river with the rest? Or is the narrator's visualization not so exact as that? Cf. Roadrunner's "leaving the water" in 15 to run over the land.
[29]Kasunyo. The identification is not certain. "A long-legged duck."
[30]Also unplaced.
[31]"Wolf's or Mountain Lion's cave." This may be an actual geographical place name, not a mythological one. See 5:1 (UC-AR 11:1, p. 41) and 16A, note 14, and part II, B, 3 below.
[32]"Wet-tunyíve." But Raven calls himself by his secular Mohave name, Aqāqa.

[33]Unplaced and untranslated. It is possible that the first element of the name should have been written Matavilye-.
[34]"He named him that because this bird's flight is slow and heavy."
[35]Amaṭ-hamak, according to J. P. Harrington, is a small range paralleling the river on the W, S of Eldorado Canyon.
[36]The blocking of the river recurs in 19, though there he also dams and widens the river. In both cases he is nearly dead. The idea may be that he holds his followers back because he is too ill to go on. In 36 a white beaver tries to obstruct the procession, then led by Halykūpa.

dived. He emerged again. He continued to dive and emerge. The birds following him did not ask, but they looked at him and thought: "I think he has become sick from what he has been telling us. What he has taught us has returned[38] to him and made him sick." (6 songs).

19. Yellak again blocks river, now at Ha'avulypo.— From θaweve they continued to go down the river. Now Yellak's body was entirely dead, only his heart was not yet dead. He continued to dive and emerge.[39] All the other birds knew that he was dead. The one who was going to take his place[40] when Yellak died held everything in his own heart, but as yet he did not tell it. He asked Yellak: "Do you still know?" He thought Yellak was already dead, but Yellak said: "Yes, I understand you." Now he wanted to stop. Then he stretched his wings and so stopped the water from flowing and damned it and made it wide.[41] Then all the birds stopped: here they were going to talk. This was at Ha'avulypo.[42] (10 songs).

[37]θaweve is not exactly located, except that the present context puts it upriver from Ha'avulypo, Eldorado Canyon. In 8:192 (UC-AR 11:2, p. 105) it is called θavêve and is made the point farthest N on the river to which the defeated former residents of Mohave Valley and Northerners flee; from there they turn east into the heart of the Walapai country N of Hackberry. 6A (UC-AR 11:1, p. 46) puts θaweve on Cottonwood Island but is almost certainly inexact.

[38]"Has come back on him," like a reflection. Almost anything one interferes with, especially what is unaccustomed, may react in this way.

[39]This body, already dead except at the core, continuing to dive and emerge like an automaton, is a strange image.

[40]Halykûpa: cf. 20.

[41]Cf. note 36.

[42]Ha'avulypo is where Matavilya, the first god, father of Mastamho, died, was cremated, and his ashes washed away

20. Yellak dies at Ha'avulypo and Halykûpa takes his place.—Now Yellak died and lay on the water belly up. Then Halykûpa,[43] who was the one who would take his place, said: "I know that he has died, because this is the place where someone[44] died long ago. Two (rock) posts stand here. They were once his house posts. I heard this. Someone lived and died here, and then they wanted to make it that the house would be washed away. But they were unable to wash it away entirely, and these two house posts still stand. I have not seen them before but I have heard of it. The man who built the house was Numē-numá'a.[45] He was the one who died here. Then Amaṭ-kapes'ara[46] burned the house. Now Yellak has died here. His skin will sink down into the water. There it will turn into something: it will become animals. When we come to the end of our way I will tell you more about them, but now I do not yet know."[47] (10 songs).

by the river. Cf. Tale 9, Origins. Most myths start with a reference either to Ha'avulypo or to Avikwame.

[43]I got a slightly uncertain identification of Halykûpa as the Western Grebe. Cf. 7:96 (UC-AR 11:1, p. 66). In 77 below he turns into a slough bird that flies badly; which seems to confirm the identification. However, it seems wisest to retain the native name.

[44]Matavilya. One suspects there is a connection between their dying at the same place, but I do not know what the connection is in Mohave thinking.

[45]This name of Matavilya is otherwise unknown to me. Nume is Wildcat.

[46]In 7:22 (UC-AR 11:1, p. 56) he is called Amaṭ-kapisara, an insect, and digs the postholes for Mastamho's house at Avikwame.

[47]These gods and heroes are not omniscient. They and the world are yet young. They think things out, and wait for knowledge to come to them. The beings into which Yellak's body parts turned are met with, or at least heard, and named below in 61-63. Reference to them is made in 33.

B. Grebe Leads the Birds Past Mastamho (21-32)

21. Halykûpa orders Han'ava to cry for Yellak— Halykûpa said: "I know what made Yellak die. He became sick from the sky, the clouds, the earth, the water, and the wind.[1] I know that. Now all call him Umas-ahaim-takyeve.[2] It will be the last time. All say it. Then do not say it again, because he is dead.[3] Now cry. Cry with the sky and with the wind. As anything makes a noise, a sound of its own, cry with it.[4] Who will be the one to cry first? You, Han'ava-kumêitse,[5] cry first." Then Han'ava-kumêitše began

[1]As Yellak himself thought in 17, above, though the birds thought differently in 18.

[2]A mythological fabrication: "Child-wet-takyêve."

[3]Taboo of name of dead or of reference to them.

[4]Wailing has to be suggested to start.

[5]This first mourner has six names:
   Han'ava-kumêitse, cf. the final name.
   Amaṭ-kanivê, reference to the ground.
   Nyat-nyī-môm.

to cry. Then they cried with him, all who were there. Then Halykûpa said: "Next, you will be Amaṭ-kanyivê. That will be your name." Then he said: "Next you will be Nyat-nyī-môm. Next you will be Nyat-nyī-qwênye. Next you will be Nyat-nyī-lye. Next you will have the name Han'ava."[6] (10 songs).

   Nyat-nyī-qwênye.
   Nyat-nyī-lye—these three seem made up.
   Han'ava, the usual form, a locust or cicada. Above, in Origins, 9:13, he is called Han'ava. In Chuhueche, 13:14, there are two of these wailers, called Hayunyé, and they become the heroes of the story.

[6] "He had six names, but was one man, who changed, like a tadpole to a frog, and became different, because he was not finished at first. When he first cried, he was Han'ava-kumêitse, yellow, like a horsefly (sic; cicada?) in the arrowweeds. Then he was Amaṭ-kanyivê because he came out of the ground where there was moist, soft sand at the foot of the post of the former house there. When he was Nyāt-nyī-môm, he was silent. As Nyāt-nyī-qwênye he looked yellow, with yellow wings."

22. <u>Minse'atalyke leads some into side channel.</u>—
Then Halykŭpa said: "That will be all. Now let us
stop crying." Then they all finished. He said again:
"I am the one who will tell you what I know. I will
be the leader." So he started again. As they went
downriver, there was a bird among them named
Minse'atalyke.[7] Then Halykŭpa said to him: "Perhaps
you have dreamed well. Perhaps you will be a doctor.
I want to divide these here and let you take half of
them." Then Minse'atalyke said: "I will follow the
water to the right: I will go west. You behind me can
come behind. And the (main) river will follow me,
going in a different direction."[8] Halyekŭpa said: "It is
well. I will go on the eastern side; I will go the true
way. You can go your way. But you will meet me
again. I shall not lose you." So they stood there and
disagreed. Then Halykŭpa said: "I will give this place
a name: Aha-kekatšvoδáuve."[9] (10 songs).

23. <u>They meet again:</u> <u>Halykŭpa warns of Mastamho</u>
<u>at Avikwame ahead.</u>—Then Minse'atalyke went to the
west. He did not know much; he was not going really
to be a doctor; but he thought he was a great man.
Halykŭpa said: "Sakataθêre and Av'akwaθpı̄ne,[10] you
can go with him. Go with Minse'atalyke." Thus many
went with Minse'atalyke. He went straight along, not
telling them anything on the way; but on the eastern
stream Halykŭpa talked to those following him. He
came to Waθalye,[11] and there Minse'atalyke arrived
also: they came there at the same time; so they had
all met again. Then Halykŭpa said: "Do you see? You
are not much. You will not be anything. You have not
dreamed, you know nothing: you have met me here
after all. Now all will follow me and I shall be sole
leader." Then Halykŭpa said: "I have heard that there
was one who went away.[12] I have not seen him, but I

have heard of him. I have heard it said that he would
be a great man, a brave man, a man with supernatural
power. I heard that he was at Avikwame, but I do not
know who he is. When we arrive there, perhaps he will
overcome us. Perhaps he will not let me pass by. When
we come there, perhaps I will be caught." (14 songs).

24. <u>He names the river.</u>—Halykŭpa said: "I heard a
great noise, but nevertheless I go on. And, I will give
a name to this river. I call it Nyahaim-soδóma. And
I give it the name Myahaim-tšumême.[13] That makes
two names." (5 songs).

25. <u>He lines them up in file.</u>—As they went on from
there Halykŭpa said: "Get into one file and follow me.
I will look back and if you are in a crooked line I shall
see it." Then, when he looked back, he said: "That is
right; that is what I wanted. You have obeyed me. You
are going in one straight line. I call that Nyahaim-
elóye."[14] (5 songs).

26. <u>They proceed despite sounds from Avikwame.</u>—
They continued to go south. Then they came to Ahai-
kuso'érve, also called Malykát-uδáuve.[15] Then Halykŭpa
said: "We have come here on the water. I will call
this place by another name: Nyahaim-hoāme.[16] Now we
will go on. I hear a noise from Avikwame: nevertheless
I will go on. We will pass by and go straight south."
(4 songs).

27. <u>They swim past Avi-kunu'ulye.</u>—They went on.
Halykŭpa said: "I will give a name to this place so
that all will know it. When you are alive,[17] you will
know the name of this place. This, here on the east,
will be Avi-kunu'úlye.[18] That on the other side of the
river, on the west, will be Qotase."[19] (5 songs).

28. <u>Hoping to pass Avikwame safely.</u>—As they went
on down from there, he looked for a good place from
which to look about[20] but did not find it. He said: "If
he overcomes me and catches us and takes us up on
his mountain, perhaps we will become something. Perhaps we will dream and have supernatural power. But
if he does not overcome me and take me, we shall go
past and on. We are not far from there.[21] Now I will
give a name to this place, so that everyone will know

---

[7]Minse'atalyke is red-headed like a woodpecker, but is
evidently a water bird. The full form seems to be Miny(e)-
sa'atalyke, as in 7:96, note 155 (UC-AR 11:1, p. 66).

[8]He was taking (or making?) the western channel.

[9]At the head of Cottonwood Island.

[10]Sakataθêre reappears in 66-75 below, and 7:96 (UC-AR
11:1, p. 66). He is not identified. Av'akwaθpı̄ne is a duck,
perhaps the Scaup. Cf. 7:10, 36, 96 (UC-AR 11:1, pp. 54, 58,
66).

[11]At the downstream end of Cottonwood Island.

[12]Mastamho. It is not clear why the oblique allusion, why
the fear of being caught or overcome by Mastamho as they
pass Avikwame, and how they do get by in 31. There is no
doubt that Mastamho is greater than Yellak and Halykŭpa,
who are after all his creatures through being born with the
river that Mastamho makes. They are perhaps conceived as
rebelling against his superior power, and therefore having
something illegitimate about them. The Yellak singing is
sometimes classed as shamanistic and therefore ambiguous
in its social desirability (Handbook, p. 766). At any rate,
after Halykŭpa has returned from the sea but has been defeated in trying to take farmland in Mohave Valley, he goes
to Mastamho who gives him his ultimate transformation
(73-77). The tale closes with Mastamho's own final change
(78-82), just as it opened with him (1). The whole Yellak-

Halykŭpa cycle (2-77) is therefore encapsulated in a thin
shell of Mastamho's doings.

[13]Untranslated.

[14]-elóye seems to refer to the straight file.

[15]Malykat-uδauve, "Jimsonweed (Datura) stands" or "where
it is."

[16]Wet-hoāme.

[17]Have become what you will finally be.

[18]"Tumescence-rock." It recurs in 7:89 (UC-AR 11:1, p.
65), in a context of lewdness. It was described as a small
sharp peak 6 miles N of Hoatšavámeve, which is close to
the river in Arizona, "opposite" Avikwame.

[19]Amái-nye-qotáse is mentioned in 8:191 (UC-AR 11:2,
p. 105) but seems farther S than Qotase here.

[20]"To see the whole earth."

[21]Avikwame, which he is worrying about.

it. I am a bird, but I will give it a name. I call it
Maθuvêlye. I call it also Ayáts̆-uváuve.[22] It has two
names." (8 songs).

29. <u>Halykūpa urges them not to listen to Mastamho.</u>
—When they went on from there, he said: "Do not go
off to a distance, do not go aside, follow me! When
you hear something being said west of the river, do
not stray off there. If you hear it and go, they will
do something to you. Then perhaps you will possess
great supernatural power. But listen to what I say
and you will be good and happy. Listen to me and
follow me. Do not go aside and it will be well. What
you will hear there is wrong. I am afraid you will go
there, therefore I will come to land on this east side
of the river. And I give this place the name Nyahaim-
ikílyke."[23] (6 songs).

30. <u>Traveling and resting.</u>—Then they started to go
on again. Halykūpa walked[24] around them on the water.
He said: "I will tell you how I want you to walk. When
you walk, I want you to stop and rest for a time. I
will give that names. I will call it Nyahaim-iwāse and
Nyahaim-ināke."[25] (10 songs).

31. <u>They pass Avikwame: he reveals Mastamho's</u>
<u>names.</u>—They went on and came to Himé-ke-huvíke.[26]

Halykūpa said: "The one who made this river with his
staff has four names: Pahuts̆ats̆-nyahaim-kuváya,
Pahuts̆ats̆-nyahaim-kuváts̆kye, Pahuts̆cats̆-nyahaim-
kuvats̆éits̆ye, and Pahuts̆ats̆-nyahaim-kuvapáye.[27] He
has all the large birds with him up there.[28] Do not
look in that direction, do not listen. He keeps all those
birds with him, and instructs them how to do something.
We will pass right on to the sea far down below.
Pahutsats̆ is saying: 'I want you all to come here to
me because it is I who have power.' But do not do it;
come with me down to the sea." (10 songs).

32. <u>They sleep in Mohave Valley.</u>—Then they went
on. And soon Halykūpa said: "Now it is well. You have
not listened to him and we shall get by." When they
came near where Fort Mohave now stands, he said:
"The sun is nearly down; it will soon be dark. Then
we will stop and sleep." They went on down, just below
where Fort Mohave is; at that time there was low level
land there, and no mesa. There they stopped and slept.
In the morning Halykūpa said: "We have come to this
place, Aqwáq-iyóve. I will give it a name. I call it
Nyahaim-e'áqma.[29] (13 songs).

_____

[22]Maθuvêlye and Ayats̆-uvauve seem not to be mentioned
elsewhere for what must be Avikwame, or part of it.

[23]Wet-ikilyke.

[24]"They walked on the water and he walked around them."
Cf. Section A, note 14.

[25]-iwāse was said to refer to stopping, -inake to alter-
nately walking and stopping.

[26]Hime- is foot, leg; huvike perhaps is double or pair.

They must be where the river comes out of its canyon into
the rather narrow upper part of Mohave Valley, below the
present Davis Dam. The place is mentioned also in 8:170,
171 (UC-AR 11:2, p. 103) as Himike-huvike on the W side.

[27]Páhuts̆áts̆ is Mastamho as in Section A, note 3; nyahaim,
wet, moist, as before; the remaining four elements are -kuva-
ya, -kuva-ts̆kye, kuva-ts̆eitsye, kuva-paye.

[28]At Avikwame. "Large" may refer to eagle and the hawks.

[29]"Wet-e'aqma." Aqwaq-iyove, "deer-see," is a well-known
place in upper Mohave Valley, UC-AR 11:2, Map 1, site E,
E side, and p. 139.

C. Grebe Leader Farther Down River (33-51)

33. <u>Sounds far south come from Yellak's body.</u>—As
they went on down the river again from there, Halykūpa
said: "You can hear a noise far in the south. Everything is happy and joyful there. When Yellak died, his
feathers and his skin and his claws sank in the river
to turn into animals. I think it is they who are far
below there. I do not know it, but I hear them and I
think that."[1] He told them this so that they would go on
with him. He thought that perhaps they wished to return,
but that if he told them they would go on. (18 songs).

34. <u>Gnatcatcher left to become Mohave.</u>—As they
went on down, they came to Hats̆ioq-waṭveve.[2] Halykūpa
said: "Who will take this land? It is a good place and

level. When the river recedes, there is soft mud (to
plant in)." Then Gnatcatcher[3] said: "I take this land. I
will own it. I will take it on both sides of the river."
All heard him. Then, after him Ts̆aiqwatarqe said: "I
want the bottom land, the overflowed land,[4] for I am
the youngest. You are older. You can have the high
land on the (first) terrace, but I want this near the
river." He and Pilpiyo and Qeiδiδo[5] said they wanted

_____

[1]Those that his remains turned into (20) are told of in
61-63. They appear to be salt-water invertebrates.

[2]Hats̆ioq-waṭveve is mentioned again in 71. It is the site
of a Mohave settlement, about halfway between Fort Mohave
and Needles, UC-AR 11:2, Map 1, F, west, and p. 140.

[3]Han'avets̆ípa. He is probably Gnatcatcher, as in 7:70 (UC-
AR 11:1, p. 62). He is described there as building nests with
small openings, in the mesquite rather than in the willow-
cottonwood association of the valley, and as being sharp-billed
and nearly as small as a hummingbird.

[4]He and his two companions wanted the valley bottom,
annually overflowed and farmable, whereas Gnatcatcher was
to be on the lowest of the terraces, which cannot ordinarily
be farmed by Mohave overflow methods, though the mesquites
on it penetrate to water.

[5]Pilpiyo and Qeiδiδo are unidentified birds.

the low land. They said: "We shall be Mohave and we want this land." But Gnatcatcher said: "No. I took it first." Halykūpa heard them quarreling thus, but he did not say a word. Only after he began to go on, he said: "I will let you stay here. I will leave you. You say you will be Mohave, you four. When I return, I will give you names.[6] (10 songs).

35. Halykūpa sees tract he means to farm later.— Then, as he went on, he did not tell his people anything. He did not speak to them as before. He continued going. When they passed Avi-halykwa'ampa[7] he saw wet ground on both sides of the river with good growth on it. He looked but could see no one there. Then he thought: "That will be my food. I will own this land when I return.[8] No one will take it, for no one is here." (10 songs).

36. At Topock they pass White Beaver's damming.— So they went on down. At Hayekwire-hiδo[9] there was White Beaver.[10] He said: "I am the chief of all. I am better than you. You cannot pass here." He turned his tail on edge and with it stopped the river so that it stood still and flowed back. Halykūpa tried to pass but could not: the river flowed back northward. Then Halykūpa said: "He cannot stop me. I will go to the side[11] and back, and again to the side and back, four times. Then the river will run through southward again. You will see. He will be unable to stop me." Then he went east and west and east and west and the river ran by that place again, southward, and they all went with it. (6 songs).

37. A stop to rest.—They went on. A little farther on it was the middle of the afternoon.[12] Then Halykūpa said: "We will go to the land here.[13] The name of this place is Iδúlye-iδáuve."[14] (4 songs).

38. They pass a nesting rock.—They went on down and passed by Kweyo-weye-hatápmeve[15] without stopping.

[6]He returns and tries to take their land away from them but fails in 71, 72.

[7]Avi-halykwa'ampa, UC-AR 11:2, Map 1, H, west, and p. 140, is about 4 miles S of Hatšioqwatveve and 5 miles N of Needles, by the mesa.

[8]He does return in 69, but fails to take up the tract.

[9]Hayekwire is a species of rattlesnake, and (h)iδo is tooth. The place is one of the pinnacles called "the Needles," or perhaps the group of them, on the east side below Topock (Mohave: Tupak, "bridge," the informant called it in 1905) where the Santa Fe R.R. and Highway 66 cross the river (UC-AR 11:2, Map 1), just above where this enters a long gorge—an ideal place from which to flood the valley.

[10]I do not recall White Beaver's appearing elsewhere in Mohave myth, nor do I know his motivation nor what he symbolizes. He lived there.

[11]First east, then west.

[12]Anyá-tonya'ím.

[13]Reason for the stop not clear.

[14]Iδúlye-(i)δáuve is mentioned also in Yellak II:35, below.

[15]I suspect that Kweyo-weye-hatapmeve is named after the cannibal Kwayū, cf. 6B (UC-AR 11:1, p. 48), and 15:13 below. Cf. also G. Devereux, p. 247 of Mohave Coyote Tales, JAFL 61:233-255, 1948.

Halykūpa said: "I have finished. I will stop talking. When we come to a place to sleep, I will think some more." Then they arrived and slept for the night.[16] Then Halykūpa spoke. He told how there would be more and more birds, and how they would grow. He said: "If we go straight on without providing, there will be no more like ourselves. So I will pull out feathers and stick them up. They will be here forever as rock. When you lay eggs, come here. You do not know about it now, but when you come to the end of the way, you will learn. You will know when to come back, and you will know this place." That place was Himé-qo'áṭa.[17] (10 songs).

39. Their feathers begin to sprout.—In the morning they all went south again. When they came to Hatše-humêve,[18] they stopped. All were holding their wings in the water. Then Halykūpa said: "Lift your wings. I want to see." Then they raised their wings and he saw their feathers beginning to grow. Halykūpa said: "That is why I wanted you to raise your wings: I wanted to see that. When you arrive at the end of the river, you will be full-grown birds with wings and feathers. But you do not yet have them here." At this place they stopped. (5 songs).

40. They look back and see Avikwame.—They went on down again and came to Takhapoδínke. Halykūpa said: "Do not look back but follow me." They went on until they came to Omaka.[19] There Halykūpa said: "I want you to form a line and not to look to the north until I look." He stood west of them. Then he looked northward and saw Avikwame.[20] But at that time it was only a high hill of sand. He said: "I see Avikwame far away. I can see the land from which I have come and where I belong." Then all the others looked north too. They said: "We have left the place to which we belong. We shall never return to it." (6 songs).

41. They remember where they came from.—Then Halykūpa said: "Let us start. I hear a noise far in the south." He went on and they followed. When they came

[16]This is the second night they sleep on the way (the first time in 32 at Aqwaq-iyove), but the leader "thinks" and keeps them awake. Most song-cycle tales, including the Yellak II outline below, content themselves with one night of sleep, no matter how long the itinerary.

[17](Hi)me-qoata is a high rock or crag, with bird nests all over it, mentioned also in 1:104 (UC-AR 11:1, p. 19) and Yellak II:37 below. See UC-AR 11:2, Map 2, 17, east and p. 142.

[18]Hatšehumêve has been entered as Ha-tše-huwêve, no. 17a, on UC-AR 11:2, Map 2, and p. 142.

[19]Takhapoδinke is unplaced, but has been entered by interpolation on UC-AR 11:2, Map 2 as 17b (p. 142), but Omaka or Umaka (the first syllable long and accented), no. 18 on Map 2, is mentioned also in 8:159 (UC-AR 11:2, p. 101) and in 11:50, above. It is in or opposite Chemehuevi Valley, upstream of a bend in the river, and now under water of Lake Havasu from Parker Dam.

[20]It is possible that the top of Avikwame is actually visible from so far down as this, in spite of intervening mountains and the gorge.

to Aspá-lye-pú'umpa,[21] he said: "Stop and stand here.
I am sorry for my own land that I left. I will tell of
my land. After that we will go on again." Then they
stood still and he went around them. Four times he
told of the way they had come from their country.
(4 songs).

42. Halykūpa insists they will become birds.—Then
he said: "Let us go." They went on and came to
Selye'áye-kwamé.[22] A little beyond, where there was
a good level place, he said: "Let us rest: we will
stay here awhile." Now they all wanted to go up the
bank on to the shore, but Halykūpa said to them: "No,
do not go up. Stay under the bank, in the water." He
himself remained out in the river. Then he felt of
their wings.[23] He said: "Now you are different. Your
feathers have grown. Now you cannot any longer see
the place from which you came. You can look to the
north, but you can see nothing there any more, because it is too far. And after a time you will entirely
become birds." Then they thought: "How shall we be
birds? How can we fly? I think we shall remain as we
have been. I do not think this can be done."[24] But
Halykūpa said: "Yes, you will be birds and you will
fly." Some of them argued with him, saying: "We cannot be birds. We shall never fly." But he told them:
"Yes, you will be birds. I will make you so that you
will be able to fly. You will see. I shall bring it
about." (6 songs).

43. Woodpecker flies off east.—They started downstream once more. When they came to Hakutšyêpe,[25]
they rested. When they were ready to go on, one of
them decided to remain behind. He said: "I will give
myself a name. I call myself Umás-nyahái-tasúme.[26]
That will be my name." He was about to be Woodpecker.
Then he flew up; but he was unable to fly high because
his feathers had not yet grown enough: it was too early.
Halykūpa said: "He is finished. He will be a bird from
now on. He will not return, but be a bird." Four times
Halykūpa spoke thus. Then Woodpecker flew up in the
air, off to the east. (4 songs).

44. Quail goes off west.—Then they went, and as
they traveled Halykūpa told them: "Follow me in a
straight file. Then the river will be narrow. But if
you go abreast, in rows one beside the other, the
river will be wide. Only if you go straight one behind
the other, will the river be narrow. I tell you this
that I want you to know." Then they came to Avi-
hãmsokwálype.[27] There one of them said: "Now I will
tell you. I am going to become something. I will call
myself Umase-mítše. Here is where I will tell you
my name and tell you what I will do. I will go away
and make my living in my own way." Then he went
out of the river and stood on the west shore. He was
about to become Quail.[28] He told them what sort of a
noise he would make, so that all would know him when
they heard him. Now it was nearly sunset. Halykūpa
said (to the birds): "Do not sit down, but stand."[29]
(6 songs).

45. They sleep: Oriole tries to wake them.—Then
they went on down past Kovesôkwe-hunāke,[30] but they
did not stop. Not far below they came to Aví-soqwílye-
hātái.[31] Then the sun set and they slept. They did not
go on the land to sleep but slept on the water.[32] Halykūpa did not sleep, but thought. He was covered by the
water; only his head was out. They wondered who might
be the first to get up in the morning. Then Oriole[33]
was the first to awake. He began to say: "It is daylight. It is a good time for everyone. All will feel
good and happy." They heard him, and liked what he
told them and wanted to say the same. But Halykūpa
said: "No, do not listen to him. He has become different. After a time you also will change." (6 songs).

46. Night-hawk tries to wake them before dawn.—
Then Night-hawk[34] awoke. He said: "It is day." Then all
awoke again and looked about and saw that it was not

[21]Aspa-lye-pu'umpa, mentioned also in 8:159 (UC-AR
11:2, p. 101), is a mountain (aspa means eagle), below the
bend, UC-AR 11:2, Map 2, 20, east (see p. 142).

[22]Selye'aye means sand, and -kwame is probably the same
element as in Avikwame. Exact location and side of river are
uncertain, but I have ventured to enter it on UC-AR 11:2,
Map 2 and page 142 as 22a between 22 and 23, east.

[23]"Arms."

[24]The pupils doubt, the leader knows the future. The change
to ultimate form is gradual. Cf. above 39, and 48-50, and, for
Halykūpa himself, 75, 77, below.

[25]Mouth of Bill Williams Fork (or more recently "Williams
River") into the Colorado, UC-AR 11:2, no. 24 on Map 2, and
a natural landmark (now drowned by Lake Havasu), some of
whose mentions are listed on UC-AR 11:2, p. 142.

[26]Child-wet-tasume. The ordinary Mohave name was not
recorded, so the species remains uncertain. Isoná is the
name most frequently translated as woodpecker.

[27]Unplaced; (Hamsokwalypa) between 25a and 25c of UC-AR
11:2, Map 2. For the widening and narrowing of the river, see
also Yellak II:51 below, 7:12 (UC-AR 11:1, p. 54), and 9:19
above.

[28]Ahmá.

[29]"In the water."

[30]Kovesôkwe-hunāke is again not exactly placed, and it
may actually have been nearer Parker than its place between
26 and 27 on UC-AR 11:2, p. 142 and Map 2 indicates.

[31]Soqwilye-hatai(ye) is one of the great swift hawks (probably not a falcon) whom warriors dream of; see 74. Avi-
soqwilye(-hatai) is the bold, free-standing little mountain or
butte east of Parker City and known as Black Peak. It is
mentioned also in 3:36 (UC-AR 11:1, p. 35), and 15:17 (Avi-
sukwílye) below, and as no. 28, UC-AR 11:2, p. 142. It is not
where shown on UC-AR 11:2, Map 2 by no. 28, but as indicated by the 1000-foot contour line E of Parker. I had not
been in the vicinity of Parker when Map 2 was drawn.

[32]Their third sleep; the first in 32, the second in 38. Did
they sleep standing in or floating on the water? Halykūpa's
sleeping under water with his head out above may reflect
some habit of the grebes.

[33]Sákumaha.

[34]Orró.

yet morning. "It is not yet day," they said. Then Night-
hawk spat on his hand and rubbed white streaks on his
upper arm and across his jaw, and blew saliva over
himself.[35] "It is morning," he said again. But they saw
that it was not yet day, and that he had lied to them.
(6 songs).

47. Mockingbird really wakes them.—Now a bird in
the middle flew up. He sat still[36] in the air and said:
"I will talk a little and it will be day." Then he talked
and it became light. When he finished talking it became dark again. Four times he did this; then it was
bright daylight. He was Mockingbird.[37] (10 songs).

48. River widened but their bodies still unfinished.—
Now it was a fine day. Halykūpa said: "When we go,
all go abreast. Do not go in line as we came down
before. I want to have the river wide here and to
make good wide level land."[38] Then they went down
abreast. He said to them again: "You think the sky is
far off but it is only a short distance. You think the
(end of the) earth is far off, but it is only a short
distance. I hear the end.[39] I hear a noise there." So
he told them as they went on down the river. They
went on without speaking. He said: "I am not speaking to anyone else for there is no one here. I tell
what I say only to you." So he continued to tell them,
and they came to Avi-vatáye.[40] Then he said: "We will
go up on the land. I want to see you walk." He wanted
to see how fast they could walk and how they looked.
Then he made them walk four steps. He said: "That
will not do. It does not look well when you walk." He
felt their bodies. "Your feathers have not yet all
grown: they have not come out all the way.[41] In time
they will all grow and you will be entirely birds. Now
let us go on the water again and go on." Then all went
on the river once more and started down. (6 songs).

[35]Accounting for his present appearance.
[36]Hovered.
[37]Sakwaθa'ālya. There is a chance that this is the magpie
rather than the mockingbird. Both birds chatter much and
variedly, which is what the Mohave chiefly mention in characterization.
[38]River widening also in Yellak II:51 below, above in 44
and in Origins, 9:19, and in Mastamho, 7:12 (UC-AR 11:1,
p. 54); see note 27. This happened where the wide bottomland is now on the Parker Reservation.
[39]Of the river, probably: the surf, perhaps.
[40]Avi-vataye: Riverside Mountains, west side, opposite
Poston. UC-AR 11:2, p. 142, no. 32, but misplaced on Map
2: actually opposite entry 35.
[41]This is the third time: in 39 and 42 before.

49. Halykūpa will finish their bodies.—They went
downriver and came to Avi'ivêre.[42] Halykūpa said: "You
are not finished yet. You have no toes, no hands, no
throat, no teeth, no tongue, no head. I will tell about
those and you will have them. When I finish you will
have tongues and toes and teeth and hands. When I say
that you have hands you will have hands. When I say
that you have toes you will have toes. When I say that
you have tongues you will have tongues. When I say
that you have throats you will have throats. When I
say that you have breath you will have breath." (8 songs).

50. He tells them how to make eggs.—They went on
down and came to Aha-ku-tinyáme and Aha-selye'aye,
one place with two names.[43] Now Halykūpa, thinking
that when they arrived where they heard the noise in
the south they would become something else, said:
"When you turn to birds how will you grow? If you go
straight on down (without learning), there will be no
birds after you. We will stop here and I will give myself a name. Before we reach that place I will make
it so that you will lay eggs and there will be more
birds. I will tell you how you will do it." Now the birds
wanted to make eggs by spitting in the female's mouth.
But Halykūpa said: "No." Then they said: "We will raise
the right wing and flap it against another's wing. I think
that is how we will make eggs." But Halykūpa said: "No,
I will tell you how you will make eggs. Look at me.
Lift your wings, then strike them on the water. Strike
them and make foam. It is only in that way[44] you can
make yourselves lay eggs." (8 songs).

51. Mudhen lays eggs.—Then Mudhen[45] said: "I am
going to begin to make eggs." Then she[46] did as Halykūpa had said and struck her wings on the water. Then
she laid an egg. Four times she did that and laid four
eggs. Then Halykūpa said: "Yes, that is how I want you
to do." Mudhen said: "You will all do this. I did this
and laid eggs. You can do the same. Now I will tell
you my name so that all will know me. My name is
Yamasām-alūka."[47] (4 songs).

[42]Avi-'ivêre: Big Maria Mountains, also on west side,
opposite Moon Mountains on east; on UC-AR 11:2, Map 2,
back of F on river.
[43]"Dark-water" and "sand-water," UC-AR 11:2, Map 2,
nos. 46, 45, east side, below Ehrenberg, and p. 142.
[44]Evidently referring to courtship tactics of ducks, and
the like. The reference to the physiological function is almost
prudish in its indirectness.
[45]Hanyiwîlye, the mudhen or coot.
[46]Mohave of course does not distinguish "he" and "she."
[47]Meaning?

D. Grebe Leader to the Sea (52-65)

52. <u>Far south they hear the beings from Yellak's body.</u>—Then they went on down and came to Aha'ṭ-kwatpárve.[1] Mudhen did not go with them. She stayed behind where she had laid eggs. Now Halykūpa said: "You can hear someone in the west." The others said: "There is no one in the west." Then he said: "Put your ear toward the east: you can hear someone." Then they listened toward the east but heard nothing. Then he told them: "You can hear it in the south." So they listened toward the south and heard a noise. "Yes, we hear it," they said. He told them: "I know what it is. When Yellak died, his body and his skin sank. They have become something. They have turned into living beings." (3 songs).

53. <u>They walk over the ground.</u>—Then when they started from Aha'ṭ-kwatparve he said: "Now all go in line so that we will make the river narrow." When they got to Kúvukwīlye[2] he said: "You hear a noise in the south; those are your brothers.[3] You think it may be someone else, but it is your brothers. Let us go to the west shore. Let us walk on the land off the river, instead of going on the water." (3 songs).

54. <u>Halykūpa makes rain to refresh them.</u>—Then when they walked on the land they did not go far before it was hot, and they were not used to it. "It is hot," they said, "for all the way here we were in the water." They could hardly move. They lay down, went on, and lay down again. "How shall we reach the place where the noise is? It is too hot for us; we shall not be able to arrive." Then Halykūpa said: "I will do something for you." First he stretched his hand toward the west and talked far to the west where the day was cool and good and there was rain. Then it came from there: rain came and wind came. Then he stood and looked to the east and called to the cold wind, the pleasant wind (and it came). Then he looked to the north and talked toward that and brought hail[4] from the north. When he had done this he stopped. Now all the ground was wet. The birds put their wings in

the water and shook them. He told them: "Now you feel good. You are cool. I told you that I would do it." (4 songs).

55. <u>A spring flows where they huddle.</u>—They were all in one place there, crowded together in a little hollow. When the rain had fallen on them their feathers swelled up so that they looked like large birds. All around was water as if from a spring. Then Halykūpa said: "When we leave this place there will be a spring here, forever. It will not go dry. Now I give it a name: I call it Ahá-kumī̄θe."[5] (4 songs).

56. <u>They go on to To'oske.</u>—Then Halykūpa said: "Now let us go. The earth is pleasant and cool and the sky is pleasant and cool." Then they went. Then he gave a name to a place. "The name of this place is To'oske."[6] At that time there were no mountains and no rocks; everything was sand. (3 songs).

57. <u>They try to fly but leave tracks in the mud.</u>—Then as they went on down he said: "Let me see you fly." Then they all flew up, but could not rise high. Their toes touched the ground; their wings flapped but they did not rise. Then he told them: "If you are like that you will not be able to fly high. Try it again." Then again they could not rise. Again he told them: "If you cannot rise and fly up (now) you will always be thus." Four times he made them try to rise but they could not fly. Their toes remained on the ground. Now it was muddy where they were and their tracks showed on the ground where they had tried to rise. Halykūpa said: "Your toes are like Yellak's toes. Your bodies are different, but your toes are like his. I call this place Yéllak-imé."[7] (6 songs).

58. <u>They return onto the river.</u>—As they went on down they came to Aha-θauvarūve.[8] Halykūpa said: "If we keep on in this way, if we continue to walk, it will be too far and we shall not be able to arrive. It may be too hot and you will become thirsty and die. I think it will be best if we go back onto the river. It will be quickest." (4 songs).

59. <u>Again they hear noise ahead.</u>—Then they went into the middle of the river and on down again. "Now

[1]Aha'ṭ-kwatpárve here, Aha-kwatpave (cottonwood-grove?) in 2:4 (UC-AR 11:1, p. 24), where it is the point farthest S in the Vinimulye tale. UC-AR 11:2, Map 2, no. 50, and p. 142, east side, not far from the latitude of Palo Verde, some 60 miles above Yuma, so that hearing anything in the ocean is a supernatural event.

[2]Kuvukwīlye: at Picacho, on west side, where the customary foot travel crossed the river. UC-AR 11:2, Map 2, site K, west, and p. 143. Mentioned also in 1:57 (UC-AR 11:1, p. 11), 8:86 (UC-AR 11:2, p. 88), and Yellak II:59 below. This is a long jump from the last place.

[3]Kwora'āk-moêvits is what he said. Kwora'āka is old man; o'evitš, "brother," in address; m-, presumably "your."

[4]Hôatše. They are on a land-route cut-off away from the river, hence their exhaustion.

[5]Aha-kumī̄θe: UC-AR 11:2, Map 2, site M, west, and p. 143. Mentioned also in 1:58 (UC-AR 11:1, p. 11).

[6]To'oske (Tôske): UC-AR 11:2, Map 2, site O, west, and p. 143; cf. 1:60 (UC-AR 11:1, p. 11). They are still on the short-cut trail W of the river.

[7]Apparently "goose-foot," "goose tracks," though the second member of a compound modifies in Yuman, and the meaning should therefore be "track-goose." UC-AR 11:2, Map 2, site P, west; cf. p. 143 and 1:61 (UC-AR 11:1, p. 11).

[8]Aha-θauvarūve, for "aha-hoбae-erūve" [sic]; Aha-θavarúve in Yellak version II:73. UC-AR 11:2, Map 2, site Q, west, and p. 143.

everything is well. Now we feel well. We look far off
but it does not seem distant. You look to the east and
think it a little distance. You look north and you think
it only a little distance. You look to the south and see
no one, but you hear talking, a noise from there. It is
near, at Nyimkutavâve.[9] (4 songs).

60. Wondering how they will look when transformed.—
Then as they went down on the western side of the
river they said: "We have gone far, nearly to the end
where we hear the noise. It is not far to there. What
colors shall we be? Shall we be white or blue or yellow
or striped?[10] We want to know that." Halykûpa said:
"Wait until I tell you. I will tell you how you will be,
whether you will be white or blue or striped or black.
You will have an appearance. But now I give this place
the name Avi-kunyûre."[11] (4 songs).

61. One they hear ahead is Pakyêt-pakyêt.—Then
they went on down to Hukθilye.[12] Then Halykûpa said:
"Now you hear it. I hear talking and you hear it. I
knew it. When Yellak died, his skin and his claws sank
and went to the sea and turned to beings. They are
talking now. I know who it is; I know the name of one.
It is Pakyêt-pakyêt."[13] (4 songs).

62. Another is Aha-nyi-sata.—Then as they were
about to start he stood and talked. He made them into
four companies. He said: "When we reach the sea you
will enter it and become something. I shall go with you
too, but I shall not turn into anything. I will return."
When he had said that they started. They went on until
they came to Kwenyô-kuvilyô.[14] Then Halykûpa said
again: "I know who is talking. I do not see him but I
hear his sound and know him. His name is Aha-nyi-
sâta."[15] (2 songs).

63. And another is Qwilolo.—Again they went on and
came to Amaṭ-kutkyêne.[16] Then they heard someone.
Halykûpa said: "I know him. His name is Qwilolo.[17] He,
too, grew from Yellak's claws." (4 songs).

64. They are eager to enter the sea.—Then they
went on once more. They saw the sea.[18] It was not far
away and the birds heard a noise and saw someone
there. Then all wanted to be the first to reach it; each
one wanted to be ahead of the others. But Halykûpa said:
"No, do not hurry. Wait until I tell you. The sea is not
good water; it is salty. If you jump into it at once you
will not be able to fly. I want you to be well off." (5
songs).

65. They follow Snipe and stay in the sea.—Then
they went on and reached the sea. One of them was the
first to dive into it. He went to the bottom and brought
up ahtšilye shells. These he tied around his neck, from
which it is white. Then he sat up on the water with his
head raised so that all could see it. He was Snipe,
Mȋn-turís-turíse.[19] He said: "My name is Umás-e'áse.[20]
All will know me. If I am not known in one place I will
be in another. People will see birds like me and know
me." Now the birds on the west[21] flew up and into the
sea. Only three did not enter it. They merely went up
to it, four steps from it, and started back. Halykûpa,
Sakataθêre,[22] and Han'emo[23] were the three who stood
there and looked. Then Halykûpa said: "Now you who
are in the sea, and it is salty, your feathers are salty
too, and you will not be able to fly (far away).[24] You
will stay here: this ocean will belong to you. I call
you Umás-nyahái-tatšume.[25] (6 songs).[26]

[9]Nyimkutavave, UC-AR 11:2, Map 2, site R, west, and
p. 143.
[10]The Mohave seem sometimes to specify "color" when
they have in mind total appearance. Note that four alternative "colors" are mentioned, but that they reappear just
below with one substitution and one change of order. In short,
four is favored, but there is no fixed scheme: any four colors
are improvised. But note that red is not among them; nor in
12:2, nor in 12:14, nor in 13:15, above.
[11]Avi-kunyūre: UC-AR 11:2, p. 142, Map 2, no. 60, east
side. Somewhere near Imperial Dam, some 15 miles above
Yuma city.
[12]Hukθilye: mentioned as no. 62 on UC-AR 11:2, p. 143
but not entered on Map 2. It seems to be Pilot Knob, at the
southward bend some half-dozen miles below Yuma city;
called Xuksil in Yuma—x for h, l for ly, and Yuma s regular
for Mohave θ.
[13]Pakyêt-pakyêt "looks like a fish, but has like feathers
along his sides; his body is fishlike." A crustacean? or insect
larva? This is the first of the three beings into which the
skin and claws of dead Yellak (20) transformed, as mentioned
in 33 and 52.
[14]Kwenyô-kuvilyô, far downstream, in Cocopa country;
(Kunyokuvelyô) mentioned also in 8:83 (UC-AR 11:2, p. 87).
[15]Aha-nyi-saṭa, "water-its-saṭa" (?). Saṭa or asaṭa is a
staff or rod or cane, such as Mastamho made the river with.
The animal "looks like a fish, has a sharp nose, an edge
along its back." This might also be a crustacean. See 6B

(UC-AR 11:1, p. 48, fn. 20); Hal(y)kutāta; and below, fn. 33:
ha-ly-k-ataṭa.
[16]Amaṭ-kutkyêne: last station before the sea. Yellak version II:77; UC-AR 11:2, Map 2, site 72, west, and p. 143.
[17]Qwilolo "has a shell with little holes, is like a ball, and
white." It identifies as a sea urchin. Its ordinary Mohave name
is Ahanemaθîre. It evidences curiosity about distant things,
that the Mohave should know and name an unornamental and
useless thing like a sea urchin occurring two hundred or
more miles from their habitat.
[18]Haθo'ilye. The Gulf of California, of course, in this case.
[19]"Has a white and brown stripe on his throat, long bill
and long legs, lives at edge of ocean, shakes his head."
Appears also in 1:103 (UC-AR 11:1, p. 18) and in 13:85 above.
[20]"Child-e'áse."
[21]Why west?
[22]Sakataθêre (cf. 23), unidentified, occurs also in 7:96 (UC-
AR 11:1, p. 66).
[23]Han'emo, occurs also in 7:10, 96 (UC-AR 11:1, pp. 54,
96) denotes either ducks in general or, specifically, as here,
the pintail or wood duck.
[24]Salt-water birds of course do not come inland to the
Mohave country. This is expressed as not being able to fly.
[25]"Children-wet-tatšume." Any connection with Child-wet-
tasume for Woodpecker in station 43, section C, fn. 26?
[26]As the narrative was written down, this was the next-to-
the-last set of songs mentioned, but on later review the informant said it was the last. It seems a logical stopping
place; the birds have reached the sea, their journey is over,
the songs should end. What follows in E-F, 66-82, is after-
math about Halykûpa and Mastamho, supplementary to the
main theme.

E. Grebe's Return to Mohave Valley and Mastamho (66-77)

66. Halykūpa, Sakataθêre, and Wood Duck plan to return north.—Then Sakataθêre said: "The sky is not very far away. The earth is not very far away. It is only a short distance. I think I will go back. I want to return to where I came from in the north, to Avikwame. I want to return and be a Mohave." Halykūpa said: "When we arrive at that place perhaps he[1] will make me into something. Perhaps he will give me supernatural power or do something else for me." Sakataθêre said: "I think everything is finished here. We will go upriver again and in the north it may be completed too." Halykūpa said: "It is well, but if you want to go, find something good to take along. Look for shells, for hakwehaye, kwasinuva, aha-nya-ham'okyê, and ko'olykumuna shells.[2] Find those and we will take them back with us." Then Sakataθêre found shells of all those kinds and put them on. Then he wanted to try to fly up high. He flew up and looked to the north. Then he said: "It is not far." Then as they were about to start, he took four steps to the west and back; then four to the south and back; four to the east and back. Then he looked north[3] and said: "Let us go north where we came from." (4 songs—?)[4]

67. They fly up and see the oceans.—Sakataθêre said: "I am all made. My feathers are complete. I have the things that I want to take with me. I am ready." Then the three of them, Halykūpa, Sakataθêre, and Wood Duck, jumped four times. They leaped high up, half way to the sky. They looked down and saw the ocean in the west. "Did I not say so? The sea is there, not far away," they said. They looked east. "Did I not say it? The sea is there, not very far away." They looked north and saw the sea[5] and said: "It is not very far." Then they looked down and saw Avikwame below them.[6]

68. Try to alight on Avikwame but miss it.—"That is my place," they said. Then two of them hovered there, but sent Halykūpa ahead. "Go down first and stay at Avikwame until we come," they told him. Then Halykūpa flew downward. He tried to reach Avikwame and stand on top of it, but he did not reach it.[7] He arrived at the mountain Avi-kwahwáṭa[8] and stood on that. Now the two others, who had stayed up above, started for Avikwame and thought they would settle on it, but they also did not reach it. They too came down where Halykūpa was, and all three stood there.

69. They go to the tract Halykūpa claimed on the way down.—Now they wanted to go somewhat farther north. Sakataθêre said: "I think we will go up the middle of the river on the water. What shall I do with these things that I have obtained at the sea?" Halykūpa said: "When we arrive where we are going you can give them to the people that own that place, for we want that land for ourselves." Sakataθêre said: "No, I want to wear them myself. That place which we want, did we not take it[9] when we came down the river? No, I will not give up these things for the land. I will wear them." Then they went up the river.

70. Sakataθêre makes the place white with shells.—When they came to Savetšivūta,[10] Sakataθêre took the shells which he had brought and rubbed them in his hands. He crushed them fine and threw the dust on the ground; so he made the earth white there.[11] Then Halykūpa said: "We will sleep here. Tomorrow we will go on. When we came down the river we claimed that (other) place but went on down. The four who stayed

[1]Mastamho. Withholding of the name by Halykūpa is almost certainly deliberate. Compare the indirect allusions in 23-30 until they have passed Mastamho on Avikwame, after which Halykūpa tells his four ritual names.
[2]I cannot identify the species. Aha-nya-ham'okyê means "water pestles," evidently a columnar shell or columella.
[3]Antisunwise circuit beginning with W.
[4]The four songs here were subsequently denied by the informant in a review of the song structure of the story, no doubt correctly. See fn. 26 of part D. However, the three remaining birds have not yet begun their return and are still at the ocean, whence, presumably, the confusion of statement.
[5]The western ocean is the Pacific, of which the Mohave knew, and which they probably saw occasionally, even in pre-Spanish times. The northern ocean is puzzling, unless there was belief in sea being all around the land. An eastern ocean would have been learned of from Spaniards or American whites long before 1905.
[6]They have flown back all the way to Avikwame, but not to their place of origin at the source of the river. Mastamho, so anxiously avoided on the way down, after all draws them there by his superior power.

[7]Halykūpa's attempted first surrender to Mastamho ends in a misfire.
[8]There is said to be an Avi-kw-ahwaṭa, "red rock" or "blood mountain," in the vicinity of the railroad bridge and Needles peaks, but the reference is more likely to a red rocky bank of the same name in Nevada, at the sharp bend of the river below Hardyville and above Camp Mohave, shown in UC-AR 11:2, Map 1, and p. 140, as C, west side. This is only some 7 miles from Hokusave of 73, fn. 22. At that, Halykūpa has missed Avikwame by nearly 20 miles short. If the going "N" and "up" the middle of the river in the second sentence of 69 is to be taken literally, and not as a slip, it would argue that they had landed below Needles city and that therefore Avi-kw-ahwaṭa was the lower one of that name. In that case they would have missed Avikwame by about 50 miles.
[9]That is, did we not claim it in our minds on the way down? See 35. At that time, no one was there, Halykūpa said.
[10]Savetšivūta is 3 miles upriver from Needles city, on the same side, west:UC-AR 11:2, Map 1, J, west side, and p. 140. On the way down, in 35, reference is to fertile land seen on both sides as they pass Avi-halykwa'ampa.
[11]The mesa (terrace) at Savetšivūta is whitish. But why has he crushed his shells and thrown them away when just before he refused to give them up because he wanted to wear them? Another case of typically erratic (or elliptic?) motivation in Mohave storytelling.

in this country[12] occupy it. It does not belong to them but they live there. They think we are not coming back. Now when we return perhaps they will say to us: 'It does not belong to you. You cannot have this land. It is mine. Go away.' I think they will say that. Perhaps they will do something to us."

71. <u>They come to Gnatcatcher: he tries to feed them.</u>—Then in the morning they went on up. Now they did not travel on the river but on the land. Then they came to Mahoat̯-aha θêve.[13] There they stopped. Now the four men who lived near there (Gnatcatcher, Tšaiqwatarqe, Pilpiyo, and Qeiδiδo) were at Hatšioq-wat̯veve, only a little north of where Halykūpa and his two companions had stopped. Then Gnatcatcher saw them resting there. He said: "Why do they not come? I have something ready for them to eat." He had seeds, akatáye, aksāmta, and ánki.[14] Those he and his people made into bread and mush, and lived on that. He said: "I want them to come before noon. It will be too hot if they wait. I want them to come early." Then Halykūpa, Sakataθêre, and Wood Duck went on up and arrived at Hatšioq-wat̯veve. They came into the house and Gnatcatcher gave them to eat what he had, but they, because they were birds, did not know that kind of food and did not eat it.[15] Then Gnatcatcher wondered what they ate. "What do you eat?" he asked them. They pointed to the earth and to sandbar willows[16] and said: "Mud and willow leaves." Then those there went and gave them that and they ate it. That was what they lived on and liked.

72. <u>Stick-fight for Gnatcatcher's land: he keeps it.</u>— Then the three who had come said: "We want this place: it belongs to us." But Gnatcatcher said: "No, I own it. I live here. I plant and raise crops here. This is where I live.[17] If you say that, we will fight. If you overcome us, you can have the place." Then they fought with sticks.[18] Then Gnatcatcher was hurt and Wood Duck

was hurt,[19] but nevertheless the four living there beat the three who had come from the south.[20]

73. <u>They turn to Mastamho.</u>—Then when they stopped, the three said: "We are going on. When we came down-river we heard that there was a person over us.[21] He has brought many to Hôkusave[22] and they are all there with him. I have not seen it but I know it. He will do something for every bird. Perhaps if we go he will make us into something."[23] Thinking that, they went to Hôkusave.

74. <u>Mastamho is transforming Hawks.</u>—Now Mastamho was there already and all of them stood about him. Halykūpa and the two with him arrived and saw him standing in the middle. Mastamho called to them: "Come here: sit down!" Then he said: "Now I will make you all into birds. I will make you fly." Then he took Soqwilye[24] by the right arm and threw him up. Then he flew, turning to a bird. "He cannot become a man again," said Mastamho. Next he took Soqwily-akatai in the same way and threw him up and he too flew off. Thus he did to the birds who are lucky.[25]

75. <u>He transforms Halykūpa, Sakataθêre, and Wood Duck.</u>—Then he said to Halykūpa: "I give you the name Atšiyêre-hakwinyu-verêrqe." To Sakataθêre he said: "I give you the name Atšiyêre-hakwinyu-vapinye. Han'emo, I will give you a name also. Your name will be Atšiyêre-hakwinyu-kwatcavaδa."[26]

76. <u>He transforms other birds.</u>—Then he said to all the others there: "You will all become birds now and your names will be different. I call you Atšiyêre-ma'im-kunu-ya, Atšiyêre-ma'im-kunu-tšetše, and Atšiyêre-ma'im-kunu-tkyê." Those were the names that he gave to all the others there.[27]

---

[12]Gnatcatcher and the three others who fell out to settle at Hatšioq-wat̯veve, in 34.

[13]Badger-ahaθêve? Evidently below Hatšioq-wat̯veve, and on the west side.

[14]Wild plants, though also sometimes sown or aided.

[15]An endlessly repeated theme: what one does not have the habit of, one just does not eat.

[16]Ihore.

[17]In spite of the squabbling in 34 when his three companions want Gnatcatcher to give them the bottomland while he goes up on the terrace, he is first in the tract and is now in control. The dispute then evidently referred to the type of vegetation that the four species of birds actually frequent preferentially.

[18]"Stick-fighting," described in Handbook, p. 745, as tšetmana'ak, was a device for settling intratribal quarrels over land or shaman-killings. Fatalities might result, but ordinarily there were only some bloodied heads or broken collar bones; and feeling having given way to fatigue and winding, the losers withdrew peacefully. Long staves or limbs were used to beat down on heads. This was called a'im hatšioq-wat̯vevek, with-sticks hit-one-another; whence the place name. It may be assumed that an actual contest between groups of Mohaves once occurred there; or could

consistent localization in the same spot of the myth episode of the birds' fight have given the place its secular name? —as it apparently named Hokusave of 73.

[19]One injury on each side.

[20]Halykūpa's role is far from glorious, apart from his bowing to Mastamho. He talks of taking land only after Gnatcatcher has actually chosen his and settled on it; then, coming back, he fails to occupy his tract and claims Gnatcatcher's, but fails to take it from him.

[21]Again the indirect allusion to Mastamho.

[22]Hokusave is E, west side, UC-AR 11:2, Map 1, and p. 140, and means "nose pierce." It is only a couple of miles upstream from Hatšioq-wat̯veve, just before the Nevada boundary is reached. It is where in another tale (7:83, UC-AR 11:1, p. 64) Mastamho floated to, then, having grown feathers, flew away from it as Bald Eagle.

[23]More dependence on Mastamho: they cannot of themselves adequately achieve their own transformation.

[24]Compare the long section on hawks and war power, in Mastamho, 7:59-69 (UC-AR 11:1, pp. 61-62), and War, 15:17 below. The Soqwilyes seem to be hawks and not falcons, which are called atšyora.

[25]I.e., give luck and power in war, when they have been dreamed of.

[26]Tšiyêre is bird; -hakwinyu-, ?; the varying third element of the names is verbal.

[27]Again Atšiyêre; -mai'm-kunu-, ?; plus -ya, -tšetše, -tkye; -kunu- may belong with this last element rather than with -ma'im-, which perhaps means "give."

77. Halykūpa goes into a slough.—Then Mastamho told them all to fly up and away, and all flew off except one. Halykūpa tried to fly with the rest but could not: he could only walk. So he walked off and jumped into the slough and he did not leave the water again. He lives there, unable to fly (well).[28]

[28]An inglorious end. But so is Mastamho's, both in this tale and in 7:84 (UC-AR 11:1, p. 64), and 9:50 above. When grebes are approached on the water they rarely fly, but usually dive and reappear at a distance.

F. Mastamho's End (78-82)

78. Mastamho returns to his staff, makes fish.—Now they were all gone. Mastamho was alone. He said: "I do not know where I will go to change.[1] I think I will go where my staff is which I left standing in the ground where I made the water emerge." So he went up to that place. In four steps he arrived there at Waθāi'otāpma.[2] Now he stirred the water with the staff and made a fish.[3] Then he threw the fish on the water so that it splashed; he wanted to make many fish. "If I did not do this there would be no fish," he said.

79. Mastamho makes rock and desert.—When he had done that, he stood[4] on the end of his staff as it stuck there, and looked around. He thought: "If I became something different now it would not be well; so I will finish everything before I change." Then he took mud and threw it, to become rocks.[5] He took a handful of sand into his mouth and blew it out; so he made sand over the land. The mud which he had thrown, he now felt of and it was hard and dry. "Yes, that is how I want it," he said.

80. Mastamho ponders.—I will go north to the end of the sky and stay there and it will be good. No, I do not think I will go north to the end of the earth and the end of the sky." Then he thought in the same way about the other directions, east and then west.[6] Then he said: "No one can do what I can. If I left before everything was completed, no one could finish it. So I will make everything; then when everything is good, I will turn into something else. Then all will know me."

81. Mastamho throws his staff.—Now he had got wings and was a bird; but he still had his staff. He said: "I will throw my staff."[7] So he threw it to the north and it stood up straight in the ground. He said: "I will give a name to that place. My staff will be something now: I call that place Amat-nyahaim-asaṭ."[8]

82. Mastamho becomes Sakwiθêi bird.—Then he drew four marks on the ground with his foot. He stood north of them and said: "Now I will go. I will run four steps—then I will fly." Starting from the last mark, he ran four steps. Then he rose up and flew and now his name was Saqwiθêi.[9] He said: "I have finished everything. All of them have flown away. Now I too will fly off and be a bird."

[1]Change to his final form.
[2]It is not named at the beginning of the story except for four "ritual" designations. In 81 Mastamho gives it the name Amaṭ-nyahaim-asat, "staff-wet-place." In Mastamho, 7:10 (UC-AR 11:1, p. 54), it is called Hatasaṭa, again with reference to the staff or cane. The making of the river by plunging the staff occurs also above in Origins, 9:18, and below in War, 15:4. I cannot translate the present form Waθāi'otāpma. The sources of the river in Wyoming and Colorado are of course far beyond Mohave travel knowledge; all their reference to it are bound to be more or less fabricated.
[3]In the full Mastamho story, 7:10 (UC-AR 11:1, p. 54), four kinds of fish are named, and they come out when he first plunges and withdraws the staff, followed then by four waterbirds—whereas here the fish are like a last-moment afterthought.
[4]Sic: he literally stood on its end to be higher and look around better, probably; rather than merely leaning on the staff.
[5]In 7:13, 14 (UC-AR 11:1, p. 55) Mastamho makes Avikwame and other mountains from mud—but again, early in his career.

[6]Not four directions, and not in circuit.
[7]It is certainly dreamlike to throw with an arm which has just turned into a wing.
[8]See fn. 2.
[9]Unidentified. Saqwiθei is "near houses, unafraid of people, knows human beings." It might be Magpie. Contrast the Bald Eagle, Saksak, of 7:82-84 (UC-AR 11:1, p. 64) and of 9:50, above.

YELLAK SONGS RERECORDED IN 1908

For purposes of record, I append the catalogue numbers of cylinders of songs rerecorded from Aspa-sakam at Needles on March 1, 1908, as repetitions of specified songs selected from Yellak as first sung by him in 1905. Songs were identified by place name and event.

1905 Songs		Cylinder Catal. Nos.	1908 Songs	Cylinder Catal. Nos.
I	1	14-139, 140	1	14-975
I	2	141	2	976
I	6	145	3	977
II	1	146	4	978
II	2	147	5	979
III	3	174	6	980
IX	1	169	7	981
XVIII	1	178	8	982
XXXVIII	1	189	9	983
LIX	1	222	10	984
LIX	4	225	11	985

The words of some of these repeated songs are:

Yelak, 3: inyamaṭ (my land) kañiyaviδau

5: himañau(tš) tawemañai inyamauṭ hañaii—for iamk, go, matawemk, go.

6: nahaiyamim kuvaiyañhim tinyamautš kwiδauvañai—for nyahaim-kuvare (place name) hav'ak amaṭ kuvi'iδauk.

8: kumikumayi mikañai ipanha—said to be, when spoken: cry im im han'ava (insect) paika'ave (all hear)

9: kañinu-kwirañ; for nyemnukwere, walk on edge.

11: inañau   emerge
    hulomañai   dive, ilom
    hañiñau
    kañisañan   look, isamk
(Looking back from the ocean they see Avikwame).

YELLAK II

On March 3, 1908, near Needles, I recorded on cylinders 17 songs and an itinerary or outline of the Goose story from an old man named Hakwe, who called himself a "relative" of Aspa-sakam who had told me the foregoing full version. Hakwe appears to have been Aspa-sakam's father-in-law. He said that Yellak was his only singing.

He listed 89 stations, all but four of them with songs. For a good many of these he specified "many songs" (indicated in the outline by "M"), or said "many, but I can make it four (or three, or two) here" (listed as M or 3, etc.). There were 17 such cases of "many or less," plus several of 5, 8, 10 or less; and 15 instances of just "many." With "many" counted as only 6, the aggregate comes to over 400 songs; counted at 10 songs, the total runs up above 500. This is a really large number of songs on one theme and pattern. Hakwe said it took him two and a half nights to sing the series through.

He also differed from most informants in that his groups consisted of 1, 4, or 8 songs rather rarely, but that groups of 3 or 5 songs were numerous. This is the distribution:

Songs in group:	0	1	2	3	4	5	7	8	10	M	M or 3	?
Stations:		4	1	10	11*	3	18	1	1	4	15	18	4

*One instance of "2-3."

This is not the same distribution as for Yellak I, but is similar.

As for the nature of the songs, I am incompetent to describe this as compared with those of Yellak I;

but other Mohave who have heard the records, at once recognized both as being Goose.

Hakwe, perhaps realizing that if he was to complete even an outline in a day, besides singing a number of songs, hastened from station to station with a minimum of dwelling on what happened at each; but he mentioned the place of each with unusual frequency, nearly 70 times, plus 10 more where an event is specified that can be inferred as occurring at the place last mentioned. This makes it that all but about a dozen of his stations are placed along the river in at least consecutive order; and some proportion of them are absolutely locatable through other sources. This in turn constitutes a fairly firm list of geographical identifications, many items of it corroborated by Yellak I, Tumanpa, Nyohaiva, Cane, the Epic, etc. (tales 14, 11, 3, 1, 8).

The comparison of Yellak I with II is a more internal matter of intratale variation. This will be taken up after the itinerary outline of II has been presented.

Outline of Yellak II

1. At Nyahaim-kiyume (wet-see), Nyahaim-kuvatše, Nyahaim-kumaike, and Nyahai-'irreme [these are mythical, not known geographical spots], there were nearly-hatched eggs lying in the ground. When they hatched, many ducks and water birds came out, but only Yellak "told of his ways" and the four names of the place. (M) (Cylinders 959, 960)

2. They went on the river at Nyahaim-θare-ketšupatše and Selye'aye-ketšupatše (wet and sand ketšupatše). (M) (Cylinder 961)

3. Ikiny-umas-haitukyive was Yellak's name before he hatched, when he was underground. (?)

4. Ikiny-umas-haitšume was his name when he swam off. (?)

5. Ikiny-umas-satukyetš was his name when he told of Mastamho's making the river. (?)

6. At Satuδuk-kwi-nyamasave, white rocks in the river canyon. (?)

7. At Aha-kwitšqove. (2) (Cylinder 962)

8. At Ativ'ilye-kutšehwire. (5)

9. At Aha-qumlaye. (5)

10. At Nyahai-tšupatš (cf. name in no. 2), another river slough. (3)

11. Ikinye-umas-kumatinyeye is what he called himself. (2)

12. And Ikinye-sampumtša. (2)

13. At Avi-kitšu'uke. (M, or "I can make it 4 songs here.")

14. At Avi-kuhupave. (M or 3)

15. At "Lizard Mt.," Avi-qwatulye. (5)

16. At Qwilyeθki. (M or 3)

17. At Nyahai-ku-qwirpe: about Roadrunner. (2) (Cylinder 963)

18. At Hamuθkwilye-ivatše. (3)

19. At Ava-k-tinyam, "dark house," [evidently referring to Matavilya's house at Ha'avulypo or possibly Mastamho's on Avikwame]. (M or 3)

20. Tinyam-hware-hware and Han'ava were crying in the house when they saw Masahai-atšume (this is what they called Yellak) coming leading many birds downriver. [Masahai means a grown girl; a young man is mahai]. (5) (Cylinder 964)

21. At Avi-kwinyasave. (3)

22. At Haihanuesupai. (8 or 3)

23. At Kwapaṭa. (M or 2)

24. At Selye'ayi-ta. (10 or 3)

25. At K-amai-ave-te hihu ta-hayahaya-ve. "Amaiavete's head where-rolls (?) to." (5)

26. At Meke-huvike. (M or 2)

27. At Koyak-havasu, "Blue (or green) koyak. (5 or 2)

28. At Avi-kutaparve. (7) [UC-AR 11:2, p. 140, Map 1, no. B, west]

29. At Qara'erve. (5) (Cylinder 965). [UC-AR 11:2, p. 138, Map 1, B, east]

30. At Waθakupay. (5 or 3) (Cylinder 966)

31. At Avi-kunapatše. (3)

32. At Avi-haly-kwa'ampa. (M or 2) [UC-AR 11:2, Map 1, H, west]

33. At Mat'are ("Field"), here at Needles city. (3) [Near K, west, of UC-AR 11:2, Map 1]

34. At Hayikwir-iδo ("Rattlesnake's teeth," the Needles pinnacles east of the canyon below Topock). (3) (Cylinder 969) [UC-AR 11:2, Map 1, below Z, east]

35. At Iδulyeδauve. (5) (Cylinder 968)

36. At Hokyampeve. (5) [UC-AR 11:2, Map 2, no. 2, east; p. 141]

37. At Me-koaṭ. (M or 2) (Cylinder 969) [UC-AR 11:2, Map 2, no. 17, east; p. 142]

38. At Ahamtinyemve. (3)

39. At Katuvere. (5) [UC-AR 11:2, Map 2, no. 19a, east; p. 142]

40. At Sanquvanye. (5) [Possibly UC-AR 11:2, no. 6, east; p. 141; but the order does not tally]

41. There he made himself white. The river bank there is white, and Goose thought he himself was white like the seagulls, but he was not. (10 or 2)

42. At Ahmo-kwatay. (10 or 2) [UC-AR 11:2, Map 2, no. 19, east; p. 142]

43. At Hakutšyepe. Here Yellak went on straight, many of the others went off in a slough to one side and had to come back. (10 or 2) [UC-AR 11:2, Map 2, no. 24, east; p. 142]

44. At Kutuδunye. (4 or 2) [UC-AR 11:2, Map 2, no. 34b, east; p. 142]

45. It was dark here. They looked all about. Some thought that was how this place always was, others said it would become light again; so they disputed. (3 or 2)

46. Owl (δokupita),Tokoke, Koθweke, Satšyake, and Minkutiruirui went out into the night; five birds that call at night. Goose told about them. (M or 2)

47. He told of Orion, Pleiades, the stars. (M or 2)

48. The birds were asleep. (3)

49. Goose awoke, was happy, he had dreamed he was at the ocean, told the others about it. (M or 2)

50. Dream good tell-of, sumatš ahotk kanavek, and they all started to swim to the ocean. (M or 2)

51. All abreast, they came to where the river was widest, going south. (M or 2)

52. About Land-ahuitšem and Sky-ahuitšem, about Sky-Analyem (mesquites) and Land-Avilyó. (?)

53. At Moon Mt. (Avi-hely'a) [UC-AR 11:2, Map 2, no. 39, east; p. 142] and Sakwarepa. (M)

54. About Sky-see (Amai-uyuma) and Land-see (Amaṭ-uyuma): "they had never seen that sky and country before. (M or 2)

55a. About Land-hatusalye, Sky-samuδi, Land-samuδi (sameδi appears to mean "not know"), and Amai-humak-mily-ivatšk-vi'itayam (going to a new world). (5)

55b. About the place Hatusalye [cf. 55a and UC-AR 11:2, Map 2, 49a, east; p. 142] where they would come to the ocean and how their feathers would be wet as they sat on the shore. [Future; they are not yet at the ocean] (3)

56. They would be all in a row abreast going on the ocean—many birds, but only one Goose. (3)

57. Going abreast, with legs, nose, feathers, body all finished, so each bird said. (5)

58. Finished, and each with a name, so Yellak said. (5)

59. At Kuvukwilye. (2) [UC-AR 11:2, K, west, near Picacho; p. 143]

60. Mastamho was waiting for them there, with many birds. Goose said they would not live there but would fly to a cooler place. So they left. (M or 3)

61. He was trying to look N, E, S, W (sunwise circuit) for a good place to live and take them along, because he did not want to stay. (M)

62. "Goose arrive," Yellak kuv'ove [name of place? or event?]. (M)

63. He went into the SE corner (of the house), wanting to tell about his steps and walk. (2)

64. Hanyevunye nyamaθam hilvi katšupatše, "water-its-road white appearing make" [description of event?]. (M or 2)

65. At Aha-kumiθe. (4) (Cylinder 970 probably records the first of these 4 songs)

66. At Aha-tšuvauve: he called it that. (5 or 4)

67. To'oske. (4) (Cylinder 971) [UC-AR 11:2, Map 2, no. O, west; p. 143]

68. Haθo'ilye isamk, "ocean see." (4)

69. Goose dreamed he saw the ocean, but others said it was only the bank of a mesa. So they disputed. (5)

70. Then they came to that place: Yiminalyek, the Mohave call it; Yimutšyenek, the Yuma. (4) [UC-AR 11:2, Map 2, no. 63, east; page 143]

71. At Lakime (for Yellak-ime, Goose-foot, Goose-track). All were happy, said they had found a new land. (1 long song, sung over and over) (Cylinder 972) [UC-AR 11:2, Map 2, no. P, west; p. 143]

72. At Kuyaly-kuv'ave. (5)

73. At Aha-θavaruva. (2) [UC-AR 11:2, Map 2, no. Q, west; p. 143]

74. At Haskulyí. (2)

75. At Aha-kyulye, "Long-water." (M or 1)

76. At Avi-ku'a'a and Nyim-kutavave. (M)

77. At Kutkyene [UC-AR 11:2, p. 143, no. 72] and Avi-aspa [UC-AR 11:2, p. 143, no. 73] (M) (Cyl. 973)

78. At Selye'ai-kutene. (M)

79. At Avi-savet-kyele. (M)

80. At Hatšupak-kuminye. (M)

81. "At Hakwatšθarve, where they started [sic]; they have gone back there." (M)

82. At Horkutpatš. (M)

83. At Avi-kwoha'á. (—)

84. At Hatane. (—)

85. At Tšitšupite. (—)

86. They go to fly, have feathers. (—)

87. At Ihu-lye avtauve. (M)

88. At Hokusave ("Nose-pierce"). (M) [UC-AR 11:2, Map 1, no. E, west; p. 140; above Needles, not quite in Nevada]

89. At Minyoraive, well N of Needles, behind (N of) Avikwame. (M) (Cyl. 976 is last song of this group and of the entire cycle)

Comparison of Content of
Versions I and II

The second version is so bare of incident in its scant outline that comparison with the first is difficult. Fifteen stations correspond in locality, from the mythical source of the river to the sea, to return upriver to vicinity of Avikwame, and including final transformations at Hoku-save in Mohave Valley. In version I the birds sleep three times in their journey, in II only once, but this

is in the same stretch as the third night in I. Now
and then there is a song theme mentioned in both
versions, like Roadrunner in I:15 and II:17. But
whether Gnatcatcher's land taking at Avi-haly-kwa'ampa
in I:34 and the White Beaver at Hayekwir-iðo in I:36
occur when the same places are mentioned in II:32
and II:34 remains uncertain because no incidents are
recorded for II. The incident of taking the wrong
channel (I:22, 23) recurs but much farther downstream,
below instead of above Mohave Valley, in II:43.

Other parallels are: widening or narrowing the
river or valley by travel abreast or in file, I:44, 48,
53, II:51; feathers etc. finished, I:16, 67, II:57; feathers
wet at ocean, I:64, 65, II:56; telling of steps and walk,
I:48, II:63; Mastamho waits for them but they pass
him by in I:23-29 and II:60.

The most marked difference is that in I Goose
dies early in the journey (20) and Grebe takes his
place all the way to the sea and back until his
own transformation (77), whereas in the II outline
Grebe is not named, Goose continues to be mentioned until the Yuma country (69), and by inference
remains leader until the very end (89). Also, version I has two songless sections at the end, about
Grebe's return (66-77) and Mastamho's transformation (78-82), of which especially the last bears only
slight relation to the rest of the story.

All in all, Yellak I and II clearly are versions
of the same plot, and not two plots with a common
name; but they show at least one major and some
minor differences.

Correspondences in Itineraries of Yellak I and II

I		II	
2	Nyahaim-kwiyuma, etc.	1	Nyahaim-kwiyume, etc.
14	Hatekulye-nyi-kuya		
17	Amaṭ-hamak	15	Avi-kwatulye
18	θaweve		
19	Ha'avulypo	19	Ava-k-tinyam, dark house
23	Waθalya		
27	Avikunu'ulye (7:89, UC-AR 11:1, p. 65)	24	Selye'aya-'ita
27	Qotase (8:191, UC-AR 11:2, p. 105)	25	Amaiaveta's head
28	Avikwame	26	Mekehuvike
		28	Avi-kutaparve (UC-AR 11:2, Map 1, B, west)
32	Aqwaqa-'iove (UC-AR 11:2, Map 1, E, east)	29	Qara'erva (UC-AR 11:2, Map 1, B, east)
	Sleep 1		
34	Hatšioq-watveve (UC-AR 11:2, Map 1, F, west)		
35	Avi-haly-kwa'ampa (UC-AR 11:2, Map 1, H, west)	32	Avi-haly-kwa'ampa
		33	Playfield at Needles
36	Hayekwir-iðo, Pinnacles	34	Hayekwir-iðo
37	Iðolye-ðauve	35	Iðulye-ðauve
		36	Hokiampeve
38	Hime-koaṭa. Sleep 2	37	Me-koaṭa
40	Omaka (UC-AR 11:2, Map 2, 18)		
41	Aspa-lya-pu'umpa (UC-AR 11:2, Map 2, 20, east)		
43	Hakutšyêpa (UC-AR 11:2, Map 2, 24, east)	43	Hakutšyepa
		44	Kutuðunye (UC-AR 11:2, Map 2, 34b,* east).
			Sleep
45	Avi-sokwilye (UC-AR 11:2, Map 2, 28, east).		
	Sleep 3		
48	Avi-vataya (UC-AR 11:2, Map 2, 32, east).		
	Riverside Mts.		
49	Avi-vera (UC-AR 11:2, 33a, Map 2, east).		
	Big Maria Mts.		

I (cont'd)   II (cont'd)

50   Aha-selye'aya (UC-AR 11:2, Map 2, 45, east)
50   Aha-kutinyam (UC-AR 11:2, Map 2, 46, east)

                                                              55b Hatusalye (UC-AR 11:2, Map 2, 49a, east)
52   Aha-kwatpave (UC-AR 11:2, Map 2, 50, east)
53   Kuvukwilye (UC-AR 11:2, Map 2, K, west)   59   Kuvukwilye
55   Aha-kumiθe (UC-AR 11:2, Map 2, M, west)   65   Aha-kumiθe
56   To'oske (UC-AR 11:2, Map 2, O, west)   67   To'oske
57   Yellak-ime (UC-AR 11:2, Map 2, P, west)   71   "Lak-ime"
58   Aha-θauvarave (UC-AR 11:2, Map 2, Q, west)   73   Aha-θavaruva
59   Nyim-kutavave (UC-AR 11:2, Map 2, R, west)   76   Nyimkutavave
60   Avi-kunyure (UC-AR 11:2, Map 2, 60, east)
61   Hukθilye (UC-AR 11:2, Map 2, 62, east),
     Pilot Knob
62   Kwenyo-kuvilyo (UC-AR 11:2, Map 2, 71, east)
63   Kutkyene (UC-AR 11:2, Map 2, 72, east)   77   Kutkyene.
                                                              And Avi-aspa (UC-AR 11:2, Map 2, 73, east)
65   At ocean   78-80 (?) At ocean
66   Return upriver   81   Return upriver
70   Savetšivuta (UC-AR 11:2, Map 1, J, west)   85   "Tši-tšupite," same?
73   Hokusave (UC-AR 11:2, Map 1, E, west): trans-   88   Hokusave: transformations
     formations
65   Last songs (at ocean)   89   Last songs, at Minyoraive

          *No. 34b, east, on UC-AR 11:2, Map 2, but in 1953
     it was placed on E side river below Head Gate Rock
     and above Parker (28), so that its proper position
     would be No. 27b.

Narrative 15
ORIGIN OF WAR

INFORMANT AND CIRCUMSTANCES

This narrative is unfinished, but it was carried far enough to show its general character. It is an institutionalizing myth about Mastamho giving lengthy lectures at Avikwame. There are no songs.

The narrator was Tokwaθa, or Musk Melon, an old man with a war record, and, like Nyavarup, narrator of stories 9 and 10, a historic character in the sense of being mentioned in the literature. He was one of nine Mohave hostages imprisoned in Yuma in 1859. When I knew him he lived near the pump house of the waterworks at Needles. On Sunday, June 21, 1903, a mourning commemoration was held half a mile north of Needles for another old warrior who had accidentally shot himself on June 15 and who was cremated the next day. I was notified and came to witness the rite of "preaching" and running by the mourners. The next day Tokwaθa told me his recollections of the captivity of Olive Oatman, the white girl who lived five years among the Mohave in the 1850's.[1] The day after, June 23, during the afternoon, Tokwaθa narrated to me "what he had dreamed about how war began." As almost always with Mohave informants, he underestimated the time required for a full telling—besides of course failing to allow for the time consumed by the Englishing to me. When the afternoon ended, he thought that there still remained a day's telling. But apparently I had arranged to return to the university that evening; and the myth remains a rump.

My accustomed friend and interpreter, Jack Jones, was not available. A young man served me whom I recorded merely as Jim. On general Indian precedent he is likely to have been a younger kinsman of Tokwaθa. The straight factual story about Olive Oatman on the preceding day he did not hesitate at. But this origin myth in English evidently troubled Jim a bit. Its first paragraphs are somewhat bald, and a few passages uncertain in meaning. About halfway, Tokwaθa began to "preach" in the jerky, shouting, ritual oratory of the Mohave, repeating what Mastamho had told him in the same manner. Footnote 21 tells more of this manner of speech. It is ejaculatory, elliptic, and disconnected, and must be very difficult to convert into con-

tinuous "prose." Jim therefore helped me record in Mohave as many of the phrases as we could get down, and then translated their allusions as best he could. Jack Jones, a middle-aged man with more assurance, might have asked the informant to tame his rhetorical manner into a narrative rendering of the same substance. It was therefore perhaps just as well that he did not officiate on this occasion. It is of course an old working rule that an ethnographer ought not depend too exclusively on one interpreter—though when good rapport has been established, the temptation is strong to do so.

ANALYSIS

Paragraphs 1-9 are a prelude, a somewhat sketchy account of origins and Mastamho, along the lines of Mastamho, 7 (UC-AR 11:1, pp. 50-68), and, above, Origins, 9, the first section of 13, Chuhueche, and the beginning and end of 14, Goose.

In 10-12, Mastamho begins to "preach." In 10, whose purport seems to be general and to refer to the act of speaking itself, a balancing of the sense and sound of phrases is marked: umasesála, rib; akatšepíre, shoulder; atšilyámet, jaw, esūkyávet, jaw; yimtšeδum, sing, nyimtšám, say "he͂"; hitšôvesik, scattered, himsálvek, scattered; and a double pair referring to tongue motion in speech: pronounce, twist, bend, move. Some of these Mohave terms more or less rhyme. Compare the distorted words in Mastamho, 7, as reviewed on UC-AR 11:1, page 67, and the pairing and jingling of proper names in the Epic, 8, UC-AR 11:2, page 132. The Luiseño in ritual passages like to double deity, essence, ritual act, or artifact, naming a pair of designations—though usually without rhyme or jingle —much as the Mohave often use twin names for a single locality.

In 11-12 there is an account of the instituting of the patrilineal totemic clans of the Mohave. This accounts for only about a third of the total number, but those named are mostly the larger clans. The only other myth reference to the beginning of clans is in Nyavarup's Origins, 9:48 above; and of course in the "historical" epic, 8:173-176 (UC-AR 11:2, pp. 103-104).

---

[1]Published as "Olive Oatman's Return," in Kroeber Anthropological Society, Berkeley, No. 4, 1951 (pp. 1-18).

Nyavarup, however, named only three clans: Kuts̆-hoalye, Maha, Owits̆; then broke off with the statement: "I was there, but I did not listen. Other old men know all this: I do not know it." Tokwaθa lists seven clans.

Paragraphs 1-12 together form an abbreviated account of origins, as Table 1, Origins, 9, above, shows, which lists corresponding episodes in Origins, 9, Mastamho 7 (UC-AR 11:1, pp. 50-68), the present 15 (War), and 16G, Sky Rattlesnake.

Paragraphs 13-15 are straight narrative again—and somewhat overcondensed—of the Kwayū-Crayfish episode, known also from 6B (UC-AR 11:1, p. 48). They serve however to introduce the subject of intertribal war: Kwayū, though a cannibal, is a Mohave, living just south of Mohave Valley: Crayfish is from the sea, near which are the Kohuana and Cocopa, historic enemies of the Mohave and Yuma.

The remainder of the tale, 16-20, reverts to Mastamho's preaching, all of it general in character though with direct reference to war. There is no action whatever, only Mastamho's directives.

Here the fragment ends.

THE NARRATIVE

1. Before there was dry land, before Matavilya, that is when we were all born. The way it was, we were born in one place; all tribes were born at Avikwame[2] —the Mohave youngest, other tribes older. This is what I know from what I was told and what I dreamed: we were like children; that is how fighting began.

2. When Matavilya died, Han'ava[3] came up out of the ground where he grew; he came up to make people feel consoled by his mourning crying; that is why we cry. But you white people did not receive that from him, so you do not wail (at death). Han'ava gave us Mohave not so much[4] as to the Yuma, Pima, and Kamia, but he gave the whites none at all.

3. When Matavilya died, there was no sun or light, everything was dark. They carried him out of the house and set him down. Now they were wanting to burn him; that is why we burn dead persons. Mastamho said: "Let us try to discover which way is north, or east, or south, or west"; for he was only a little boy.

---

[2]All beings were born of heaven and earth along <u>with</u> Matavilya, <u>before</u> he led them; this seems to be the meaning of the first sentence. The second seems to contradict this, but literally the tribes were segregated out at Avikwame by Mastamho only after Matavilya's death; cf. 5-8 below, 7:51-55 (UC-AR 11:1, p. 60), and above, 9:43-44.

[3]Cf. 9:13 for Han'ava.

[4]The Mohave do have less formal mourning ritual than the Yuma and many Californian tribes—no use of images or "dolls," for instance.

So he went to lift the body a little, but it fell back with a noise.[5]

4. As the body burned, Mastamho thought: "What shall I do that we may forget him? This will be best: to let him go (from remembrance); then they will always do like that. So let me go up." Then he went upriver (north), stuck his cane into the ground, and water came out and flowed through the ashes where they had burned Matavilya (and washed them away). So there came to be this river.[6] And Mastamho led and carried all the people on his hands, his back, his shoulders (above the water).[7]

5. When he came downriver from here, he thought: "What shall I do that will help them most? The tribes in the desert, let them go west." Now the river had fallen and there was mud in places; there he sowed wild seeds of kwaθapilya[8] for them to live on there. This first dry land was called[9] Akwe'im, Aha-kulye-masāve, Hakovĭlye, Hukθara-'ats̆hwerve.

6. His first name, which his father[10] gave him, was Ikĭnye-masam-vats̆iδ ômā.[11] Now he said: "Let us go back to where we were born." So he took (carried) them all back to Avikwame, and the river (flood) had gone down. Then the first thing they saw were Hana-pūka[12] Ants moving around, working, raising the ground.

7. Then he did something for the Walapai to the east, at Ki-yarayara. [At] Yikitakmĭve, Ese'ewĭ, Tove-kuva, and Kumtālyva[13] he made seeds of kwaθapilya, ma-selye'aye, ĭδĭts̆a, and ts̆elyepêve[14] to grow.

8. He was still taking care of four tribes: the Mohave, Yuma, Halts̆iδ ôma, and Maricopa;[15] he kept them all around his lap. He said: "I will do more; I will teach you. You Maricopa, I give you a good language that you will use. And I give you a name, Coming Near East,[16] Hatpa-'inya. You Halts̆iδ ôma will speak a little differently. And you, I will give you the name

---

[5]The passage is not clear. Cf. above 9:11, 13:11, 12. The circuit is sunwise beginning in the N, ending W.

[6]Cf. 7:10 (UC-AR 11:1, p. 54), and above, 9:18, 14:1.

[7]Cf. 9:20, and, as done by a human hero, 8:22 (UC-AR 11:2, p. 78).

[8]For kwaθapilya, cf. 7:15 (UC-AR 11:1, p. 55), and above, 9:22, 24. It is sage, chia.

[9]Translations uncertain. Hukθara means coyote.

[10]Thus usually for the relation of Matavilya and Mastamho.

[11]A similar name occurs in 9:11 (note 31) as one of two companions of Mastamho; but that passage may have been misunderstood, additional <u>names</u> of Mastamho having been confused with <u>associates</u>.

[12]They were specified as white, which would make them termites. In 9:27 above, two kinds of ants play the same role. Hanapūka are mentioned again below in 15:20, note 49.

[13]My recording was overcondensed. I have assumed these four are place-names and have supplied: "At."

[14]Three of the same four seeds are made by Mastamho for the Chemehuevi to the west in 7:15 (UC-AR 11:1, p. 55); malysa there replaces the present ĭδĭts̆a. Cf. also 9:22, 24.

[15]They form a dialectic group. Cf. my Classification of the Yuman Languages, UC-P Linguistics 1:21-40, 1943.

[16]Hatpa-'inya seems literally to mean "East-Pima," though the Maricopa were always west of the Pima.

Kutšyāna (Yuma); you will speak not loud, but low.[17]
And you Hamákhava, you will speak my Mohave language, apart from all the others."

9. Then he led these four tribes in four rows,
saying: "Now there will be dry land, and I will make
a house to live in, as I dreamed it. I saw it in a
dream; and I say to you that no one else saw it."
Standing in the center, he had the four companies[18]
around him. And he was wise.[19] So he said again: "I
am going to level it here; I will try to build a house.
I have already given each tribe its name. Now I will
bring out eagle, and the sun, and give you all, of the
four tribes, common words."[20]

10. Now Mastamho said this to me [in the oratorical,
emphatic, shouted, interjectional style of formal Mohave
ritual]:[21]

umasesála, rib

akatšepíre, shoulder

patšumí, companions

itšesumáyúm, give (good) dreams (luck)

hĭmva'ĭm

makame-tšeqwá'ra, how (I will) talk

atšilyāmet, jaw

esūkyāvet, jaw

yimtšeôum, sing (one way)

nyimtšām, say "hẽ" (well)

lili, sound (of talking starting)

iqátš [for iha-tš, spittle?]

hitšôvesik, scattered

himsálvek, scattered

amaiy-emiák, speak up (loudly)

kwĭne, smooth (sound of talking)

sukusūk, pronounce (with tongue)

pahepa'h, twisting back and forth

hemályk, bend back

hemkwĭlk, moving around

amaiy-emiák, speak up (loudly)

patšemitš-ka'āvek, companions hear

itšemĭm, rafters

ava-tšutārve, small cross rafters

ava-tšusĭqa, brush covering of house[22]

ihatš-hatšĭny-ik, [spittle boy]

ihatš-ikĭnye, [spittle girl]

11. Mastamho said: "I will tell you everything for
you to live by. Take the name of the moon, halyá; for
that you will have[23] Hoálya [as the women's name of
a clan]. Also, for sun, anyá, you will have Nyórtše
when (the women are) old, Nyó'iltše when they are
young[24] (in that clan). And you will have Halypôta."[25]

12. He said:[26]

Etšeqwárek, I talk

apôtem

ihátš, [spittle]

mūha, Moha

mathāk, north

hipā, Hipa

ihatš-masávem, ihatš (spit) white (cloudy).

pĭve

lūle, floating in air [clouds]

ōwitše, Owitš

ihatš-pĭve

qáṭa, Kaṭa[27]

[17]Perhaps it means "unclearly, not plainly."
[18]Companies: tribes, rows. Cf. 7:52-56 (UC-AR 11:1, pp.
60-61), 9:35.
[19]"Like a witch, weather-wise," said the interpreter; i.e.,
supernaturally wise.
[20]The meaning was said to be that the word for eagle,
aspa, and that for sun, anya, is the same in all four languages.

[21]In this ejaculatory oratory, the accented syllable is
clearly enunciated, the other syllables in the word or phrase
are hurried and much less clear, the whole is shouted
abruptly and fervently; then there is a pause before the next
phrase is uttered in the same manner. It is a highly charac-
terized oratorical delivery. The Mohave speaking English call
it "preaching"; "exhorting" might describe it better. It is
always used in the funerary commemoration for brave men
(Handbook, p. 750: nyimi-tšekwarek—I have also recorded
kohotk); at formal cremation bewailing by those who have
dreamed; and sometimes in myth recitation not accompanied
by singing. So far as I know the content is always dreamed
myth of origins. The words may be distorted somewhat as
in songs. I am under the impression that this stylized speech
is not fully grammatical. At any rate, it is—like songs—not
fully explanatory of its meaning but moves unjointedly from
word to word, leaving part of the continuity of sense implicit,
to be inferred or supplied from previous knowledge of the
context. The translations here given are those of the interpreter, and no doubt sometimes connotive rather than exact.
Translations by myself are enclosed in square brackets, thus
[ ]. The ritual "preaching" is referred to on UC-AR 11:2,
p. 133.

[22]In 7:23 (UC-AR 11:1, pp. 56-57), iqumnau, av'a-tšutara,
ava-tšusive occur for itšemim, ava-tsutārve, ava-tšusiqa here.
[23]Allusion is to the "totemic" reference, such as haly'a,
moon, corresponding to the female clan name such as Hoalya
though the clans are patrilineal.
[24]Nyo'iltše-Nyortše is one of very few clan names that
change with age of the bearers. Nyo'iltše has four totem
references besides sun: fire, eagle, deer, beetle.
[25]Frog is the "totem" of the Halypôta clan, but mention
of it got lost here.
[26]This paragraph continues the institution of clans and
their names. But at that only seven clans are mentioned, as
against some twenty recorded at one time or another for the
Mohave. The four additional to those in notes 23-25 above
are Moha, Hipa, Owitš, Kaṭa.
[27]This paragraph agrees partially with what was obtained
from other informants—see Handbook, p. 742, and 8, Epic
(UC-AR 11:2, pp. 114-118).

Clan name	Meaning here	Meaning, Handbook
Moha		mountain sheep
Hipa	north, wind	coyote
Owitš	float in air	cloud
Kaṭa		tobacco
(Mat-hatšva)		wind (mat-ha)

13. After Mastamho had told these things, Kwayū,[28] a Mohave, a large man,[29] also born at Avikwame, went downriver to Mukiámpeve[30] and lived there by himself with his two sisters. One of these had two eyes, the other only one eye, and she lived in from the river, but the two-eyed one close to the river, and there she watched.[31] Now Kwayū used to go downriver to the Kuhuana tribe, and there he caught people, squeezed[32] their necks, brought them home (and ate them): that is how he lived. So he began the fighting between tribes, by killing others to eat.

14. Now Halkutāṭa[33] lived in the sea, just beyond the Kuhuana. There he sang; and he was wise, and knew what to do. So he came upriver, and approached Kwayū's house in the river,[34] and raised it up, and took and killed Kwayū, and carried his body back with him. In the middle of the sea he stood up the feathers which Kwayū had had all over his body. He stood them up in a circle, like a house, and went inside.

15. But when Mastamho heard about it he was angry, because he and Kwayū were of the same tribe. "I will go and kill him," he said; "he ought not have killed him." So he went downriver and looked about but at first could not find Halkutāṭa. But then he saw him, far in the sea, lying in his house of feathers. Then Mastamho chewed coyote-grass,[35] spat it into the sea, this dried up, the feathers appeared, and there he found Halkutāṭa and killed him. That was the beginning of war.[36]

16. Mastamho said:[37]

Ava-tanêva, a place to southeast, in Yavapai country

Avi-qara-'ôtata, Monument Mountain, to south in California

Matha-lye-vaδôma, to south, in Arizona

Tāha, "monument-stick-(place)"[38]

takwĭse, cactus species

ho'ūlye, cactus species[39]

āve, rattlesnake

háltoṭa, black-widow spider

ata-kwanamĭ, (make) brave[40]

itšámve iv'áum, put it on, stand

hêt'éka, have said

satôlyikwa, pull skin (?)

tšatšúkunve, hurt

hatšoārve, throw stick at

sathoālyka, playing shinny

ahwaĭ-evūnūk, war begins

17. He said again:

iθáve, arrowed[41]

ata-kwanamĭ, (make) brave

ánalye, mesquite wood

ata-kwanamĭ, (make) brave

a'ĭse, screw-mesquite wood[42]

ata-kwanamĭk, (make) brave

itšámve iv'áum, put on and stand

hĭmni tšamāneka, they begin

amat Avĭ-h-elye'á, in Moon Mountain country

Avĭ-vatáye, Great Mountain

[28]Kwayū, Meteor, is always evil or dangerous, usually a cannibal. See 1:37, 74-83, 104 (UC-AR 11:1, pp. 9, 12-16, 18). See also 6B (UC-AR 11:1, p. 48), which contains the substance of the present 13, 14, but further identifies Kwayū with Coyote, perhaps erroneously. See also G. Devereux, Mohave Coyote Tales, JAFL 61:233-255, 1948, where Kwayū is killed by Patcakarawe, who in turn is the hero of my tale 6A (UC-AR 11:1, pp. 46-47).

[29]A "giant," in Devereux, just cited. I found in 1953 that the Mohave were equating kwayū and giant generically.

[30]The Needles pinnacles, as in 6B (UC-AR 11:1, p. 48). See also UC-AR 11:2, Map 2, no. 2, east, and p. 141.

[31]For passersby for her brother to catch?

[32]Sic; broke? choked them?

[33]Halkutaṭa is probably crayfish or a similar crustacean, as per 6B, note 20 (UC-AR 11:1, p. 48). See also 14:62 above, Aha-nyi-saṭa. In 1953 halkutaṭa was again described, as barely of finger length, which suggests a prawn rather than a crayfish; but are there freshwater prawns in the Colorado? Or is it a caddis or dragonfly larva? The etymology seems to be "water-in-cane" or "-staff," ha-ly-k-atata.

[34]"His face covered with foam." Kwayū's face? Or his own?

[35]Ohutšye.

[36]Now at last the story has reached its professed subject, war. The Devereux Kwayū episode also refers to the institution of war.

[37]Paraphrasing into prose, the interpreter told: Mastamho said: I stand here at Avataneva. I will divide the land, so much to each (tribe), and you will fight (over it). Where the tracts end you will set up monuments (of stones or stakes), and (from that) you will have wars.

[38]Of these four places, I cannot add more precise identification for (1) Ava-tanêva. (2) Avi-qara-'ôtata I recorded in 1953 as Avi-qor-otat, as the name of two erosion pillars or monuments in the Whipple or Monument range between Mohave and Parker valleys, running, in California, more or less west to east about end-on with the Bill Williams Fork flowing in on the Arizona side. One of these pillars is conspicuous from Parker and much of the Colorado River Reservation. This one the Mohave say is the sister; the brother is less tall; the Halchidhoma or Halchadhom "worshiped" (feared) them. These pillars (and the range of which they were part) constituted the boundary between Mohave and Halchadhom while the latter still lived on the Colorado; if either crossed it, it was for an attack. (3) Matha-lye-va-δôma I have not been able to identify further as a place. The word may mean "North-in-dwellers." Compare Matha-lya-δôma as the northern half of the Mohave tribe in Mohave Valley, as against the Kave-lya-δôma or southerners, in Handbook, p. 746. The tribal name Halchidhoma or Halchadhom is a similar formation: perhaps Ha-ly-tša-δôm(a), "river-at-(?)dwellers." (4) Taha is a conspicuous bell-shaped peak standing somewhat off the main range of the Turtle Mountains, to the west of the Needles-Parker highway. Some Chemehuevi took refuge on it in the 1860's after killing a Mohave near the Blythe Intake, and were vainly beseiged by the Mohave, who had not expected that the Chemehuevi would be able to find water on top. The place is mentioned in Tortoise, 19:29, 35.

[39]Ho'ūlye may not be a cactus, but evidently is a second stinging plant, as the two animals that follow bite.

[40]Kwanamĭ means brave, liking to fight. Seven lines below, ahwaĭ, "war," seems to be cognate with ahwé, "foreign, enemy."

[41]For arrows.

[42]The mallet-headed club is of mesquite, the simple cylindrical club of screw mesquite, Handbook, p. 751.

Avĭ-sukwĭlye, Hawk Mountain
Avĭ-aʼĭse, Screwbean Mountain[43]
atšavaðθkitšam, I divide (the mountains)
at-ahwaik itšamĭm, for war ready
avĭrk viʼivʼāum, finished I stand here
maṭ-m-iθave-ha nyaʼimvi viʼivʼaum[44]

18. Mastamho said again: "Now these feathers,[45] this pile of them, I make them into four heaps, one here, one there, and put them about, giving you something to quarrel over, to make you ready to fight."

kwányume nyāyum, (I give you) more yet
viʼivʼāum, standing here
iʼĭθ mítak avékwmotê, not to retreat
môhmohe, raven-beak ornament[46]

esukūlyk, put on head
aqāqa, raven
hihuntakírtem váʼwe, its beak cut off

19. And Mastamho broke a gourd in half, big enough to cover the forehead, and painted a mark on it, and said: "Put it on (across the forehead), go to war, and when you start, do not retreat!"[47]

20. He said again:

kwányume nyāyum, (I give you) more yet
viʼivʼāum, standing here
totšūlye, raven-feather ornament[48]
hiðáuk mátek hatápek, I hold and put on
viʼivʼāum, standing here
tšámeðulye, piss ants
ata-kwanamí, brave
hanapūka, white ants[49]
amaṭa hiatokíre, where the land began.[50]

---

[43]The translations given are etymologies. These four mountains surround the Parker Reservation, where the Mohave used to come to fight with the Halchidhoma. Avi-k-elyeʼá is Moon Mountain, E of the river. Avi-vatáye is Riverside Mountains, west of it. Avi-sukwĭlye is the isolated dark peak behind (SE of) Parker where Nyohaiva transformed, 3:36 (UC-AR 11:1, p. 34). Avi-aʼise is downstream of last, running south from Bouse Wash, facing the river.

[44]Translated as: I will give you something over which to get angry at each other.

[45]Sivilye.

[46]The môhmohe is described as consisting of the beaks of ravens or crows mounted on a stick and worn as a headdress. If I understood correctly, the wearers might not retreat: something like the bearers of crooked lances in the Plains.

The Mohave also carried a straight, double-pointed feathered lance called ukwilye to war as a no-flight symbol, and ran with it in warriors' funeral commemorations.

[47]The forehead gourd, of which I appear to have no other record, is another no-flight decoration.

[48]Cut raven feathers strung on a thong, worn hanging from the neck.

[49]Cf. section 6, above.

[50]The two species made the earth grow and be dry. The account breaks off here, unfinished.

Narrative 16
VARIOUS FRAGMENTS

I present here various fragments and scraps from several informants, distinguished as 16A-16G.

These are, in order:

    A. Mountain Lion's and Jaguar's Powers.
       By Nyavarup.

    B. Coyote and the Moon.
       By Nyavarup.

    C. Oturkepaye.
       By Jo Nelson.

    D. Bittern and Doves.
       By Robert Martin.

    E. Vinimulye-patše II.
       By Kutene.

    F. Nyohaiva Song Repetitions.
       By Eagle-Sell.

    G. Sky Rattlesnake: a Doctor's Dreaming.
       By Achyora Hanyava.

16A. MOUNTAIN LION'S AND JAGUAR'S POWERS

This account is from the doctor Nyavarup who gave the accounts above of Origins, 9, and Alyha, 10. It is a somewhat rambling mixture of myth, description of tribal custom, and dreaming of personal powers, not easily segregatable, but strung on the thread of what the two great felines originated.

Hatekulye is somewhat uncertain between Wolf and Jaguar, as discussed under 5, Deer, on UC-AR 11:1, page 41.

This is what Nyavarup said in 1902:

The Mohave do not eat desert tortoises—they are afraid to. Paiutes do eat them, also red-spotted lizards. There are no tortoises east of the Colorado River; that is because Mastamho said so: he gave them as food to the Paiute. And he gave the Walapai rats to eat. And he said to us, I tell you what is good for you to eat: eat fish! So the Mojave eat fish; but the Chemehuevi and Walapai eat no fish. If Mastamho had said, Eat everything, the Mohave would be eating everything.

There were Numéta, Mountain Lion, the older brother, and Hátekúlye, Wolf (? or Jaguar), the younger brother. These two told the Paiute (Chemehuevi) to kill and eat rabbits and birds. Mastamho appointed these two to tell the Chemehuevi what to do.

These two gave to the Walapai also: they gave them good eyes, to see plainly with, and far. And likewise the Chemehuevi, when they hunt, can see game from far off.

Numéta and Hatekulye are also animals—"mountain lions." Therefore [because they helped mostly the desert tribes] there are no mountain lions about our land here.

When the Chemehuevi dream, they have bows and arrows and kill with them. When it becomes day and they go out, they kill game: it is because these two gave it to them. When they see game, the animals cannot run fast, or they sit down so the Paiutes can take them with their hands; they want to be caught. The same with the Walapai. But if Mohave go to hunt, the animals run swiftly away.[1]

Among the Mohave, some men can catch fish well. I am one of these. It was given to me. I can catch fish better than others. I learned it at Kuyak-úilta,[2] downstream of Ha'avulypo where Matavilya died, east

---

[1] This paragraph illustrates well both the sharp consciousness of tribal differentiation prevalent in the area and the underlying general concept that all special abilities must be due to "dreaming," that is, supernatural experience, both as originally ordained and as personally experienced.

[2] Kuyak-uilta is unplaced, and the word seems mangled. There may possibly be a connection with Kuyal-katš-vapítva of 8:171 (UC-AR 11:2, p. 103), there placed "at Eldorado Canyon," but from its association with Havirepuka more likely on or near Cottonwood Island.

of the river. It was Numeta and Hatekulye who taught me. They came to Kuyakuilta and wanted to build a house.

They were thinking about birds. "Let us go to Aví-θekwínye," in the mountains to the northeast,[3] they said. "When we arrive there, we want to make a dark round." They meant a house. They arrived there and made the house. Then they wanted to make birds. They made them from their breath, blowing it. They made many birds.

Then they called their names. They stood before the house, and the birds too. They held out their hands (extended together edge to edge), and called to the birds to come sit on their hands. Dove, Hoskyíve, was the first one they called. And they called him by a second name: Ikinye-humás-e'ála.[4] Then you are next: your name will be Qámtôska,[5] they said to another. Then they called Kaθevéme; then Roadrunner, Tálypo; then Blackbird, Haθ'íkwa.

Then they called and named one after another Utúr-ke-payi, the one with two little white stripes on his crown which he got from carrying about on his head his pair of gambling poles;[6] Hitokupi'lyewaku, who has a little red on his head; Tšieq-véor-veore; Hútukuro, Curve-billed thrasher;[7] Is'úna, Woodpecker; θinyére; Sukwílye-katai, Hawk; Tápire; Kukhó, Yellow-hammer;[8] Minsá'an, who is red all over; Sakweθa'álye, Mockingbird; Aqáqa, Raven;[9] Hanemó, (Wood) Duck; Haníwilye, Mud-hen; Hitšui-kúpuye; Hwat-hwáte; Pūk-havasó, "Green-necklace," Mallard (?); Yahilyétaka; Anyákwiyú; Atšqeyuke, Bittern;[10] Yélaka, Goose;[11] Sakúre; Ahá-nye-masaha; Asei, Buzzard; and Ahmá, Quail.[12]

They did not make many kinds of birds in this country: that is why there are not many kinds here in the valley. They did not make eagles here; that is why there are not many seen about.

There is a place Aví-kunyihóre[13] in the west, before one comes to San Bernardino. There Numeta and Hate-

kulye made deer. After making the birds at Avi-θekwinye, they had gone on to Hatekulye-náke[14] north of here, near the river. There they were thinking of making more animals. They looked for a good place for that, and so they went to Avi-kunyihore.

Others, if they dream about Numeta and Hatekulye, may get ill from the dreaming. But I dreamed of them and did not become sick. Therefore I can cure those that do get ill of it.[15]

Some men—not doctors—dream of deer, and are taught songs by them, and sometimes at night they will sing Deer, and dance to it, and they tell what the Deer did.[16]

And so some sing Birds, Tšiyere, and some sing Raven, Aqaqa. They learn this (by dreaming) of Avi-kwame; but it is not for doctoring.

When I dreamed of Numeta and Hatekulye, they were like men. They told me how to take fish. They said, Let us show him, then he will know it. After they had given me this, they began to turn into animals: Their hands became hairy and claws grew out for them to catch rabbit and deer.[17] They gave me an íhulye net to take the fish with. The Walapai dream of them too, some of them, and then they can hunt and kill game, and their wives wear buckskin and have rabbit-skin blankets; and the Paiutes too. The Walapai will not eat fish, the Mohave will not eat Walapai seeds.

16B. COYOTE AND THE MOON[18]

This is also from Nyavarup.

Coyote has three names: Húk-θara, Hipá, and θára-veyó.[19] He thought, How can human beings stand up? How can they go without fur? They are poor things:

---

[3]This would be in Walapai territory, but I seem to have no other record of Avi-θekwinye.

[4]"Boy-child-e'ala," a characteristic mythological name. Dove is usually a girl in Mohave myth—see 16D below—but ikinye is a boy.

[5]Qamtôsqa is mentioned in several contexts but I have no identification of the bird. It is described as brown and calling "tos, tos." Devereux's may be an interpreter's guess with a familiar English name, based on similar size. I do not know whether robins visit deserts.

[6]Oture or utura. For the bird, see 16C, below.

[7]Important in 7:79-81, 85-101 (UC-AR 11:1, pp. 63, 64-65).

[8]Or Flicker; kukhó is the secular name of Satukhota, 18, below.

[9]Subject of story 4 (UC-AR 11:1, pp. 37-40).

[10]See 16D below.

[11]Story 14, above.

[12]It was clear that this list, especially its last part, did not represent any order memorized by the informant.

[13]Avi-kunyihore is mentioned in 5:2 (UC-AR 11:1, p. 42) as Avi-kwin-yehore, one of 4 places "W of," that is, near,

San Bernardino, where the same two gods make deer. That act is mentioned here also, but only referred to.

[14]Hatekulye-nake, elsewhere translated as "mountain lion's cave," was recorded as -naka in 5:1 (UC-AR 11:1, p. 42) and as -nyikuyá in 14:14, above. According to 5:1, it is upriver from "Lizard Mountain," Avi-kwatulye. According to 14:13-19 it is upriver from Ha'avulypo and Hatavilya- (or Matavilya-) kutšhwerve, and only ritually designated places are named above it.

[15]Illness from exposure to supernatural power is cured through treatment by those who have had similar exposure but have assimilated it. This idea is widespread from northern California to the Southwest, but is not particularly accentuated by the Mohave.

[16]As in story 5 (UC-AR 11:1, pp. 41-45).

[17]This sort of temporary and visible transformation of the deity is more characteristic of the Plains-to-California region in which the personal guardian spirit is an animal than it is of the Mohave.

[18]Compare the Coyote stories for children, 6C to 6H (UC-AR 11:1, pp. 48-49).

[19]The 3 names are mentioned also in 6A, footnotes 5, 7 (UC-AR 11:1, p. 46).

He said, None of you can jump over the moon! But I can! They all said, No, you can't. You may fall in and never come back. He said again, It is you who can't do it. But the people answered, Neither can you. I can too, he told them. Well, let's see you, they said. And all looked as he got ready. He ran four steps from the east and leaped and fell right in the middle of the moon and was gone—everybody laughed. He is sitting in the moon, now, with his head turned and his mouth turned, and his yellow knife (of flint), ahkwétša-θilye, hanging from around his neck.

16C. OTUR-KEPAYE

This fragment is from "Baby's Head," also known as Jo Nelson, who in 1903 dictated the long Mastamho story 7 (UC-AR 11:1, pp. 50-68); also a memory history of actual tribal warfare; and a sort of gazetteer of alien tribes. I was trying to get him to identify the Tólkepaya, as Corbusier and later Gifford called the Western Yavapai. He could not do anything with the name, and finally suggested it might refer to a small bird (song sparrow, possibly) about which there was a story telling how he engaged in a war or stick-fight within Mohave Valley. In this feature, the episode resembles Yellak 14:70-72, above, where two sets of birds about to transform—one of them into Mohaves—fight over farmland in Mohave Valley. However, all the birds mentioned there and here differ completely in names. It is therefore likely that there is no connection with Yellak, other than that the general idea of birds fighting about land was a floating theme in Mohave myth. This theme was then drawn upon—but with different actors—here, in Yellak, and (with change to insects fighting against birds) in Tumanpa, 11:4-6, above.

Otūr-kepáye, Tokupílye-wake, Tšérqwa'orveóre, and Tôske-ipa[20] lived at Avi-hakwahamve[21] and wanted to go to Tasilyke[22] to play hoop and poles. "Who will carry the poles?" they asked. Then Otūr-kepaye balanced them on his head and carried them there: that is why he has two white stripes on his head.[23]

These four lived at a terrace on the west side of the river. They had many people with them, but did

not tell them: they wanted to cross the river at Hwatitotahuere[24] to fight with those upstream on the other side. So they reached Ha-sôδape,[25] then turned downstream to Aha-pêne,[26] from there upstream a little to Qavkuaha,[27] and a little farther to Sa'ontšive.[28]

This is a long story; we will tell it later.[29]

16D. BITTERN AND DOVES

This fragment from Robert Martin at Valley School, below Parker, was recorded in 1954:

Two Doves, Húskive, were pretty and wanted to get married. Many birds came, good-looking ones, and vainly tried to make them laugh. Then came Bittern,[30] Atšqéuqa, who was ugly and wore a necklace of fish. But he made them laugh and married them.

Now when an ugly man marries a pretty wife, and is teased about it, he says: Atšqéuqa nya'ím, Bittern gave it to me.

This is the episode told also in Mastamho, 7:91 (UC-AR 11:1, p. 65), where it is put in context and localized. There is agreement even to the necklace of fish worn by Atšqeuqa: in 7:91 he catches four little ones, threads them on blackwillow "leaves" (twigs?), and wears them as a headdress. The woman won in Mastamho is Tortoise, Kapeta; but immediately after, in 7:92, a Dove girl arrives and is told that women who dream of her will be kamaluik, loose.

16E. VINIMULYE-PATŠE II[31]

In March, 1908, at Needles, as part of a program of obtaining records of songs from parallel versions, or duplications of specified songs repeated by the same singers from several years earlier, I found a youngish

[20] Four birds, all unidentified. Tšaiqwatarqe of Yellak 14:34 above may be corrupted rendering of the same form.
[21] Avi-hakwahamve is unplaced, unless it be a very bad spelling of Kwamhaθeve, UC-AR 11:2, Map 1, 29a, W, a couple of miles below Needles City.
[22] Tasilyke (Amaṭ-tasilyke) is UC-AR 11:2, Map 1, J, E, half a dozen miles upstream of Needles, opposite side.
[23] Otūr-kepaye is a small bird; twitters in the bush, not loudly; the two white stripes run fore-and-aft atop his head. Otūr is the poles; hapaik, "carries on head."

[24] Unplaced; the form sounds corrupt to me. My rendering of Mohave was still pretty crude when I worked with Nya-varup in 1902.
[25] Ha-sôδape is UC-AR 11:2, Map 1, H, E, maybe 10 miles above Needles and 5 below Fort Mohave.
[26] Aha-pêna is unplaced.
[27] Qavkuaha is Qāv-k-uvaha of UC-AR 11:2, Map 1, I, E, two miles downstream of Ha-sôδape.
[28] Sa'ontšive is UC-AR 11:2, Map 1, 24, E, two miles below Qavkuvaha. The range of places visited is on the east side about opposite the spots visited and fought over on the west side in Yellak 14:34, 70-72, above.
[29] Unfortunately, we never got around to recording it. The informant thought it might be part of the Migration Tale or Epic, no. 8 (UC-AR 11:2); but so far as versions of this are known (no. 8, and fragmentary versions A, B, C, E, UC-AR 11:2, pp. 134-136), it has only human actors.
[30] American bittern, or great blue heron; see UC-AR 11:1, note 145, p. 65.
[31] This fragment has been briefly discussed on p. 135, UC-AR 11:2.

man called Kuténe who knew Vinimulye-patše. He was married to the daughter of Kunalye, an old man from whom I secured part of a "Great Tale" or Migration or Hipahipa Legend which is published in Handbook, pages 772-775, and discussed on page 134 of UC-AR 11:2. He agreed to sing for me a dozen Vinimulye-patše songs: the cylinders were subsequently catalogued at the University as nos. 946-958. The Vinimulye-patše story told to me by Hiweik-kwinilye, which is published as No. 2 in UC-AR 11:1, states the number of songs at each station, but I had no phonograph available in the bottomlands north of Camp Mohave school in 1904. Kutene's songs therefore supplement rather than parallel Hiweik-kwinilye's.

He sang eight songs from the beginning of the series, two from around the middle, two from the end.

The first eight songs are from Avi-ahnalye, "Gourd Mountain, beyond Avikwame northwest in Nevada, 200-300 miles off." The first of these songs tells of the place, the second of their walking, the next two of the approach of sunset and darkness, the fifth of the sun still shining on the mountains on the east side of the valley (cf. below 19:4), then three more about their being on their way.

The two songs from the middle of the tale (cyl. 955-956) were sung at Avily-kwa'ampa, upriver from Needles where the mesa meets the river. This is UC-AR 11:2, Map 1, H, W (Avi-halykwa'ampa), 6-7 miles above Needles. This place is mentioned in the full version, 2:16 (UC-AR 11:1, p. 25) as where the pursued and the victors crossed the river from west to east.

The last two songs of the story (cyl. 957-958) are from four places in Chemehuevi country to the west and northwest of Mohave Valley: New York Mts. or Aví-waθá; Kómota; Harákaraka; and Charleston Peak or Sávetpílye, the great mountain northwest of Las Vegas from which atomic explosions are now observed. This geographical ending agrees with the 1904 version, except that the terminal tract is much wider in range to the north in II. The New York Mts. are the northern continuation of the Providence Mts. where Hiweik-kwinilye's version I ends. Since all the places mentioned are in Chemehuevi homeland,[32] I now assume that the theme of Vinimulye-patše is that of a clan lineage or "band" or horde of Mohave moving from Mohave Valley into the historic Chemehuevi desert to settle, returning to fight victoriously with their former fellow clansmen or neighbors, and then going back once more to live in the desert—to become Chemehuevi perhaps, or Desert Mohave (Kroeber, UCP-AAE 47:

[32]Charleston Peak in fact, and perhaps Harakaraka, are in territory of the "Las Vegas band" of the Southern Paiute.

294-307, 1959). This is a theme obviously kindred to that of the Historical Epic, and accounts for the similarity of Vinimulye-patše to that, as for instance in its absence of supernatural elements.

While the 1904 informant began his story in Mohave Valley (2:1, 2, UC-AR II:1, p. 24 at Aha-kwa'a'i, UC-AR 11:2, Map 1, no. 28, east), his station 3 was already far west of the Valley, at the Providence Mountains, and he volunteered that he usually omitted the songs from the two first stations and began with the third. This brings versions I and II into closer accord as to major geography and imputed tribal appurtenance.

It has occurred to me that the distinctive part of the name Vinimulye-patše might be Aví-ny-imúlye, "mountains their names." I suggested this to some Mohave in 1954, and they were inclined to agree, though they had not thought of it before and were not sure.

16F. NYOHAIVA SONG REPETITIONS

In 1908, Aspasakam sang over for me at Needles half a dozen songs which I had recorded from him in 1905; which are here listed for record.

1905 Songs	Cylinders	1908 Songs	Cylinders
1:3	230	1	986
2	231	2	987
14	243	3	988
30:1	259	4	989
31:2	261	5	990
31:4	263	6	991

The only word of "1" is isuma, for sumak, dream. Song 5 (31:2) runs (ñ = ŋ):

amatuaña	sumakwaña	sumakahuwam
amaṭ-ya'ama	sumak	sumak
place name	dream	dream

16G. SKY RATTLESNAKE: A DOCTOR'S DREAMING

In Handbook, 1925, pages 775-777, there is an account volunteered by Achyora Hanyava, narrator also of myths 11, 12, 13, telling how he acquired the ability to cure bites by white ants, scorpion, black-widow spider, and rattlesnake. These animals all derived from the body of giant Sky Rattlesnake when he was decapitated on Avikwame mountain. This narrative of how these four animals acquired their harmful powers is followed by exposition of how they exercised them and how the

informant counteracted them. This is professional
rattlesnake-shaman's theory and practice.

But the narrative of Sky Rattlesnake's ambushing
and decapitation is current myth, which Mohave lay-
men all knew something about, and it is in turn preceded by an account of Matavilya and his death and
funeral—for which Sky-Rattlesnake was blamed and
killed—and which formed part of the Mohave origins
myth. In the Handbook, the information was cited as
an illustration of shamanistic beliefs, and the intro-
ductory general myth was therefore given only in
condensed summary. This general myth is reproduced
here in full, as written down in 1908, and its com-
parability with myths No. 7 (UC-AR 11:1, pp. 50-68)
and 15 above is indicated in Table 1 above (in the
discussion of No. 9, Origins). On the other hand, the
informant's shamanistic account is not repeated here,
except so far as needed as a framework to make
intelligible matter omitted from the more generalized
publication of 1925 but now presented; or as reinter-
pretation of data published then.

The Narrative

1. I begin to tell of where Matavilya died, at
Ha'avalypo. Matavilya made a dark house, with posts
and rafters; Matavilya and Frog (Hanyiko) did that;
all the tribes were there inside that house.

2. Frog said: "He is my father." Frog was a woman
doctor. She made Matavilya become sick and die: she
took away his "body" (soul, shadow).

3. Before Matavilya died, he had said: "I am going
to die." There were six there who heard him say that,
six kinds of Singings: Long Tumanpa, Short Tumanpa,
Chuhueche, Salt, Avaly'unu [of the Yuma] and Nyavaóók.
These six were men. When Matavilya died, they began
to sing their six kinds of songs.

4. After Matavilya died, Mastamho said to Gopher
(Takse): "Get wood to burn him with." So Gopher sank
underground, in a deep hole. There he made four logs;
he made them out of his own saliva.

5. Then Mastamho said: "I am going to burn him.
I want a trench, with wood above it for burning. I
want someone to dig the trench. He called one, like a
wasp, Amaṭ-kepísara: "You dig it." So that one dug;
he threw out the earth west and north and east, and
south.[33] Then he said: "I want a name for digging it:
I call myself Amaṭ-kepisara."

6. Mastamho said: "There is no fire. In the west,
across the desert, is a great mountain, Fire Mountain
(Avi-a'auve); that [Mountain] is a doctor, and there is

[33]Clockwise circuit beginning in W.

fire there all the time. You get fire there," he said[34]
and pointed at Coyote. So Coyote went off west.

7. After he was traveling, Blu-fly, θily'ahmó-kavasú,
a woman, plucked a shred from the right side of her
bark skirt, rolled it four times [on her thigh? between
her palms?], and made fire.

8. Then they took arrowweeds and put them at each
corner of the trench and logs and lit these. Salt did
that: his name is Aθ'í-meqáyere,[35] because he lit it.
While the fire burned, all the tribes stood off from it,
all about, and watched.

9. Matavilya had said: "When I die, you will know
nothing. You can go where you want to—I don't know
where. Perhaps you will go and turn into rock, or
water, or wood: I don't know." That's what he said.
Now some of them said: "I am going east." Some said:
"I am going north"; some: "south," some: "west."[36]

10. But we, the Mohave, did not go away; we stayed
here. The others all went off, but we stayed, we Mohave.
We stayed till the body was burned to ashes, and the
ashes were covered with earth. The peoples that went
west, south, east, north[37] did not cry much; they cried
a little and went off and did not see the ashes, but the
Mohave stayed and kept crying and crying until the
fire was burned out and covered up: only the Mohave.

11. K-amáy-avé-te, Sky-Rattlesnake, watched the
burning too. When he saw it all covered over, he went
off. There was no ocean then. It had rained and there
was a lake from that, but no ocean. Sky Rattlesnake
went there, beyond the Cocopa, that was where he went.

12. Mastamho was still there, [at Ha'av'ulypo]. The
house was gone, but the posts still showed. He thought
about it. "What can I do so there will be no house, no
posts? I want to remove them so no one can see anything. Well, I will go north," he said. And he went
north and gave the place four names: Aha-nye-atšpátš-
keve, Ha-móxa, Aha-kwa-yereyérve, and Kwavasú-
vilyepátše."[38] He drew a staff out of his body. He
plunged it in the ground, and when he drew it out,
water flowed. A boat came with the water: he called
it kaθ'ukyé. He walked ahead, and the water and the
boat followed him, zigzagging. He kept going like that
until he came far south beyond the Cocopa [to the
Gulf of California]. Then he returned and went to
Avikwame mountain. As he came he saw the river
running that he had made in the north.[39]

[34]There appears to be no such actual mountain; it is evidently invented ad hoc to be rid of Coyote who is mistrusted.
[35]"Salt-meqayere," recorded above in 12:1 as Aθ'i-meka'ere,
oldest of the four Salt brothers. Cf. 19:48, note 26, below.
[36]Nearly anticlockwise circuit beginning in E.
[37]Anticlockwise circuit beginning in N.
[38]The first three compound names begin with the word for
water, the fourth with that for blue or green (havasu).
[39]Riddance of Matavilya's ashes is not mentioned; and the
house posts, petrified, still stand at Ha'av'ulypo.

13. He had made the earth low in the south, and the water ran there, ran for four days. Mastamho said: "In four days there will be much water. It will rise and cover the mountains; there will be no earth showing."

14. Mastamho got four tribes together: the Mohave, Walapai, Chemehuevi, Yavapai. He made himself taller where the tribes stood and gathered up two or three men at a time in his arm and set them on his shoulders, his head, his arms, to keep them above the flood. The water rose up on him half way up; he "stirred" it with his hands, and it fell and went back down to the ocean; it made the ocean.

15. And he made that great high mountain, Avikwame. The water could not cover that. It was what he stood on when the water rose. Now he left the four tribes there, on the mountain. It was dry land. Seeds grew, and there were mesquites, willows, cottonwoods, all kinds were growing.[40]

16. Mastamho said: "I will build a house on this mountain: I will make a young house, av'á humark." This was just a shade roof, not like the round house [with sides and sand roof] where Matavilya had died. Mastamho said: "Matavilya died, but he was not knowing. He only told some things. He made [song-cycle] singers. I do not know about that; but I do know this: I want some men to be curers. I will tell about that. You listen to what I am going to say and you will be able to do that, to cure." So he made some men to become doctors.

17. Mastamho said: "I have built the house. It is finished. Now I want someone to go downriver to get the man there, Kamayave·te, to come, because the house is done." So he sent Quail woman: she was to tell him: "Matavilya is sick and wants you to come and doctor him." Quail went, but Kamayave·te answered: "He is dead already"; and she returned.

18. Then Mastamho sent Quail man to say the same. Kamayave·te said again: "Why, he is dead. I saw him. That is why I came here." He meant that he had not liked to stay around Matavilya's corpse.

19. Mastamho sent Aθa-kwe'ataye[41] to say the same, but Kamayave·te's answer was the same.

20. Then he sent Spider, Halyto·ṭa, who said: "I will bring him." He was on top of the river, and he ran down on that.[42] When he returned, he said: "He is coming."

21. Quail man said: "I will kill him." Quail woman said: "No, I will kill him." They had a kimatše, something like an ax.[43] When Kamayave·te put his head inside the house, they cut it off: Quail woman did it.

22. Kamayave·te had said: "I know they will kill me: they will cut my neck. But my tears will fall, and the sweat will come out of my body and drip onto the ground, and from those my body will be restored. I shall go there and be killed, my head will be cut off, but I shall become alive again."

23. Now his head rolled down eastward to the river from Avikwame, but the body was part inside and part outside the house. The body tried to return to life. Wind came out of it. It was trying to stand up and live; he tried and could not. He rolled about trying to make hard wind and rain to revivify him; he was not yet dead. But when the sun was beginning to descend, he died. He died there and his body dried up.

24. But the head, below to the east, rolled along the bottom of the river, back downstream to where it came from. It tried to bring Kamayave·te to life again. It could not do that, but it did something. It became like a snake in the ocean, a snake with legs. It lives there now, but I do not know its name.

25. Nobody buried the body. Its blood had dripped, sweat had run out, the glue in the body joints dropped on the ground. The blood made little round red eggs, which were alive, and these became rattlesnakes.

26. Four kinds came from Kamayave·te's body. Atsyeqa, the little yellowish ant [white ant, termite?] came from the eggs [of the liquid in the joints?] and was the oldest. The hot sweat became Scorpion, Mení·se, the second in age. Hálytoṭa, black-widow spider, came from the foamlike fat—not flesh—under the skin. The youngest, Rattlesnake, Avé·, came from the blood that dropped on the ground when Kamayave·te's head was cut off.

[40]Flicker's wet tail feathers are not mentioned. Food plants just grow, in this version, instead of being made for human beings as in other versions.
[41]Aθa-kwe'ataye may be meant for θonoθakwe'atai, Yanaθa-kwe-'ataye, or Tonaθaqwataye of 1:35, 3:4, 5:6 (UC-AR 11:1, pp. 9, 29, 43).

[42]Spider is later mentioned as one of the four born from the substances of Sky Rattlesnake. Specifically, Halytoṭa is the poisonous black-widow spider, but the present messenger may be a different insect with a similar name. His running on the river surface may indicate him as the water-boatman bug; and (a)ha-lye means "on or in water." Possibly I misheard here the more familiar word Halytoṭa, black-widow spider, for the Hal(y)kutāṭa of 15:14, 15, above, who lived in the sea to the south, killed Kwayu for his cannibalism, and was killed in revenge by Mastamho in his own stockade which he had built of Kwayu's down-feathers; see also note 20 to No. 6B (UC-AR 11:1, p. 48) and notes 33-35 to No. 15, above. The suggested etymology would be "in the water staff," and the animal perhaps be a crayfish or prawn. Note that its later home was, like Sky Rattlesnake's, in the southern ocean (Gulf of California).
[43]From Spanish hacha, ax? Some knowledge of steel axes (with which alone a neck could be severed at one blow) must have reached the Mohave soon after 1770 as a result of the Spanish expeditions from Sonora to settle Alta California passing through Yuma territory.

27. The people there were in four rows, six, ten, or twenty in a row. Mastamho told them to dance: "Pound the earth with your feet!" Then he taught them the names of three sicknesses: hayekwire, which is also the name of a species of rattlesnake; isumá, "dreaming"; itšhulyuye, referring to beaver. He would say to a man: "Can you say that word?" If the man said he could not repeat it, Mastamho did not want him. If a man could pronounce it, Mastamho wanted him for a doctor. Some of them would say: "Hayekwire" or "Isuma," and he would tell them: "You have it right." Four times he taught them.

28. While he was teaching, the four that were to come out of the eggs that dripped from Kamayave·te were underground, to the north, not yet hatched; Mastamho heard them talking as he stood there. They emerged to the west and sat there. They were doctors, but he did not teach them to be so. They came from Kamayave·te who was a doctor, out of his blood and body parts, and it is from that that they are doctors.

This ends the general myth underlying Achora Hanyava's exposition of his personal shamanistic powers. This narrative will now be discussed, after which some unpublished additional data and interpretations of his shamanism will be presented.

Discussion of the Myth
or Dream

This version of world origins is on the whole closest to No. 9, above. It is briefer on Matavilya, but not as brief as is No. 15, above, or wholly lacking like No. 7 (UC-AR 11:1, pp. 50-68). It is longer on Sky-Rattlesnake, because it is ultimately on him that rattlesnake doctors' power rests; Nos. 7 and 15, not being concerned with that power, simply omit the entire episode. Again, this version agrees with No. 9 in largely lacking the culture institutings by Mastamho and his delegates which make up the body of No. 7, but which No. 15 also treats scantily except for the institution of warfare.

The principal specific differences and variations are as follows.

The six personified song cycles present at Matavilya's death in Sky-Rattlesnake paragraph 3 are enumerated above by the same narrator also in Chuhueche 13:3 but mentioned as a group by no other informant. They are in contrast with Mastamho's teaching of doctor shamans in 7:57 (UC-AR 11:1, p. 61), and above 9:32, 36, and 16G:27.

In paragraph 4, it is Gopher who makes wood to cremate Matavilya with, as against Raccoon who brings it (and Badger who digs the cremation trench) in 7:1 (UC-AR 11:1, p. 52); above in 13:7 (same informant as in 16G:4), it is Gopher again.

In paragraph 5, as above in 13:9, the insect Amaṭkepisara digs not the post holes for Mastamho's house as in 7:22 (UC-AR 11:1, p. 56), but the trench for Matavilya's cremation.

Coyote's leaping over the short men Badger and Raccoon to steal Matavilya's heart (7:4, UC-AR 11:1, p. 53) is omitted from the present narrative, though paragraph 6 mentions his being sent off for fire, perhaps in precaution against his greed. Again 13:13 above agrees with the omission.

In paragraph 10, the Mohave are the last tribe to go off, because they mourn longest; in other versions, they are kept longest by Mastamho to be taught more, No. 7 (UC-AR 11:1, pp. 50-68), and No. 9, above.

Making of the river, 12, is much as in other origins, even to a boat, here called kaθ'ukye, coming out with the water; but Mastamho leads this zigzag instead of riding and tipping it as in 7:12 (UC-AR 11:1, pp. 54-55) and 9:19 above.

In 14, 15 the mountain remaining uncovered by the flood is Avikwame instead of Akoke-humi (9:20 above), and the tribes on it are the Mohave plus three desert tribes, instead of all tribes. He lowers the flood by "stirring" it with his hands instead of motioning with them (9:20).

The messengers sent for Sky-Rattlesnake in 18-21 and his executioner differ from those named in other versions.

These variations are about what we have learned to expect in repeated versions of tales of American Indian tribes, except where there is institutionalized teaching of origins.

Additional Shamanistic Data
from the Informant

While the narrative in paragraphs 1-28 is straight narative myth, the informant's account of his personal shamanistic powers is an interwoven tissue of Mohave myth, of his personal beliefs and dreams, and of statements of what he did in practicing his cures. The Mohave just have no purely shamanistic beliefs independent of their tribal mythology. Their individual shamanism is deeply imbedded in their general mythology as they all more or less know, narrate, or sing this. The distinction between the preceding and the present section accordingly is actually not a difference between myth and shamanism, but is the difference between super-individual narrative belief and world view having no specific applicability to activity as such, on the one hand, and individually held beliefs validating a set of practices applied to cure poisonous bites, on the other hand. At least half of the exemplification of "shamanism" that follows consists of myth-type narrative not experienced by or shared with other Mohave.

These data supplement and extend those printed in the Handbook, pages 776-777, and include some new or revised interpretations.

<u>a</u>. After the four poisonous ones emerged and set off to the west, Mastamho stood before the people and taught them. Four times he stopped, and each time the four had grown larger. The fourth time, they stood up. They were doctors by themselves; Mastamho did not make them so. In fact, what he was teaching the people was to dance, using the right leg and arm, whereas doctoring was with the left hand, which must not be used in dance singing.

<u>b</u>. When Mastamho led the people from Avi-kuta-parve on the river to Avi-hamóka, Double Peak in the Tehachapi Mountains, he went by way of Aha-kuvílye, Paiute ("stinking") Spring, and Avi-waθá, the New York Mountains. The four traveled separately, parallel to him.

<u>c</u>. At Avi-hamoka, Mastamho made a metate for Tortoise, Kapéta, a woman, to grind Kwaθepilye and maselye'aye seeds. He made the metate roundish, not squared as it is today;[44] and the Paiute and Chemehuevi were to use it, for their seeds. Because Tortoise ground for them, these tribes now eat tortoises, but the Mohave do not.

<u>d</u>. Bittern, or Blue Heron, Atsqeuqa, came to see the seed grinding. He stood behind Tortoise and said: "A good-looking woman is grinding." She looked back and smiled. Then everybody said: "She is married now." And Bittern gave himself another name: Pahu-tšatša-yamasam-tahu'irve, Food-white-tahu'irve.[45]

<u>e</u>. The Handbook account tells how Rattlesnake painted himself with cloud and wind. This was for war, which he liked for its killing, and which Mastamho instituted, with a boundary against the southern tribes at Koskilye, Monument Mts.[46] Rattlesnake was leader

in the first foray, and arranged for a dance at Tehachapi over two scalps taken; it was after this that he often thought of war and wanted to bite (kill) someone. "I like him and want him with me as a friend," is what he says then. But he has to ask permission of Tehachapi Peak; and only if the mountain assents is there no cure and the bitten man will die and his shadow come to stay with Rattlesnake; if the mountain is silent, the man will recover. This gathering in of shamanistic victims, and the authority of personified mountains, have been discussed in my Ethnographic Interpretations 1-6 (UC-AAE 47:2, 1957).[47]

Rattlesnake is the youngest but most virulent of the four, and presumably is dealt with first for that reason.

<u>f</u>. It was Buzzard, Asei, who scalped one of the two foes.[48] It was after the scalp dance at Tehachapi that Rattlesnake, till then a man, transformed into a snake. He said: "I am happy. I eat wind and dust and cloud. I can live on them: they make me fat."

<u>g</u>. Another one who transformed then is Kamay-huekatš-hwunitšve, who became the little fly with two feathers projecting from its tail, which dances in swarms toward sunset in the desert. The scalps were kept there at Tehachapi and turned into rocks.

<u>h</u>. As for Spider, if there is no confusion in the record of the text, he must get permission to kill from "the chief of the Rattlesnakes" (<u>sic</u>), Ampota-nyamaθam-tamakwa, at Lyehuta (otherwise unmentioned), north of Avikwame.

If Spider bites without permission, the man lives and Spider dies. His shadow, full of breath and legless, becomes a round thing called "dust-yara," which rolls in the clouds and makes rain. This whole set of beliefs, like almost all the Sky-Rattlesnake myth, is full of meteorological references.

Spider, Halytoṭa, is represented as dangerous enough to make clear that he is the black-widow species.

<u>i</u>. The account also mentions another Rattlesnake and another Spider that went off to one side, so that the informant did not dream about them. Both have to do with war: Brave-warrior-Spider, Halytoṭa-kwanami, causes diarrhea; and brave men rather than shamans dream of him. The other is a "short rattlesnake," called Ave-hákθara, who was also a brave man.

<u>j</u>. Scorpion grew out of Sky Rattlesnake's sweat, which is harmless, so Scorpion now lacks power to kill. His four roads are underground, and at the ends of them he set Firefly, Tarantula, and two other spiders,

---

[44] The Mohave and Yuma are the only historic tribes in California that used a neatly rectangular metate. It is not known whether they devised the shape after they got metal tools or took it over from the Pueblos earlier.

[45] This episode recurs in 7:91 (UC-AR 11:1, p. 65) and 16D, above (with Doves in place of Tortoise).

[46] In the full text, this boundary is specified as running from Ahpe-δave (a flat mountain, at SW end of Mohave Mountains) and Ta'ha (a bell-shaped peak E of main range of Turtle Mountains) on the W, through Koskilye, to Malyho-

ha ("water pipe," UC-AR 11:2, Map 2, no. 26, E, and p. 142) and Kumaδiδe on the E. The southern enemies are attacked at Ahpe-xwelyeve (mountain S of Blythe Valley); Aha-kwaθo'ilye (Laguna Palo Verde); Hu'ulye-sama (unplaced, possibly in Cocopa country).

[47] UC-PAAE 47: 226-233, 1957.

[48] Buzzard is scalped, also in 11:5 above.

who own winds and clouds as breath, which make bitter rain—more meteorology. Scorpion asked authorization to kill from four rattlesnakes, but they remained silent. These four were first, "Two-persons," Pa-havike, or Hopamily-kwa-havike, at Aví-haly-kwa'ámpa;[49] second, "Blue-tooth," Hiδó-kwe-havasú, at Kutšuvave;[50] third, Asétime, the kind of rattlesnake now known as Ave-kwetšitšukyave, in his house Ava-axwai-tšivauk ("house-war-put") in Monument or Whipple Mts., Koskilye; and fourth, he went to Aví-vatáye, the Riverside Mts.[51] SW of Parker. From there, Scorpion returned to Tehachapi.

k. The oldest of the four products of Sky Rattlesnake, Atšyéka, kills less directly than the others. His roads, like Scorpion's, are also underground; and he sank down to Amaṭa-hiwa, earth's heart, and there his shadow or soul is now, as Night-body, Ku-tinyam-himaṭa, whereas what he transformed to came up again as Atšyeka, who has his house in the heart or roots of dead fallen trees.

---

[49] "Lie prone on water mountain (or 'rock')," in Mohave Valley N of Needles, UC-AR 11:2, Map 1, H, W, and p. 140.

[50] A dozen miles W of the river, at the W end of "Chemehuevis Mountains," which are sometimes included in "Mohave range."

[51] UC-AR 11:2, Map 2, 32, mistakenly shown there E (instead of W) of river. The four rattlesnakes live in four mountains.

Then he saw himself, yellow and bright, and called himself Shining Body. [This suggests that Atšyeka is a termite, a "white ant," especially as he is expressly differentiated from the large and small ants, Tšamaδulye and Hanepuke.]

1. Atšyeqa attacks not by biting with his body but with his underground shadow, his night body. [Termites are harmless.] This shadow of his goes through a vein to the person's heart, eats that, and the man begins to die. The cure is by blocking his road with a very fine earth, amaṭa-napáka, put on the patient's body. [It is clear that this is a material treatment against a psychic danger, whereas the three other animals are actually poisonous.]

However, the informant evidently also confused termites and ants, because he spoke of Atšyeqa gathering the seeds of cultivated plants and semidomesticated ones (aksamta, ankika, akataye), which he carried home, rolled four times, and thus turned them into more atšyeqa. "You can see him carrying the seeds home." [This reference is to harvesting ants; termites do not travel above ground or collect seeds; they live by eating wood, within which they live. But the confusion is easy; many of us who are not entomologists look upon white ants as ants.]

Narrative 17
CANE REPEATED

CIRCUMSTANCES
OF RECORDING

In 1908, on February 21, 24, 25, 27, I obtained at
Needles, from Tšiyêre-kavasūk or Blue Bird, 140
phonograph cylinders of songs of Ahtá'-amalya'é, the
narrative of which he had narrated to me four years
earlier, as I finally published it as the first one of
Seven Mohave Myths on pages 4 to 23 of UC-AR 11:1.
Leslie Wilbur interpreted for us in 1908. I did not
attempt to secure every one of the 182 songs that
Blue Bird had mentioned in 1904; but I did record at
least one song out of every group or block ("station"
or "paragraph") of narrative, and often more. Nor did
I hold the singer to his exact listing of 1904. Instead,
I explained and he agreed to what I wanted: a represen-
tative selection of the Cane songs, each identified as
to its place in the story. This involved his telling, for
each group of songs, at least an outline of the paragraph of the prose narrative to which the group of
songs related, or a reference to an identifying incident.
Particularly did I try to secure the place at which the
song groups were supposed to have been sung in the
story: this as a convenient identification.

This procedure was calculated to give me not only
a record of most of the Cane songs but also a somewhat reduced outline version of the narrative. The plan
worked well, except that instead of 104 song groups, I
obtained in 1908 mention of only 76, with some attendant
variation and addition of narrative contents. The shrink-
age was caused by omissions due to oversight (like the
getting of the fourth wife in 17b and 18a, UC-AR 11:1,
p. 7, of the original version), or to suppression of
minor incidents (as of 85, 88, UC-AR 11:1, p. 16), or
deliberate denials in 1908 that songs accompanied
important passages of narrative (such as 102-104,
UC-AR 11:1, p. 19, the end of the tale).

On the whole, however, the later and shorter listing
followed the order of the older one and confirmed it
as to narrative content. This was particularly evident
in the long travelogue or itinerary constituting section
G (paragraphs 38-68, UC-AR 11:1, pp. 10-11), where
incidents are sparse but place names abundant.

However, it has seemed worth while to compare the
two versions in detail, though as compactly as possible,
as a study of how versions can vary in the mind of the

same narrator. Yellak I and II (narrative 14 above)
are from different individuals, and incidentally differ
far more from each other than do Blue Bird's two
Cane renditions. I therefore give, first, a paragraph-
by-paragraph outline comparison or concordance of
story content in Cane I and II, or narratives 1 and
17, or 1904 and 1908; and, second, the full recorded
text of fifteen paragraphs of the latter, where this
departs more significantly than usual from the earlier
version.

CONCORDANCE OF CANE I*
AND II (TALES 1 AND 17)

1a (0 songs). At Avikwame: Kamayavêta killed. — II.
Lacking.

1b (4 songs). At house there: parts of the house.
— II:1 (4 songs). At Tšehotave, Kapet-tuδumve:
house at Ha'avulypo (?). [These 2 places were
mentioned in 1904 (as Tšohatave and δokupíta-
tuδūmpe) in UC-AR 11:1, note 97, p. 18, as where
the boy hero stood at the east end of Avi-mota
when he destroyed his foes by fire lightning.]

2 (3 songs). N a bit: Groundsquirrel. — II:2 (2 songs).
At Avi-kutaparve. No Groundsquirrel. — II:1a (3
songs). Hunt, reach out and "take" mayu sacks (cf.
I:5) and baskets.

3 (2 songs). N a bit: Rat. — II:3 (3 songs). Rat.

4 (3 songs). Rat eaten, house built of saliva. — II:4
(3 songs). At Tšehotave, Kapet-tuδumve, Ava-tševau-
vunuk, Korenyeva'ím: build house.

5 (1 song). Hunt, "take" mayu sacks, uncle Yellow-Pima
joins. — II. Lacking, except mayu in 1a.

6 (1 song). Bet arrows. — II. Lacking.

7a (0 songs). Corn taken from SE, wheat from NE.
— II. Lacking.

7b, 8, 9, 10 (1 song each). Tšese'ilye (or his daughter)
in W has hwetše-hwetše bird, brs. go, quarrel over
her, y. br. gets her, brings back home. — II:5 (4
songs). To Ivθe-kupaye, y. br. gets girl, mocking
bird (?).

11, 12 (2 songs each). Sun's daughter in E has bird,
cock (masohwaṭ in 1:86), y. br. gets her, has 2
wives. — II:6 (said 2 songs, sang 4). E, Sun's

*Cane I is UC-AR 11:1, pp. 4-23.

[93]

daughter, Masohwat is nyahaṭ, her pet, y. br. gets
her, o. br. Sunayūmoṭem has nothing.

13 (2 songs). On way home, about the stars. — II:7
(1 song). On way, stars.

14 (1 song). New wife grinds corn. — II:8 (1 song).
She wears beads.

15, 16 (2 songs, 1 song). N for girl with yellowhammer,
o. br. gets. — II:9 (3 songs). To N, yellowhammer,
o. br. gets.

17, 18a (1 song). S, hotokoro bird, o. br. gets. — II.
Lacking, probably oversight.

18b, 19 (1 song each). Go for cane, find it. — II:10,
11 (1 song, 2 songs). Same.

20, 21, 22, 23 (1, 2, 2, 1 songs each). Quarrel for
butt, o. br. makes knife, they struggle over cane,
return. — II. Lacking. [Not in I:] II: 12, 12a (2
songs each). Marking cane for flute.

24, 25 (1 song each). O. br. makes y. br. ill, spoils
his birds. — II:13 (said 4 songs, then 1). Y. br.
sick, spoils own birds. (See below.)

26 (1 song). Nume-peta arrives for the death, sends
for "tim-ahutši" wood. — II:14 (1 song). Kwatšya-
kwatšya and Tinyam-kwespi sent to Avi-mota for
"ahutšye" brush for bedding for dying man.

27, 28 (1 song each). Y. br. tells of his bones, o. br.
and Nume-peta cut out his bones, kill him, wives
cut hair. — II:15, 16 (1 song each). Y. br. speaks,
dies, wives cut hair.

29 (1 song). Sun's d. returns home, Tšese'ilye pregnant,
unborn boy sings in her. — II:17 (1 song). Tšese'ilye
goes home, boy sings father's song in Sun's daughter.

30 (1 song). Makes rain to have privacy at birth. — II:
20 [sic] (1 song). Same.

31 (1 song). Emerges. — II:18 (1 song). Is born, sings
of that.
— [Not in I:] II:19 (1 song). Sings of house and its
parts.

32 (1 song). Spared because disguised as girl. — II:21.
Baby names Pukehane, Nume-peta, Kwatšā-kwatšā,
Tinyām-kwaθpil when they come to inspect him.

33 (1 song). Suckled as if a girl. — II:22 (1 song).
Mother quiets baby singing to it as girl, about
cradle.

34, 36, 37 (2, 1, 2 songs). Shinny played with f.'s
knee-cap, boy turns self into halye'anekítše lizard
and steals it, knocks it as fire ball W into mts.,
kills people there. — II:24, 25a (1 song). Similar.
(See below.)

35 (2 songs). Boy sends his mother off with coals in
pot, then grieves for her. — II:23 (3 songs). M.
leaves with coals, boy thinks of her as tired.

37, 38, 39 (0, 1, 2 songs). Boy runs to Avi-kutaparve,
crosses river on 4 piles of sand, goes down to

Qara'êrve, sleeps, hears tinyam-hwarehware insect
sing. — II:25b, 26 (2 songs). Same. His name is
Ahta-kesu'me.

40 (1 song). Travels to Selye'aya-kumitše. — II:27.
(1 song). Same.

41 (2 songs). At Hanyo-kumasθeve, frightened by rattlesnake. — II:28 (2 songs). Same.

42. (5 songs). Wears snake as belt, sees wildcats at
Kamahnulye. — I:29 (2 songs). Same.
— [Not in I:] II:30 (2 songs). Wild cats run off to
Avi-veskwi.

43 (1 song). Met by horsefly at Aha-kuminye. — II:31
(1 song). Horseflies.

44 (1 song). At Hotūrveve, hummingbird. — II:32 (1
song). Same.

45 (1 song). S to Sampuly-kuvare. — II:33. (2 songs).
Sings of sand there.

46, 47 (1 song each). Clouds at Sacramento Wash and
on way to Gourd Mt. — II:34 (1 song), 37 (2 songs).
Clouds at Atsqaqa; sees Gourd Mt.

48, 49 (1 song, 5 songs). S to Screwbean Spring on
Akoke-humí. — II:35 (5 songs). Same.
— [Not in I:] II:36 (2 songs). Not getting tired on
way. (For 37, see I:46, 47).

50 (2 songs). To petrified men at Ahwaṭa-kwimātce.
— II:38 (2 songs). Same.

51 (2 songs). Ahtoṭa wolfberry "grapes" at Kuhultoṭve.
— II:39 (2 songs). At Kohwiltotve, no ahoṭa mentioned.

52 (1 song). At Bill Williams Fork, meets badger.
— II:40 (1 song). Same place, meets Numeta.
— [Not in I:] II:41 (1 song), to Halye-motate, sandy,
by river.

53 (1 song). To Avi-su'ukwilye, jackrabbit. — II:42
(1 song). Same.

54 (3 songs). S to Avi-melyehwêke. — II:43, 44 (3 songs,
1 song): Sees, reaches Avi-melyehwêke.

55 (2 songs). Sleeps, on to Avi-hupo. — II:45 (2 songs).
To Avi-kuhavak, sleep not mentioned.

56 (1 song). To river at Selye'aya-'ita. — II:46 (1 song).
Same.

57 (3 songs). Crosses on sand piles to Kuvukwilye.
— II:47 (2 songs). Same.

58 (1 song). S to Aha-kumiθe. — II:48 (2 songs). Same.

59 (1 song). To Amaṭa-hiya, Earth-mouth. — II:49
(1 song). Same.

60 (1 song). To Tôske. — II:50 (1 song). To "Toske
rock."

61 (1 song). To Yelak-ime, Goose-foot. — II:51 (1 song).
Same.

62 (2 songs). Near Yuma, sees cane. — II:52 (1 song).
Same (Kutcan-eva).

63 (1 song). Past Cocopa Mts., Enpeθo'auve. — II:53
(1 song). Same (Anpeθauve).

64 (3 songs). To Gulf of Calif., sees surf, crane.
— II:54 (3 songs). Same, thinks crane is eagle.

65, 66 (2 songs each). E, sea shells, ducks. — II:55
(1 song). Same.

67 (2 songs). Hatompa'auve in lagoon. — II:56 (2 songs).
Same. (See below.)

68 (1 song). NE to A'ĭ-kumeθĭ catsclaw trees. — II:57
(1 song). E to same.

69 (5 songs). Finds tracks of Sun's 4 wives. — II:58
(5 songs). Same; he sings their names (cf. I:71).

70 (2 songs). Finds house, hides, blows himself out as
a bit of cane, leaves shadow indoors. — II:59, 60
(1 song each). Finds house, sleeps, fears birds are
enemies, whirlwind conceals him outdoors.

71 (2 songs). Women return, oldest warns of him; he
calls their names (cf. II:58), — II:61 (2 songs).
Shadow indoors, return, warns others.

72, 73, 74 (2, 2, 1 songs). Y. sis. finds him rotten,
o. revives, feeds him tobacco. — II:61 (2 songs).
Same except tobacco.

75 (4 songs). Women warn him of husband Kwayū.
— II. Lacking.

76 (2 songs). Kwayu comes, fails to kill boy, gives
him tobacco. — II:61 (2 songs). [see also above].
Sun comes home, refuses to give boy tobacco.

77, 78 (2 songs, 1 song). Kwayū leaves, Sun comes,
wants gamble, sees beads hidden in boy's hair;
loses 4 women, then belongings in sky-sack, then
own body; rises to escape, hurls heat, boy matches
with ice, turns Sun double (sun dog). — II:62, 63
(1 song, 2 songs). Sun now gives tobacco, wants
gamble, sees hidden kwinkalaka "baby clothes";
loses 4 wives, belongings, own body; rises to
escape, boy reaches E for light to burn sky, Sun
checks with ice [note inversion from I]; Sun becomes double sun dog; boy puts winnings in sack,
ridicules won pet beaver. (See below.)

79, 80 (2 songs each). Boy inspects winnings: beaver,
scorpion, bees, mirror, sees he is ugly. — II:64
(1 song). In mirror sees he is ugly.

81, 82a, 82b (4, 0, 2 songs). Boy dives in won pool to
N W S E, now beautiful, reaches N E (S) W for
apparel; the 4 women successively find, embrace
him, carry home; he prefers oldest for not reject-
ing him before; morning starts E, thinks wives
encumbrance, makes rain to kill them. — II:65 (2
songs). Dives 4 times, beautiful, reaches N W E
for talykδpa apparel [nothing about women enamored];
morning starts E to mother, wives encumber, makes
rain to kill. (See below.)

83, 84 (1 song each). Repents, brings back sun, laughs
at mud in their sandals. — II:66 (2 songs). Same.

85 (1 song). Wives wear shell frog-gorgets. — II.
Lacking.

86 (2 songs). Mother's Masohwaṭ bird flies to meet
him. — II:67 (2 songs). Same.

87 (2 songs). Reunion with mother. — II:68 (2 songs).
Same.

88 (1 song). He tells her what happened. — II. Lacking.

89, 90, 91 (1, 2, 2 songs). Mother calls wives d-in-law;
boy questions mother's father about lightning; goes
E for 4 lightning canes, gets in hole, splits them
with nail. — II:69 (2 songs). M. gives food to wives
to grind; boy asks about lightning cane, goes off E
at night with blankets, turns to Thunder, cuts and
covers cane, returns, tells incredulous mother.
(See below.)

92 (1 song). Travels N to war on father's killers kin.
— II:70, 71 (1 song each). Similar. (See below.)

93, 94 (1, 2 songs). Meets half-brother, they identify
their relationship. — II:72 (2 songs). Similar.
(See below.)

95, 96 (1, 2 songs). They mourn together, call up
their dead father. — II:73 (2 songs). Similar.
(See below.)

97 (1 song). Leave f. in ground, go N to Selye'aya-
kumítše, see f.'s scalp, dust. — II:74 (1 song).
Same. (See below.)

98, 99, 100 (2, 2, 1 songs). F.'s o. br. sends
Kwatšakwatša as messenger to Qara'êrva, tells
terms of contest; Lizard warns them; uncle Yellow-
Pima warns them. — II:75 (2 songs). Same, except
to Avi-kutaparve; and Yellow-Pima omitted. (See
below.)

101 (1 song). Lizard wins first contest with scalp,
opponents challenge boy to cane dice. — II:76 (2
songs). Same. (See below.)

102, 103, 104 (2, 10, 2 songs). Boy's lightning cane
stronger, burns up opponents on Avi-mota, fire
stopped at Iδo-kuva'ire by ghost-arrow plant; with
lightning cane he turns m., 4 wives into Pleiades,
half-brother into Snipe, Yellow-Pima into Soθêrqe
bird; he first wants be Kwayū meteor, but goes
into rock Mekoaṭa by river below Mukiampeve.
— II:77 (apparently no songs). Similar except in
details. (See below.)

EXCERPTS OF VARIANT PASSAGES FROM CANE II
(References to 1 are to UC-AR 11:1, pp. 4-23)

II-13. [Cf. 1:24, 25.] Home again. To bed, each
with wives. Younger brother becomes sick; calls the
morning, makes it day. He pulls the feathers off the
birds that the wives had (from before their marriages);
they fall to the ground. [In version 1:25, the older
brother partly skins five named birds kept by younger.]
The younger, leaning on a cane, asks how the cane

can be marked. They reach eastward to take something to mark with. The younger gets darkness (Tinyam), which does not show on the cane, he is angry, throws it away to the north. This is what was making him sick. The older reaches and gets white (morning) "from takurave" and paints his cane with that. The marks are tulituli. (Said 4 songs, sang 1, then said 1 only).

II-24. [Cf. 1:34, 36, 37.] The baby slept. In the morning, young men crowded around, playing shinny. The baby tried to take away their shinny ball and run back with it to where he was born; they tried to kill him and were close behind. He started to knock it N, E, S (sunwise circuit), did not like it, then struck it W. There was loud thunder, the people were scared, and some (2, 3, 'havĭk, hamŏk') were killed. He did that because his father had been killed. (1 song).

II-56. [Cf. 1:67.] He followed the ocean beach S, saw a great Hatŏmpa'auve, and sang of that. It is like a horse, very large, has 4 legs, ears. [Possibly a cayman, which occurs in rivers of the middle Gulf of California.] (2 songs, the first containing the word lomelom, raise head.)

II-62. [Cf. 1:77, 78.] Sun gave him a large clay pipe, full; the boy smoked it at one draft. Then Sun said he wanted to play him hoop and poles for their apparel. The boy said he had nothing. Sun said he saw the boy was carrying his kwinkalāka "baby clothes" inside his body (a string over one shoulder, under other); he could bet that. So the boy agreed. They played, and he won; then he won Sun's four wives, and Sun wanted to bet his body: "if you win you can kill me"; but the boy said, "That would be no use to me." Nevertheless, they played; and soon Sun had only one more cast before he lost his body. They threw, Sun lost, the boy went to kill him, Sun fled, leaped to the sky. So the boy reached east and took light to burn the sky with, Sun threw down ice, put out his fire. Then the boy clubbed him; he sang of that. (1 song.) — 63. Sun became double (anyatš havik, two-sun, sun-dog); everyone looked, all tribes saw him, called him two-sun. The boy took all he had won and put it in a small sack. And he had won a beaver: he made fun of that. (2 songs).

II-65. [Cf. 1:81, 82.] The boy went to the little lake [he had won], dived in to the north, south, east, west [sic], and each time he came out with longer hair, until it reached to his hips, and he looked fine; and he called a wind to dry him. Then he reached his hand north and took beautiful white feathers and put them on; then west

for fine ahtšilye shells, then east for fine apparel (talykŏpa), and said, "Now I am a good man like others. And when he returned to the house where his four wives had cooked, he was handsomer than others. [Nothing about his staying out and being embraced as the four women find him]—Then it was afternoon, and they ate, and slept. —In the morning he said he wanted to go east to see his mother, but his wives should stay. But the women said they would go with him. So they ate, and started.—Then he thought, "I am still only a boy. How can I have four wives and nothing to feed them with?" So he meant to kill them, and called clouds and rain. (2 songs).

II-69. [Cf. 1:89-91.] So they sat there. And his mother had grain, and told the wives to cook it for the afternoon meal—people used to eat two meals daily: breakfast and early supper. So they ate and lay down to sleep. So during the night he asked his mother where he could get ahta-kurrave, lightning cane. His mother would not have him go because he might get killed. But when his mother slept, he rolled up his blankets and went off east. After he had gone a way, he changed himself into Thunder with a great noise [sic—he does not as in 1:91 go into a hole made in the ground by lightning at Thunder's place]. Then he cut four pieces of the cane and covered them with his blanket. Then he returned to his mother, lay down, and covered himself. After a time he told her that he had been and got the cane, but she did not believe him. (2 songs; the first about the color of his blankets: itš-avasuitš, itš-ahwaṭ, masukwalype).

II-70. [Cf. 1:92.] [The next day?], when he came home in the evening, his wives were waiting and cooked supper. They ate and went to bed; at night, the boy awoke, and said about his cane: "Mother, you know about the cane I got. Well, there will be war. I am going to leave you." His mother looked at his face, but said she would not be left: she would go with him. So in the morning they all started north. As they went, they came to low and to high places; he sang of those on the way. (1 song). [The hero is throughout referred to as humare, boy, not by his name.]

II-71. They came to a large, wide hill, Kwanak, and he sang of that. (1 song).

II-72. [Cf. 1:93, 94.] They went and went, and then they came to another boy, one from the east. He had come to this place and made a fire there; he did not know who it was coming, and ran off. But the one with four wives called him to come back. He called long, and then that one began to return and stood near, and they looked at one another and asked, "Who are you? Whose son?" First the one from the east sang and then the one with four wives. The one from the east said: "Kwatšákwatšā and Tinyam-koθpily raised me." The other said, "Pā-kwaθ [viz. Hatpā-'aqwaoθtce] raised me." (2 songs.)

II-73. [Cf. 1:95, 96.] The one with four wives was Ahtá-kesúme; the one from the east was called Ahtá-háne. Both of them burned their clothes and belongings, and all of them cried: their tears ran like rain, until the burned property was covered wet with them. They were two [half-] brothers: they told of their father, how he looked, and how he had been underground now for four years, but they had been on top of the earth; and they said they would dig down and see their father. This was at Amat̩-iya-kwatat̩a [presumably a coined place name]. (2 songs.)

II-74. [Cf. 1:97.] When they finished singing, their father kind of came alive, and emerged. He called them his sons, and told how he came to be under ground: he was the richest in possessions, therefore they had killed him and made him be in the earth; he had worn blue nose pendants of ku'cô. His older brother had taken out all his bones, left him only his "soul" (himat̩ hiviδiktik); that is why he could not walk, could not go with them, though he would like to. So they cried together.—Then they went on, and came to Selye'aye-kumítše and looked at Avikwame and saw their father's scalp hair hanging and people about it singing. Then the boys sang of that. (1 song.)

II-75. [Cf. 1:98-100.] They went on northward. They had got part way when Puke-hane and Nume-peta and Kwatša-kwatša and Tinyam-kwaθpi knew that they were on their way. "When they arrive, we will kill them," they said and waited for them.—Now Halye'anekítse, the small blue-tailed Lizard, stood close by the dancing [over the scalps], painted with clay. He waited all day, wanting to tell the boys. Then he crossed the river and called to them, at Avi-kutaparve: "If you come to where they are dancing, you will be killed." Then he returned. But the boys made songs about the names of the four men. (2 songs.)

II-76. [Cf. 1:101.] So they piled up sand in four places, kicked it and changed the land so it extended across the Colorado River, and went over toward the dance place where their father's hair was hanging. Word was sent on of their coming. Now Taksê, Gopher, was with the four men there, but Halye'anekítše Lizard was on the boy's side. Now if Gopher could lift and throw a big rock farther, they would kill the two boys.

And if Lizard failed to climb the pole and take their father's hair, they would also kill them: that is what they bet on. So the boys called to the four men that they were here and ready. Then Gopher lifted the big rock and threw it [but not far enough]; and Lizard climbed to the top; so the two boys won all their property.—Then the men there wanted to play with dice, otaha; and the four bet their bodies against the property they had lost. Now before they began, the two boys sang of their [four cane] dice: each one had a name according to its marking, and they sang of those: rainbow, kwalisei; tompilyuwaka bird; the woman die, otah-θenya'ak; and coyote teeth, hukθar-iδo. (2 songs.)

II-77. [Cf. 1:102-104.] So they began to play, the women did: one of the boy's wives and one for the other side. And the boy's wife won the bodies of all the others; and they scattered and were afraid. Then Ahta-hane [sic—now it is the hero's name!] sent his four women and the one who had won the game, five in all—he sent them home. And he threw one of his cane dice to Avi-mota and there was a great noise, and all the people there were killed. And he threw another of his two canes behind him, north to Avi-kwame, where it blazed into fire and killed all the people there. But Ahta-hane and his brother and the women made the land extend across the river again and crossed, and looked back and saw the fire and laughed, and came back to Avi-kutaparve on the east side: the fire did not cross the river to the east.—Now he still had two canes left in his hand. He struck them together and made his five women go up to the sky and become stars. They are Hatša now, the Pleiades.—And Ahta-hane made a lake: "[Hat-]pa-kwaθ[tce], go into the lake and be a Saθerke bird," he said. It is a large bird, mostly on the water, and constantly squeaking. —And he changed Ahta-kesume also into a bird, into Turis-turís, Snipe; (it is a small bird with a white collar as if it wore beads, which constantly bobs its head, along the water's edge.—And now Ahta-hane was the only one left, and wanted to become Kwayū, Meteor, or Ball-lightning, which makes a great noise and fire in the sky. So he leaped up into the sky, to go to the ocean or the sky. But when he came to Hokyampeve, Needles Peaks, he dropped into the Colorado, thinking he would like to change to rock or something there. So he floated downriver, with his leg sticking up, and became stone, and now is Me-koat̩a, "Leg-projects," a rock at a big bend in the river. Cranes have their nests there now at high water. (No songs mentioned.)

DISCUSSION

What is there that the two versions differ in, other
than the sort of oversights or small changes of context that almost any person would be likely to make
in retelling a complex, several-day-long story after
several years?

Differences occur above all in the names of the
personages, their kin relationships, occasionally their
identity; and—not in itineraries but where events are
of interest—in geographical localization also.

The following will substantiate.

Puke-hane is the older brother in both versions;
the younger is Tšitšuvare in 1:2, Kovitšivare in 17:1.

The posthumous son of the younger brother is
finally named as Ahtá-háne in 1:95, but as Ahtá-
kesumé in 17:25. This is confirmed in 17:73, where
Ahta-kesume is identified as the one who arrives
with four wives, while Ahta-hane is his half-brother
by the same father who comes from the east. In 1:93,
this half-brother is Tšese'ily's son and is called Ahta-
kwasumé. In short, the narrator had between 1904 and
1908 interchanged the names of his principal hero and
this late-appearing kinsman; but in 1908, before he got
through his second telling, he had changed back again!
But in 17:77, the names are interchanged once more:
It is now Ahta-hane who has the wives and is the
active hero! This fits with the hero being told of
simply as humare, boy, all the way from 1:29 to 1:95,
and mostly from 17:27 to 17:72.

In 1:29 it is Tšese'ilye who bears the posthumous
son, her cowife Sun's daughter having gone home. In
17:17 it is the other way around: Tšese'ilye leaves,
Sun's daughter stays and bears the hero. But in 1:90,
when the boy meets his mother again, she is Sun's
daughter, as in the 1908 version.

There are two Suns in 1904, one of 1:11a, 1:90, the
other of 1:77, 1:78, as already discussed (UC-AR 11:1,
page 21).

In 17:59-61 the boy hero falls in with Sun's four
wives, then in 61-63 Sun comes home, gambles with
him, and loses. In 1:75-78 the four women are the
wives of Kwayū, meteor and cannibal, who returns and
gives the boy tobacco; but having gone again, Sun comes
and does the gambling.

This extra Kwayū of 1:75-78 is somehow a duplicate
of the boy-hero himself (as well as of Sun); for the
boy knocks his father's knee-cap away as a destructive
meteor (1:37), and plans to become a meteor at Mukiampeve himself (1:104) before he actually transforms
himself into the rock Me-koaṭa.

In short, it is evident that it is a matter of relative

indifference to the narrator-singer what the names of
his personages are, and precisely how they are related,
and in fact whether they are identical or distinct. He
has his general plot fairly well in mind, and his scheme
of songs; but who his characters are and what they are
called is superstructural and not particularly relevant.
A certain name or type of name or kinship has suitable
association or connotation, and is brought in for its
"decorative" effect and affect; but its intrinsic significance as means of identification is so small that the
name can be and is applied at times to another person.

Probably significant also is the narrator's refusing
to give his boy hero's name at all until he has him
meet his half-brother in 1:95: he "as yet had no name"
(UC-AR 11:1, note 87, page 17). It is when the half-
brothers first meet and inquire into their identity that
the couplet Ahta-hane and Ahta-kwasume is appropriate;
but which one is which is so unimportant that the narrator gets mixed over it.

He also is mixed about geography. Avi-kwame and
Avi-mota belong to the villans, Avi-kutaparva, Icokuva'ire,
Qara'erva to the heroes; but the inconsistencies which
I tried to straighten out (UC-AR 11:1, p. 21) cannot be
wholly reconciled, whether they relate to the northern
origin or to the southern desert, because their geography was hazy in the teller's mind. Where it is a
matter of a mere travelog on which to hang minute
incidents, as in 1:38-68 and 17:25-57, the versions are
precise, agree, and can be used as a geographical
manual. But before and after this formal itinerary,
geographical references are intermittent and imprecise:
Blue Bird was interested in other things. If he knew
the name of each spot where something happened in the
emotional parts of his narrative, he often did not think
it worth mentioning. I believe that often it was not in
the focus of his thinking at all.

I ought perhaps to explain why this second Cane
version was not used in 1948 in connection with Cane
1 (UC-AR 11:1, pp. 4-23), or even alluded to there.
Frankly, it had been forgotten in the forty years between
its recording and the publication of Cane 1 in 1948. It
was forgotten because, except for a few pages of Eheme-
huevi notes (which I happened to dispose of by prompt
publication—Jour. Am. Folklore 21:240-242, 1908) the
Cane 17 version was all that I entered in a substandard
size notebook (no. 86) which got misplaced and forgotten.
It was perhaps just as well that it came to my attention
again after I had worked over my Mohave narratives
as a whole between 1946 and 1953, instead of before:
Earlier I should probably have worried over trying to
reconcile the two versions, instead of analyzing the
variability and the form that they took.

Narrative 18
SATUKHOTA
(1953)

THE RECORDING

This narrative was secured under different circumstances from all the others in this volume except no. 19: forty-odd years later, and through an interpreter speaking excellent English.

In February 1953, I revisited the Mohave at Needles and visited for the first time that part of the tribe—by now forming a large majority—living around Parker on the Colorado River reservation. I had last been at Needles in 1908, and was interested—and somewhat fearful—to see what changes time had brought to the tribe. Also, there were many specific points of native geography to check and explore with informants, and I wanted to see with my own eyes some of the country that the myths had told about.

On Sunday, February 8, 1953, I sat down at Parker with a seventy-three-year-old Mohave to inquire into place-names and related matters. He was named Avé-pūya "dead rattlesnake," in Mohave, Pete Sherman in English. His simulye or patriclan was Nyo'iltše. He had been born on the reservation at Kusol-iδau, close to Poston. He did not remember at what spots in Mohave Valley his parents had been born and raised. He spoke some English and understood more, and could sign his name, though he wrote it vertically for horizontal reading. He wore his long hair tied up in a blue bandana, which he would not remove for photographing. He was approachable, friendly, on the phlegmatic side, with a twinkle in his eye. He lived perhaps a mile or two from reservation headquarters, in a house of his own adjacent to that of his married niece.

Robert Martin served as interpreter. He told me that his father was an agency physician; and that when he went to the agency school in the first decade of the century, feeling against half-breeds was still so strong among the Mohave that he and one or two others were much persecuted by their schoolmates. However, his appearance is wholly Mohave: I should never have suspected any admixture of white blood. He is fully identified with the tribe, genuinely interested in their history and culture, eager to serve as interpreter, and excellent at it.

As the day, fruitfully devoted to ethnogeography and matters flowing from it, drew to a close, I asked Pete Sherman whether he would tell me his Satukhóta story. He was agreeable, and Martin wanted so much to hear and interpret it that he got leave of absence from his regular government job for the next day.

I suppose that for me it was partly a case of the old hunter again sighting quarry. Also, it would obviously be of interest to ascertain how much four decades had changed the old native culture in its ritual and aesthetic aspects: most of the Parker Mohave are now successful cash-crop irrigation farmers of hay or cotton. On this point I may say at once that, to judge by this case, the song-narratives that have been remembered at all have not changed significantly in quality or manner. A few minor innovations are mentioned in the notes. The difference from the past most useful to me was that Pete Sherman had more sense of time than the Mohave of an older generation, and was willing to merely mention the second, third, and fourth tellings of an episode instead of repeating them verbatim in full. He also appeared to condense the end of the story somewhat. He was probably led to do this by Martin's desire to complete the tale, since he would have been unable to resume interpreting the next day. Without this pressure, the telling would almost certainly have consumed a day and a quarter to a day and a half.

After Pete had spoken of variant versions at one point (par. 52a) and of songs his kinsmen did not sing for him because they were not good (64), I assumed he would admit he had learned the tale and songs from others. However, to make the record formally complete, I asked the question: and he gave the stock old-time answer: Yes, he had dreamed it; and then his old folks had said he had dreamed it right. Evidently the Mohave feel that the two statements are not in conflict but supplementary on different levels—like physiological and spirit paternity in Australia and the Trobriands.

After I had the story on paper, I was doubly satisfied to have secured it, because of its parallels among the Diegueño and Halchidhoma, whose versions, in spite of innumerable variations in detail, are really remarkably similar in plot and orientation, considering the

complex structure of the tale. In fact I first heard of
Mohave Satukhôta after I had read Constance DuBois's
Diegueño story of Chaup (or Cuya-homarr) in the
Journal of American Folklore of 1904 and was struck
by its resemblance of manner to Mohave narratives,
and inquired of the Mohave if they had something
similar. The result was that Jo Nelson, narrator of
tale 7, Mastamho (UC-AR:1, pp. 50-68), told me what
I put into the Handbook of Indians of California, page
764, in the following words.

> Satukhota has much the same plot as the Diegueño
> story of Kuya-homar, but the Mohave know nothing
> of this, and connect their series with a Maricopa
> version called Satukhota [for "Maricopa" read
> "Halchidhoma now merged among the Maricopa."]
> Its geographical setting indicates that they are
> right. The story is said to begin at Aha-kutot-
> namomampa near the Bill Williams Fork of the
> Colorado [the present version confirms, although
> the particular place was not mentioned]. Kwa'akuya-
> inyohave, 'west old woman,' surviving alone after a
> flood [left alone after tribal migration], gives birth
> to two boys, Para'aka and Pa'ahane, who grow up,

take cane, make flutes, and attract the two far-away
daughters of Masayava-kunauva [Patuk-sata], who
lives at Koakamata, near Maricopa Wells [Koaka-
matše (8: 14, 81—UC-AR 11:2, pp. 78, 87) is at Gila
Bend; in the present version they are Pimas at
Aha-Kupinye near Sacaton, farther up the Gila].
They marry the girls, go off with them, and are
killed by their wives' kin in the Papago [Pima]
country, but are avenged by their son Kwiya-humar.
Satukhota and 'Cane' appear to have much plot in
common [true, especially toward the end]. The
Satukhota singer smites his palm against his breast.

In 1933 the longest of a series of tales published
by Leslie Spier from the Gila Yuman is the same
story, which he calls Flute Lure. It was told him by
Kutox, a Halchidhoma by descent among the Yuman
tribes of the Gila who collectively are now generally
known as Maricopa.

I give now first the text of Mohave Satukhôta; then,
instead of discussion and summary of it, a concordance
of common elements and analysis of variations in the
versions of all three tribes; and a review of problems
raised by these.

THE SATUKHOTA STORY[1]

A. Birth of Twins

1. When all people were at Avikwa'me after Māta-
vilya died and his place was destroyed, they came
southward, hitherward, sorrowing.[2] They were the
Yuma, Cocopa, and Kamiá.[3] When they came to
Tšesahā,[4] an old woman, Kwakúi-nyuháve,[5] said she

would stay. So she was left there, and lived alone in
a kuyá or cave.[6]

2. The old woman had put mud[7] on her head,[8] then
went down to the river to wash it off. After that, she
walked out on the sandbar. There she nyahwāpilk.[9]
Then Gopher[10] smelled that, traveled underground,
came up where she sat bare-rumped with her bark
skirt spread around her. He emerged and had intercourse with her. She walked home pregnant.[11] When
her time came, she bore twin boys. The older was
Para'āka, the younger Paraháne.[12]

B. Eagle Pets

3. They grew up. The old woman preached[13] to them
about eagles[14] as pets at Avi-samakwiôîke,[15] far up the

---

[1] In answer to an orientation query, the informant said:
"Satukhôta is the name of a kind of a song. I don't know what
kind of a looking or colored bird it is. Kukhó (red-shafted
flicker) is a bird, but Satukhôta means just a singing." I
interpret this statement to signify that Satukhôta is a ritual
or song designation for the Kukho flicker. The informant
obviously did not wish to make the identification explicit. See
notes 172, 174.

[2] The universal mourning for Matavilya, the first death, is
referred to in 7:3 (UC-AR 11:1, p. 53), and 9:13, 13:14, and
16G:10, above.

[3] The three river tribes south of the Mohave, after the
flight of the Halchadhom and Kohwan. The Mohave are not
mentioned, though tribes come in fours: evidently because
they stayed in Mohave Valley, while the three named
went on southward.

[4] Tšesaha is in California more or less opposite the mouth
of Bill Williams Fork. In a list of place names upriver from
this mouth, it was preceded only by Amaṭa, "earth," and by
Ahma-va-ahwêre, "quail run," two spots very close together
about a half mile above the turn of the river at the entrance
of the Fork. Next to Tšesaha was Avi-korotata, or Avir-
qorotat, two natural "monuments" or pinnacles that once
marked the northern boundary of the Hálchadhom or Halchidhoma.

[5] Kwakui is "old woman"; nyuhave might mean "her going
through" or "west"; paragraphs 63, 64 (see note 191) make
the latter more probable; but no translation was obtained.

[6] This kuya reappears in the name of her grandson, Kuya-
humare, "caveboy," in 65a.

[7] Maθ'e-hupink.

[8] Either to kill lice or, with mesquite gum mixed in, to
make the hair lustrous. Handbook, p. 729.

[9] Menstruated.

[10] Here called taksé kunyóre, marked or striped gopher.

[11] Hutuivek.

[12] Meanings unknown. The names are similar to those of
the two Cane brothers, Púke-hane and Tšitšuváre (1:2, UC-
AR 11:1, p. 4), and the latter's posthumous child Ahtá-hane
(1:95, UC-AR 11:1, p. 17).

[13] Instructed them at length, insistently.

[14] Aspa. Eaglets are meant.

[15] Samakwiôîke is SW of Parker, behind (beyond) the Riverside Mountains, "across from" Rice. It was also recorded as

cliff of that mountain. The two boys went into the river, washed their heads, combed their hair,[16] using charcoal at the bottom (of a bowl) of water as a mirror,[17] and put on[18] their apparel.[19] They wore bow, arrow, club, hip belt, surkôva, and quiver.[20] Then they stood ready and equipped;[21] stood at the back of the house.[22] (4 songs.)

4. Then they started, traveling west. Now the old woman at the house, their mother, was a doctor,[23] and caused a deep canyon to be before them, one they could not cross: they stood at the edge and looked down. They stood talking about where they had expected to play.[24] Then Para'āka, the older, started to go east along the canyon edge; he went on and on, but the canyon did not end. So he returned. Then Parahane, the younger, went west along the edge. He too returned.[25] (4 songs.)

5. Now they were going to cross the canyon by magic,[26] and sang of that; and they crossed it. Then as they were going toward Avi-samakwiɓīke, the old woman turned it to be behind them: it was like a mirage. The older brother said, "We did not really pass it already. It is our mother's doing, she is making us think we passed it." (2 songs.)

6. As they went, they saw mountain swallows[27] flying about the mountain and coming toward themselves. They stood and watched them and said, "They must be angry." (2 songs.)[28]

7. The swallows went back into their nests, but with their heads out, looking down at the boys, who had bewitched them,[29] and were going on. (3 songs.)

8. As they went, they saw the mountain of the eaglet pets which they were going to: it was white standing,[30] (they said); they had not reached it yet.

Then they saw the eaglet pets as they went.[31] (4 songs.)

9. When they came near, they heard the eaglets saying "Sauk." (2 songs.)[32]

10. They came to the foot of Samakwiɓīke Mountain and looked up a high cliff. Parahane, the younger, was ready to climb it; but the older brother said to him: "You said you were a doctor; in your dreams you said you could fly back and forth over the earth." Then the younger brother used magic, rolling on the ground, putting earth on his head and rubbing it into his hair, and became the Gray Racer Snake;[33] he lay there like that. Then he began to climb (the cliff). He went up four steps,[34] lay still, and told his older brother he would be unable to get up to the nest. He knew he could reach the eaglets, but he said he could not.[35] "This is my mountain, it is my eagles. I shall die here. You will return and tell our mother, or she will miss us." (No songs mentioned.)[36]

11. Now the younger brother came down and stood at the foot of the cliff and watched his older brother turn himself into the male Red Racer.[37] Then the older began to climb, and said the same thing about four steps and being unable to reach and to tell their mother.[38] But he went on climbing and came to the nest. The two eaglets were scared; he chased them to the end of the nest, and took hold of one. The eaglet[39] struck and bit his hand: he let it go and cried. (3 songs.)

12. The younger stood below and sang toward him above. The older came down bringing two eaglets, and dropped one on the ground. Now Parahane got the older eagle, but Para'aka the older got the smaller one.[40] Then Parahane looked about for mountain sandbar willow,[41] found it, made a baby bed of it, tied his bird on, carried it so as they started home. The older brother wanted the older eagle, but his younger brother had

---

Avi-sumá-koɵīke, "lying root mountain," still a part of the Riverside massif, away from the river. Part II, B, 2, below.

[16] The comb was of root of sutcive, a dry hill grass.
[17] Sanyīka hatcuītša halioyi, the last meaning mirror.
[18] Mat-uwai, reflexive.
[19] Nya-sonātš.
[20] Respectively: otīsa, ipa, nya-kelyexwaya, suyūla, surkôva, nya-kopêta. Surkôva is something put around the body of warriors; neither informant nor interpreter was quite sure what. The quiver was of deer hide, aqwaq teɵkwīla, or of wild cat.
[21] Mat-uwaik, tcivérk muv'ôk; cf. note 18.
[22] Av'umak kūv'ok.
[23] Kwaɵiɓêi.
[24] Satmulyeu kunūve ikwe-nyuɓaumk matha-nyuɓaumk ipā-tapmak. Ikwe, matha, ipa, apmak are cloud, wind, arrow, shoot.
[25] Takavek ivāk nyuvok vuv'ok. These may be the words of what they sang. The verbal forms seem to be dual.
[26] ɵatwitš was heard here, ɵavītšk in section 7, below; cf. note 29.
[27] Hamkye avi.
[28] Mat-itɵāvtcum huyôk suv'ok, angry stood watched. These are evidently the words of (one of) the two songs here.
[29] ɵavītck; cf. note 26.
[30] Nyamaɵav haquwāk. This and the next phrase are evidently the words of the songs sung here.

[31] Aspa nyaxaṭ hisamk vatayêmk.
[32] Himīm ha'avk vatayêmk.
[33] Kwatníalk; it climbs trees. This was also the personal name of Jack Jones who was my usual interpreter from 1900 to 1910.
[34] Stylistic: the Mohave are always making four "steps" in myth or song, even up this cliff.
[35] Deference to his older brother? The motivation is unclear.
[36] The nonmention is perhaps an oversight.
[37] The gray and the red racer are female and male (ipa) of the same kwatnialk species, in Mohave.
[38] Here is one of the differences between the tellings of 1900-1910 and 1953: straight duplications and repetitions are now summarized or merely mentioned as the same. This was begun by the interpreter Robert Martin, but Pete Sherman, who understood English, and spoke some, soon grasped the method, and by afternoon, when time was becoming short for completing the tale, he used the shortcut to bring us to the end that day.
[39] They were eaglets, but the word used was aspa, eagle. Mohave seems to have little tendency to use diminutives.
[40] The situation is like that in Cane, 1:8-14, 18-22 (UC-AR 11:1, pp. 5-6, 7), in which the younger brother gets the first wives and the butt instead of tip of the cane.
[41] Avī ihore.

got it and he was angry over it. He came behind,
holding his eagle by the feet and swinging it, sulking.
He was saying, "You will never reach home and have
its feathers; I will make it so. I will make rain.[42] I
will make it by kicking up dust, kwahā weed, kam'umka
brush, creosote bush.[43] They will go up and clouds and
rain will return.[44] And so it was raining. (12 songs.)[45]

13. Then he was going to make the clouds and rain
stop. The clouds were afraid,[46] they hung over the mountain. The sun shone through them; he looked at the sun;
but he was going to make the clouds return. (1 song.)[47]

14. So it began to rain again, heavily, and they held
their eagles in their arms to cover them. But when
they came to Hoatše-wamveve,[48] it hailed and both
eagles were killed; but they still held them. The older
brother said, "They are both dead, why do we go on
carrying them? It gives us pain, it slows our travel,
our bodies are weak." As they stood there, he said,
"I will bury it." He dug a hole elbow[49] deep, dropped
his eagle in, also his bow, arrows, club, and the rest,
and covered them over. Only he kept his tokoro cane.[50]
The younger did the same, also leaving himself his
cane. Then they said, "We will call this land Savat-
kiale, and Amaṭ-savehê and Hoatše-wamveve:[51] they
will be called so forever." (3 songs on the death of
the eagles.)

15. They started on homeward again, crying for the
loss of their pets. (1 song.)

16. As they came on crying, they stopped to look
up, and saw their dead eagles flying: it was their
ghosts,[52] it was their shadows[53] they saw. (2 songs.)

17. They walked on home to Tšesaha, went into the
house, and lay down on their faces. Their mother was
cooking (outdoors), and when she was ready called
them, but they did not answer. When she did not see

them come, she called in to them, "I know what happened
at the eagles' nest and about your pets dying; I saw it
all while lying here." Then she made by magic[54] two
piles of earth, took a tokoro cane,[55] pushed it elbow-
deep[56] under a pile, and there was an eagle on top,
alive; and the same with the other. Then she called,
"Come on out and see your eagles alive!" The boys
inside thought, "It is bad of her to be talking like this!
Is she lying or not?" So Parahane the younger spied
on his mother whether she spoke truly, and looked out
of the house. He saw the eagles, ran out, seized the
older bird. Para'aka also ran to take the older bird
but did not get it. Then he did not take the younger
one but stood and watched.[57] When the old woman saw
that he was angry, she said to his brother, "You are
the younger. When I used to make arrows for you, yours
had no feather because you were small, but for your
older brother I put feathers on his arrow. When you
were little and hunted eggs, I said, 'The older one will
get the older bird, the younger the young one.' That is
how I used to tell you." After she said that, the younger
gave the older eaglet to his older brother and took the
younger one for himself. Then the old woman said, "They
will not be like that, little and big, when they grow up:
they will be the same size."[58] (2 songs.)

18. It was sundown, it was dark, and the old woman
was still telling them, "Go up through these washes and
you will find the long-eared jackrabbit. Kill it and bring
it to eat; I like it. And the big spotted collar lizard,
bring that, and the chuckawalla lizard; and the desert
tortoise;[59] bring those for my food, those four. (2 songs.)

19. After the eagles were grown, they flew high,
dancing with the wind.[60] (2 songs.)

20. Their mother said, "Catch your eagles and tie
them, else they will fly back to the mountain where
you got them and you will not see them any more." So
the boys caught and tied up their eagles. Then she made
a partridge[61] and gave it to her two sons to eat. When
the older had finished, he was ready to pick the feathers
off his eagle. (1 song.)[62]

21. The younger did the same. They were still at
Tšesaha. (1 song.)

[42]Kuv'au mat-ke'êre, rain make.
[43]Ivθe is creosote bush, <u>Larrea</u> <u>tridentata</u>, locally known
as greasewood.
[44]Ikwe kuv'auk vatavĩk.
[45]The narrator first said 3 songs, later changed to 12.
[46]Ikwe-tc-elehaik, clouds were scared.
[47]The narrator here asked how many songs he had mentioned. I listed them, totaling 27; it was then he raised the
number for paragraph 12 from 3 to 12.
[48]North of Samakwiδĩke, halfway or more home. See note
51.
[49]See note 56.
[50]Tokoro (see also notes 55, 155) was here described as
a walking stick or cane with a crook at one end. Cf. tokoro
or tukoro in Epic (UC-AR 11:2, pp. 156-164, notes E-28
"straight cane," F-24, I-26 and 50, J-92).
[51]Savat-kiale is not mentioned otherwise; Amaṭ-savehê
was recorded the day before as Sovhe, a half mile or so
from Koskĩlye, an inland pass through the Whipple Mountains,
traversed by the old Needles-to-Parker wagon road; Hoatše-
wamveve was then said to mean "hail stones" (as in the
story here) and to be on this same road where it crossed a
strip of malpais lava.
[52]Nyaveδaik.
[53]Mat-kwisayo, shadows or souls.

[54]"Witched," the interpreter said.
[55]See note 50.
[56]See note 49.
[57]Sulking; see note 28, above.
[58]Matter-of-factness in a fantasy situation.
[59]The four animals are: akūly, matcĩ (they are pale, live
in the hills), hamθulye, kapeta. She says "for my food"—to
feed the eaglets?
[60]Mathai'imak.
[61]Sic: suvĩ.
[62]It is evident that most of this paragraph is narrative
about tying up eaglets and eating partridge, and that the sole
song, matched by the younger brother's in 21, probably refers
only to being about to pluck feathers.

22. Then they did pluck their feathers. The eagles were ashamed,[63] hung their heads, for they were picked clean. The old woman said, "If you hang their feathers against the wall of the house, smoke and dust will stick to them and they will look bad.[64] When you go hunting, there is a long-tailed one[65] that you can kill; bring it and I will skin it, and if you put your feathers in it, it will be good, they will not soil." She meant the swift-fox.[66] So they went to hunt it. (1 song.)

23. As they started, she said, "Do not shoot at it. Stand and call the swift-fox to come to you, and hold it down. Its skin will not be bloody then." So Para'aka the older called it, and caught it. Then Parahane was going to do the same and called it, but saw that his swift-fox was not white but green in its body,[67] after he held him down. They skinned them, carried them home, put their feathers in, hung them on the wall. (1 song.)[68]

C. Hunting and Cane

24. The old woman said: "Isamā pakê, isamā tinyām, ismā ire,[69] if you can get those, bring them, burn and put them on the tracks of deer. Then the deer will weaken[70] and not travel far and you can kill them. You can call those three, they will come to you." So Para'aka did that, he called them and made a whirl-wind[71] and (by it) got those three. (1 song.)

25. And the younger did the same and got them: they themselves were still at Tšesahā. (1 song.)[72]

26. When they had reentered the house, she said, "There are three more, growing in the east: isamā

pakê, hat'alāya, isamā ire.[73] It has three names but is one thing. If you bring that, like willow but from the mountains, and stronger, I can make bows from it."[74] (2 songs.)

27. She preached to them again, "As you go hunting, you will see ironwood.[75] It is strong; but later it falls down, dead. So it is with people: some day they lie down and die. The mountains are strong and of rock, but even their banks cave, their sides fall.[76] So it will be with human beings." (No songs mentioned.)

28. She preached[77] again. "Go east, get cane,[78] bring it to me, we can make flutes,[79] and play on them. With that you can get women." So they went after it, and arrived where it stood, and saw it tall and green. Then Para'aka sang about it. (1 song.)

29. And Parahane sang about it. (1 song.)[80, 81]

30. They cut a cane out of the growth, Para'aka taking the butt, Parahane the upper end.[82] So they came back to their house at Tšesaha, and the old woman cut the cane with her fingernail,[83] and breathed through it: they both watched her. She blew, but no sound came, it stayed in. (4 songs.)

31. The mother handed the cane to her older son. He began to play on it, then gave it to the younger: they both played. Then two girls heard it far off at Aha-kupínye[84] near Sacaton; they were Pimas.[85]

This is the end of the story of the two boys in this country.

[63]θatūnyukvik, because there were two, the interpreter said; a single one ashamed would be θanyôk.
[64]Watcamesaik, alaik.
[65]"Animal."
[66]Kókho, not to be confused with kukhó, the red-shafted flicker referred to below in note 127.
[67]Havasuk tšamahaik, "green of body," the interpreter said, although havasuk also means blue. There is no overt symbolism in the white-green contrast; only a concrete re-enforcement of balance in the pairing. Compare the differently colored birds or bird cages of the Cane brothers' girls in 1:7b, 12a, 16, 17b (UC-AR 11:1, pp. 5, 6, 7).
[68]The teller first said "one song" after Para'aka caught his swift-fox, but then postponed it until the younger had caught his and they had got home.
[69]When asked what these were, the narrator said, "I don't know what they are. They are the old woman's names, she knew, I don't." That is, they are circumlocutions that help put the story and songs on a ritual or at least nonsecular level. The interpreter did not venture on a translation. Two of the three names recur in another group of three in 26. As there, the three probably denote one thing.
[70]Aqwaq ny-ītatšm.
[71]Matha-yekwīre.
[72]Both brothers' songs presumably mention only the whirl-wind and the three names of what it brings, not their mother's instructions.

[73]As compared with 24, hat'alaya replaces "night isamā." It is evidently a desert tree.
[74]By design or ōversight, the narrator did not mention the expectable securing of the bow wood by the boys.
[75]Axpalyka, probably palo fierro, either Cercocarpus betuloides, a mountain mahogany, or Olneya tesota, desert ironwood.
[76]In a recorded historical account of wars, mountains and the sun are contrasted with men as enduring; but the social mood there is one of "not wanting to live long," of throwing one's life away.
[77]Tšeqwārek yukanāvek, "told and said," spoke formally, usually Englished as "preaching."
[78]Ahtá.
[79]Also called ahta here, but taltal below in 42, note 125.
[80]Again a pair of songs, perhaps identical in their words, but attributed one to the older and one to the younger. I assume they merely describe the appearance of the cane, not the mother's instructions.
[81]We stopped here for the midday meal, and the narrator asked the total number of songs he had mentioned. I said 57 —but now count 59. We had sat for 150 minutes, of which he and the interpreter each used about half.
[82]In Cane, 1:20, 22 (UC-AR 11:1, p. 7), it is the younger brother who wants and gets the butt end—as here in 12, 17, above, he gets the larger eaglet.
[83]In Cane, 1:91 (UC-AR 11:1, p. 17), the hero splits lightning cane with his fingernail.
[84]"Warm spring."
[85]Hatpa; as against Hatpa'nya, "east (?sic) Pima," who are the Maricopa; and Hatpa'amai, upper Pima, who are Papago.

D. Girls Journey West and Return

Now I begin the story of the two girls in the East.

32. Two girls ran out to the spring; the older said, "Jump into it, catch fish." When the younger entered the water, the older sister heard the playing here in this country. She stood, listened, called her younger sister out of the water. "Listen! It is like some kind of animal,[86] but I think it is human." Both listened. As they started home, they spoke of how their people were not taking care of them right. "If we go there[87] (to the playing), we don't have to tell them, because we are treated like orphans."[88] Now their father was called Patuksāta.[89] And the girls were Amkyêlye Kosa-pāya, the older, and Amkyêlye Kwesa-yūmpa, the younger.[90] At the house, though they said, "We do not have to tell our father or mother," the younger was picking bits of charcoal from the ground to use in parching corn to carry for a lunch.[91] After grinding the corn, they baked it in hot ashes.[92] As they were about to start, they stood behind the house and sang. (4 songs.)

33. Then they started. They came to a shade[93] and saw Ground-squirrel.[94] The older girl thought, "It might be he that we heard playing: he looks like it. As we come toward him, we will hear how he plays, how he talks." They went on step by step, like spying. Ground-squirrel tried to make with his mouth the sound of a cane flute, but it was unlike. As they stopped to listen, he told them, "I am the one that was making that music. Toward morning, the people left to go home, you can see where they went; they threw water on the ground." But it was not so; it was his urine that he had spilled. He said again, "It was not my voice that

you heard; but if you will go on that hill where the ocotillo is growing, I will climb around among them and it will be my true voice." They said, "We have traveled far, but if it is true what you say, we will go over and hear it." When they all got on to the hill, Ground-squirrel ran up and down the ocotillo stalks four times while they both watched.[95] Then he lay on the ground. The girls said, "We are going on. We have far to go, you have lied to us, it is getting late. You are no good." And they left him, going on. Ground-squirrel lay there face down, looked after them. "It should have been told if they had married me; it would have been a coyote story;[96] but it wasn't." (2 songs, by the girls.)

34. As they went on, they came to Big Tree Lizard.[97] Here the same happened. "It was I making the music," he said. (2 songs.)

35. Next it was Woodpecker,[98] the same way. (2 songs.)

36. Next it was the large slow hawk Hūmaθe. (2 songs.)

37. As they came through Black Mountain Wash,[99] here near Parker, the younger sister menstruated.[100] The older asked her, and she wouldn't tell, but the older saw blood down the inside of her leg. "I knew that was happening," she said, "but you wouldn't tell me." (4 songs.)

38. They came to Ahmo-ketceθile.[101] There, at the river, they stopped and ate their provisions (and drank).[102] (No songs mentioned.)

39. The two boys were hunting (across the river), and becoming thirsty came down to opposite Movālya,[103] and there, at Ahmo-ketmasava,[104] they drank. They were carrying deer on their backs. The older sister said, "They must live far from the river; if not, we

---

[86]Itcípaya; itc- is something, some kind.

[87]Pi'ipa.

[88]Kwimūlevek.

[89]Patuk-sāta (or Patek-sat—Patak—may be correct) recurs in tale 6A (UC-AR 11:1, pp. 46-47) as "a name of Coyote." He is, there, an old man, beyond Phoenix, with whom lives a woman who gives birth to a hero boy, whom the old man later wants to kill, but is himself killed by "the Mohave." This story is garbled, and was denied by other Mohave as a Coyote tale; I have discussed it on p. 136, UC-AR 11:1, and on p. 176 in notes 6 and 7 to Part VII of the Epic, UC-AR 11:2. Note 7 refers to Devereux's Mohave Coyote tale in which one "Maricopa" leader is called Pataksat. Spier's Maricopa "Flute Lure" tale (p. 367 of Yuman Tribes of the Gila River, 1933) also contains two girls who travel and Patukcut (pp. 381, 392), their father. In every case the name is that of an old man on the middle Gila.

[90]I cannot translate any part of the two names. Kwesa- and Kosa- are phonemically equivalent.

[91]Provisions to carry on a journey.

[92]Grind, tawãm; ashes ax'ổ.

[93]Ava-matkyulya, the flat brush roof usual in front of houses and sometimes standing alone.

[94]Hum'ïre.

[95]It is not clear why he ran up and down the ocotillo (Fouquieria splendeus, of Candlewood family) to improve his music, nor why he should have tried to bring made-up visitors into his pretense.

[96]Evidently: a trickster story.

[97]Ahateθilye.

[98]Is'ôna.

[99]Avi-soqwilye hatai. Black Mountain is an isolated hill 4 miles behind Parker, as seen from the river.

[100]Mat-areik.

[101]Ahmo-kutšeθilye, also recorded as Ahmoketaθilye, is about 1/4 mile downstream from the headgate and reservation dam, Movālya in Mohave, about two miles upriver from Parker. The name means "soft-(rock)-mortars" or "sandstone-mortars." By it is Ha-θïtšive, "where drink water." In listing geographical names, the informant had previously said that here is where "they" crossed the river in the Satukhôta story. In the next paragraph, the boy heroes come down to the river at Ahmo-ketmasava opposite Ahmo-ketaθilye.

[102]By Ha-θïtšive, as indicated in note 101.

[103]Movālya is the Headgate rock at the dam, on the east side, said to be "called Movara by Americans."

[104]See note 102.

will find it out." At sunset, the girls crossed[105] to where the boys had drunk. As they went on up from there, the sun was down, and they saw ghost (light) flickering[106] in the west. They followed that, called to it, "You will stay around in the canyon and be like that. It will be your name, Ghost-flickering." (4 songs.)[107]

40. They came to the (boys') house, but did not go in: they stood behind it. It was night, but the old woman knew it and called to the boys, "We have visitors."[108] They did not believe her. But they came out, stood before the house, tore the sky open,[109] looked through it, and told their mother, "There is no one here." The old woman said, "It cannot be virgins, they must be whores, they have been married before."[110] (4 songs.)

41a. When the old woman sang these four songs,[111] the girls heard her, walked around to the door, and put the old woman to sleep.[112] Then they went and lay with the boys. Toward daybreak, they both said, "We are going back to our home." Parahane had cohabited with the younger sister, but his older brother Para'aka did not want anything to do with the older girl, though she played with him. "I would no longer kill anything in my hunting," he thought.

41b. When it was day, the two girls started home. As they went, the older asked the younger, "Did you have intercourse?" She would not say, but when she micturated the urine flowed straight to the ground instead of breaking, and the older sister knew. At the Colorado River, they bathed, then returned by the same way they had come.[113]

[105]By swimming. This was so commonplace in Mohave life as to be taken for granted.

[106]Nyaveδĩk husulye. It may be the zodiacal light, or sunset sky reflection on rock walls; husulye possibly means "gleam" rather than "flicker."

[107]These songs may refer to several of the events of this paragraph, or only to the ghost-flicker.

[108]Pi'ipatš ivatšk viδauk.

[109]Amai ūδãpk. What this means is wholly obscure to me, and the informant said he could add no information.

[110]English and Mohave word meanings do not correspond here. I doubt if Mohave natively had a simple word for virgin or virginity. The term used by the informant was masahai, which means girl, without reference to being married or unmarried, but applicable only to a grown-up young woman who had not borne a child. The second term, kamalui, is generally translated whore, in its older English sense, but not in the sense of prostitute, which the Mohave did not have. "Married before" is presumably a euphemism in English for "sexually experienced."

[111]This remark shows that Mohave cycle songs do not attempt to summarize the narrative immediately preceding them, but that, normally if not always, they express the words of a personage in a story. They might be compared to a string of slightly varied lyrics interspaced in a prose recitative, the lyrics being speeches, but the recitative both narration and dialog. The Mohave songs correspond to the Poetic Edda, which consists of metrical dialog or rhapsodical utterances; the narrative, as I give it in the present publications, to the Prose Edda.

[112]Hav'or θupānyay.

[113]We are here in a long stretch of narrative, in the middle of which the thread of the girls is dropped and that of the boys picked up.

E. Consequences

41c. The two boys also came out of the house and started for the river. The older also asked the younger, "Did you cohabit?" and he would not tell. But the older saw that he had, because his urine did not stream out strongly.[114] At the river, they washed their hair, then returned to the house. As they passed the fire place, a drop from the younger one's hair[115] fell on the coals (and hissed), and his mother said, "See, you had intercourse with that girl. I knew[116] it would happen like that."[117]

41d. Next morning, they went to hunt. Para'aka, west of the river, killed a deer before noon and carried it home. Parahane, on the east side,[118] had his arrow break whenever he shot, or the game escaped, and he could kill nothing. He kept on trying, however, until he came to Ah'a-kwatpave.[119] There he killed an akwes-kanāme,[120] and that only, and brought it home. But his mother had already seen his trip, and said to him, "Now you see, you can't kill because you have had intercourse. It is always like that, and will stay so."

41e. The old woman began to skin the older brother's deer with her knife.[121] But she kicked the deer around to make it come alive.[122] It did come alive, jumped, and ran off. The boys took their arrows, pursued it, but they were angry[122] at their mother and shot to miss. (6 songs.)[123]

42. They followed the deer to Ahtcye-kuθuke[124] this side of Phoenix, did not kill it, and started home, still angry at their mother. The younger one saw the smoke (of where the girls lived) and wanted to go there; but

[114]The reverse of the effect on the girl, in the preceding paragraph.

[115]The connection is not quite made clear, but there seems no reason to suspect any very deep symbolism.

[116]The eternal "I told you so."

[117]He had his way in spite of her disapproval of the girls.

[118]There seems no special reason for his taking the opposite side, except as part of the balancing contrast between the brothers that is constantly being worked in like a rhythm of symmetry. It is not a case of consistent association with directions, for in 4 it is the younger brother who takes the west side.

[119]Or Ah'a-tkwatparve, "cottonwood grove," once mentioned as "15 or 20" miles below Ehrenberg, which is opposite Blythe. Ehrenberg itself is about 45-50 miles by air from Tšesaha near Monument Mountain in the Whipples. The story takes license with distance here, as it has in the girls' trip.

[120]Some kind of an animal, I don't know what, said the narrator.

[121]Ahkwe-θkwutšakware or Ahkwe-tšeθilye, two names.

[122]The three of them are always falling out but loving each other again. There was no doubt more of this between close kin than the generalized accounts portray; the tales evidently reflect life in their emotions even if their motivations are not always explicit to us.

[123]I assume that the six songs refer only to 41e or part of it, not to 41a-d.

[124]Given in 44 as Utšekoθũke; see note 131. It is evidently somewhat nearer to the Colorado than is the warm spring "near Sacaton" at which the girls are said in 31 to have lived.

the older said, "No, we must return and tell our
mother before we go off anywhere." So they went
home and told her, "We are going where the girls
are. If we die you will see our dry deer hide, hanging
there on the wall, move, and you will know we are
dead. If we die, our flute(s)[125] will split and scatter
over the house and tell you. And our feathers will
scatter, and so will the cottonwood tree down,[126] and
you will know. And our yellowhammer[127]-feather headdress which we are wearing, if we are killed, yellowhammer birds will return here carrying blood on their
mouths." (2 songs.)[128]

F. Twins Journey East and Die

43. So they started (to go east), but turned and
looked back and saw their mother coming behind. So
the two of them made a whirlwind which carried her
back to her house.[129] Looking at her, they said (sang),
"The old woman is still bothering[130] us as we travel."
(1 song.)

44. They went on, and before sundown came again
to Utšekoθūke.[131] The younger said, "Let us arrive even
if it is night," but the older said, "No, we want to
arrive in daytime." So they stayed there, and Para'āka
built a fire of brush. His younger brother was angry,[132]
threw his weapons down, and lay down to sleep; but he
sat up and watched. Then Nighthawk, Urū,[133] was singing. Para'āka told about that in songs. (6 songs.)

45. Then he told[134] about Owl, δokūpīt: He was afraid
of it; it was lying[135] to him. (6 songs.)

46. In the middle of the night, a bird flew overhead,
going west. In his singing he told about it: "Night
owl[136] is flying over me." (2 songs.)

47. Toward morning, the older brother stood up,
ready to go. "It is daylight," he said. "No, it is not,"
said the younger. So they disputed over that.[137] (1 song.)

[125]Called taltal here, simply cane in note 79.
[126]Kamainy-itšyê-vta.
[127]Kukho, red-shafted flicker. This is the satukhóta that
names the song-cycle and story; but satukhóta refers to
these, the bird itself is called kukho.
[128]Presumably about the omens only.
[129]In 24, note 71, she had taught them to use the whirlwind.
[130]Nyimevek.
[131]Variant recording of Ahtšyekuθuke of 42, note 124.
[132]At their resentments again.
[133]The interpreter called it "nightingale." It is a favorite
subject of Mohave song.
[134]In song.
[135]It seems to be considered generically deceiving.
[136]Tinyām kaḷṭesky(e) or kaltšyesk, the large bat. The
small one is qampany.
[137]Argument how perceptions are correctly construed is
a recurring motif.

48. When it was light enough to see, the Owl δokūpīt
sat there. He looked like he had horns.[138] (6 songs.)

49. At daybreak, he saw Urū nighthawks coming overhead. "We must have been staying on their road,"[139] he
sang. (6 songs.)

50. Now it was full light. "How shall we go?" they
said. Both[140] took an arrow, broke off a little end of
feather, blew it where they were going to, became that
wisp, so floated there. (1 song.)

51. As they floated, they dropped to the ground a
little short of the (girls') village. So they picked cottonwood down,[141] and became and floated as that. When
they reached the house, they did not enter the door,
but an opening at the corner (of the roof). They dropped
through that, became boys again, and found the girls.
(No songs mentioned.)

52a. Patuksāta,[142] the girls' father, was thinking.
Porridge was cooking outdoors, and it boiled over.
Now some who sing this say it was a dog, some say
it was his own son's little son, who picked up from the
ground what boiled over and ate it.[143] I think it was his
son's son, not a dog.[144] Now the older sister[145] got up
and said, "If we lie here like this, how will we ever
get anything to eat?" and took a pottery dish to bring
live coals, but when she saw the porridge boiling over,
she scooped the spillings from the ground four times.
The old man her father stood and saw her, and wondered,
"How is it that she is like that? She never was like that,
to take up and eat spillings instead of carrying (the pot)
in to feed them."[146] So he sent his son's son Itšamām-
sokóve[147] to see why his daughters did not come out.
The little boy took along pumpkin seeds to nibble on
his way to the house but ate them up before he got
there, so returned without entering, and reported, "There
is no one in the house except the girls." His grandfather

[138]Hīkwe. Perhaps that is one way in which the owl is
deceiving or lying (note 135).
[139]Av'unye is way, path, road.
[140]Huvik, both.
[141]Amainye-atšê-ku here, Kamainy-itšye-vta in note 126
to 42. The difference probably is partly grammatical.
[142]Cf. note 89.
[143]Itšamām-sokóve is one who eats such spill or waste.
The term itšiãlt, "glutton," was also given.
[144]The narrator here recognizes two versions; which certainly exalts tradition over dreaming as the source of the
story.
[145]In my notes here I used an abbreviation which might
be read either as "older sister" or "the old woman" (his
wife). The former makes better sense, but not altogether
clear sense.
[146]There is something omitted or misexplained or misunderstood here. Both the older sister and the little boy eat
the spilled food. Who has set the porridge on the fire? Why
does the girl not feed her sister and the two boys, but only
snitch for herself? This is clear: The girls are in the house
with their lovers, their father is outside at a little distance
or in another house. The boiling pot is outdoors, where the
Mohave normally cook.
[147]See note 143.

put some tepary beans in his hand and sent him again, and a third time with maize, but he came back saying the same. The fourth time he gave him pink beans[148] which are hard and slow to eat, and he had not finished them when he got to the house. So he went in, saw the boys, was scared,[149] ran back crying, and told of their being there. His father's father said, "Yes, now you see,[150] you were lying to me before." (No songs mentioned.)

52b. So the old man stood up, put on his owl-feather headdress and black face paint,[151] also his hulyêpa belt,[152] because there were enemies[153] in the house. And nye-sa'ôra,[154] he told his wife to bring him that, and brushed it off, and it made a noise like cracking: it is like a walking cane, is the same thing as tukoro,[155] perhaps this is the Maricopa or Yuma word for it.

52c. Then he started to tell the news to three "hawks,"[156] warriors: they were his "brothers."[157] These were Coyote, Hukθara or θara-veyo;[158] Raven, Qwaqāqa;[159] and Setkuwāka.[160] He went out and came to Coyote's place. Coyote told his wife to cook; but the old man slung[161] the sweat off his body and said, "I did not come to eat; I have visitors and want to give them a good time."[162] He meant he wanted to kill them. Then he went to Raven and to Setkuwāka and said the same thing. So those three started for Patuksāta's house, flying.

52d. The two boys knew it. They heard the wet earth moving,[163] a strong wind knocking the trees down, from these three coming. The boys saw them, bewitched

them so they could not do anything to them, as they lay along the inside of the wall of the house.

52e. Patuksāta started out again. This time he went to Falcon,[164] the grayish one.[165] Falcon started to serve him jackrabbits, but the old man said, "I did not come to eat, I came to entertain visitors." Then Falcon sank into the earth,[166] took up red clay and painted his hair,[167] rose up to the sun and looked down. He saw that the three "hawks" had not killed the boys. So he shot down to the house making a noise like thunder and darted in through a corner, not by the door,[168] and killed the two boys. (4 songs.)

That is the end of the story of the boys.

G. Their Mother's Mourning
and Departure

53a. The boys did not wholly die right away. The girls took them up in their arms, carried them about in the house, weeping without noise: the tears ran down their faces. When they were dead, Setkuwāka said, "I am the one who killed them," and rubbed his club in their blood.[169] But his two companions disputed with him.[170] Patuk-sāta returned, came in, and said to the girls, "There is no reason for you to be sorry for them." He dragged the boys' bodies out and threw them aside. The people crowded around where they lay, touched and played with them, laughed, and had fun.[171] Dust was (raised and) blown from (the gathering) there.

53b. They had said to their mother, "If we die, Satukhôta[172] will bring our blood." So now Satukhôta came alive in the quiver (where the headdress of its feathers was carried) and emerged between the people's legs. They wanted to chase it, but Patuk-sāta forbade it.[173] (2 songs.)

54. Satukhôta flew to the old woman their mother at Tšesaha, stopped, blood spilled from its mouth[174] into

[148]Marik-uta ("short [?] teparies").
[149]The scare is unmotivated here, except in so far as a small child might be startled by finding unexpected strangers. In the Halchidhoma and Diegueño versions however (see below), the boys shine with stars which they have put on.
[150]Once more, a variant of the "I told you so."
[151]Kwinyahily.
[152]In 3, note 20, the war belt is called suyūla.
[153]Ahwe, strangers, foreigners, enemies.
[154]Nye-sa'ôra, probably: his sa'ôra."
[155]See note 50.
[156]Soqwilye, the word used here, denotes hawks, generically, of several species. Warriors become such by dreaming of hawks. The term here accordingly is a straight metaphor.
[157]Kwora'āk-o'êvitš, from kwora'āka, old man.
[158]Huk-θara is the usual Mohave word for coyote; θara-veyo seems to be used in myth and song. Cf. tale 6A (UC-AR 11:1, p. 46, note 5); 7:2 (UC-AR 11:1, p. 52).
[159]Aqāqa is the usual Yuman form, apparently including both raven and crow (most Mohave do not know the English word raven). But compare in 6A (UC-AR 11:1, p. 46 and note 8), Qwāqāta as the name of a woman at Avi-kwa'ahāθa (a mountain beyond Phoenix) associated with Patak-sata, Hipa-hipa, and coyote. And Devereux, in JAFL 61:233-255, 1948, mentions a woman Kwakak, mother of Patcakarawe, associated with the Maricopa country.
[160]Neither narrator nor interpreter—nor I—could give any explanation of Setkuwāka.
[161]Wiped with the edge of his palm and slung off it. He had been running, presumably.
[162]Probably a saying or standardized ironical statement.
[163]Why "wet"? Was the earth still young and moist??

[164]Atš'ôr-nyamaθave, either the prairie or the true falcon.
[165]The Mohave say it has "hooks" on its elbows to strike with.
[166]To get his red paint? Perhaps also to show his power?
[167]"Covered his head with it."
[168]As the boys themselves had entered.
[169]I do not know whether this was a custom.
[170]This is surer as a Mohave habit.
[171]A sort of unorganized Yakaθa'alye, victory dance or gloating over a killing.
[172]Here at last the narrator brought in the bird after which the song-cycle is named—or rather its proper ritual name. It is of course, by context (cf. 42), the kukho or red-shafted flicker. When, before we began, the narrator seemed to deny this (see note 1), he was only parrying my inquiry that seemed to him improper. "Everything in its place."
[173]Motivation not clear.
[174]Here the bloody mouth clinches the identity of Kukho and Satukhôta.

the fire. The old woman cried, knowing what her sons had said. (2 songs.)

55. She stood, "I will tell of my sorrow." (2 songs.)

56. She told of their looks and color.[175] (2 songs.)

57. She addressed them: "I don't care; I told you often what would happen."[176] (1 song.)

58. She told of their weapons and clothes. (2 songs.)

59. She went back into the house and lay down. Then she heard her two boys coming in: it sounded like real. She went to their bed places, felt around, they were empty: it was only their souls.[177] She told of that. (3 songs.)

60. Then she sang of the house: of its earth pushed against the walls, of the arrowweed thatch, of its walls,[178] of its rafters.[179] (4 songs.)

61. Then she left home for her sorrows.[180] She started to go north, but the way did not seem right and she came back. She started east, then south, and it was the same. When she started west,[181] she found it felt better. She went on, but stopped, thought of not just leaving her house like that, and came back, and set fire to it at the four corners. She thought, "I will burn up and die with it" and lay down in it. But when the fire became great, she jumped out and stood there; she did not want to die.[182] She lay down and was scorched: the fire almost reached her. "My house is dead,[183] I wanted to die in it and could not." (2 songs.)

62. She stood and sang about the house burning. (3 songs.)

63. Now she started west, carrying a little pottery kwaθki with live coals in it.[184] "I will keep going. I might starve or be killed by enemies, but as long as I live I will go on westward." She went and went, then stopped and built a fire. "I have sorrow, I have lost both my boys, I cannot keep my hair." She had no knife, so she fired weeds, rolled her hair in the flame, burned it off close.[185] When she saw her shadow, she said, "I

look like a ghost.[186] My ears stick out."[187] (1 song.)

64. She went on again.—From here on, they never told me the songs: my kinsmen said they were not good and did not sing them for me.[188]—She went on, through Oq'ōq, a tribe or village, and through Sahamkyêta, the tribe beyond.[189] When she reached the ocean, she went right on into it, to Haθo'īly-uvĭvk, Ocean's Middle. One can see her there: she never died. When she is old, she becomes a girl again,[190] over and over. She is Kwakui-nyuhāve: all Mohave know her name.[191]

That is the end of the story of the old lady.

H. Kuyahumare

65a. Now the younger of the two sisters had become pregnant. Her father Patuk-sāta said, "If it is a boy, I will roast and eat him. If it is a girl, I will let her live." When the child was born, it was a boy. But his mother pulled his privates between his thighs and told the old man, "It is a girl: she will carry water and grind corn for you."[192] His name was Kuya-humare.[193]

65b. The child grew. As he played around, he came to where his father's bones were lying about. He took up a knee-cap,[194] played with it, and danced with it, till evening; he did not know it was his father's bone. He did this for three days; and again on the fourth. But now his mother's older sister suspected what he might be doing, went to spy on him, saw him dancing, and

[175]Mat-inyōre, "self markings, own appearance."
[176]A way of speaking—she does care, of course. "You would have it so though I tried to prevent it." It is a reproach of affection for causing grief to the survivor.
[177]Matkwisa, literally shadow, also soul.
[178]Which she will shortly burn.
[179]The four components are, in order, tapūk, suve īka, sopaik, tcuqah. The order is from outside inward.
[180]Yamkumaik.
[181]Sunwise circuit beginning with north.
[182]The Mohave give their emotions rein, but are biologically naturalistic as well as fatalistic.
[183]Ny-eva-tš-ipuik.
[184]A dish of coals for starting a fire (it could be replenished on the way by bits of sticks), or a glowing firebrand for warmth as one ran, were customary for women and men respectively.
[185]She might have drawn a glowing stick across her hair, but rolling in the flames is emotionally more satisfying.

[186]Nyaveδi-levĭk, ghost resemble.
[187]Women's free-flowing hair habitually covered their ears. However, the remark is also in line with Mohave interest in vivid, concrete observation.
[188]To us, this would be plain admission that he learned the songs and tale from his older kinsmen. However, after we were all through, I said to the interpreter, "Then he did not dream this?" and the old man replied, "I did dream it. Then (when I sang and told it) the old people said I had dreamed it right." The case for what constitutes "dreaming" can be rested there.
[189]Neither name is identifiable as an otherwise known tribe or settlement. Sahamkyêta may have been Gabrielino or Chumash, or just a name.
[190]I do not recall hearing of any other such cyclic rejuvenation. Could it be American influence toward happy-forever-after ending? The standard Mohave ending is a transformation (itštuātšk) into an animal or rock.
[191]"Old Woman of the West" is indicated as meaning by the context here. See note 5.
[192]Cf. Cane, 1:32 (UC-AR 11:1, pp. 8-9).
[193]The interpreter translated as "Cave-child," from kuya(m), cave. This agrees with his grandmother's being left in a cave, kuya, at Tšesahā, note 6. It is more reasonable than my former conjecture that Diegueño Cuya-homarr was by transposition from Kwayu (Kayu, by metathesis kuya); even though Kwayu meteor occurs in the Diegueño and Halchidhoma versions, and in the related Mohave Cane story. To the Mohave of 1953, incidentally, kwayu has come to mean "giant."
[194]Cf. Cane, 1:34 (UC-AR 11:1, p. 9); Nyohaiva, 3:15e (UC-AR 11:1, p. 31).

told him, "That is your father's bone you are dancing
with." (1 song, sung over four times; it is what the
boy sang on the four days.)

66a. The boy cried, came home, lay down on his
face.[195] He thought what he should do. Then he made
it rain.[196] It rained so heavily that there was a flood
all over except where the two sisters lived, his mother
and her older sister. All the people[197] perished.

66b. Then he took his mother and her sister and
started with them to go to his grandmother, his father's
mother. He was thinking of her. He came to Williams
Fork mouth[198] and followed the Colorado up a little way
to opposite Amaṭa.[199] Here he was going to cross the
river; but he could not take the two women along.[200]
So he turned them into Snipes, Turísturís.[201]

66c. He himself swam over, but nearly drowned.
Then he called Dragonfly[202] to help him. Dragonfly
flew to him, took hold of his back hair, and carried
him across to Amaṭa; and from there he went on to
Ahmaly-avêre.[203]

66d. Now he already knew what his grandmother had
done, so he went on westward past (where) her house
(had been at Tšesaha).[204] He went and went, passed
through the same tribes, reached the ocean, walked into
it, and got to his grandmother's place. There they both
live, immortal:[205] formerly people used to see them.

Asked to sing a few songs, Avêpuya reflected, then
chose "six" (actually he sang five) from paragraph 45,
in which the older brother told Owl it was lying to him;
then followed with the two from 46 about the Kaltšyesk
Bats. His voice was a deep bass, very resonant, without
marked stresses or intervals, almost a great hum. He
accompanied himself with a barely perceptible beat of
his right foot; no instrument is used with the Satukhôta.

[195]Ashamed, depressed, angry.
[196]Cf. Cane, 1:30, 82b (UC-AR 11:1, pp. 8, 15-16).
[197]Cf. Cane, 1:37, 102 (UC-AR 11:1, pp. 9-10, 18).
[198]Hakutšyepa. It is now drowned out by Lake Havasu
behind Parker Dam.
[199]Amaṭa was only a half mile above Williams Fork mouth
and the turn of the Colorado where Parker Dam was built.
The name means simply "earth" or "land."
[200]Cf. Cane, 1:82b, 103 (UC-AR 11:1, pp. 15-16, 18).
[201]Cf. Cane, 1:103 (UC-AR 11:1, p. 18).
[202]Sakotít, described as red-winged.
[203]Ahmaly-avêre or Ahma-va-ahwêre, "quail run," just
downstream from Amaṭa, perhaps 100 yards.
[204]Cf. note 4.
[205]Not a usual Mohave ending; see note 190.

COMPARISON WITH
DIEGUEÑO AND HALCHIDHOMA
VERSIONS

The 1953 recording of this tale from the Mohave
makes the third full-length version of it available from
as many Yuman tribes.

The first was published by Constance G. DuBois in[206]
the Journal of American Folklore in 1904, under the
title of "The Story of the Chaup." It fills 26 pages, and
contains mention of 89 songs, plus 4 others inferred,
plus a notation of some having been omitted toward the
end. By 1904 I had recorded part of the present collection of myths, and Miss DuBois's Chaup story at once
struck me as remarkably Mohave-like. I made inquiries
about it among the Mohave, and was told of a similar
song-tale called Satukhôta, as stated above. At the same
time, it was evident that the Mohave Cane story also
contained some elements of Diegueño Chaup.

The second version was got by Spier between 1929
and 1932 and published by him under the appropriate
title "Flute Lure" in 1933 in his Yuman Tribes of the
Gila River. It occupies 30 pages slightly smaller than
DuBois's. It is much the longest tale given by Spier.
A good many songs were mentioned by the narrator,
but not systematically, it would seem.[207] The narrator
was an old man, Kutox—he is pictured in Spier's plate
1,—who was not Maricopa but Halchidhoma in descent.

My Mohave version now renders possible a comparison of the three. It is extraordinary how alike these
three tellings are, both in general outline of a really
complicated plot and in dozens, perhaps hundreds, of
concrete and original touches. No one can doubt that
we have before us three renditions of a single story:
if there is any marvel, it is how faithfully it was preserved in its intertribal wanderings. Yurok narratives,
which I have frequently secured in several versions,
even when relatively brief, vary more within the tribe,
than these three Yuman ones. However, we also know
that oral tradition, unless it insists on verbatim fidelity,
cannot hand substance on unchanged; especially where
aesthetic motivation is stronger than the ritual com-
ponent. So there are also hundreds of differences: items
lost, others added, new twists, variant emphases.

I have therefore instituted a two-fold comparison.
The first is a synthetic Concordance of Common Elements, given relatively briefly. The second is a longer,
more detailed list of Variations in the Three Versions.

[206]JAFL 17:217-242.
[207]I count 17 in the part of the story before the girls
come.

These are grouped under 11 heads, I to XI[208] with
lower-case-lettered subheads, according to the order
of the Common Elements list. In this first list I give
the "paragraph occurrence" of motives and items. For
Mohave, the paragraphs are those of my text. For
Diegueño and Halchidhoma, the paragraphs are not
numbered in the printed texts, but represent a numbering in my annotations. However, their approximate
place in the two printed texts can readily be found,
and they serve to indicate relative sequence, and hence
changes in order. Thus the episode of the twins'
mother turning herself into a stump and being almost
shot by them (IIf), is paragraph or item 13 in the
Halchidhoma version and comes after the IIIa-c episode of the revivified deer, 11-12 in the Halchidhoma
versions, whereas in Diegueño, it is 6 and the deer
incident is 8. Similarly, the deer episode in Mohave
is 41e, almost two-thirds of the way through the tale,
instead of near the beginning. (I list the paging in
Spier on which items 1-75 of the Halchidhoma version
are printed: 1-3, p. 367; 4-8, p. 368; 9, 10a, b, p. 369;
10c, d, p. 370; 10e, 11, p. 371; 12, 13, p. 372; 14-16,
p. 373; 17, p. 374; 18, 19, p. 375; 20, 21, p. 376; 22-25,
p. 377; 26-28, p. 378; 29-32a, p. 379; 32b-d, 33, p. 380;
34-36, 37a, p. 381; 37b, p. 382; 37c, p. 383; 37d, p. 384;
37e, p. 385; 38-40, p. 386; 41, p. 387; 42-45, p. 388;
46, 47, 48a-d, 49, p. 389; 50-51, p. 390; 55-56, p. 391;
57-62, p. 392; 63-66, p. 393; 67-69, p. 394; 70-73, p.
395; 74-75, p. 396.)

Concordance of Common Elements
in Plot of the Three Versions
(D, Diegueño; H, Halchidhoma; M, Mohave)

I. Birth of the Twins
   a. Mother left, alone. D 1; H 1; M 1.
   b. Bathes, impregnated by Gopher. D 1; H 2-4;
      M 2.
   c. Twins, one called Parahane. D 1; H (5); M 2;
      cf. M Cane 2 (UC-AR 11:1, p. 4).

II. Growth of the Twins
   a. Mother makes cradle, etc. D 2; H 6.
   b. False claimants of paternity. D 3; H 7.
   c. Boys kill quail from cradle. D 5; H 8; M
      Coyote 6A (UC-AR 11:1, p. 46); M Chuhueche
      (Tale 13) 79.
   d. Cry till she cooks quail. D 5; H 9; M Chuh.
      (Tale 13) 79.

   e. She makes bows for them. D 7; H 10; M Chuh.
      (Tale 13) 79.
   f. Is almost shot as stump. D 6; H 13.
   g. Boys successively kill larger game. D 7;
      H 10.

III. Revivified Deer
   a. Boys kill deer. D 8; H 11; M 41e.
   b. Mother revivifies, sends off. D 8; H 12;
      M 41e.
   c. They follow, angry. D 8; H 12; M 41e.

IV. Eagle Pets
   a. Mother sends boys to cliff. D 9; H 14; M 3.
   b. Interferes by making: Canyon, M 4. Mirage,
      H 15; M 5. Rain, D (8); H 16, 22.
   c. Younger tries climb as racer snake, falls.
      D 10; H 17, 18; M 10.
   d. Older climbs as racer, takes eaglets. D 10;
      H 19; M 11.
   e. Younger seizes better eagle; quarrel. D 10;
      H 20, 21; M 12.
   f. Angry, they make rain against each other.
      D 11; H (22); M 12, 13.
   g. Eaglets die, buried with weapons. D 11; H 22;
      M 14, 15.
   h. Mother draws revivified eaglets from ground.
      D (12); H 23; M 17.
   i. They disbelieve her, but find them. D 12;
      H 24; M 17.
   j. She adjudicates renewed quarrel. H 25; M 17.
   k. Instructs them to bring her food. M 18.
   l. And tie and pluck eaglets. M 20-22.
   m. And get swift-fox skins for eagle feathers.
      M 22-23.

V. Cane and Flutes
   a. Coyote sent for arrow canes. H 26.
   b. They are straightened, feathered, shot with.
      H 27-29.
   c. Boys sent for deer magic, bow wood. M 24-26.
   d. Sent to get large cane. D 13; H 30; M 28-29;
      M Cane 18a-19 (UC-AR 11:1, p. 7). From in
      sea. D 13; H 30.
   e. Y. br. tries to get and fails. H 31.
   f. O. br. meets 4 underwater beavers. H 32.
   g. O. br. blows away water and animals. D 13.
   h. Both brothers cut cane—butt, tip. M 30; M
      Cane 20-22 (UC-AR 11:1, p. 7).
   i. (Mother) cuts cane with nail. H 33; M 30; M
      Cane 91 (UC-AR 11:1, p. 17); M Chuh. (Tale
      13) 76.
   j. Mother decorates canes as flutes. D 13; H 33;
      M Cane 24 (UC-AR 11:1, p. 8).

---

[208]These parts of the story in the intertribal comparison
are designated by Roman numerals to prevent confusion with
the somewhat different parts or section of the Mohave tale,
which are designated by capital letters.

k. Mother plays flute. D 13.
   Fails M 30.

l. Twins play flute. D 14; H 34; M 31.

m. It surpasses birds' songs. H 34.

n. Girls attracted, smell bad, sent away. D 14.

o. Two girls. D 14; H 35; M 31.

p. Daughters of Patuksata. H 35; M 32; cf. M
   Coyote 6A (UC-AR 11:1, pp. 46-47).

q. Daughters of Buzzard. D 14.

VI. The Girls Visit the Twins.

a. Two sisters swimming. D 14; H 35; M 32.

b. One hears music, draws other out. D 14;
   H 36; M 32.

c. Talk of leaving home, not tell father. M 32.

d. Father suspicious. D 14.

e. They leave. D 15; H (36); M 33.

f. Obstacles, incidents on way. D 15, 16.

g. They meet pretended flute players. D 16;
   H 37; M 33-36.

h. Go on, see twins drink, follow them. M 37,
   39.

i. Mother forbids girls, criticizes, hides door.
   D 17; H 38, 39; M 40; M Chuh. (Tale 13) 71.

j. Mother sends boys out to see. D 17; M 40.

k. Mother calls girls d.-in-law. D 17; M Cane
   89 (UC-AR 11:1, p. 16).

l. Mother put to sleep. H 40; M 41a.

m. O. br. refuses o. girl. D 17; H 40; M 41a.

n. Although she wakes him with insects. D 17;
   H 40.

o. Because it would spoil hunting. M 41a.

p. Y. br. does fail to kill deer. D 19; H 42;
   M 41d.

q. Girls leave, y. unwillingly. D 18; H 41; M
   41b.

VII. The Boys' Visit: Omens, Journey.

a. Y. br. wants his wife, o. goes with him.
   D 19; H 43.

b. O. br. tells mother. H 43; M 42.

c. They leave omens: headdress. D 20; H 44;
   M 42.

d. Mother tries to impede going. D 21; M 43.

e. One br. angry at other. D 22; M 44; M Cane
   20-22 (UC-AR 11:1, p. 7).

f. Sleep on way; sing of owls, etc. D 23; H 45;
   M 44-49.

g. Put stars on body. D 23; H 46.

h. Fly to girls through roof. D 23; H 47; M 50,
   51.

VIII. Death of the Brothers.

a. Father hears girls laugh, curious. D 24; H 48.

b. Sends grandson to see. D 24; H 48; M 52a.

c. Bribes him with handfuls of food. D 24; H 48;
   M 52a.

d. Gluttonous child returns for more. D 24; H
   48; M 52a.

e. Sees brs. shining. D 24; H 49.

f. Is scared, returns. D 24; H 49; M 52a.

g. Old man paints and prepares for war. H 50;
   M 52b.

h. Asks aid of Coyote. D 25; H 50; M 52c.
   Falcon. H 50; M 52e. Others. D 25; H 50;
   M 52c.

i. Dialogue of old man with allies. H 50; M 52c.

j. Coyote fails to attack. D 25; H 51-52.

k. Falcon to sky, swoops in roof hole, kills.
   H 52; M 52e.

l. Both brs. killed. D 26; H 52; M 52d, e.

m. False claimant to killing. D 27; H 53; M 53a.

n. Brs.' corpses abused. D 27; H 58, 59; M 53a.

IX. Twins' Mother Mourns and Leaves.

a. The omens are fulfilled. H 54; M (53b).

b. Flicker's bloody mouth. H 56, 57; M 53b, 54.

c. She mourns. M 55-59.

d. Burns house. D 42; M 61-62.

e. Goes off. D 43; H (69, 73, 75); M 63, 64; M
   Cane 35 (UC-AR 11:1, p. 9), with coals in
   dish.

X. Kuyahumar's Career

a. Y. sister pregnant. D 19, 28; H 60; M 65a;
   M Cane 29 (UC-AR 11:1, p. 8).

b. Her f. will eat child if boy. D 28; H 60; M
   65a; M Cane 32 (UC-AR 11:1, p. 9), will kill.

c. Is dressed and raised as girl. D 29; H 61,
   M 65a; M Cane 32 (UC-AR 11:1, p. 9).

d. Mother's f. tries kill him. D 30; H 64, 65.

e. Retrieves m's f. (m's br.)'s gambling. D 34;
   H 70, 71.

f. Kills m.'s f. D 35; H 66; M 66a.

g. Dancing with f.'s bones. D 31; M 65b; M Cane
   34 (UC-AR 11:1, p. 9); M Nyohaiva 15e, f, 27
   (UC-AR 11:1, pp. 31, 33).

h. Kills gr.f.'s people. D 34, 35; M 66a; M Cane
   37, 102 (UC-AR 11:1, pp. 9-10, 18).

i. Knocks f.'s bone far. D 32; M Cane 37 (UC-
   AR 11:1, p. 9).

j. Evokes his f.'s shade; useless. D 37; H 67,
   68; M Cane 96, 97 (UC-AR 11:1, p. 17).

XI. His Reunion with Grandmother

a. Goes to join father's mother. D 36; H 69; M
   Cane 87 (mother) UC-AR 11:1, p. 16.

b. Various adventures. D 38, 39, 41; H 70-72;

M 66c; M Cane 69-82, 97-101 (UC-AR 11:1, pp. 11-15, 17-18).

   c. Transforms mother (and her sister). D 40; M 66b; M Cane 103 (UC-AR 11:1, p. 18).

   d. Finds grandmother. D 42; H 69; M 66d.

   e. They live together. D 43; H 73; M 66d.

   f. He is meteor or comet. D 43; H 74; M Cane 104 (UC-AR 11:1, pp. 18-19).

Variations in the Three Versions
(D, Diegueño; H, Halchidhoma; M, Mohave)

I. Birth of the Twins

   a. D, 2 sisters have pool (doublet of section VI a,b); in IIc,d older is lost. —H, she can no longer follow people; is Sinyuok inyuxava ("west woman"?), at "Blue-water." —M, Kwakui-nyuhave, "West (?)-old-woman," stays behind as mourning tribes travel S.

   b. H, She mocks Yellow Gopher, Ce-akwas; fourth time he seizes her; she sends him away, then regrets it. —M, Taksé-kunyore, striped gopher.

   c. D, Twins called Para-han and Ashatahutch; both are Cuya-homarr (sic). —H, not named. —M, Para-hane (y), Para-'aka (o). —M Cane 2, 95 (UC-AR 11:1, pp. 4, 17): Puke-hane(o), Tšitšuvare(y); latter's son Ahta-hane.

II. Growth of the Twins
(Lacking in Mohave version)

   a. D, reach N for red knife, S for blue; N for rough hat for o. br., S for fine for y. —H, she sings and makes 4 parts of cradles.

   b. D, Coyote, then Wild Canary, claim paternity. —H, animals bring wood, she rejects, but takes Gopher's.

   c. D, boys kill quail from cradle with hailstones out of ears. —H, fillip with dirt out of ear. —M Coyote 6A (UC-AR 11:1, p. 47), Patša-karrawa in cradle kills quail with black balls he makes of his breath. M Chu-hueche (Tale 13) 79, pellets of saliva kill (an indubitable but thin echo of the episode).

   d. D, mother thinks quail are from suitor, angry, throws them away. —H, she scolds, throws quail out.

   e. D, younger's bow better.

   f. D, mother turns into stump to watch, hence her name Sinyo-hauch (sic). —H, turns into stump.

   g. D, in order: blue-breasted lizard, wood rat, rabbit, jackrabbit (deer). At first they are frightened and run off. —H, in order: mice, amilk, pack rat, rabbit, jackrabbit (deer).

III. Revivified Deer

   a. D, twins kill deer at end of series of small animals. —H, same; then they sing to make deer light to carry to their mother to skin. —M, incident transposed to later in the tale, VIp, after the girls have come and gone, and y. br. fails in hunting.

   b, c. D, resuscitated deer runs to E ocean, then W, enter it, is safe; boys return angry. When they kill a deer, they eat it, give mother rabbits. —H, M, m. resuscitates deer, they chase, apparently angry.

IV. Eagle Pets

   a. D, the ignorant boys bring crows, horned owls, common owls, buzzards instead of eaglets. —H, on Vi-taxa mt. (Avi Taha'?). —M, on Samakwiðíke Mt.; they dress and arm with care.

   b. M, mother, having sent them, blocks them by an impassable canyon. —H, M, see a mirage (M, made by mother). —D, H, mother makes rain, as again in H, IVg.

   c. D, y. br. climbs, falls, smashed, o. revives; "I only slept." No mention of snake. —H, y. to climb W side, o. E; y. gathers feathers, o. makes him discard; y. turns into gwitnyialk snake, falls. —M, y. makes magic rolling on ground, turns into female Racer (kwatnialk), knows he can climb, professes inability, comes down.

   d. D, o. br. "gets" red snake, pacifies snakes on mt., ties feet of 2 eaglets, throws them down. —H, o. br. turns into (cottonwood?) down, floats up while y. worries, brings down 2 eaglets. —M, o. turns into male Red Racer, follows eaglets to end of eyrie, is struck by one, brings both down.

   e. D, y. br. tries keep both pets, but cedes black one. —H, y. takes bright eaglet, o. insists (sic) on dull one, they quarrel. —M, y. takes larger eaglet, o. wants it; y. carries his on cradle frame, older by feet, sulky.

   f. D, o. br. brings rain from W over y., then y. makes thunder storm from N over o. —H, mother makes rain on them. —M, o. br. makes rain, sun, heavy rain, both try cover their pets.

   g. D, both eaglets die, are buried with yellow paint and twins' hair. —H, M, both eaglets die, are buried with twins' weapons. —M, on way, see eaglets' ghosts.

   h. D, twins home, sulk. —H, mother draws revivified eaglets out of ground with stick. —M, she pushes stick into heap of earth, resuscitates eagles.

   i, j. D, mother says eaglets are returning; twins disbelieve, but find them; o. again gets black one. —H, M, twins think mother lying, angry at her, quarrel over birds, m. makes y. br. give up better bird.

k, l, m. M only: mother sends twins hunt 4 kinds of small game; eaglets fly dancing with the wind. Eagles tied, plucked, ashamed; m. sends boys to hunt swift-fox as container for feathers.

V. Cane and Flutes

a, b. H only: mother sends Coyote east for crooked arrow canes, she straightens and feathers them, has twins practice shooting.

c. M only: she sends twins to bring deer hunting magic and bow wood.

d. D, H, she sends to get "tree" (D), cane (H) deep in sea. —M, simply sent for cane.

e, f, g, h. D, o. br. blows away sea and animals. —H, y. br. dives, fails; o. dives, passes red, white, black, yellow beavers on sand of same colors, cuts cane. —M, no difficulties, both cut, o. br. butt, y. tip. —M Cane 20-22 (UC-AR 11:1, p. 7), cut cane, quarrel over precedence.

i, j. D, mother shapes and decorates flutes; H, same, plus pointing 4 directions antisunwise beginning S. —M, mother cuts with fingernail; M Cane 91 (UC-AR 11:1, p. 17), hero splits thunder cane with nail; Cane 24 (UC-AR 11:1, p. 8), o. br. decorates cane flute with saliva.

k. D, mother plays flute. —M, she tries and fails.

l, m. D, twins play to 4 directions. —H, they surpass birds. —M, both play.

n, o. D, girls come from 4 quarters but are sent back because smell bad from their food, except 2 from E. —H, M, 2 girls come from E, from near Sacaton, Pimas.

p. D, girls are daughters of Ithchin, Buzzard. —H, M, of Patokcot(u), Patuksāta. —M Coyote 6A, 3 (UC-AR 11:1, p. 46), Pataksata is old man E of Phoenix, finally killed by "Mohave" from W (p. 47).

VI. The Girls Visit the Twins

a, b. D, 2 sisters at pool, y. hears first. —H, o. sis. hears, pulls out of water. —M, y. in spring fishing, o. hears flute, calls y. out.

c, d. D, father suspects, asks, they allege willow bark gathering. —M, girls feel abused by parents and free to run off, pick up charcoal bits to parch corn for way.

e. D, leave, sing of home; blow night away (cf. M (Satakhota) 40 above, boys tear night sky open) with smoke from pipes (taken) from their ears. —M, sing behind house.

f. D only: brush and thorns hurt them, no road, high trees (song material); sand hill, they slip back, o. sis. roughens with fur blanket reached for.

g. Pretenders at flute playing. D, Rattlesnake (only rattles), Raccoon (offers snake as food), Horned Owl (same), Frog (large, blocks pond, girls drive off with caps to drink). —H, Xomase Hawk (whistles, kills prairie dogs), Xa'-ndaseilye Lizard (offers mesquite), Ground Squirrel (xumir, runs up and down pole), Small Screech Owls (sit in row, push), Horned Owl (sits, hoots). —M, Groundsquirrel (whistles, runs up and down ocotillo), Aha-teθilye Tree Lizard, Woodpecker, Humaθe hawk. —In all cases, the point is the ludicrous failure of the imitative pretenders.

h. M only, perhaps because the only localized account: the journey, Satukhota 37-39; y. sis. menstruates; they eat at Colorado River; see twins, hunting, come to river for drink; cross, follow them, see ghost-flickering light.

i, j, Mother's negative attitude. D, m. knows girls coming, warns sons against; owls, coyotes howl, she sends sons out to see. —H, m. sees girls coming, covers up door, girls step on ashes, warm hands. —M, m. tells sons of visitors, they disbelieve, tear sky open to see (cf. VI, e, Diegueño), report no one there; mother declares girls unchaste. —M Chuhueche (Tale 13) 71, o. br. calls y. br.'s new wife unchaste.

k. D, girls silent as twins' mother uses kin terms to them, until she calls them daughters-in-law; she sends them into house to boys. —H, M, lacking. —M Cane 89 (UC-AR 11:1, p. 16), calls son's wives d-in-law.

l. H, y. twin puts watching mother to sleep with "bag"; awaking, she calls him Paru-xan. M, girls put o. woman to sleep.

m, n, o. D, o. twin does not "greet" girl; she sends fleas to bite him (and keep awake). —H, o. keeps face down, silent, though girl makes ant hill and scorpion to move him. —M, on account of hunting luck, o. refuses intercourse, though girls play with him.

p. D, morning, y. br. unable to kill game, pines, wastes, m. restores by throwing in pond. —H, y. on hunt does not try, plays music with bow. —M, y. cannot kill, except an akweskanāme.

q. D, girls go home, o. because not married. —H, o. sis. prevails on y. to go home. —M, go home, o. knows y. had intercourse.

VII. The Boys' Visit: Omens, Journey

a, b. D, y. br. persuades o. to go with him to wife. —H, same, though o. knows girls' people are

enemies; tells mother. —M, o. br. kills deer, m.
instead of skinning kicks it alive, it runs off, twins
pursue, angry at m., far E, see smoke of girls, y.
wants to go to, o. persuades him first to notify m.,
they return to her.

c. Omens left with mother: D, o. br. hangs headdress, will wave if dead; y., feather rope will break.
—H, beads and arrows will break in storm from E.
—M, hanging hide will move; flutes will split; feathers
and cottonwood down will scatter; headdresses they are
wearing will turn into yellowhammer birds coming back
with blood in mouths.

d. D, m. tries to keep them, reaches to sky for
hailstones as play things; they set up grass dummies
of themselves, she embraces, faints. —H, lacking.
—M, m. follows, they make whirlwind to carry her
back home.

e. Brothers quarrel: D, o. tells y: drink at
Frog's pond with eyes shut, intends push and drown
him (unmotivated), y. sees. —H, lacking. —M, y. wants
to push on to girls, o. makes camp, y. angry; o. sits
up, watches; they quarrel whether it is dawn. —M
Cane (UC-AR 11:1, pp. 7-8), brothers quarrel over
cane on trip, 20-22, o. bewitches y., 24-28. —M Chuhueche (Tale 13) 45, 52, 71, 75, 76.

f. D, at night, owls and coyotes; they sing of
them. —H, at their camp, horned owl falls in fire, y.
thinks it sign of death. —M, o. br. sings of Owl,
Night hawk.

g. D, twins reach to sky, put stars on their
bodies. —H, put on large stars for eyes, small over
body. —M, lacking.

h. D, they rise, fly over people, through roof
hole into girls' house; people think are "meteors"
(chaup), girls' father says human. —H, girls are dice-
gambling when boys enter by smoke hole, sit beside
them. —M, they blow themselves as broken arrow
feather, then as cottonwood down, float in at corner
hole of roof, find girls.

VIII. Death of the Brothers

a. D, H, girls laugh, father in other house hears,
is curious.

b. D, f. sends grandson to see. —H, sends crooked
and greedy daughter's son to see. —M, o. man sees o.
d. come out, eat spilled boilings over, wonders, sends
gluttonous son's son (or dog—"variant version").

c, d. D, bribes boy with wheat, then maize to eat
on way. —H, bribes him with handful of pumpkin seeds,
then 2 of maize, then 4, then 8 of palo verde seeds;
boy eats all but last on way, returns without entering.

—M, bribes with pumpkin seeds, tepary beans, maize,
reports no one in house; then with pink teparies, only
these last him to house.

e, f. D, boy sees twins' star eyes shining, scared,
runs back, tells. —H, boy peeps, sees shining, girls
throw dirt at, he falls, sobs, is scared, runs. —M, boy
sees twins, is scared, runs back, reports; gr. f. tells
him he lied before.

g, h. D, o. man asks aid of Coyote, Hawks, Bear.
—H, he paints for war, seeks 3 tribes, Coyote, Tcora-
huwak Hawk (Falcon). —M, he dresses and paints for
war, notifies his "hawk-warrior brothers": Coyote,
Raven, Setkuwāka.

i. H, Coyote and Hawk knock old man down with
gambling poles. —M Coyote (52c), Falcon (52e) tell
wives to cook for him, o. man says he came to entertain visitors.

j. D, Coyote, Hawk, Bear successively come to
attack twins but see shining and desist. —H, Coyote
starts with weapons, arrives, sits down with 3 tribes
admiring twins. —M, Coyote, Raven, Setkuwāka shake
earth and blow trees down, but twins lie inside house
wall and with magic paralyze the attackers' efforts.

k. H, Falcon rises to sky, drops through smoke
hole, clubs twins dead, swoops out by hole. —M, Falcon
paints, rises to sun, swoops down with a roar through
house corner, kills the twins.

l. D, old man tunnels to his daughters' house, it
begins to fall, twins fly out, he follows, catches y. br.,
kills with magic; o. br. now wants die also, sits, is
killed.

m. D, Coyote, the people, claim to have killed
twins, but girls' father stands on their bodies and
boasts. —H, Coyote strikes y. br.'s body, but is derided
as false claimant, then threatens crowd and is named
Saramiyo. —M, Setkuwāka claims to have done the killing, but Coyote and Raven deny it.

n. D, people there cut up and eat twins' bodies.
—H, old man Patukcut stakes bodies up; blood drips
on pumpkin seed meal, which is eaten by all (a "Maricopa" custom; the Mohave attribute it to the Halchidhoma while on the Colorado). —M, father takes bodies
from weeping daughters, throws out, people touch, play
with, taunt corpses.

IX. Twins' Mother Mourns and Leaves
(Scant in Diegueño)

a. H, arrows and bead strings break, storm from
E, twins' mother sings in mourning.

b. H, Yellowhammer pecks bodies, bloodies his
feathers, flies to mother to tell, she reviles him, he

shakes earth at her. He sleeps, ants crawl on him, he tastes them, picks them up, becomes bird who does that. —M, Yellowhammer (here Satukhôta, not Kukho) comes alive from feathers in quiver, emerges, dashes between peoples' legs, flies to mother, spits blood into fire, she cries.

c. M, mother mourns in a series of songs (55-59).

d. (D, her house, dirty, is burned for her later by her grandson Kuyahumar.) —M, she burns her house, tries to burn herself (60-62), burns off her hair (63).

e. (D, she flies off on Kuyahumar's back.) —(H, grandson overtakes her, goes off with her.) —M, she goes to W ocean, enters, lives there, rejuvenates (63, 64). As she travels, she carries coals in dish—as in M Cane 35 (UC-AR 11:1, p. 9).

X. Kuyahumar's Career

a. D, H, M, y. sis. pregnant. —M Cane 29 (UC-AR 11:1, p. 8), y. br.'s first wife is pregnant.

b. D, grandfather will eat brains if boy. —H, M, will eat him. —M Cane 32 (UC-AR 11:1, p. 8), will eat if boy.

c. D, H, M, M Cane 32, boy declared girl, so raised. Also: D, boy grows fast, cries for piece of father's flesh to eat. —H, water poured on fire to keep gr. f. from seeing child is boy; he discards head ring, plays with bow.

d. D, gr. f. has boy swim in water with stakes, throw a crushing rock, but fails to kill him. —H, gr. f. tries lose boy, push in fire.

e. D, H, gambling reversal by boy for m.'s f. (D), m.'s br. (H); the episodes seem out of place and loosely attached.

f. D, boy kills the local people, apparently incl. gr. f.; boy shoots his m.'s m. for dancing dressed in his father's bones. —H, boy shoots up, arrow falls on old man. —M, old man's death not specified, perhaps included among his people in 66a.

g. D, it is his m.'s m. who dances in father's bones. —M, the boy dances with them in his innocence. —M Cane 34 (UC-AR 11:1, p. 9), mother tells him he has been playing with f.'s bone; M Nyohaiva 15e, f (UC-AR 11:1, p. 31), finds f.'s bone, wrestles for it, wins; 27 (UC-AR 11:1, p. 33), will fight on account of.

h. D, he exterminates them in two lots, with different magic, not fully motivated. —M, he makes heavy rain and drowns all except m. and her sis. —M Cane, he exterminates people with struck shinny ball becoming kwayu meteor, 37 (UC-AR 11:1, pp. 9-10),

and with thunder cane burning them up, 102 (UC-AR 11:1, p. 18).

i. D, boy whistles f.'s heel bone to him, knocks it W into ocean, then kicks f.'s br.'s heel for E. —M Cane 37, see preceding paragraph Xh.

j. D, owl and ants guide him to spot; f.'s voice speaks; boy tries to fit bones together, leg missing, f. can't stand. —H, lies prone, 4 times fills hole with tears; draws f. and his br. up from ground with an arrow where cremated; they hang head in shame, too weak to help boy. —M, lacking. —M Cane 96, 97 (UC-AR 11:1, p. 17), boy makes ground open, f. rises, boneless, cannot walk, embraced, weeping, farewell, f. returns.

XI. Reunion with Grandmother

a. D, H, leaves mother and her sis. to find gr. m. —M, takes them along. —M Cane 87 (UC-AR 11:1, p. 16), boy rejoins mother.

b. D, reaches house of "lions," almost killed, makes house fall on them; to pond with blackbirds; crane swallows boy, buzzard rescues him (perhaps buzzard is his m.'s f.); these adventure episodes are poorly integrated into the narrative, and not always clear. —H, see Xe. —M, he nearly drowns crossing river, is rescued by dragonfly, 66c. —M Cane 69-82 (UC-AR 11:1, pp. 11-16), boy marries, contests with Kwayu and Sun; 97-101 (UC-AR 11:1, pp. 17-18), contests with father's foes, revenge.

c. D, his mother follows him, tired, he stretches his bow as bridge for her over lake, twitches her off and drowns her (unmotivated). —H, last mention of m. when he leaves her to go to gr. m. —M, at river, he cannot take m. and her sis., turns them into Snipes. —M Cane 103 (UC-AR 11:1, p. 18), turns m. and 4 wives into Pleiades, half-brother into Snipe, uncle into Snowy Owl (?). —M Chuhueche (Tale 13), 85, m. turns into Snipe.

d. D, gr. m. is blind, he sits on her lap, cries; her house is dirty, he burns it for her. —H, gr. m. has gone NW, he overtakes her. —M, follows her to her perpetual ocean home.

e. D, he flies with her on his back to San Bernardino Mts., they live there now. —H, they go off together; she is morning star, at whose rising the aged die (? idea of rejuvenation). —M, they keep renewing their youth.

f. D, he is Chaup fireball. —H, he becomes red comet in N—though Kwiya-homar seems to mean meteor (kwiyu) boy. —M Cane 104 (UC-AR 11:1, pp. 18-19), he will be a flying meteor, kwayu, but turns into rock Me-koaţa (leg projects) on Colorado River.

Reconstruction of Source of the Tale

The question arises whether the analysis made throws light on the history of the tale among the three tribes.

In the Common Elements list, the following appear:

D and H share items, 16; M only, 11; total, 27.
H and M share items, 11; D only, 6; total, 17.
D and M share items, 8; H only, 5; total, 13.

This makes Mohave definitely the most aberrant, Halchidhoma probably the least so.

A count of details in the Variations list would evidently increase these figures considerably, but presumably without much changing the proportions.

During the past hundred years or more, the geographical position of the three tribes has been triangular, with the Halchidhoma-Diegueño base somewhat longer than the two other sides. This would put the Mohave nearest to median position. However, before 1830, the Halchidhoma, in 1826 still on the Colorado River, were in median position geographically, as they remain "median" in the twentieth century in the form in which they tell the tale. We may therefore conclude that they served as intermediaries between the Diegueño and the Mohave before about 1828-30.

Of course, one or more other river tribes may also have been involved in the spread—the Yuma or Kohwan especially, or both—but the tale failed to be collected from them. The Yuma are likely in this connection because the Kamia, who are desert Diegueño, were in the habit of farming in Yuma territory on the Colorado when their own backwaters in Imperial Valley failed them. The Kohwan are indicated as probable participants because their dialect is of Cocopa-Diegueño group, and because between 1776 and about 1830 they lived sometimes near the Halchidhoma in the Blythe-Poston-Parker region.

The Diegueño are almost precluded as the original tellers of the complex story, which in length and total character is unique among them, but is characteristic of the river tribes. For instance, the specification of nearly a hundred songs at precise places in a hero and adventure narrative has not been paralleled among any coastal or mountain tribes of southern California.

If the Mohave had devised the tale and passed it on first to the Halchidhoma, it would be hard to understand why it was transmitted by them to the Diegueño with less alteration than during the first step; especially so since in subsistence, war habits, and general attitudes and total culture the river Yumans were more similar to one another than to the Diegueño.

All in all, then, an origin in the region of the Halchidhoma, Yuma, and Kohwan is indicated, and at a time before the Halchidhoma were driven out to take refuge on the Gila some 130 years ago.

This also fits with the consistent localization of the visiting girls in middle Gila drainage. This localization makes more poetic sense with the twin heroes somewhere on or near the Colorado than if they were also on the Gila, where the Halchidhoma arrived soon after 1830. Unfortunately, the Mohave version is the only one specifically localized throughout. If the heroes of the original story were thought of as living on the Colorado, the Diegueño would have had little to say about the geography, because they did not often visit the river (except for the desert Kamia going to the Yuma). The Halchidhoma version is strangely unlocalized, for a tale told in such detail; and I would assume the reason to be that in the century that elapsed between the flight of the tribe from the Colorado and Spier's recording of the narrative, the Halchidhoma remnant on the Gila had got hazy about their great-grandfathers' geography on the Colorado.

Finally, the Mohave localization of the tale in the region of the Whipple Mts. and Parker, old Halchidhoma territory that the Mohave later occupied, fits in well with the reconstruction reached.

Satukhota and Cane Relations

It is also clear that the infection of Mohave Cane by Satukhôta happened most markedly in ideas taken from the final two sections of this latter tale, those sections dealing with the posthumous son of the younger brother, Kuyahumar. The majority of episodes about him recur in the Cane story; but they are there distributed between the father Tšitšuvare and his son Ahta-hane. Farther, there are five episodes that the concordance shows to be original in Satukhôta-Flute-Chaup, but to have dropped out of it in Mohave (at least in the version recorded), while being preserved in Cane. These are episodes Vj, VIk, Xi, Xj, XIf of the concordance—all of them post-eaglet-pets.

I may add that as we got into the last two sections of the recording, interpreter Robert Martin turned to me and said: "This *is* almost like Cane here."

Narrative 19
TORTOISE
(1954)

THE NARRATOR

Perry or Peter Dean, who narrated the Kapeta or
Tortoise tale on January 31, 1954, seemed at that
time about 65 years old. He did not know when he
was born, except that it was in the early spring. He
said that he was younger than Pete Sherman, who had
told me Satukhóta and was born about 1880, but that
he was older than Judge Burton, He did know precisely where he was born: it was at Tupák-ulĉle, "old
bridge" (of the Santa Fe R.R.), called Qasa'óqa in
pre-American days. This older name is not entered
on UC-AR 11:2, Map 1 because I did not record it,
but it is probably the same as Kwisa'óqa, "V" on
Map 1, there entered as 7 miles below Needles on
the east side, though some Mohave estimated the distance as only 4-5 miles. The very first or pre-
Topock railway bridge may have been some 3 miles
below Needles.

Perry Dean was of clan Móha; his wife was Sú'ulye.
He moved from Needles in 1942 to Parker, to a ten-
acre irrigable allotment that his wife had received.

Perry Dean is smallish for a Mohave, spare and
wiry rather than large. He evidently understands and
perhaps speaks some English, but I preferred to ease
the work relationship by having skilled and interested
Robert Martin interpret. Perry impressed me as a
good general informant, concise but to the point and
reliable.

He is a doctor, in other words a shaman, and is
said to have treated white people for broken bones. He
specializes in fractures, arthritis, tuberculosis, and
pneumonia. The Needles or Parker school football
team used to take him along when they played in San
Bernadino. Once, when a player got his cheek bone
crushed, Dean's first treatment was to blow on the
spot, which gave some relief. Then he sucked to draw
the dented bone back into place: the player felt it give
and return.

Dean seems to have left Needles for Parker Reservation because of the following reported episode. There
was trouble about a woman, whose husband, correctly
or erroneously, considered himself wronged. He was
one of the large, heavy Mohave: seizing Perry by his
long hair, he dragged him to the railroad track to
throw him under a train. But Mohave bystanders inter-
fered and stopped him. Perry, who makes the impression of a man of spirit, then turned on the assailant
and told him he would not live long: in a month, at
five o'clock when the railway-shop whistle blew, he
would be dead. The big man seemed to continue per-
fectly well; but when the day came, he had dressed
himself in his best coat and pants, and was sitting on
his bed, talking with friends, when the whistle blew
and he fell backward, dead. This story is hearsay; but
the best clothes and the bed as the critical hour ap-
roached indicate the influence of Perry's suggestion.
At that, his prediction did not make Dean in the least
liable under American law. But to the Mohave, he had
caused his opponent's death by shaman's power; and
he knew that some kinsman of the dead man was likely
to kill him—by overt means—in revenge. Hence his re-
moval to the Parker Reservation, where distance, a
less involved population, and the Agency policemen
increased his protection.

NATURE OF THE TALE

Tortoise as told by Perry Dean is thin in plot. Incidents are few and unimpressive. Mostly it is a journey,
from Matavilye's death to transformation of the two
brothers. The songs tell where they came, what they
saw, and what they felt or said on the way. These
sights, feelings, or statements are referred to—perhaps
more often hinted at, or abbreviated—in the words of
the 316 songs. The narrative, for all its conciseness,
is more explicit about them than about deeds. Prominent in it are a series of visual images of the appearance of nature—especially the land, air, and sky. These
are discussed below in the Content Analysis of Emotion,
Nature, etc. (Part II, A).

The route traveled is given in detail in the Geographi-
cal Appendix. In summary, it begins at Ha'avulypo in
Eldorado Canyon, goes west to the vicinity of Tehachapi
Mts., then returns eastward to overlook northern Mohave
Valley, sidles southward west of the river nearly to
Whipple Mts., then east to the Colorado at Chemehuevi
Valley, and down the river to just above Bill Williams
Fork; which, the river crossed, is ascended into the

southern end of Walapai country. Here the route becomes indefinite, and in two or three stages the mountain Ikwenyeva, "Cloud-home," is reached, to the southeast in southwestern Walapai territory near the Yavapai border, or again, according to other statements, much farther off in Gila drainage, in or near Maricopa territory—the Mohave seem to know two mountains called Ikwe-nyeva, or to place it variably in two different tracts (see Part II, B4). Here the Tortoise brothers build a house and stay, except for a trip south to the ocean for shells; after which they transform.

THE TORTOISE NARRATIVE

The singing begins in the north at Ha'av'úlypo and ends in the East at Ikwényeva. When I have sung all night, I arrive at daybreak at Táha and (A)tší'ára (29, 35), the peaks west of Parker. In the evening, I have come to Ikwenyeva, well up Bill Williams Fork; and next morning, I finish.

Young men, relatives or sons-in-law, may sing along with me. If they have dreamed Tortoise, they learn it and remember all the songs. If they did not dream it themselves, they forget the songs, or remember only a few and skip around with these.

1. At Ha'av'ulypo was Matavilya. With him were his four children: they had not named themselves yet. They sang four songs; on the fifth, Matavilya's arms and legs [gesture of passing hand in front of limbs] were dead—only his heart [informant pointing to his own] was still alive; on the sixth song, Matavilya died. The two oldest of his sons went off; the two youngest he had called to sit beside him. The older ones went underground, far out under the ocean [Gulf of California], and came up there and turned into the Water Turtle, Haly-kov'á, and the small, spotted, long-legged Frog, Hany-itšq'urq [not the bullfrog]. (6 songs.)

2. His two younger sons carried Matavilya out to the pyre and burned his body, until there were only coals (útšets) and ashes (hama'úlye). (1 song.)

3. Then they sang: He has gone, perhaps he has become wind, or rock; I do not know which. (1 song.)

4. They dried as they sang. Then they walked four steps west and turned and looked at the mountains to the east, where the sun, already set, was still shining on them and they looked red (ahwát meδárek; anyá tciδarek). (1 song.)

5. Still standing there, they sang of the sun. Is he older, or the moon? Sun must be the older because he shines more. (3 songs.)

6. They moved farther west from there and sang: The sun is set; it is dark, night-crazy (tinyám yamómk); if anyone dreams of these crazy nights, he will steal and rob. (4 songs.)

7a. They stood and sang more, about the night halfway to midnight, of the night time that is good, that is finished (fully arrived?), of the sound of the night moving (tinyám ahótk, tinyám mátavírek, tinyám hotšámk). Those who dream of these (times of) night will have luck and will prosper. (Songs 1, 2 of 8.)

7b. Still standing there, the younger sent his older brother ahead on the way: he is going, walking (mátayemk, úv'ak). Songs 3, 4 of 8.)

7c. They went on, looked around, saw the sky, the earth also (amái kutiδómk isámk kwiváuk; amaṭ). Songs 5, 6 of 8.)

7d. We are coming, we shall be there [at Avíhamóka]. (Songs no. 7, 8 of total of 8 songs.)

8. They saw clouds lying in the east, then rain; and the younger said to the older: The clouds in the east are the ghost of our father: when he was burned, the smoke became clouds.

> ikwétš anyá-kaδín hopám íδik, clouds in east
>   lying there.
> ikwé tú'atc mathá tú'atc, cloud gone, wind gone.
> ikwé-nyaveδái mathá-nyaveδai, cloud ghost,
>   wind ghost.

And he said to his older brother, See over there, the clouds are white, are yellow, are red, are black[1] (nyamasáve, akwáθa, ahwáta, nyéilyk). (6 songs.)

9. Now they stood at Avi-hamók, three-mountains at Tehachapi,[2] and told of the dark of the night, and reached out[3] and took a basket, kárri' [beaten in time to the songs];[4] this is not of the Mohave, it is of the Chemehuevi and desert tribes to use for their food and to carry. Sometimes the older brother spoke, sometimes the younger; but this now—the younger sang, for the older knew nothing. (4 songs.)

10. Then they saw the places Kohóye and Pákye to the southeast.[5] (4 songs.)

11. They were on the way back, going east. (3 songs.)

[1]A four-fold color sequence, without directional correlate. The sequence is from light to dark. It recurs below in 19:69a, note 41.
[2]The name is generic for the region of Tehachapi. It derives from what we call Double Mountain, south of Tehachapi Pass, plus a nearby mountain appearing of about the same height; these are conspicuous as a trio for a large part of the highway from Barstow to Mohave.
[3]A favorite way of producing or making objects out of nothing, in myths.
[4]This was mentioned first in 4, but was said properly to enter the tale here.
[5]Kohoye is on or near Mohave River, 24 miles above Barstow; cf. 8:2, UC-AR 11:2, p. 77, and also p. 143 (IV). Pakye is unplaced.

12. They were going, though they did not know which way; but they were coming here, southeastward. The younger said: Look, take the straight path! And he pushed him along. (3 songs.)

13. Coming along, mátaδík, in the dark. (6 songs.)

14. They did not know where they were going, nor where they were. They said (sang): Beyond the sky, beyond the earth, amái kotón, amaṭ kotón. (20 songs.)

15. Looking down, then up, they saw the Pleiades, hatšá, going into the hole of heaven, amái kukópk lyépuk, "sky hole enter."[6] They were little girls playing, singing, dancing on the way;[7] that is why they traveled slowly. (3 songs.)

16. They took four steps, then looked to the southwest[8] and up and saw the three stars Ammo, Mountain-sheep [belt of Orion], and said, We know you, we call you by name, Ammo; in the sky, in under its arm, you are lying, amáinye supónye mahák háδivk. (4 songs.)

17. They went on, they sang of their travel. (3 songs.)

18. It became day and they saw the mountains and recognized them, but did not say their names. (1 song.)

19. They sang about traveling through the desert, kwánākw. They were in the flats (playas, lake beds) between the mountains, where the railroad now runs, around Ludlow and Amboy. (4 songs.)

20. They stopped under a high range, Aví-kavasú, Providence Mts. It is our mountain, the clouds hang around it, we look up at it. (2 songs.)

21. And there they told of the desert people's food, which there would be. There are rock and sand, but when the clouds and wind (mist) pass over, something will grow for them. (4 songs.)

22. They told of traveling on. (2 songs.)

23. They stopped and looking southeast saw a high mountain that looked like it had been scooped up and dropped. They asked each other its name, and called it, and another, Kaδáreδare and Aví-mota.[9] (2 songs.)

24. The younger kicked the [little sand] hill [at the feet] of his brother, and the earth and sky were blazing from the north: amáya upílyta, sky white hot.[10] (1 song.)

25. And the younger took the stalk of ghost-arrow, nyaveδí-nyipá, like tule sedge but furry, and marked it across, and laid it as a barrier to the sky blaze.

And he laid red clay, maθé-hwata, in four lines, and stopped the heat coming to them. (1 song.)

26. They came to Ha'íva, "water unite,"[11] and to Iθáva-kukyáva, "arrowweed bunched," (two places where the railroad comes up from Needles northwest to the pass near Klinefelter), and to a spring near there, Hapurúi-kutokópa, "water jar with a hole;" it is our Mohave land, and the spring is for us to drink. (2 songs).

27. Now they were on the top of the divide and looked down on the Colorado River. But there was a fog over it, móhoi tcúmitc,[12] and they were afraid to come down to it. So they started to go back westward.[13] (3 songs.)

28. In a canyon, west of Needles, at the north end of Ohmo, Sacramento Mt., he told his older brother: Go ahead, look for a good place to walk; you seem exhausted. (1 song.)

29. On top of the divide,[14] looking south, they saw the mountains Táha and Atší'ara[15] west of Parker, and the younger told the elder: It is another country, far away, we do not know it. (4 songs.)

30. On the ridge of Sacramento Mountain (Ohmo), there is a sharp point Asei-ismáve, Buzzard-roost (sleep).[16] They turned that, and to the west, not far away, they saw two hills and named them Ahmáta-tu'itše, Pumpkin-pile, and Ahá-tatuámpa'ámpa, Water-upside-down. They were now near [upper] Chemehuevi Wash, west [?] of Atší'ara. (5 songs.)

31. As they went on, the younger made rain. Before it came, he said: I dreamed it would rain; but he had really (iδútše) made it. It came, heavy, and soaked them. I dreamed it would happen, he said. (1 song.)

32. Then the big boulders were loosened and rolled down and crashed, and he sang of that sound. (1 song.)

33. Then he sang, It rains on us as we travel in another land (túwaik), but soon it will stop. (1 song.)

34. They went on: My dreams come true, I told you so. (2 songs.)

35. A little farther, they came opposite the mountain Taha. I name it: people will travel, and will call it Taha.[17] (3 songs.)

36. They stepped on four steps, to where now the

---

[6]"Entering the hole of the sky" seems to mean they had risen so far.

[7]An idea that is practically universal in native California, but I do not recall previously recording it from the Mohave.

[8]Error for southeast?

[9]Aví-motá is Manchester Mountain, S of Avikwame, N of Piute Wash, bounding the N part of Mohave Valley on the west. See Cane 1:101, 102, notes 97, 98 (UC-AR 11:1, p. 18); also 7:14, note 29 (UC-AR 11:1, p. 55). Ka-δáre-δáre is unidentified.

[10]Compared by the interpreter to the atomic bomb. The idea, and the checking of fire with ghost arrow in 25, recur in Cane, 1:102, 103 (UC-AR 11:1, p. 18).

[11]Or: "springs join."

[12]"Fog (or steam) as if put there."

[13]Or SW?

[14]Sacramento Mountain.

[15]Táha is a bell-like peak on the W flank of the Turtle Mountains range; and Atší-ará, "fish tail," is an associated peak, W or NW of Parker some miles—but apparently E of the Needles-Parker highway. It seems a detached element of the Whipple Mountains, dark colored and with a jagged comb that might suggest a fish tail.

[16]Fifteen miles or so S of Needles, not far from the Parker highway.

[17]Cf. 29.

power wires cut across the Needles-Parker road, and
saw a mountain far south (I)sam-kusaveve—I do not
know where it is. But there they saw[18] the dust raised
by Blackbirds, (a)θíkwah, scratching the ground. "It is
they, they were with us [at Há'av'úlypo], they are our
havík, our kwora'ák-o'éve, our brothers, I know them.
(3 songs.)

37. They came down Chemehuevi Wash (amát Aθóve)
into the [river] valley where there were many mesquite
trees; and [going on south along the river] they named
a place Ahmá-vawére, Quail-running.[19] (8 songs.)

38. They took two steps, looked across the Colorado,
saw a little peak by the river, called it Ho'áu-nye-
vátše, Horseflies' houses.[20] (2 songs.)

39. They reached the river bank a little below
opposite Hakutšyepa, mouth of Bill Williams Fork,
and went up the Colorado a little way on the west
side. (2 songs.)

40. They went down to the river's edge at
Omotukílye, each with two bunches of arrowweed
[gesture: thickness of thigh], one under each arm,
to swim across by. (1 song.)

41. They entered the water and swam. An undertow
took them down, turned them over four times, brought
them back to where they had started. (1 song.)

42. On the bank they stood and the younger brother
said: I know this river: I will bewitch it (ahón θávitšk),
make it still. So he witched it, and the river ran on,
but without undercurrent (hatšpón). And they went in
again, and it carried them south, then north, then east
across, and they landed a little north of Hakutšyepa
at Kúhotóte and Sávetohe.[21] (3 songs.)

43. They dried themselves, then took white earth,
amáṭ-nyamasáve, and put it on their faces; but it did
not suit them. Then they picked up white paint earth,
amaṭ-eh'e (diatomaceous clay?) and painted their (face
and) hair, and then black paint, kwínehílye, over the
white, and were satisfied. (2 songs.)

44. Then they started again, from near Hákutšyepa,
and to the east saw a big mountain, Aví-ku-vatáye,
and next to it another, Tšivutaθ-'imave,[22] and coming

at the foot of them, ghost(s), nyaveδítš, kicking along
a great ball, far up toward the sky, then to the south.
The younger brother said: I know him. He is our
brother, kwora'ák-o'éve. He will be like that and travel
all the time, because he has no home. He is (Hi)mé-
kut-asínye, Single-foot.[23] (2 songs.)

45. They took two steps from the mouth of Bill
Williams Fork and listened. In the mountains east
they heard people talking.[24] They said: We don't know
who they are, but they are from where we came from
and have traveled here. We don't know the name of
their tribe, but we hear them. (2 songs.)

46. They stood again, a little from the mouth, and
saw black willows, sandbar willows, cottonwoods,
arrowweeds (iδ'ó, ihóre, ah'á, iθava—the characteristic
riverbottom growth), all green. (4 songs.)

47. They traveled up the bank of Bill Williams Fork,
four or five steps upstream, and looked down at it and
a snag of driftwood, íhne, and on it the clear-winged
dragonfly, Ahtá-koδósk, "he who carries a cane on his
back."[25] Who is he? What is it? asked the older; and
the younger said: I know him: he is our brother,
kwora'ak-o'éve. He will be like that, he will travel
above the water, he is to be that way. (4 songs.)

48. They took four steps east, then saw a ghost,
Nyaveδí kúsu'ulye, coming toward them, then going
north, blazing up, subsiding, then blazing up, traveling
on;[26] and they called his name. (4 songs.)

49. They went on east, up Bill Williams Fork, singing of how they walked, stepped, as they traveled.
(2 songs.)

50. Still going on, they came to mountains and
canyons, and said: We are in the land of another tribe
now; these mountains belong to the Hoálye-paya.
(2 songs.)

51. They went on, then stopped. These mountains
have names, they said; but they did not tell the names.
(2 songs.)

52. They went on about three steps, to between the
mountains. Amáṭ Kwóata, Amáṭ Si'wí,[27] those are the
names of the mountains we are among, they said. They
were on the west side of the south end of the Walapai
(Hualpai) Mts. (2 songs.)

---

[18]This is magical seeing, impossible without a telescope.
[19]Ahmava-were was mentioned in 1953 as Ahmáva-ahwére,
"Quail-running," a short distance above and opposite the
mouth of Bill Williams Fork in California. It is 15-20 miles
below the mouth of Chemehuevi Wash and Chemehuevi Valley,
which was famous for its mesquite trees and is the Aθove
mentioned in 37.
[20]Ho'áu-nye-vatše—see 3:12 (UC-AR 11:1, p. 30), and UC-
AR 11:2, p. 142, no. 27. It is not far above Parker.
[21]This is a namesake of the Sávetohe listed on UC-AR 11:2,
p. 139 as Savot-toha, "O," in Mohave Valley opposite Needles,
and mentioned also on UC-AR 11:1, p. 29, note 10, where the
present place downriver is referred to but not placed.
[22]The two mountains were not identified further, unless the
first name, Avi-ku-vatáye, which means "great mountain(s),"
is the same as Avi-vatáye, the Riverside Mountains—which

is probable, since they are in the vicinity, next downriver
from the Whipple massif.
[23]An appearance that hops along, but is not dangerous.
[24]This hearing is analogous to seeing what people are
doing fifty miles away.
[25]In Satukhóta 18:66c, note 202, Sakotit is the redwinged
dragonfly. Ahtá-koδósk is from háδosk, carry on back or
hanging from head.
[26]The interpreter had seen this phenomenon at night,
traveling along the mesa (gravelly river terrace). It seems
to be a harmless kind of ghost—that of a man who in life
lit funeral pyres; cf. above, 16G:8, note 35.
[27]Otherwise unidentified.

53. Going on eastward they saw a great mountain, and they saw the birds and animals on it, and the water there that these drank. They called the mountain Apén-ik-ha.[28] (2 songs.)

54. They stood and said: That water will always be there. It is the animals' (tšípai); it was given them. Mostly they will be called Coyote (húkθara); they will travel about and drink that. (2 songs.)

55. They went on toward it; and standing on a little hill, they saw the mountain Cloud-home, Ikwé-nyeava.[29] (2 songs.)

56. They went on three steps, four steps, to the foot of the tall mountain and saw the clouds and wind that hung about it. (1 song.)

57. Ikwé-nye-vá is like Aví-kwamé. They stood and said, All tribes living here will dream of this mountain, dream well of it. The mountain will plan for them, work for them. I will build a house on it. — There were no trees there, but they (reached out and) got rafters, a'vá tšútara, and poles, av'a tšúsive, posts, of yellow pine, hoalye,[30] and built it. —Mostly it is the Mohave who will build like this,[31] they said. But this mountain will give luck, in games, in races, in everything, this Ikwé-nye-vá. (4 songs.)

58. On the mountain, they said: Now the house is finished. Who will hear about it, who will go to bring apparel (sunákutše)?[32] Now the small round hairy spider that jumps when touched, δo-noso-kwatáye—the name means "many tears"—was human then. He ran his saliva like a path to a named mountain in the north, to a named one in the south, then to another; and he said, I will travel that saliva road (ihá-kulúlk, web) and get that apparel. —He came back with a blanket. (13 songs.)

59. At Ikwé-nye-vá, Kapeta, Tortoise,[33] said: I know how to get that apparel. I will travel to the ocean, I myself, and will bring necklaces, ear ornaments, nose ornaments. So he got to the [southern] ocean, and into it, and reached the two older brothers who had gone off first. He said: I know them, they are my brothers, they traveled underground to here and became Water

Turtle, and the other one Spotted Frog; that is what they turned into, but they are my older brothers. (15 songs.)

60. On the return from the ocean, the people at Ikwé-nyeva saw Kapeta and δo-noso-kwatáye coming far off. They said, It looks like them coming, they are halfway (kwánavek havatúyek). And Kapeta and δo-nosa-kwatáye saw them at the mountain too: We are coming, we will arrive, you will see us, they said. (14 songs.)

61. So they arrived, carrying what they had brought, and the people followed them around to see, but they did not set it down. (3 songs.)

62. Reaching up, they pulled it off their necks [gesture] and threw it down: Well, see what we brought. (2 songs.)

63. The people opened it up: These are things we do not know. They belong to old people.[34] We have not seen them before; they are not found here, but are from the ocean. Poor people like us cannot wear them. (2 songs.)

64. There were ahtšílye shells, and round káyāra, and kú'ulye kamenáye also called nepúka, beads, and flat hollow tomása from the beach.[35] (4 and 3, total 7 songs.)

65. On the mountain, they were telling about it, that they would name them. (1 song.)

66. Hanemitšá, the wasp[36] that catches horseflies, was human then. He said: I will travel and follow them. They were many, they have gone.[37] (5 songs.)

67. Owl, δókupít, and Humtályewai who owns the night—he is like Night-hawk, Orrú, but larger—were there. Humtályewai said: It is dawning; but Owl said: No. Humtályewai said again: Yes, I can see the Milky Way (ahtcílye-kwiya-nyúnye, the road by which they get shells) has turned in the sky. And the Pole Star, Amáisekaháva,[38] too. But Owl told him: No it is still dark. But I will make the night longer, and you can fly a way still. (4 songs.)

---

[28] Two interpreters could do nothing with Apen-ik-ha. The first element sounds like "beaver."

[29] On Ikwé-nye-vá, see Part II, B, 4.

[30] Heard mentioned by the narrator, not translated by the interpreter.

[31] True, as compared with the Walapai. But the Mohave of course use cottonwoods, not yellow pines, which grow many miles away.

[32] Sunákutše seems to be a form of honáktše, to wear as a necklace.

[33] From here, the interpreter consistently used only the singular, whether saying "brother," "tortoise," "he," or "I"; but the original pair of brothers is undoubtedly meant. Animal names like Kapeta are identical for one or many. Also, the younger brother has throughout the story been the active one.

[34] "Old people" in the sense of "the aged." These seeming jewelry objects were signs of dignity or social importance rather than being beautifiers of the young.

[35] These shell ornaments are difficult to identify from descriptions. Ahtšilye are small univalves, probably Olivella. Káyāra were thought by one informant to be abalone, Haliotis. Tomása he had never seen, but knew to be shells. For kú'ulye kamenáye and nepúka he reacted only with hu'ú'lye, cholla cactus, and nepúka, ocotillo. Clamshell disk beads of wampum type, not mentioned here, he knew as qosó.

[36] Hanemitšá is "like a bee," according to the interpreter. Another informant called it nam'itšá and said it had holes in the ground, was bigger than a bee, smaller than a bumblebee (θampó-kwiníly) and not a yellowjacket (θampó-akwáθe). In 7:22, note 42 (UC-AR 11:1, p. 56), Namitša is a large reddish wasp (?) that throws earth as it burrows.

[37] We interrupted the telling here for the midday meal, and the telling was more compressed in the afternoon.

[38] "Pointing toward the sky," the North Star, but I am not wholly convinced of the identification.

68. Humtályewai said: I know it is morning because
I have marked my wings and my mouth with it. I own
night, and I know it is dawn now.[39] (10 songs.)

69a. After Tortoise had gone to the ocean and
returned, he[40] changed himself: he would tell later
into what. He had a long beard and he acted like a
child. The beard was first white, then yellow, red,
black.[41] (4 songs.)

69b. He was thinking of transforming. If I could go
far under ground (amáṭa tcíuk), to ground gold stone
(amáṭa hitšívk), I could become something there, and
people who knew me would be doctors—but I don't
want that. —So he came out again. A second time he
sank in, to his knees, but came out. Then he thought
he wanted his body to be so that [desert] people could
eat it. (2 songs.)

69c. Then Tortoise took a walking-cane with crook,
nyakwaθi'á, made a bundle of his apparel, carried it
over his shoulder on the cane, cried, and walked about
in circles.[42] (3 songs.)

69d. My paths, where I am going, I will leave them
after me. (2 songs.)

69e. He stood and became altogether childish. He
had lice in his hair; they bit him,[43] made the blood
flow, it hardened, "like cement," [to form Tortoise's
shell]. (1 song.)

69f. He went out of the house ("about 100 yards"),
turned around and looked at it, hearing a noise. He
said: It is my own spirit (matkwísa, shadow), I know.
I am dead already, but I know it. It is following all
my paths [that I trod in life], thinking I am dead.[44]
(1 song.)

69g. He [his spirit] stood there with his bundle on
his cane over his shoulder, and went up to the sky.
(1 song.) (69a-g, 14 songs.)

70. So he turned into the common [i.e., animal]
Tortoise. "I name myself and the color (appearance)
of my back." (4 songs.)

These were the two younger brothers that started
from Há'av'úlypo and came here to Ikwé-nye-vá.

[39]The owning of night is claimed also by Bat in 71, below.
The informant pointed out that there was a lot of detail in
the groups of songs here which he was omitting.
[40]Cf. note 33 above.
[41]This sequence of four colors repeats that of 8, above.
[42]As part of his childishness.
[43]The combination of lice and witlessness at transformation recurs for the great god Mastamho in 7:84 (UC-AR 11:1,
p. 64). What is here called "childish" in translation there is
"crazy," yamômk. It is the animal body or species that loses
rationality; the "shadow" or spirit leaves it and survives.
[44]On death, the soul retraverses every way gone by the
body during life. "He" sees his soul doing this, thinking that
its body is dead! Yet "he" is about to go up to the sky in
69g, and to transform into the animal Tortoise in 70. I
assume that, at least in our terminology, it is his soul or
spirit (Mohave matkwisa) that goes up in 69g, his body (imaṭ)
that transforms in 70.

Annex[45]

71. Bat, Tinyam-qaltšeôkw, said: I will tell about
daylight. No one knows about that but I, for I own
night. (6 songs.)

72. He said: The sky is different, the earth is different, because it is dawn. (4 songs.)

73. In the dawn I can see the mountains and the
sun shining behind them. (4 songs.)

74. I stand: It is daylight. (6 songs.)

75. I stand: It is day; now there is light all over.
(6 songs.) This is the end of the songs of dawn.·

76. Kaθvém, a night bird, sat listening to dance
songs. At midnight, he thought that the logs he had left
in flames would be burned through.[46] I had better go
back to look after them, he said. When he arrived, the
sound of singing at the house was still in his ears.
(6 songs.)

SYNOPSIS AND ITINERARY

1-3. At Há'avúlypo. Matavilya dies, is burned.

4-5. Four steps W; sun has set.

6-7a. "Farther" W; night times.

7b-d. On way west to Aví-hamóka, "three mountains,"
viz. Double Mt. of our maps (UC-AR 11:2), S of Tehachapi Pass, which with an adjacent unnamed peak is
visible as triple for many miles east in the Mohave
Desert.

8. See colored clouds in E, which suggests it is
day, but in 13-16 it is still (or again) night, and they
see and name stars.

9. Stand at Double Mt., get basket to beat for accompaniment to singing.

10. They see to the SE places Pákye, not otherwise
located, and Kohóye, 24 m. from Barstow, on or near
Mohave River, mentioned also in 8:2, UC-AR 11:2,
p. 77 and also p. 143 (IV).

11-15. Going E, then SE, it is dark, they see the
Pleiades.

16. Four steps on, to the southwest (SE?) see Orion.

18-19. Daylight. In playas around Ludlow and Amboy,
on Highway 66.

20. At foot of Providence Mts., Aví-kavasú. The S
end of these is about 30 m. NNE of Ludlow.

[45]The relation of this Annex (71-75 about Bat and 76 about
the night bird Kaθvém) to the Kapete story as a whole is unclear. It is somewhat repetitious of 67-68 about Owl and
Humtalyewai—which in its turn interrupts the thread of the
main plot. The informant was increasingly abbreviating his
narrative as he approached the end, so that connections or
relations clear to him were lost in the recorded text.
[46]In the pre-ax days logs could presumably be cut through,
for house posts and rafters, chiefly by burning.

23. To SE they see two mountains, one looking as
if scooped up and dropped, and they call one Kaδáreδare,
the other Aví-mota; the latter is Manchester Mt.,
bounding northern Mohave Valley on the west, and
mentioned in 1:101, 102; 7:14 (UC-AR 11:1, pp. 18, 55).
They are probably conceived as standing at Piute range
and looking across the desert valley through which
Highway 95 now runs. Piute range is perhaps 30 m.
somewhat N of E of Providence Mts.

24, 25. At Mt. Manchester, they make the sky blaze,
and then stop its lightninglike spread with the ghost-
arrow plant; as in Cane, 1:102 (UC-AR 11:1, p. 18)
and 17:77, the hero hurls his lightning over Mt. Manchester to annihilate his foes.

26. South of Mt. Manchester, near Klinefelter on
the railroad, they come to three springs or water
holes at Ha'íva, Iθáva-kukyáva, and Hapurúi-kutokópa.

27. From the top of the divide there, they see the
Colorado River, but fear a mist on it and turn away
W (or SW).

28. They go on S to the N end of Ohmó, Sacramento
Mt., W of Needles City.

29. From its summit they see two peaks to the S,
Táha and Atší'ara ("Fish-tail"), E and W of the highway from Needles to Parker and Blythe; the first is
a bell-shaped peak off the eastern flank of Turtle Mts.;
the second, a serrated ridge on the SW side of Whipple
Mts.

30. On the ridge of Sacramento Mt. they pass the
peaklet Asei-ismáve, "Buzzard roost," see two hills to
the W which they name "Pumpkin-pile" and "Water-
upside-down," and then approach upper Chemehuevi
Wash, W (or NW) of "Fish-tail Mt."

32-35. They make it rain as they go on S and come
abreast Táha peak, which they first saw in 29.

36. Four steps onward brings them to where the
high-power wires cross the Needles-Parker road as
of 1954, and they see far S the mt. (I)sám-kusavéve
(which the narrator could not locate specifically), and
blackbirds raising dust there.

37. Descend Chemehuevi Wash to the mesquite groves
by the Colorado River, which by 1954 had been drowned
in Havasu Lake by Parker dam. This is Chemehuevi
Valley, Aθóve, near the mouth of the wash. The informant's geography is in error, however: Chemehuevi Wash
and Valley are N of the two mountains sighted in 29
and reached in 30 and 35, and would have been reached
before the mountains. The alternative is that after
coming abreast the two mountains, they backtracked N
(and E) to Chemehuevi Valley. From there they go S,
along the river to Ahmá-vawére, "Quail-running." (See
below, Part II, B2, W side.)

38. On to S, two steps, see on the E bank of the
river the little peak Ho'áu-nye-vátše, "Horseflies'
Houses," mentioned also in 3:12 (UC-AR 11:1, p. 30),
and UC-AR 11:2, p. 142, no. 27, and below, Part II,
B2, E side.

39, 40. Descend to river's W edge opposite Hakutšyepe,
Bill Williams Fork mouth on the E side, then go a bit
upstream to Omotukílye.

41, 42. Try to cross on bundles of arrowweed, the
current carries them back to shore, but they finally
land at Kúhotóte and Sávetohe, a bit above the mouth
of Williams Fork. Savetohe is mentioned on UC-AR
11:1, p. 29, note 10. There is another place of the same
name upstream in Mohave Valley, opposite Needles City,
"O" on UC-AR 11:2, p. 139 and Map 1.

44. To E they see the prominent Riverside Mts.,
Aví-ku-vatáye, and another mt. Tšivutaθ-'imave, unplaced—perhaps a peak in the Riversides.

45. Go two steps from the mouth of Williams Fork
and listen.

47. Four or five steps up the Fork and see the
dragonfly "cane-carrier" on a driftwood snag.

48. Four steps more upstream (E) and see a ghost.

50. On up Williams Fork, among mts. belonging to
the Walapai.

52. About three steps on E to Kwóata and Si'wí,
said to be mts. W of the S end of the Hualpai range.

53. Farther on E, they see a great mt. Apén-ik-ha,
unidentified. It is not clear whether this is merely like
Ikwé-nye-vá, Cloud-home, of 55 seq., or is another
name for it.

55. They see Ikwé-nye-vá, Cloud-home Mt.; 56,
reach its foot; 57, 58, build a house on it. There are
two mountains of this name (see Tortoise II, below;
also Part II, B4); but the present one is constituted
by a part of Artillery Mountains, N of the Williams
Fork and on the W side of lower Big Sandy creek or
wash, which combines with the Santa Maria to make
Williams Fork. Ikwé-nye-vá is in Walapai territory,
and the Walapai call it a cave.

58, 59. Tortoise and "Many tears," the hairy leaping
spider, travel to the southern ocean (Gulf of California)
to secure apparel and shell ornaments.

60-65. They return with the goods.

(The remainder of the tale has no geography, except
for Tortoise going a short distance (69f) outside his
house at Ikwé-nye-vá to transform.)

67-68. An episode whose relevance to the tale is
not clear. Horned owl (δókupít) and Night-owner
(humtályewai, a larger sort of night-hawk) argue
about duration of the night.

69a-g, 70. Tortoise gives up attempts to sink into the
ground. He turns into a child, blood flows on his head and
hardens to become (a desert tortoise's) shell. He hears
and sees his spirit (shadow) leave the house and rise to
the sky, while [his body] becomes that of a tortoise.

   Annex 71-75. Bat (tinyam-qaltšeskw, night owner)
sings of dawn.

76. Kaθvem, a night bird, has the singing at Ikwé-
nye-vá ring in his ears after he leaves.

COMMENT ON TORTOISE

Most of this narrative is pure journey—a straight itinerary. There are mentions of how places and the sky look,
reflections on past or future, slight enlivenings of stretches
by dancing along or making it rain; but there are no adventures, not even happenings, nor do the principals meet
other personages—only the cloud ghost of their father (8),
or a one-legged ball-kicking ghost (44), or a fitfully blazing
harmless ghost (48).

The heroes are the two youngest of Matavilya's four
sons (1). The younger has the initiative, does all the talking, and orders or pushes the elder around (7b, 8, 9, 12,
24, 25, 28, 29, 31, 42). After their "Cloud-home" destination is reached and they have built themselves a house on
it (57), the narrator consistently used the singular, and the
interpreter said "he"; the older brother seemed forgotten,
or merged in the younger.

The one event in the story seriously involving action
(24, 25) is an unmotivated making the sky blaze and then
stopping the spread of the destruction with ghost-arrow
stalks. This episode is probably a borrowing from Cane,
especially so as both narratives associate it with Avi-mota
Mt. But in Cane it determines the final triumph of the hero
and the destruction of his long plotting enemies. In Tortoise no one is mentioned as foe or as liquidated; the act
is more like an atomic bomb test in its irrelevance.

The final transformation has been influenced somewhat
by the transformation of Mastamho, as is discussed in
note 43.

Travel seems to go on through night and day; there is
no mention of lying down to sleep, as in so many other
narratives.

Traveling on for "two, three, or four steps" is mentioned again and again in Tortoise. This phrase occurs
occasionally in other tales, but nowhere so often as here.

I do not rid myself of a feeling that this song-narrative
has shamanistic undertones, as indeed might be probable
from the narrator's being a practicing doctor. There are
references to three different kinds of ghosts, as already
cited. Hairy spider, Tortoise's coadjutor toward the end,
makes saliva roads and travels them (58, Handbook pp.
776-777); the younger Tortoise leaves his paths behind
him after his death or transformation (69d); when the eddy
carries the brothers back to shore, he "bewitches" the
river and they cross it without difficulty (42).

TORTOISE II

In March 1908 I phonograph-recorded a dozen Tortoise
or Kapeta songs (cylinders 934-945) at Needles. The singer
was Doctor's Sack or Kwaθiδe-nye-hamalye, also called
Hawk's Tracks (Road) or Hawk-nyutaṭ-nyune. Besides Tortoise, he also sang Salt and Jackrabbit, was a curing doctor,
and could sing about this power.

Kapeta was a man and a Mohave, he said, and the story
and singing about him are Mohave, not Chemehuevi. From
the full series, which took a night and a day to go through,
he selected five groups of songs to sing into the phonograph.
These five he located in four places, as follows.

At Avikwame, where all tribes and animals began.
Kapeta came out last and went westward. That is why the
Chemehuevi eat desert tortoises. Songs 1, 2, cyl. 934, 935.

He came to Tšarreyo, four sharp points in a row in the
ridge Avimota, south of Avikwame, northwest of Mohave
Valley. Songs 3, 4, cyl. 936, 937.

He came to Hotáh-kunúve, "Dice-play," south of Ibis,
west of Needles. Songs 5, 6, cyl. 938, 939. It is also mentioned in 9:92 as Otahve-khunuve, south of "Ibex," where
Dove girl smoothed a round level place on a mountain (as
a gaming area).

There he decided to go east, and reached Ikwe-nye-va,
"Clouds' House," a mountain in the region of "Phoenix, in
the Maricopa (Hatpa-nya) country." Songs 7, 8, cyl. 940, 941.

There he built himself a house and sang of that. Songs
9-12, cyl. 942-945.

The last two songs run thus:

   Cyl. 944:

Kwinyavai, Ikwe-nye-va
ku-tinyam hakwink, dark imagine, i.e., build a
   dark thing (house) by imaging it.
havasu, blue—"said just to fill in the song."

   Cyl. 945:

hinyore, markings, on tortoise's shell
hiama, for himaṭ, body
aqwaθ, yellow, spots on back.

Comparison with Version I

As compared with the full version, the present one sub-
stitutes Avikwame for Ha'avulypo as point of departure.
Then they both move westward.

Tšarreyo is not mentioned in the full version, but Avi-
mota, of which it is part, is seen and named in 19:23.

Hotah-kunuve is not named in version I, but its localization must be in the vicinity of 19:26-28. The same place is
mentioned in Chuhueche, 13:45.

In I, Ikwe-nye-va is first seen in 19:55, has a house
built on it in 19:57, and remains the abode of the Tortoise
brothers until the end in 19:70. There are two sites for
this "cloud-home" mountain, both in Arizona, in version
I it is up Bill Williams Fork, in II in Gila drainage. See
Part II, B, 4.

PART II: DISCUSSION

PART II: DISCUSSION

A. Content Analysis of Some Features of Mohave Narrative

EMOTION, NATURE, MAGIC, DIDACTICISM

I have tabulated the frequency in the longer stories of all items, references, or episodes of certain kinds or qualities. Table 4 shows both the absolute frequencies and the converted frequencies per 100 paragraphs.

"Emotion" refers to affect shown by characters, either by explicit mention of the feeling (angry, ashamed, sorry) or as inferable from behavior mentioned (wept, laughed, cursed).

TABLE 4

Qualities in Narratives

Tale and No. of Paragraphs	Emotion	Nature	Magic	Didactic	Em	Nat	Mag	Did
					Per 100 Paragraphs			
1. Cane, 111	40	3	35	3	37	3	32	3
2. Vinimulye-patše, 29	8	...	...	...	28	...	...	...
3. Nyohaiva, 41	8	...	12	9	20	...	29	22
4. Raven, 34	1	6	3	2	3	18	9	6
5. Deer, 36	4	5	7[a]	1	11	14	19	3
*7. Mastamho, 102	3	...	16	88[b]	3	...	16	88
*8. Epic (197). Main, 162	34	1	14	[c]	21	1	19	...
Gambling Boy, 35	30[d]	...	...		86	...	...	
	(20)				57			
*9. Origins, 50	...	...	26	20	...	...	52	40
10. Alyha, 24[e]	...	...	5	18	...	...	21	75
11. Tumanpa, 55	3[f]	...	7	8	5	...	13	15
12. Salt, 25	1	3	6	...	4	12	24	...
13. Chuhueche, 85	13	4	23	9	16	4	27	11
14. Yellak I, 82	6	4[g]	12	50	7	5	15	61
*15. War, 20	1	...	5	12	5	...	25	60
18. Satukhota, 79	28	6	34[h]	9[i]	35	8	43	11
19. Tortoise, 82	2[j]	14	12	2[k]	2	16	14	2

[a]Five of the 7 by Cats, 2 by Deer.
[b]All except 12 paragraphs.
[c]Many explicit speeches, very little outright didacticism.
[d]Thirty instances in twenty separate paragraphs.
[e]Excluding paragraphs describing ritual.
[f]Excluding paragraph 22 about kumaθe hawk feigning.
[g]Excluding six references to noises or sounds not described.
[h]There are six other cases of unwilled magic.
[i]Eight of the nine cases in paragraphs 17-29.
[j]Excluding childishness of 69a, e.
[k]In paragraphs 8, 22.
*No songs.

TABLE 5

Rank Order of Tales by Frequency of Qualities
(Per 100 paragraphs)

Emotion		Nature		Magic		Didacticism	
*Epic, Gambl. boy	86	Raven	18	*Origins	52	*Mastamho	88
Cane	37	Deer	14	Satukhota	43	Alyha	75
Satukhota	35	Tortoise	14	Cane	32	Yellak	61
Vinimulye-patše	28	Salt	12	Nyohaiva	29	*War	60
*Epic, main	21	Satukhota	8	Chuhueche	27	*Origins	40
Nyohaiva	20	Yellak	5	*War	25	Nyohaiva	22
Chuhueche	16	Chuhueche	4	Salt	24	Tumanpa	15
Deer	11	Cane	3	Alyha	21	Chuhueche	11
Yellak	7	*Epic, main	1	Deer	19	Satukhota	11
Tumanpa	5	Vinimulye-patše	...	*Mastamho	16	Raven	6
*War	5	Nyohaiva	...	Yellak	15	Cane	3
Salt	4	Tumanpa	...	Tumanpa	13	Deer	3
Raven	3	*Mastamho	...	Tortoise	12	Tortoise	2
*Mastamho	3	*Origins	...	Raven	9	Vinimulye	...
Tortoise	2	Alyha	...	*Epic, main	9	Salt	...
*Origins	...	*War	...	Vinimulye-patše	...		
Alyha	...						

*No songs.

"Nature" refers to an image of natural landscape, such as reaching behind one's back to obtain a needed tool, rocking a boat to widen the valley, crossing the river by dropping four handfuls of sand, transforming into a bald eagle.

"Didactic" will be self-explanatory. It is most frequent in the Mastamho tale, No. 7 (UC-AR 11:1, pp. 50-68), where there is a great deal of outright teaching—besides telling of an intention, executing it, and then telling that it has been done. This element is, expectably enough, most heavily developed in tales purporting to account for origins.

In Table 5 I have ranked the several tales in order of the strength in them of these four elements or qualities, by frequency per 100 paragraphs. It will be seen that the tales differ considerably. These differences will now be analyzed.

It should however first be stated that I have divided No. 8, the Epic (UC-AR 11:2), into a main narrative (paragraphs 1-30, 66-197) and the story of the Gambling Boy (paragraphs 31-65, parts D, E, F), these two parts run quite different in tenor, as has been mentioned on UC-AR 11:2, pages 124, 129, 154. Also I have not counted didacticism for the Epic, because while there are numerous explicit and informational speeches, there

appear to be none that are made to be generically instructive or ordaining for the future.

EMOTION

Much the more frequent expression of emotion (86 per 100 paragraphs) occurs in the Gambling Boy portion of the Epic as compared with its remainder (21 per 100). This portion is about a wayward, capricious youth, and contains 10 instances of destructive mischief by him—being with one exception the only cases of such behavior in the entire collection of tales.

Next come the adventure-plot stories: Cane (No. 1) with 37 per cent, and Satukhota (No. 18) with 35. The latter part of the otherwise arid Chuhueche (No. 13) also contains plot and thus brings the emotion frequency for the whole story up to 16 per cent.

The two war tales, Vinimulye-patše and Nyohaiva (Nos. 2, 3) also run fairly high, 28 and 20 per cent, especially when one considers the extreme conciseness and skeletonizing of the telling of the former. Being stories of war, they principally stress fear.

Tales dealing primarily with creation, origins, and institutings naturally run low in personal affect: War

TABLE 6

Kinds of Emotion, Instances per Tale

Nature of Emotions	Epic (Gambler only)	Epic (minus Gambler)	Satukhota	Chuhueche	Cane	Vinimulye	Nyohaiva	Total
Pleasant Emotions								
	3	9	...	...	12	1	3	28
Unpleasant Emotions								
Sorrow, crying, mourning	3	7	11	11	4	...	...	36
Anger, scolding, hatred	6	6	5	1	10	2	...	30
Fear	1	5	3	...	4	4	4	21
Dislike, etc.	6	5	1	...	2	...	...	14
Mischief, destruction	10	...	...	...	1	...	...	11
Shame, shyness	1	2	1	...	4	1	1	10
Sulkiness	...	...	5	...	...	...	...	5
Suspicion, foreknowledge, boastfulness	...	...	2	1	...	...	...	3
Farewell, repentence, nausea	...	...	...	...	3	...	...	3
Total Unpleasant	27	25	28	13	28	7	5	133
TOTAL	30	34	28	13	40	8	8	161

5; Mastamho 3; Origins 0; Alyha 0.

Subject matter or type of plot seems to have more effect than narrator's temperament. Thus Nyohaiva, emotion 20, and Yellak, emotion 7, were told by the same informant (compare for didacticism Yellak 61, Nyohaiva 22); and so again were Chuhueche, emotion 16, Tumanpa 5, Salt 4.

When it comes to kind of emotion, Table 6 resumes the situation.

First of all, in the six tales ranking highest in references to emotion, pleasant feelings constitute only about one-sixth of the total—28 out of 161. This includes mention of: smiling, laughing, dancing, pleased, happy, feel good, like, embrace, friendly, peaceful, unafraid.

On grouping of the negative affects, it appears that the sorrow group (mostly mourning, but also pain, grieving for, think of, miss, etc.) comes first with 36 instances. Next, with 30, comes anger (including hate, quarrel, reprove, scold, taunt, mock, triumph over, avert look, want to fight). Third comes fear, with 21; and then dislike with 14 (disapprove, dissatisfied, tired of, sneak off, uneasy, not feel right). If dislike is grouped with anger and hate, this enlarged group ranks highest.

Mischief and destructiveness, 11, are nearly confined to the Gambling Boy part of the Epic, as already mentioned. Of nearly the same frequency, 10, but of much wider distribution is shame (including bashful, shy), usually by women. Sulkiness, 5, is a specialty of Satukhota. Finally there is a miscellaneous group of emotions, numbering six in all, confined to the three adventure-plot stories, and including suspicion, acceptance of foreknowledge, lying boastfulness, nausea, repentance, and bidding farewell to a house—each once only.

When Table 6 was finished, I could not, for a while, remember anything to compare it with. Happening to meet Dr. Stith Thompson, I asked him; but his memory too slipped. Boas, of course, had in 1916 made a content analysis of Tsimshian mythology, and in 1935 of Kwakiutl.[1] Each of these analyzed the extent to which the actual culture of the tribal group was faithfully represented, distorted, or omitted in the corpus of its mythical or formal legendary tales. These analyses cover the entire cultures—material, social, conceptual; and one section cites instances from the narratives that have to do with emotions and ethics. In the Tsimshian volume, there is about twice as much on ethics

[1]Tsimshian Mythology, BAE-R 31, 1916; Kwakiutl Culture as Reflected in Mythology, American Folklore Society, Mem. 28, 1935.

TABLE 7

Comparative Percentages of Kinds of Emotion

Distribution of Negative	Mohave	Kwakiutl	Tsimshian	Five English Poets[*] (Range of percentages)
Anger, hate, dislike	33	15	0	3-26
Sorrow, grief	27	9	19	6-50
Fear	16	18	23	16-34
Shame	8	38	33	6-14
Other negative	16	20	25	10-51
Total Negative	100	100	100	
Positive percentage of total	17	16	8	13-29

[*]Shakespeare (Sonnets), Herbert, Goldsmith, Dickinson, Housman.

as on emotions; but the later Kwakiutl monograph reverses the proportion and puts "emotional life" first. As nearly as I could, I counted and grouped the cited instances under the categories used to group the emotions mentioned or inferable in the Mohave narratives.

First of all it seemed desirable to segregate positive or pleasant emotions from the more numerous unpleasant or negative ones. The latter were then divided into five categories, centering around (1) anger, hate, dislike; (2) sorrow or grief; (3) fear; (4) shame; and (5) all others. There were about 133 Mohave items, about 77 Tsimshian and 285 Kwakiutl ones. The simplest way to compare these, was to percentage them. The five types of negative emotion were expressed in terms of percentage of the negative total included by each of the five negative categories. The undifferentiated positives were then expressed as percentages of the grand total (positive and negative) constituted by the positives. The results are shown in Table 7.

It is obvious that there are marked differences between the three Indian tribal cultures. Positive or pleasant affects agree in being in heavy minority: from about one-sixth to only about one-twelfth of the total. The fear category also runs pretty even, at about one-fourth to one-sixth of the total negative.

For the Mohave, the heaviest representation is in the anger-hate group; sorrow or grief is second; and shame is low. Among the Kwakiutl, instances of shame predominate heavily; both anger and grief are decisively lower. With the Tsimshian, shame is also easily highest, though the percentage is lower than with the Kwakiutl. Sorrow and fear in the Tsimshian, however, are both higher than among the Kwakiutl—in fact in the aggregate they approach the Mohave, although the proportions

are inverted. Most remarkable for Tsimshian is the complete absence of notations of anger or hate. I have wondered whether a stack of slip entries, or a page of manuscript covering this category, did not get inadvertently lost. However, we can only accept the record at face value.

However, the Tsimshian seem given to tender or introvert emotions. Pity appears, uniquely, with 4 percent of the negatives, and homesickness and loneliness with 14 percent. Nearly a third of the sorrow group are actually listed as disappointed or downcast. The Tsimshian personality image seems tinged with gentle sadness.

Homesickness is mentioned also by the Kwakiutl, but only half as often as by the Tsimshian. Characteristic of the "Various" group among the Kwakiutl are envy 7 percent, sexual jealousy 3 percent, derision or ridicule 4 percent, pride 2 percent. These emotions are not named among the other tribes, except that the Tsimshian specify ridicule as one of the causes of shame. It looks as if Ruth Benedict's picture of the Kwakiutl as suspicious, envious, sensitive, and megalomanic were supported by their own narratives.

It will be noted that the largest block under Mohave "Various" is constituted by wanton, unmotivated mischief —vandalism. With this block added to anger-hate (see Table 8), the plurality of the later rises still higher to 41 percent. Further, not only is shame low (8 percent), but many cases so counted are only shyness or female bashfulness.

All in all, the Mohave emerge, in their own picture, as insensitive, easy-going, good-humored, except for the conscious value they put on aggressive warfare, which inflated their egos into anger-hate.

TABLE 8

Percentage Frequencies of Emotions Expressed in Mohave Tales and in five English Poets

	Mohave	Shakespeare Sonnets	Herbert	Goldsmith	Dickinson	Housman	Average of Five Poets
Anger-hate	33[a]	26	7	21	3	18	15
Sorrow	27	16	50	22	6	30	25
Fear	16	16	26	18	34	25	24
Shame	8	14	7	7	6	8	8
Other negative	16[b]	28	10	32	51	19	28
	100	100	100	100	100	100	100
Ratio of positive to positive plus negative, after "love" omitted	17	13	29	26	23	14	

[a]Includes "dislike, etc.," and rises to 41 percent if "wanton destructiveness" is transferred from "other" to "anger-hate."
[b]See note a.

To further broaden the comparison, I have counted the frequency of words used for the emotions so far discussed by five English poets, Shakespeare (Sonnets), Herbert, Goldsmith, Dickinson, and Housman. This is a rather simple matter accomplished by turning to the printed concordances and counting the mentions. It is much less time-consuming than making a content analysis of the Yokuts or Pomo or Maidu or Yurok myth and tale corpuses. It is also a more remote comparand, and not quite the same, because the counts depend on words used, not on mentions plus situations as in the Indian material. Still, the comparison may be of some interest.

In this comparison, negative or unpleasant emotions fare better than positive ones, because English poets have a great deal to say about love but the Mohave very little. In most English poets examined there are more mentions of love than of joy, gladness, pleasure, hope and the rest combined; occasionally, as in Shakespeare's sonnets, love is mentioned more frequently than all other emotional terms, positive and negative, put together. It seems fair to omit love from our comparison because the English poets dealt with are primarily lyricists—the Shakespeare figures are for his sonnets alone—whereas the Mohave have no poetry and their narratives treat of love only in passing and briefly.

Another factor is the enormously greater richness of English vocabulary for affective states. To compare, we must therefore group together anger, hate, dislike, irritation, fury into one unit, and again, fear, terror,

horror, fright, dismay, whereas a third unit would comprise sorrow, grief, mourning, sadness. Nouns, verbs, and adjectives must also be taken together; sad, sadden, sadness, and so on. On the Mohave side, statements about feelings and about behavior are both included: he was sad, or he wept.

Table 8 (also the last column of 7) shows the result of the comparison, with frequencies again reduced to percentages. It is evident that, with love left out of the comparison, the Mohave usage is mostly within the range of the five English poets examined. This holds even for the ratio which positive emotions (minus love) hold as against positive and negative together. The Mohave frequency for this ratio (17) is well below those for Herbert, Goldsmith, Dickinson (29, 26, 23) but still a bit more cheerful than Housman and Shakespeare's sonnets (14, 13).

Among the groups of negative emotions, the Mohave are again highest in anger-hate. In fact, they are beyond the range of any of the five English poets: 33 percent, as against 26 to 3. The figure might in fact well be raised to 41, by including "mischievous destructiveness" with anger, hate, spite.

On the other hand, the Mohave are at the low end of the fear scale of frequency: 16 as against from 16 to 34 for the poets. Their code forbids fear and exalts bravery.

But as regards sorrow and shame, the Mohave frequencies of 27 and 8 percent are remarkably close to the averages of 25 and 8 percent for the five English poets.

That the Mohave are low in negative emotions other than the four main groups of anger, sorrow, fear, and shame (and particularly low when mischievous destructiveness is transferred to anger, reducing the ratio of "other" from 16 to 8), is perhaps the effect of their much more limited vocabulary for feelings, and of the fact that their narratives, however slow moving, almost necessarily deal with behavior, with acts, more than with emotion, which are the stock subjects of lyric poets.

NATURE

Nature images come into tales perhaps less because the individual teller has a bent that way, and more because the theme is deficient in plot and the subject matter of the spoken narrative is therefore conditioned by the songs. The songs in turn tend to refer in their words to stock subjects of a static or general nature, like sun rays at dawn, wind blowing, night coming on, bats flying, the Pleiades, which can be introduced at a great many points. If human plot and adventure are developed in a story, or if it tells of fighting, or accounts for origins, there is plenty for the prose narrator to tell. If these themes are poorly developed, the narrator falls back on the songs and expands their few meager words into a declarative statement which tells where the heroes were and what they saw there, and perhaps what they thought about it. What they see may be an animal or plant or peculiar formation of the local terrain, or it may be the total prospect of land and sky. If the former, the heroes tend to address the animal or feature, saying they know it, or will name it so and so, or that it will live in such and such a way hereafter. But if what is seen is dawn, or dusk, or clouds, or a blank desert, the narrator is more likely to put into the heroes' mouths a description of the phenomenon, often in the form of a two or three word image. This, in general, is what we are dealing with under the present caption of "Nature."

Here are some examples. It will be seen that they are the sort of material which we incline to weave into formal verse or poetical prose.

Eastern mountains turn red after sunset, 19:4
The sound of night moving, 19:7a
Colored clouds lying in the east, 19:8
Beyond the sky, beyond the earth, 19:14
Pleiades moving into the hole of the sky, 19:15
Orion under the arm of the sky, 19:16
Clouds and wind moving over the desert, 19:21
Fog above the distant river, 19:27

Boulders roll and crash in the rainstorm, 19:32
Clouds hang about Ikwe-nye-va Mt., 19:56
Scared clouds hang over mt., sun shines through, 18:13
Eagles high up dancing with the wind, 18:19
Ghost light flickers in canyon, 18:39
Darkness from the east travels west, 4:32 (UC-AR 11:1, p. 40)
The hard wind whirls us as we fly high, 4:32 (loc. cit.)
It smells good, brought by the wind from the north, 5:12 (UC-AR 11:1, p. 43)
The stars are bright, it is cold, there is a little breeze, 5:21 (UC-AR 11:1, p. 44)
The surf washes into ponds behind the ocean beach, 1:64 (UC-AR 11:1, p. 11)
Looking up Mohave land with smokes all along the river, 8:119 (UC-AR 11:2, p. 94)
The mountain is pretty with clouds and wind, 13:18
The mountain is good, cool, with wind and showers, 13:66

It is evident that many of these images are celestial, relating to atmosphere or light—sometimes almost Shelleyan in propensity, however meager in expression. They certainly accord with the long vistas of the open desert. While they are mostly visual, some are auditory, olfactory, tactile, and thermal.

These are not images in the formal literary sense of being similes or metaphors, but are direct verbal expressions of recalled sensory impressions, apparently with some accompaniment of feeling tone. It must be remembered that while the Mohave have no poetry, these images are the full and clear prose expression of allusions made in the mangled words of songs.

Such images are less common, even where most frequent, than are expressions of emotion, magic, or didacticism. This is clear from Tables 4 and 5.

The five tales containing the highest percentile frequency—Raven, Deer, Tortoise, Salt, and Satukhota—are from as many different narrators. The greatest absolute number of images, 14, is found in Tortoise, but this is a considerably longer narrative than Raven or Deer. Salt with 12 percent, Chuhueche with 4, Tumanpa with 0 are from one informant; so again are Yellak, 5, and Nyohaiva, 0.

MAGIC

The introduction of elements of magic or the supernatural is of course frequent in Mohave as in all mythology. But the relative frequency of magic varies from tale to tale. The pseudo-historical Epic (UC-AR 11:2) restricts itself to magic of the sort that the Mohave believed to occur in their own actual lives, whereas song-myths like Cane, Satukhota, Tortoise revel in extraordinary and sensational powers and happenings. Vinimulye-patše, in the outline obtained, is entirely free from magic; the events narrated might really have occurred, within the frame of belief of our civilization. But again, Mohave formal creation and origin myths are as loaded with supernaturalism as such myths are elsewhere.

An assemblage of more than two hundred items of magic, as counted above, might conceivably have some value for problems, other than the folkloristic or literary aspects. One such problem is the nature of magical belief, beginning with the range and variation of such belief in general. This would involve some sort of organization of the multifarious detail. I have long been reluctant to deal with all material on magic because of the endless continuity of its itemization. The usual (Frazerian) classification into imitative, contagious, sympathetic magic is too summary (besides having its categories frequently overlap), and was evidently set up as a theory that would give a universal explanation of why prescientific cultures believed in magic.

It occurred to me that the items I had extracted primarily in order to count their frequency in different narratives, might also afford the opportunity to try whether an empirical, observational classification of utility might be developed, which, being all derived from the formal narratives of one extant tribal culture, would have a specified rooting in the time and place of the world of nature, such as are lacking from comparisons of Dayaks with Lithuanian peasants and Hesiod, for example.

I therefore proceded to group my collection of items on the old principle of putting similars together and seeing what emerged in the way of empirical classes instead of thought-out ones. It would of course be expectable that the single Mohave tribe would have or lack certain specific types of magical belief that other peoples would respectively lack or have, or possess with perceptibly different frequency. As further comparisons were made, new classes, and quite likely new major classifications, would be found necessary, until something like a natural system of magical beliefs might ultimately emerge that had general applicability. As there must always be a lonely first among comparisons, here it is. Perhaps I shall be able to supplement it with others; or some one else may be curious to see how far this classification fits or does not fit a culture he is familiar with.

It will be seen that my classes are concrete; natural first classes must be so. Again, they are coordinate only: superordination may be possible, but should follow.

Some hints at superordination are contained in the sequence of coordinate groups. There are some small groups, and a residual scattering; but in a preliminary attempt, unclassified residua are better than forcibly filled classes. The whole scheme is mainly an invitation to extend and improve the job.

Topically Classified List of Items of Magic

Reaching to Obtain Something Wanted

The act or motion is concrete, but the mechanism of attainment is completely indefinite. In other words, the magic is thoroughly infantile in that a simple kinesthetic impulse is translated into achievement without the bridge of an effectual means.

Reaching inside oneself: 1021 for a dress; 11:28 for a gourd; 13:45 for cane for dice.

Reaching in an outside direction: 7:9 (UC-AR 11:1, p. 54) behind, for a staff; 3:22 (UC-AR 11:1, p. 32) down, for white mineral paint; in specified cardinal directions: 1:7a (UC-AR 11:1, p. 5) SE for maize, NE for wheat; 1:21 (UC-AR 11:1, p. 7) W for a knife; 1:81 (UC-AR 11:1, p. 15) N for eagle down, E for a shirt and cloth, W for shell beads; unspecified "reaching out": 11:47 for paints and grease; 19:9 for a basket; 19:57 for house timbers.

Creating or Making

There is no material substratum outside the ego. The creation may be from a substance within one's body, by a particularized action or instrment, just out of nothing, or wholly unspecified.

Out of saliva or spit froth (which, outside of mythical narrative, was actually used by Mohave doctors in curing): 1:4 (UC-AR 11:1, p. 4) to make wood; 3:32 (UC-AR 11:1, p. 33) a ball, which when thrown puts people to sleep; 9:26 saliva rolled between palms into a staff; 9:47 spitting into a hole creates agricultural plants; 10:17 gaming dice; 13:8 logs; 19:58 paths, ways.

Out of breath: 6A (UC-AR 11:1, p. 47) balls to fillip as weapons.

By calling or naming: 9:31 Mastamho makes the sun; 14:47 mocking bird makes dawn and night by talking; 18:23 swift-fox caught by calling; 18:24 three objects for poisoning tracks of game got by calling for them.

By heaping sand 4 times, running in 4 directions, taking desired thing out of fourth heap: 3:34 (UC-AR 11:1, p. 34) a pole.

By turning in 4 directions: 4:4 (UC-AR 11:1, p. 38) a gourd (rattle) in the hand.

By plunging a staff into sand and withdrawing it: 7:9 (UC-AR 11:1, p. 54) river; 7:10 flow blocked 4 times with foot; 7:10 river with fish and ducks; 9:18 river; 9:19 river, with sea animals (by throwing staff into sea); 13:57 frogs with river; 14:1 river; 14:78 river stirred, fish made; 15:4 river. This is evidently a favority concrete concept.

Just made, means unspecified: Matavilya 9:3 house timbers; 9:7 sun, moon, stars; 9:47 four planting sticks (he suddenly "holds" them); 10:8 black willow; 10:13 a doll (by berdache); 13:75 maize grains and seeds in sand of house floor; 18:4 canyon to obstruct sons going off; 18:20 a "partridge"; 19:69a causing beard to change color four times.

Creating from a Material

7:13, 14 (UC-AR 11:1, p. 55) Avikwame and other mts. made by dropping mud (sand); 7:15, 16 gravel (sand) blown out to become seeds; 14:79 sand blown out, mud dropped, to make rock (or mts.); 9:12 "Frog" (sic, really Fly) makes fire twirling dress strands; 13:67 house made of darkness; 15:14 makes house in sea out of Kwayū's feathers.

Travel through Ground, Air, or Water

The relative frequency is in about the order of mention.

Underground travel: 5:1 (UC-AR 11:1, p. 42) Deer; 9:5 Hiqo (ancestral white man); 9:9 Frog, with four emergences—the only flight in the group; 11:42 old woman tunnels through mts., motive not stated; 13:8 Gopher; 18:2 Gopher; 19:59 older brother of Tortoise. —Cf. also Handbook, 1925, p. 774, fragment of a historical epic.

Sink into ground: 9:5 Hiqo sinks in, to go W; 9:50 Mastamho starts to, half in, changes mind, out; 12:8-9 two elder Salt stamp, enter permanently; 19:69b Tortoise.

Open ground, emerge from it: 1:96 (UC-AR 11:1, p. 17) hero opens it for father's ghost to rise; 4:1 (UC-AR 11:1, p. 38) Ravens grow out of ground; 9:9, 13:82 Frog emerges, the fourth time permanently; 18:2 Gopher has intercourse from underground.

Travel through air: 3:10 (UC-AR 11:1, pp. 29-30) leaps far S; 3:14 turns self into arrow, flies; 18:5 twins cross canyon produced to hinder them.

Rise to sky, clouds: 11:55 Tumanpa, as trial, but returns; 19:69f-g Tortoise knows he is dead, rises to sky.

Blown: 12:9 older Salts descending blow back brothers; 18:43 sons' whirlwind carries mother home; 18:50, 18:51 turn into down-feather wisp, cottonwood down, blow themselves to destination.

Blowing other than for travel also occurs: 13:76 blows out brother's viscera to turn him into cane (flute); 14:79 Mastamho blows sand, throws mud, to make mts. —Cf. 7:15, 16 he blows out sand to become seeds for desert tribes; 18:52 attackers blow over trees, shake earth.

Blowing is important in actual curing. The treating shaman blows breath, clear spittle, and frothy spittle on his patient. The weather shaman is most concerned with making rain and wind or stopping them—cf. the case of weather magic from myths cited below.

Through water: 8:22 (UC-AR 11:2, p. 78) Umase'aka; 8:124 (UC-AR 11:2, p. 95) Hipahipa, carry followers across river on their outstretched arms; 9:20, 15:4, 15:6 Mastamho carries ancestral tribes similarly.

Walking into ocean to live there: 18:64, 18:66b hero's grandmother, then he.

Stretching or Contracting Distance or Time

Space and time are modified with about equal frequency, but they are reduced or contracted oftener than expanded.

Widening and narrowing of river valley by Mastamho's descending boat: 7:12, 9:19 by tilting; 14:19 Goose widens river.

World measuring: 9:1 Matavilya walks 4 steps from W to middle of world; 9:2 measures middle by reaching arms to ends; 9:21 four steps in four directions to extend world (by Mastamho on mt. after flood.)

(Leaping far to S: 3:10 (UC-AR 11:1, pp. 29-30)—as ante, Through Air).

Pima girls hear flute on Colorado River: 18:31.

Speed of river slowed by singing, to enable crossing: 3:29 (UC-AR 11:1, p. 33).

Year-old footprints look fresh: 1:69 (UC-AR 11:1, p. 11).

Night made to continue: 7:2 (UC-AR 11:1, p. 53).

Precocity: 1:29 (UC-AR 11:1, p. 8) child in belly sings, talks; 1:34 (UC-AR 11:1, p. 9) 4(6)-day-old child laughs; 6A (UC-AR 11:1, p. 17) baby in cradle fillips birds, descends, returns to cradle; 6A cannot be burned up; 10:4 newly born talks; 13:77 born 4 nights after conception; 13:79, 80 baby kills birds, as in 6A.

Weather Magic

The means are unspecified, except as mentioned here.

Making rain: 1:30, 1:82b, 83 (UC-AR 11:1, pp. 8, 16) to kill fellow travelers; 3:18 (UC-AR 11:1, p. 32) by throwing one hair to the W; 9:39 by Kamaiaveta for refreshment; 13:35 by kicking up dust; 9:39, 14:54 rain and hail, for coolness; 18:12, 14, 31, 18:66a to drown foes.

To stop rain: 1:83 (UC-AR 11:1, p. 16); 13:36; 18:13.

To make wind and/or rain: 5:4 (UC-AR 11:1, p. 43) to deodorize newly created deer; 5:24 (UC-AR 11:1, p. 45) to erase tracks.

Make clouds: 1:46, 47 (UC-AR 11:1, p. 10) for coolness.

Bring whirlwind: 18:43 to carry mother home.

Make dust: 9:39 by Kamaiaveta.

Make ice, to quench fire: 1:78 (UC-AR 11:1, p. 14).

Bring storm: 18:52d blow over trees, shake earth, as part of an attack.

Make "hot sky": 19:24, by kicking sand.

This category (Weather Magic) is probably of unusual frequency among the Mohave, compared with most other peoples, because of their open-air, desert habitat.

Transformation

Here we encounter both temporary transformations to attain an end and permanent changes felt as a final coming to rest—Protean elusiveness as against metamorphoses of the Ovidian kind. The latter subdivide into transformations of oneself, of a companion, or of an enemy or opponent. Terminal transformation may be a characteristic of all mythologies, and it seems rarely to explain the mechanism of change: it is automatic, like growth.

Temporary self-transformations: 1:36 (UC-AR 11:1, p. 9) into lizard; 1:70 (UC-AR 11:1, p. 72) into a bit of cane; 1:72 (UC-AR 11:1, p. 12) into a maggoty dead body, and in 1:81 (UC-AR 11:1, p. 15) diving to rejuvenate and become handsome; 6A (UC-AR 11:1, p. 47) into a dove; 6A (UC-AR 11:1, p. 47) into a butterfly not killable in battle; 18:10, 11 y. brother turns into gray racer snake, elder into red.

Permanent self-transformations: 1:104 (UC-AR 11:1, p. 19) of Cane's son into "projecting leg" rock Me-koaṭa in river; 3:36 (UC-AR 11:1, p. 34) of Nyohaiva into "hawk rock," Black Mt. near Parker; 4:31, 32 (UC-AR 11:1, p. 40) of brothers into Raven and Crow; 7:84 (UC-AR 11:1, p. 64), 14:82 of Mastamho into bald eagle; 11:55 of the 2 Tumanpa into a pair of rocks; 13:76 of younger Chuhueche to a rock on Kofa Mt.; 13:84 of his son into cane.

Permanent transformation of kin or companion: 1:103 (UC-AR 11:1, p. 18) of 4 wives and mother into stars (17:77 Cane 11, into Pleiades); of br. into snipe (17:77); of father's br. into snowy owl (17:77, saθerke, bird); 13:85 of mother into snipe; 18:66b of mother and her sister into snipes. The plumping on this one strand-bird is notable.

Permanent transformation of opponent: 1:78 (UC-AR 11:1, p. 14) dangerous sun turned into (harmless) sun dog; 3:35 (UC-AR 11:1, p. 34) enemy head thrown away becomes Picacho Rock; 13:76 oppressive brother turned into cane.

Complete transformation: 14:74-76 (also 14:88) Mastamho at Ho-kusave, "where they pierce noses" (echo of boy's initiation?), gives birds their final shaping after making them race; there are allusions in other tales also, as in 7:94, 95 (UC-AR 11:1, p. 66), by Mastamho's delegates. There are several approaches, in the way of kinds of tribes as well as kinds of birds taking final form, in both Mastamho, 7, and Origins, 9, but the line is not sharp in these cases between specific acts of transformation and the achievement of a last stage of predestined or automatic growth.

Now and then a stage of the transformation is emphasized visually, as when Mastamho's arms begin to turn into wings in 7:82 (UC-AR 11:1, p. 64), and when feathers grow out of him in 9:50, or when he performs an act of this kind on others, as in tearing the human fingers apart in 7:48 (UC-AR 11:1, p. 60).

Finally, there is transformation by spontaneous becoming of a part of the body, without act of will: 9:41 Sky-Rattlesnake's blood turns into the ocean, his head into a mountain N of Davis Dam; 12:10, 12:25 the Salt brothers' tears turn into salt; 14:52 Goose's parts and organs become water animals.

Bewitching

By this I mean the use of internal or psychic supernatural power to bring weakness, illness, or death on others. The Mohave were sure that some men possessed this power, but they were often vague as to the mechanism of its exercise, and mostly did not connect it with any specific apparatus. Fears of it were frequent in their life; but while the belief has fair frequency in their dream narratives, it cannot be said to dominate these; it occurs in barely half the narratives; the other half are wholly without reference to witchcraft.

Rendering sleepy, unseeing, weak, or powerless: 1:24 (UC-AR 11:1, pp. 7-8) makes y. brother sleepy and ill; 3:32 (UC-AR 11:1, p. 33) Nyohaiva puts enemy to sleep by throwing saliva ball, paralyzes him by touching; 8:100 (UC-AR 11:2, p. 91) boy witched dead; 8:107 (UC-AR 11:2, p. 92) Hipahipa renders her housemates blind in order to recover a truant woman; 8:140 (UC-AR 11:2, pp. 97-98) singing at night to weaken and slow foes; 9:3, 13:1 Matavilya witched to slow death by Frog (who has swallowed his feces); 18:41a, twins' new wives put mother-in-law to sleep for night.—It will be noted that three of these occurrences are from the pseudohistorical prose epic 8 (UC-AR 11:2) which does not deal in the frankly miraculous (to the Mohave) but admits only such magic and witchcraft as the Mohave were sure occurred in their daily life.

There is also an implication appearing through tale 14, Yellak, of a contest of supernatural power between Mastamho and Goose (who dies) and his successor Grebe.

The opposite power of resuscitating: 1:73 (UC-AR 11:1, p. 12) corpse on hot sand under basket; 18:17 eaglets; 18:41d deer.

Rejuvenation when old, resulting in immortality: 18:64 twins' mother, 18:66d, son.

Souls and Ghosts

The soul is the shadow, mát-kwisa, in Mohave; a ghost, nyaveδí, is a dead soul. The terminology is clear-cut, though without evidence of a sharp line of distinction.

"Shadow" mentioned: 1:70 (UC-AR 11:1, p. 12) leaves shadow in house while he transforms his body outdoors; 11:29 Sky-Rattlesnake's shadow becomes alive, apparently as an actual snake; 18:59 dead twins' shadows visit their mother; 19:69f Tortoise knows he is dead, sees his own shadow.

"Ghost" mentioned: 1:78 (UC-AR 11:1, p. 14) Sun escaping to sky jumps up sky pole like a ghost; 5:22 (UC-AR 11:1, pp. 44-45) Deer has omen dream of flying stars striking him, he becoming a ghost; 19:44 single-legged ghost seen; 19:48 blazing traveling ghost seen.

Ambiguous term: 18:16 "the shadows (ghosts) of dead eaglets fly."

Neither term used: 1:96 (UC-AR 11:1, p. 17) dead father brought to surface of ground has no bones, is only flesh (sic), is embraced; 17:74, Cane 11, no bones, only "soul" (ḥimaṭ hiviδiktik—but himaṭ is "body").

Omens, Portents, Signs

These are only moderately frequent, and always of evil.

Predicted omens fulfilled: 18:42/18:53b, 54 twins to mother: hide will move, flute burst, feathers etc. scatter, flicker headdress become bird and vomit blood.

Omens: (UC-AR 11:2, p. 105) 8:184 nose pendant falls into sleeper's mouth—he is killed; 8:187, 188, fish in spring, 6 fighting deer—war party destroyed.

Dreamed portents: 5:22 (UC-AR 11:1, pp. 44-45) Deer: shooting stars hit body; 8:157 (UC-AR 11:2, pp. 100-101) Hipahipa: "earth-tongue" crevice.

Sign: 18:41c, drop falling on coals hisses, intercourse is known.

Hunting Magic

5:3 (UC-AR 11:1, p. 42) arrow poison slows game; 8:92 (UC-AR 11:2, p. 88) takes rattlesnakes, hangs live on belts; 8:97 (UC-AR 11:2, p. 90) antelope magic, can take with hands; 13:50, Jaguar (Wolf) steps on tracks, makes game sleepy; 13:72 hunting by pressing stick on neck of game; 18:24 poison on tracks of game.

Blocked or lost: 8:97 (UC-AR 11:2, p. 90) antelope magic blocked; 18:41d y. brother loses power.

Special War-Powers
Rather miscellaneous.

Turn butterfly, cannot be struck: 6:A (UC-AR 11:1, p. 47); hawks to wear morning star: 7:69 (UC-AR 11:1, p. 62); Mastamho gives powers: 15:15-20; Falcon kills by darting: 18:52e.

Thunder and Lightning, Fire ball, and Cane

These have a definite association: the destructive power of lightning and fireball (ball-lightning, "meteor" in the popular sense of a rolling or lying ball of fire), perhaps "sky-heat," also, can be kept in and evoked from pieces of cane. Cane is also much of a preoccupation in itself, connected with flutes and dice and girls.

Thunder and lightning: 1:91 (UC-AR 11:1, p. 17) lightning cane in thunder's hole: 1:102 (UC-AR 11:1, p. 18) lightning matched in contest; cane thrown, mts. burned up; 13:73, cane talks with thunder and lightning; 13:76 lightning flashes as cane is split. Cane II, tale 17), has variations; see 17:13, 69, 70, 76, 77.

Ball lightning, Kwayú, (cannibal, feathered, modern Mohave translate word as "giant"—see 1:76, 1:104, 6A —UC-AR 11:1, pp. 13, 18-19; 15:13-15); 1:37 (UC-AR 11:1, p. 9) Cane's son strikes ball of father's kneecap, it flies as fiery Kwayu to mts., destroys and kills there; 17:24 similar, except Thunder instead of Kwayu.

See also the transformations into cane: 1:70 (UC-AR 11:1, p. 12), 13:76, 84.

Cane cut (split?) with fingernail: 18:30; cf. 3:32 Nyohaiva beheads with thumbnail.

Relating to River or Flood

See also Travel—through Water.

Matavilya's ashes washed away: 7:11 (UC-AR 11:1, p. 54).

River crossed on 4 hand-heaps of sand: 1:38, 57 (UC-AR 11:1, pp. 10, 11). 17:76, 77.

Flood lowered: 9:20 by lowering arms; 15:15 by spitting chewed "coyote grass."

Scattered or Surprising

There is of course little unity in this group.

1:78 (UC-AR 11:1, p. 14): gaming pole stood up to fall and burn house; climb pole to sky; "heaven and earth sack"; "sky heat" in body, used to kill.

1:102 (UC-AR 11:1, p. 18), 19:25: spread of fire stopped with plant "ghost arrow."

8:79 (UC-AR 11:2, p. 87): mutually swallow nose ornaments, die (cf. Omens).

8:92 (UC-AR 11:2, p. 88): Hipahipa varies size of tracks.

9:11: direction of dead body turned by Mastamho's willing.

12:13, 15: Atise (rodent?) and Owl born from Matavilya's pulse.

13:23: ants march through Horned Toad's digestive tract (magic or natural history observation?).

13:68: Y. brother has mice efface his tracks.

14:17: Goose blocks river with wings to check followers.

14:36: White Beaver with tail blocks river to Grebe and followers.

18:5: mirage to confuse sons.

18:7: twins bewitch swallows.

18:40: twins tear open sky to see.

18:66c: Dragonfly rescues Kuyahumare from drowning.

B. New Geographic Data

Data from Pete Sherman or Avé-púya are given first; then those from Dan Welsh (marked DW), half white, a quarter Mohave, a quarter Yuma, born in 1871 at Blythe; last, those from Mary Ybarra, marked MY, Mohave, born near Ehrenberg about 1875. Sherman, of clan Nyo'iltše, was born in 1880, at Kusól-iδáu, close to Poston below Parker, of parents whose birthplaces in Mohave Valley he did not know.

1. ALONG THE COLORADO, SOUTH OF WILLIAMS FORK, EAST SIDE

Há-ku-tšyépa. DW: "water breaks out."

(Amáṭ-)kan'ú, 1 m. S of Hákutšyepa.

Malyhó-ha, "water pipe," spring, 1/2 m. S of last. —DW: malyeho-ha, straight opposite Monument Peak. —UC-AR 11:2, p. 142, no. 26, and p. 101, par. 158.

Nyapakáiteke, on the trail 1/2 m. or more from last.

Tataskyám(e), 1/2 m. S on trail, which is coming down into the river bottom. —Cf. UC-AR 11:2, p. 142, no. 31, Tataskyanve (misplaced below Parker), 2:10 (UC-AR 11:1, p. 25).

Aví-hamsú-qwa(i)lype, "bat-guano rock," 1/2 m. beyond. —Cf. UC-AR 11:2, p. 142, no. 25b, (location uncertain), and above, Yellak, 14:44.

(Ho'áu-nye-vatše, "horseflies' houses," no. 27 on UC-AR 11:2, Map 2, p. 142, and 3:12 (UC-AR 11:1, p. 30), was not mentioned by the 1953 informants.)

Hányora, "marks, designs," close to last, at the river ("aha-lye").

Sama'-úkwisa (or -okusa), next downstream on trail. This is Sama'-ókusa of 3:33 (UC-AR 11:1, p. 34) UC-AR 11:2, no. 30 of Map 2 and p. 142.

Uh'ár-kuvasáve, "watching the poor (i.e., in flesh, thin)." DW: Some Mohave were living in the little valley there, off screw-beans. Yuma came, saw them starved, said, "It will be best to push them into the river," but the Mohave pushed the fat well-fed Yuma in.

Hály-kuvíre, 1/2 m. from last. —UC-AR 11:2, p. 142, no. 29a, Aha-lye-kuirve and 8:94 p. 89).

Só-ko-honáke, "necklace," at the N boundary of Reservation, on trail. Mesquite ripened earlier here than in most places. DW: Kosó-kwe-honákwe, "put haliotis around," because a hill there looks necklaced. It is 2 m. below "watching the thin" and 5 m. above Kutuδúnye. —UC-AR 11:2, p. 142, no. 26a, Kovesokwe-hunake, 14:45.

Ahmó-ket-aθílye, "sandstone (soft-rock) mortars." With next. —UC-AR 11:2, p. 142, no. 34 (evidently misplaced downstream), Ahmo-kutš-eθilye, 3:13 (UC-AR 11:1, p. 30), 8:94 (UC-AR 11:2, p. 89). —Cf. also 18:38, fn. 101, but in 18:39, fn. 104, Ahmo-ketmasáva, though in this vicinity, is on the W side.

Há-θítšive, "drink water." With last. —18:38, fn. 102.

Movályla (said to be "Movara" in English), 1/4 m.
below, is Headgate rock through which a tunnel was
driven for the intake to the Reservation irrigation
system. DW: same, at headgate and dam; "swim,"
because the Satukhota heroes swam there. Cf. 18:39,
fn. 103.

Here the trail went up on the mesa again.

Kutuбúnye, "sit and slide," not located except between
last and next. DW: same; on mesa close by Movályle.
—UC-AR 11:2, p. 142, no. 34b, Kutuбunya, -nyve 8:158
(UC-AR 11:2, p. 101).

Aví-soqwílye, "Hawk Mt.," Black Mt., the butte ESE
of Parker. DW: same. —UC-AR 11:2, p. 142, no. 28;
3:36 (UC-AR 11:1, p. 34); 14:45; 15:17; 18:37, fn. 99.

Amáṭ-ya'áma, not mentioned in 1953. —UC-AR 11:2,
p. 142, no. 29; 3:35 (UC-AR 11:1, p. 34); 8:94 (UC-AR
11:2, p. 89); "1/4 m. from Avi-soqwilye"; 4 m. E of
Parker Agency, which agrees.

Ah'á-бokupít, "owl-cottonwood," at Old Agency, 2 or
so m. SE of Parker Agency, corresponds to Aha-
бekupiбa, "owl water" of 3:33 (UC-AR 11:1, p. 34) and
of UC-AR 11:2 p. 142, no. 33, and Map 2.

Aqwáqa-háve, "deer pass through," on Bouse Wash
9 m. from Parker, at (E?) edge of reservation, some
miles inland from river. DW: same; Bouse Wash.
—UC-AR 11:2, p. 142, no. 35; 2:9, 3:15a, 32 (UC-AR
11:1, pp. 25, 30, 33); 8:94 (UC-AR 11:2, p. 89).

Aví-'a'íse, "Screwbean Mt.," at point where it starts
at Bouse Wash, extending S. —DW: same. —UC-AR
11:2, p. 142, no. 38; 8:155 (UC-AR 11:2, p. 100), coupled
with Avi-kwa-hapama.

Aví-kwa-hapáme, "small [sic] mt.," a rock pile in
the valley, 1/4 m. from the mt. Aví-a'íse. —DW: same;
the same range as Screwbean Mt.; 10 m. N of "Ashes
Hill." —UC-AR 11:2, p. 142, no. 37; 2:8 (UC-AR 11:1,
p. 25); 8:155 (UC-AR 11:2, p. 100).

Avi-ahmó, "mortar rocks," in valley, 1 m. SE from
Valley store. "A rock pile, used to be called a pile of
driftwood, íhne."

Aví-kwa-hapáme mát'are, a bare alkali flat below
A.-hapáme.

Aví-tšórinyene, "tree-lizard rock," at edge of valley,
1/8 m. from hills. It used to look like head, back, and
tail of the lizard—the tail is gone now. —UC-AR 11:2,
p. 142, no. 36a; Avi-'itšorinyene, 3:15f (UC-AR 11:1,
p. 31).

Aví-maṭih'ó (amaṭ-eh'ó), "ashes hill, heavy sand
hill," small hill still in the valley, near mesa edge.
—DW: Aví-met-eh'ó; 3 m. N of Moon Mt.

Aví-hely'a, "moon mt.," the Moon Mt. of UC-AR
11:2, Maps 1 and 2, 5 or more m. E of river. It is
said to have its name from a moon-shaped white rock.

—DW: Aví-helye'á, 10 m. N of "Red Earth." —UC-AR
11:2, p. 142, no. 39; 2:7, 3:16 (UC-AR 11:1, pp. 25, 31);
15:17.

Aví-mat(h)a-huyáma, "Wind Strike Mt.," same as
last or part of same range. Wind from Riverside Mts.
hits Moon Mt. with a roar.

The name of a third place in this vicinity informant
PS could not remember.

Amáṭ-kw-ahwáta, "red earth," 2-3 m. from Moon
Mt. —DW: Amáṭ-kwa-'ahwat, 9 m. N of Ehrenberg.

Alapása, the former mining settlement of La Paz,
at the edge of the valley, long abandoned.

Avé-nye-va-(tše), "rattlesnakes' houses" was given
UC-AR 11:2, p. 142, no. 41; 3:17 (UC-AR 11:1, p. 31);
8:90 (UC-AR 11:2, p. 88), as being at La Paz.

Takiv'auva, 2-3 m. beyond La Paz, at the S end of
Reservation. The word was said to refer to "open
(iron) post," in other words a surveyor's benchmark
or monument, and is therefore recent. —DW: Kat'ú-
takuváuve, "scalps gone," where the Haltšaбom impaled
and scalped captured Mohave and Yuma, 3 m. N of
Ehrenberg. —UC-AR 11:2, p. 142, no. 42, Kapotak-
iv'auve etc., 2:6, 3:18 (UC-AR 11:1, pp. 25, 32).

Hóre, "gravel," the former Ehrenberg, at the river
just north of the highway bridge to Blythe. —DW: same.
—UC-AR 11:2, p. 142, no. 44; Hoore, 2:5 (UC-AR 11:1,
p. 25); 8:90 (UC-AR 11:2, p. 88).

(A)Ha-sélye'aye, "sand water," (DW only), a lake or
slough paralleling the river. —UC-AR 11:2, p. 142, no.
45, 8:90, note 30 (p. 159); 14:50.

Ahá-ku-tinyáme, "dark water," "2 m." below Ehrenberg. A historic-period Mohave called Papán lived there
who owned cattle and a mine. This was said to be the
boundary between Mohave and Yuma claims to the valley,
after the Haltšiбoma conquest. —DW: same; a "lake"
at edge of river; they used to fish there. —MY: a dark
backwater "lake" on the river, 10 m. below Ehrenberg.
Papán lived here. —UC-AR 11:2, p. 142, no. 46, 8:90,
note 28 (p. 159); 14:50.

—DW: Núme-to'óre, "wild cat sits," hills by the
river. —UC-AR 11:2, p. 142, no. 47 (Nume-ta'orve),
8:90, note 27 (p. 159).

—DW: Ak'úly-tcekapáve, "jackrabbit emerges."
—UC-AR 11:2, p. 142, no. 48, "a high hill," 3:20 (UC-
AR 11:1, p. 32); 8:89 (UC-AR 11:2, p. 88).

—DW: Aví-tšiétse, more or less opposite Ahpe-
hwelyve (no. H, UC-AR 11:2, p. 143) on W side.
—UC-AR 11:2, p. 142, no. 49 (Avi-tšitše), 3:21 (UC-AR
11:1, p. 32), 8:89 (UC-AR 11:2, p. 88).

Ah'a-(t)-kwatpá(r)ve, "cottonwood grove" 15-20 m.
below Papan's place. —UC-AR 11:2, p. 142, no. 50,
2:4 (UC-AR 11:1, p. 24), 14:52, 18:41d, fn. 119.

MY: Avá-tšúhaye, 15-20 m. SE of Cibola. —UC-AR 11:2, p. 142, no. 52, Ava-tšohai, 3:23 (UC-AR 11:1, p. 32), farthest S, 8:89 (UC-AR 11:2, p. 88).

Ye'llak-íme, "goose tracks," 10 m. below last. —Informant PS put this on the E of the river; all others put in W, on the cut-off from Picacho S. It is UC-AR 11:2, p. 143, no. P, 1:61 (UC-AR 11:1, p. 11), 14:57.

Akka, Laguna Dam.

DW: Hanyó-kyulye, "long slough," a little below Laguna Dam. (E or W side??)

DW: Avírqa, a black point, opposite Aví-kwilye-itšyese Mt. —UC-AR 11:2, p. 142, no. 61, 8:10, 85 (UC-AR 11:2, pp. 77, p. 87) near no. 60, Avi-kunyure, 15-20 m. above Yuma.

Nyam-ku-tava·va, Yuma reservation, i.e., some spot in it. —UC-AR 11:2, p. 143, no. R on W side; (Nyim-kutavāve) 14:59.

2. ALONG THE COLORADO, SOUTH OF WILLIAMS FORK, WEST SIDE

Amáṭa, "earth," place about 1/2 m. above turn of river at mouth of Fork.

Ahmá-va-'ahwére, "quail run," c. 100 yards below last.

Tšésahá, where the Satukhota (tale 18:1, see fn. 4) twins were raised by their mother. It was said to be "close to" the monument pinnacles of Whipple Mts., which probably means "abreast" of them near the river.

Avír-qorotát, "pinnacles end, finish." Two natural monuments marking the boundary between Mohave and Halchidhoma when the latter still lived around Parker. The more conspicuous rock column, visible from large areas of the Reservation, is the taller sister; a shorter one, her brother. —DW: Avír-korótat, Monument peak pinnacle.

Aví-ható, the peak of the Whipple Mts., some miles W of the pinnacles, and much higher—4,110 feet. —DW: Aví-hetó, black highest peak of Whipple Mts.

Koskílye, at W end of this range, where the old Needles-Parker wagon road or horse trail crossed it. —DW: same, top of trail over W end of range.

Sóvhe, 1/2 m. from Koskilye. —DW: Sav'he, a black hill, westernmost outlier peak of Whipple Mts. —See also 18:14 and fn. 51, (Amaṭ-)savehê.

Hoatše-wámve, "hailstones," where the present Needles-Parker highway crosses a strip of malpais lava. See also 18:14 and fn. 48, 51, where there is a second -ve suffix.

Taha', W of last and of the highway, a conspicuous bell-shaped peak standing clear of the Turtle range at its E foot. In the 1865-1867 war, the Chemehuevi killed a Mohave at Blythe Intake, then fled on to this peak, where they knew how to find water, and were vainly besieged by the Mohave. See 19:29, fn. 15, and 19:35; also 15:16.

Kuyá-k-aqwáθa, "yellow cave," 1/2 m. "this side" (S or E) of Koskilye.

Atší-ara, "fish-tail," a smallish jagged ridge, an outlier of the Monument-Whipple massif, N of Parker-Vidal highway, W of "Yellow cave." See 19:29, fn. 15.

Aqwáq-múnyo, somewhat S of "Fish-tail." —UC-AR 11:2, p. 143, no. G, much misplaced to S; 3:27 (UC-AR 11:1, p. 33).

DW: Ahpé-ðáve, a flat black mt. (? N of Turtle Mts., at SW end of Mohave range, 4 m. inland?)

Ha-talómpa, "water-bucket," near mouth of Vidal Wash into Colorado. DW: Ahá-telómve, "drip fast." There is a tale about Fox carrying water in a gourd from (?) the Cocopa, which leaked out here.

DW: Hipá-sev'auve, Vidal wash, 1 m. from last.

Aví-vatáye, "big mountains," Riverside Mts. —DW: same. —Erroneously put on E side, UC-AR 11:2, p. 142, no. 32; 14:48, 15:17.

Sumá-koθíke, "lying root," beyond, but still part of Riverside Mts. It is Avi-samakwiðike of 18:3, fn. 15, inland of Riverside Mts., "across from Rice."

Koθílye, "cement wall," a large wash entering river beyond Riverside Mts. —DW: Kusíly (Yuma form), "rough," a black point; 15 m. below Riverside Mts. —UC-AR 11:2, p. 143, no. E; 3:29 (UC-AR 11:1, p. 33); but this is upriver from G, Aqwaq-munyo.

Ahpály-kuvilyó, "broad ironwood," same place, two names. —DW: Ahpály-kúvelyove, "wide ironwood," 10 m. from last.

Aví-ivére, "strong mts.," Big Maria Mts., whose main ridge is serrated into long, jutting points. —DW: same; same mts. as last. —Erroneously given as on E side, UC-AR 11:2, p. 142, no. 33a, 14:49.

Qaleqále-viðútševe, "where Q dodged," 2 m. beyond. Qaleqale was a cannibal "giant" who came down and ate people. They could not kill him because he dodged when shot at, until he was struck in the knee, where he kept his heart. —DW: Q.-veðutšve, NE of Blythe. This seems to be a stone-outlined human figure of the maze type.

DW: Himély-qaráuve, "fast leg"; a man died and lay there (cf. last); 3-4 m. below Big Maria Mts.

Hanamaθ-nye-vá, "otter (water-raccoon) his house," at river bank abreast of last. —DW: Hanemás-nye-vá, (Yuma form), a large bad water, 2 m. from last.

Halye-pútša, "water-at pour" (obviously a modern
word). Blythe Intake, 1 m. below Otter's house. —DW:
Haly-putš, same, 2 m. below Otter's house, 1 m. up
from Ǫaleǫále-veδútšve. —MY: Haly-pútš, same.

Hapúwese, "quail-chicks' watering place," Blythe
Valley. —DW: Hapúwes. —MY: Hápuwes.

Ahmá-pályve, "striped-wild-pumpkin quail," another
part of Blythe V.

DW: Hanyó-melyeváha, in middle of Blythe V. —MY:
Hanyo-melyevá, S of Hápuwes, Blythe.

Ahpé-hwélyve, "dig up (slabs for) metates," a double
peak. —DW: Ahpé-hwélye, a mt. at S end of Blythe V.,
at (far) end of Aha-kwaθo'ilye (Palo Verde) Slough.
—MY: Ahpe-hwelyu, a sharp peak ("like Boundary
Cone") in the range W of Palo Verde. —UC-AR 11:2,
p. 143, no. I, Ahpe-hwelyeve; 3:25 (UC-AR 11:1, p. 33).

MY: Aha-kwaθo'ílya, "salty water," Palo Verde Lake;
is 5-6 m. from mt. mentioned in Handbook, p. 800, as
where the Halchidhoma were living at the time of their
defeat and expulsion by the Mohave.

MY: Sakwa-'atay(e), big lake E of Palo Verde [town];
the Mohave fished there.

Kwayú-θewénewe, "cannibal meteor 'giant' hanged
(by neck)," a rock between Picacho and Laguna Dam
[sic].

DW: Aví-kwilye-itšyése, a mt. by Hanyó-kyulye
which is below Laguna Dam (see E side list) and opposite Avírqa point on E side.

3. NORTH OF MOHAVE VALLEY

The river north of Mohave Valley is the section for
which it is hardest to straighten out the geography, in
spite of our having two Yellak itineraries that profess
to follow the Colorado from source to mouth, and
several partial ones, as in Mastamho, Epic, and Tumanpa. The older available maps are not too good; the
river and the land have changed markedly in stretches
owing both to floods and to damming—Parker Dam has
at times backed water up nearly the length of Mohave
Valley, and Davis Dam to beyond Eldorado Canyon. In
1953 I searched with Hiram McCord, a Needles Mohave,
for Iδokuva'ire and Qara'erve, the former northernmost large Mohave villages, and he could not find even
their approximate sites. We were not even sure on
which side of the river their sites now lay.

From Iδo-kuva'ire south of the bold southerly bend
of the Colorado, up to Hardyville east of its bold
westerly bend, and then on upstream north to Davis
Dam, is some eight to ten miles, probably nearer the
latter. This stretch is within Mohave Valley: it is
level and has natural growth for some distance inland

from the east edge of the river. Except at the lower
end, however, this stretch was not regularly farmed
or lived in by the Mohave, I presume because it lay
above the automatic irrigation of the annual flood.
Davis Dam I take to be at the natural upper end of
Mohave Valley, the beginning of Black Canyon in the
wider old sense of Ives. So far as I can judge from
contour maps and the looks of Lake Mohave which has
drowned Black Canyon, most of this canyon was not
as confined and steep as the 1858 accounts of Ives and
Möllhausen, and especially their illustrations, suggest.
But it held little to attract a farming or for that matter a gathering population, and there seem to have been
no residents except at Cottonwood Island (lower end
perhaps 14 miles above Davis Dam) where in 1858 a
few Mohave families were living, possibly more by
fishing than by farming, at least as compared with
those in the main Valley. Above Cottonwood Island
there seem to have been neither Mohave nor Cheme-
huevi-Paiute living permanently in the period of discovery, until the Kohóalche Paiute of the region of the
mouth of the Virgin-Muddy were reached. The Mohave
quite likely would have claimed upstream so far as to
include Eldorado Canyon as their spot of mythological
origin. But as they have never mentioned to me or to
others, so far as I know, any other historic people
(apart from the nineteenth-century Chemehuevi) actually
on the river or regularly visiting it, until the Kohóalche
Paiute on the Virgin, there would have been no need
to press or enforce such a claim. The Walapai may
occasionally have come down to the upper river, but
did not cross it to the west. Their mapped settlements
in the Black Range are mainly on the inland side, and
south of the latitude of Davis Dam.

In what follows, I am omitting Nyahaim-kwiδik and
the many other formal ritual names of probably unlocalized spots that abound especially in the Yellak versions.

We have only three fixed geographical points in this
stretch north of Davis Dam: Eldorado Canyon, Cottonwood Island, and Avikwame which is known both as
Dead and Newberry Mt. The southern end of this last
in fact is abreast Davis Dam (plate 1a, b), and its summit lies nearly six miles north of the Dam and eight-
and-a-half west.

E and W denote on Arizona and Nevada side respectively, where determined.

N1. Hatekulye-nyi-kuyá, Wolf's (or Jaguar's) cave,
den, is probably the farthest upstream place in my
lists. 5:1 (UC-AR 11:1, p. 42, Hatekulye-naka); 14:14,
16A, fn. 14. It is probably farther N than Lizard Mt.

N2. Amaṭ(a)-hamak comes next downriver in Yellak,
14:17. J. P. Harrington cites it as Mat-ha-maka, "wind's
back," a N-S range in Nevada in the vicinity of Eldorado

Canyon, apparently S of it. This might be the "Iriteba Peaks" (named after the Mohave chief also called Arateva), which touch 5000 feet as part of the Opal Mountains of the older topographic maps. Abreast the S end of this range Harrington notes "pots" in the river that were filled with fish seined farther downstream. Yellak has Amaṭahamak reached from the N before Ha'avulypo; if the narrator is right, Harrington's placing of it is wrong.

N3. θáweve, 14:18 and 8:192 (UC-AR 11:2, p. 105). In the latter, it is the farthest N reached by the people dispossessed by the Mohave after their flight from Selye'aiyi-ta, where their leaders were killed, 8:191 (UC-AR 11:2, p. 105). From θaweve the survivors remove E into historic Walapai territory.

N4. Ha'avulypo is in Eldorado Canyon, where Matavilya's petrified houseposts stand, some two miles from the river—see plate 1,e. Most narratives take it for granted as a starting reference point; in Yellak it occurs in an itinerary, 14:19.

N4a. Harrington calls the canyon—as distinct from Matavilya's housesite—Avá'pa, which might mean "person's house," and speaks of many bedrock mortars for mesquite. (I seem not to have recorded the name Ava'pa.)

N5. "Lizard Mt.," Avi-kwatulye: 5:1 (UC-AR 11:1, p. 42); 14:II:15. Harrington puts this in Arizona more or less opposite the Mat-ha-maka range in Nevada. If that range is the Ireteba Peaks, Lizard Mt. might be Mt. Davis, rising out of the canyon to a bit above 2000 feet less than 2 miles from the river, some 13 m. S of Eldorado. I think however it is more likely to be Mt. Perkins, 2 or 3 m. farther N than Davis, but 8 m. from the river and over 5000 ft. in height—the last big peak going N in the Black Range. Mr. H. F. Dobyns writes me that the Walapai by Lizard Mt. (Wi-kutula) mean the northernmost part of the Black Range, between Pilot Kuob and Willow Beach arroyo.

N6. Kwilyeθki, Y:II:16, would be next. There may be two such places or a confusion: Kwilyeθki is mentioned in Deer, 5:14 (UC-AR 11:1, p. 44) as in Mohave Valley, near Iδo-kuva'ire, UC-AR 11:2, Map 1:1:A.

N7. Ahá-kwoana is cited in 11:8, 12:20, both from the same narrator. It is on the river; Numeta and Hatekulye frequent it; and Ha-virepuka (N9, below) is S of it—distance unspecified. Internal evidence of 11:10 would put Ha-virepuka N of Ha'avulypo.

Below Mt. Davis, the river canyon widens considerably for 12 or 15 m. and is sometimes shown on maps as Cottonwood Valley. In this widening lies Cottonwood Island—really a series of three almost contiguous islands by the 1884 survey, in a stretch where the river flowed nearly SE.

N8. Aha-kekatš-voδauve of 14:22 is where the river splits and part of Yellak's following think they are leaving him. This would be the N end of Cottonwood Island.

N9. Ha-virepuka according to Harrington is the channel on the W side of Cottonwood Island. It is mentioned in Tumanpa, 11:10, and in the Epic, 8:171 (UC-AR 11:2, p. 103), along with Kuyal-kutš-vapitša, as the place where the people expelled from Mohave Valley by Hipahipa and his successors took refuge with two chiefs who later persuaded them to a counterattack. It is also mentioned as one and a fraction day's travel from Iδo-kuva'ire: going S, one slept at Kwam-haθeve, going N at "Kwaparvete" (for Ah'a-kwatθarve?). —In 1953 Havirepuka was given to me outright as the name of Cottonwood Island.

N10. Mathake-va, "north place," is the generic name for Cottonwood Island. Thus in narrative 7:1, fn. 1 (UC-AR 11:1, p. 52) and in general statement made in 1954. The people were called Mathake-pa, "northerners." The few Mohave still remaining there abandoned the island about 1865 on the outbreak of war with the Chemhuevi.

N11. Waθalye, 14:23, is where the channels rejoin, that is, the S end of the island.

Below Cottonwood Island, Harrington and I both got mention of a place on the W and on the E side.

N12. Han'uθkwily-avatša (H) or Hamuθkwily-ivatše (14:II:18) on the Nevada side.

N13. Ah'a-kwatθarve, "cottonwoods spreading" (H) or Ah'a-kwaθarve (11:11), in 1954 corrected to -kwatθarve, "cottoning"; in Arizona. —"Kwaparvete" is probably a mishearing of the last part of this place name; the only Kwaparvete recognized in 1953 is UC-AR 11:2, Map 1, I, Z.

N14, 15. In Yellak, 14:27, are mentioned two landmarks opposite each other: Qotase, "hard," in Nevada, and Avi-kunu'ulye, "tumescence rock" in Arizona. Avi-kunu'ulye was said to be 6 m. N of Hoatše-wámeve of 7:88 (UC-AR 11:1, p. 65) and Epic, 8:191 (UC-AR 11:2, p. 105). The element -qotase recurs in Amai-nye-qotáse in Mohave Valley below Ft. Mohave, UC-AR 11:2, Map 1, I, 17.

N16. Avikwame. —Qotase and Avi-kunu'ulye are reached in Yellak as Avikwame is being approached from the N. This peak is mentioned in context in 14:28, in Epic, 8:171 (UC-AR 11:2, p. 103), and as a half day from Cottonwood Island in Epic, 8:187 (UC-AR 11:2, p. 105). In Yellak II it appears under a mythological name as N16a, Ava-k(u)-tinyam, (dark house,) in 14:II:19. The main body of this impressive mountain (plate 1a, b) is 10 m. long from N to S; with its foothill approaches the length must be nearly twice as great.

The summit is near the N end.

N17. Kwam-haθeve, Epic, 8:179 (UC-AR 11:2, p. 104), is on the E side a day's travel from Havirepuka; not otherwise located. There is another one of the name on the W side of Mohave Valley, a little below Needles, UC-AR 11:2, Map 1:II:29a.

N18. Selye'ayi-ta, "big sand, much sand," E side, 14:II:24; Epic 8:191 (UC-AR 11:2, p. 105). From here the defeated flee to N3 θaweve in 8:192 (UC-AR 11:2, p. 105). There are others of the name: cf. UC-AR 11:2, Map 2:12.

N19. K-amaiavete hihu ta-hayahaya-ve, "where K's head rolled to (from Avikwame)," 14:II:25, must be somewhere near Davis Dam—I am not sure whether above or below, but presumably above. See also 16G: 23, 24.

N20. Avi-tunyore, of Epic, 8:191 (UC-AR 11:2, p. 105), "pictograph, marked rock," near Hardyville, E side.

N21. Hoatše-wameve of 7:88 (UC-AR 11:1, p. 65) and 8:191 (UC-AR 11:2, p. 105), E side. This may be upriver or downriver from the next on the W side.

N22. (Hi)meke-huvike, 8:170 (UC-AR 11:2, p. 103), 14:31, 14:II:26, W side; relation to preceding not determined. —11, note 27, couples it with our next, Avi-kutaparve.

Avi-kutaparve of 8:169 is UC-AR 11:2, p. 103, and Map 1:II:B.

Nyamasave-kwahave of 8:191 is UC-AR 11:2, Map 1:I:A1, near Iδo-kuva'ire, Map 1:I:A.

And herewith we are in the formerly farmed and settled Valley.

There are other names in the north, but without localization or place in a sequence, so I cannot do anything with them.

4. IKWE-NYE-VA, "CLOUD
HOME" MOUNTAIN

Ikwé-nye-vá, also recorded as Ikwi-nyava or Hikwe-nyeva, literally "clouds-their-house(s)," is a mountain mentioned in a number of Mohave narratives, but located in two different regions, both southeast of Needles Valley, but at quite different distances. Sometimes the Mohave are quite hazy, merely knowing that the mountain is great, remote, and somewhere in Arizona.

The first general location is in Bill Williams Fork drainage, the second in Gila-Salt drainage. These correspond respectively to Walapai border territory, and to territory of the Maricopa or of the later Maricopa-associated tribes.

Perry Dean, who narrated the unabridged Tortoise I, has his hero brothers approach Ikwe-nye-va, where they finally transform, by traveling up Bill Williams Fork to where the Big Sandy River and the Santa Maria flow together to form it; but beyond that he could not give distance, direction, or American identification, and it was clear that he did not really know where it actually was. Robert Martin, who interpreted for him, also did not appear to know, and after a random stab or two he settled on San Francisco Mt., which would be north of east instead of southeast, but at least is a mountain of the requisite greatness. I have recorded a Mohave name for this impressive massif: unfortunately it is not Ikwe-nye-va but Avi-kwa-hunapatše (14:2, n.8).

The Epic, 8, mentions "Ikwi-nyeva" as UC-AR 11:2, E 4, p. 144, no. 1, p. 146, no. I-8, p. 148, and puts it near Kutpáma which is occupied several times in the story: nos. I-7, E-4, M-0, UC-AR 11:2, p. 148, and shown on UC-AR 11:2, Map 2. "Near" is however an elastic designation; and as Kutpama is merely placed close to the confluence of the Big Sandy and the Santa Maria to form Bill Williams Fork, which is open country, the "cloud-wreathed" peak is presumably either some distance off or it is humbler than its name. The narrator of the Epic may have known pretty accurately where Kutpama was but he remained less definite about Ikwe-nye-va.

It was evidently the mountain that the Walapai (Kniffen et al., 1935, pp. 186-189) call Kwi-nya-wá and tell of its caves being used by their shamans to acquire power. They once identified it with "Artillery Peak near Signal." Along with Kwinyawá as a source of shaman's power, and apparently in the same region, the Walapai mentioned Winyakáiva. The prospective Walapai shaman spent four nights in a cave at Kwinyawá, "communicating with the spirit of the mountain." In grave cases, this Kwinyawá mountain spirit would summon Avikwame to help him. In such cases, the shaman swallowed earth (sand?) until unconscious, when Avikwame (in Walapai, Wikamé) spoke out of his mouth. (Among the Mohave this sand-eating serves the more specialized function of clairvoyance, as discussed in my "Ethnographic Interpretations 1-6," 1957, pp. 226-228).

Mr. Henry F. Dobyns of Tucson clarifies this situation and gives further Walapai information in a letter of November 27, 1956. He says that Kwinyawa', which means "clouds' home" (the etymology would be, as in Mohave, kwi-nya-wa', clouds-their-house) was so called because of a constant drip in the cave. (The Mohave narrator of Tortoise apparently knew nothing of this drip or of a cave, but told repeatedly of the water on the mountain and the clouds hanging about it: 19:53, 54, 56. And he did say that the people living around it would dream of it, and the mountain would plan and work for them: 57.) Dobyns is positive that the region was Walapai; Yavapai territory was south of Williams Fork—contrary to Kniffen, 1935.

The specific geography is complicated by there being two similar Walapai names, Kwinyawa' and Wi Nyakwa'(a) —Ikwe-nye-va and Avinyakwe in Mohave—and that in English the name Artillery was applied both to a range and a peak, the latter being a part of the range, but perhaps more often referred to. The range usually appears on maps as Artillery Mountains, and runs for about 15 m. NNW to SSE parallel with the lowest course of the Big Sandy river or wash, being some miles W of the stream, and beginning somewhat below abreast the mouth of Burro creek and, somewhat farther upstream, of the little settlement of Signal. The southern end of these Artillery Mts. is formed by Artillery Peak, which overlooks both the last of the course of Big Sandy from the W, and the beginning of Williams Fork from the N. It is Artillery Peak that was called Wi Nyakwa' and Avi-nyakwe (UC-AR 11:1, p. 93, J116, shown on Map 2 a little too far up the Sandy). Dobyns gives "waterbird mountain" as the meaning of Wi Nyakwa, that is, probably, a waterbird whose English name the native informant did not know. In Mohave, nyakwe or nyaqwe is the crane; and the name of Artillery Peak in both languages thus means "crane mountain."

The cave of Ikwényevá-Kwinyawá is about 8 miles, according to Dobyns, above the junction which forms Williams Fork; it is E of N of Artillery Peak, about 2 miles upstream of where a spur of the peak juts out to the bed of the "river"; and the cave is "in the bank of the Big Sandy," i.e., it is not a mountain cave.

Aqwaq-haθêve, F6 on UC-AR 11:2, Map 2, and p. 84 (59), is Signal Spring rather than Signal settlement, according to Dobyns. I do not know where the spring is, but a wash comes into the Sandy from the NW at Signal.

Up the Sandy a little farther, across river from the Walapai settlement Hapuk, now Wickiup, a wash comes in from the NE which on Dobyns' map is called Ha'pook. About 10 m. up this is a warm spring, Walapai Hakpin or Aha-kapin, which is the same word as Mohave Aha-kupinye, "warm spring," the name of a place designated by 25, E side, on the Map (no. 1 of the Epic, UC-AR 11:2) of Mohave Valley.

The second Ikwe-nye-va, the one in Maricopa or Gila drainage, appears in 9:9 as the far-southeast and fourth place of emergence of Frog when she traveled underground after having bewitched Matavilya. As note 26 states, this final emergence is usually put loosely around Phoenix.

Again, Doctor-Sack, who sang some Tortoise songs for me in 1908, has his story (Tortoise II) end in the house Tortoise has made for himself on Ikwe-nye-va, "a mountain near Phoenix in Maricopa country." The associated Maricopa tribes are however less accommodating than the Walapai in identifying this peak. Spier has much to say about mountains in Maricopa-Kavelchadom lore, and lists four in their territory, four more near its borders, and several more in enemy lands; but there is no "cloud-home" among them.

Finally, a version alluded to in Handbook, p. 753, which makes Tortoise a woman, has her end up, after a journey West into Chemehuevi territory, and build her final house on "Hakwi-nya-va" in Pima land.

C. Tale Itineraries

There follow itineraries for the tales in this volume, covering also those in UC-AR 11:1.

These itineraries extract the geographical references in the order of their occurrence in the tales, and present them concentratedly, convenient for geographical analysis and comparison. The new geographic data obtained in 1953, and the results of new comparisons made since 1951, as just presented, were used in formulating these itineraries. Errors and ignorances are here corrected that appeared in the texts and footnotes of the Seven Mohave Myths (Nos. 1-7) of 1948 (UC-AR 11:1). Except for tales 18 and 19, the remaining narratives (Nos. 9-17) had been recorded long before 1948, but they had not been worked over fully for all the cross-references to Nos. 1-7 that they might contain. These cross-references have now been included in the new itineraries, and often result in increased accuracy and clarification.

The numbers with which entries in the lists begin of course refer to the number of the tale and the numbered stations or paragraphs of the text of the tales. Numbers 1-7 refer to the tales in UC-AR 11:1, number 8 to UC-AR 11:2, and numbers 9-19 to the tales in the present volume.

ITINERARIES OF NOS. 1, 17,
CANE VERSIONS I AND II

The beginning and much of the end of both versions
of Cane are geographically vague, except that the very
inception is somewhat indefinitely indicated as in the
vicinity of Avikwame and its southern prolongation
Avi-mota. The middle portion of both tales, 1:37-64
and 17:25-34, follows a normal itinerary pattern, downriver from the N end of Mohave Valley to the ocean.
After that, placeless magic reigns, until with 1:97 and
17:74 we are back at the northernmost village sites in
Mohave Valley and the nearby mountains Avi-mota and
Avikwame.

Map 1 and Map 2 refer to the maps at the beginning
and end of the "Historical Epic" (UC-AR 11:2); then
follow sites, some both lettered and some numbered;
"E" and "W" denote the two sides of the Colorado;
pages are cited occasionally to aid reference to the
lists explaining the maps.

1:37-39, 17:25b, 26, Avi-kutaparve, Map 1:B, W.
    Iôô-kuva'ire, Map 1:A, E.
    Ahtšye-'iksamta, Map 1:7, E.
    Qara'êrve, Map 1:B, E.
1:40, 17:27, Selye'aya-kumîtše, Map 1:C, E.
1:41, 17:28, Hanyo-kumasθeve, Map 1:14, E.
1:42, 17:29, 30, Amai-nye-qotase, Map 1:17, E.
    Kamahnūlye, Map 1:G, E.
    Avi-veskwi, 1, Boundary Cone, E, 3249 ft.
1:43, 17:31, Aha-kuminye, Map 1:25, E.
1:44, 17:32, Hotūrveve, Map 1:N, E.
1:45, 17:33, Sampuly-kuvare, Map 1:X, E.
1:46, 17:34, Atsqaqa, Map 1:Y, E.
1:46, E up Sacramento Wash, Map 1, E.
1:47, Hanyiko-itš-kwamve.
1:47, Avi-ahvalye (17:37 seen).
1:49, 17:35, Akoke-humi Mt., 2:E2 (p. 145).
    Aha-'a'îsa, Screwbean Spring.
1:50, 17:38, Ahwaṭa-kwimãtše.
1:51, 17:39, Amaṭa-kuhultoṭve, Kohwiltotve.
1:52, 17:40, Hakutšyepa, Map 2:24, E.
1:52, 17:41, E up fork to Aha-ly-motãṭe.
1:53, 17:42, S to Avi-su'ukwilye, Map 2:28, E.
1:54, 17:43, 44, far S to Avi-melyehwêke, prob.
    Kofa Mt.
1:55, "N" to Avi-hupo.
17:45, to Avi-kuhavak.
1:56, 17:46, N to river at Selye'aya-'ita, Map
    2:56, E.
1:57, 17:47, crosses W to Kuvakwîlye, Map 2:K, W.

1:58, 17:48, S to spring Aha-kumiθe, Map 2:M, W.
1:59, 17:49, S to Amaṭa-hiya, Map 2:N, W.
1:60, 17:50, Tôske, Map 2:0, W.
1:61, 17:51, Yelak-ime, Map 2:P, W.
1:62, 17:52, Yuma settlements, Kutsyan-ava.
1:63, 17:53, abreast Anpeθo'auve, Cocopa Mts.
1:64, 17:54, to Gulf of California.
1:68, 17:57, NE (17:E) to A'î-kameðî trees.

From here, there is no localization until:

1:97, 17:74, N to Selye'aya'-kumîtše, Map 1:C, E.
1:98, to Qara'êrva, Map 1:B, E; 17:75, to Avi-
    kutaparve, Map 1, B, W.
1:102, over Avi-mota, Mt. Manchester, 17:77, to
    Avimota and Avikwame.
1:102, S to Iôôkuvaire, Map 1:A, E; 17:77, to Avi-
    kutaparve, Map 1:B, W.
1:104, S to Mukiampeve, Map 2:2, E; 17:77, to
    Hokiampeve, Map 2:2, E. to Kwayū-namau,
    2:4, E.
1:104, 17:77, Mêkoaṭa, Map 2:17, E.

ITINERARY OF 2,
VINIMULYE-PATŠE

Abbreviations are as in the last, except that ES
and WS mean E and W of the river <u>South</u> of Bill
Williams Fork.

1. Aha-kwa'a'í. Map 1:28 E.
    Amaṭ-kúsayi, or -kusayá, Map 1:G, W.
2. Iθave-kyukyave, apparently 1 day. (See 19:26.)
3. Avi-kwe-havasú, Providence Mts., apparently
    1 day.
4. Hátalompa, either in Mohave Valley Map 1:31,
    W, or more likely below Parker, WS, mouth
    of Vidal Wash.
    Ah'a-kwatpa've, farthest S, Map 2:50, E, and
    ES; probably SE of Blythe.
5. Hóore, Ehrenberg, apparently 1 day from last;
    Map 2:44, E, due <u>East</u> of Blythe (cf. UC-AR
    11:2, p. 143; in error).
6. Kapotáke-hiv'auve, 1 day from Hóore, Map 2:42,
    E; ES.
    Amaṭ-kwahoatše, another day, Map 2:40, E.
7. Avi-hely'á, Moon Mt., 1 day, Map 2:39, E; ES.
8. Avi-kwa-hupáma, 1 day, Map 2:37, E; ES.
9. Aqwáqa-háve, 1 day, Map 2:35, E; ES.
10. Tataskyánve, probably 1 day, Map 2:31, E; ES.
11: Hákutšyépa, 1 day, Map 2:24, E; ES.
11a. Selye'âya-'itá, 1 day, Map 2:12, E.

12. Hatúţve, 1 day, Map 2:5, E.

14. Amaţ-kyerekyere-kwitni, 1 day, Map 2:1a, E.

15. Kwapárvete, Map 1:Z, E.—Not so stated, but cross river to W.

16. Avi-halykwa'ampa, Map 1:H, W. Recross to E. Side.

17. Amaţ-tasilyke, Map 1:J, E; Aθ'í-kupóme ("burned salt"), Map 1:Ix, E.

   Aha-kukwinve, Map 1:27, E, c. 4 mi. from last, downstream at edge of valley.

19. Hawi. Unidentified, probably in Walapai land.

   Avi-hoálye ("yellowpine Mts."), Hualpai Mt. range.

21. Sokwíly-'ihú, Map 1:D, E.

   Selye'áye-'itš-pátše, nearby, also at Fort Mohave.

   Havatéitše-'isnáve.

22. Selye'áye-kumitše, Map 1:C, E.

24. Nyamasáve-kwoháve (-kwaháve), Map 1:3, E.

25. Avi-kutaparve, on bank opposite, Map 1:B, W.

26. Aha-ku-hulyu'i, to E or NE, spring.

27. Avi-'itšyérqe, can see Providence Mts.

28. Providence Mts.

ITINERARY OF 3,
NYOHAIVA

As always, initial numbers are those of paragraphs or stations in the tale.

1. Born at Miakwa'órve, Map 1:A, W, near end of westerly bend of Colorado. 5-6 m. above Fort. Mohave.

2. Ióó-kuva'ire, Map 1:A, E, opposite last, in bend of river from S of W to E of S; the uppermost large village in Mohave Valley.

4. Ahtsȳé-aksámta, 2 or 3 m. SE of last, off the river; Map 1:7, E.

   Selye'áya-kumitše, Map 1:C, E, a sandy place E (not N) of Fort Mohave, on the barren peneplain.

5. Kamahnulye, Map 1:G, E, 4 m. S of Fort Mohave, at foot of the mesa.

6. Sávet-tóhe or -tóha, Map 1:O, E. 12 m. S of last, also at foot of E mesa. It is due E of Needles City: about 5 m. from it on account of the E turn of the river and the width of the valley here.

7. A'í-kumnau-tšumí, not otherwise located, must be in or beyond the Black Range.

   Aha-kuvilye, "warm" spring.

8. Return to Savet-tohe, or perhaps to valley somewhat upstream of it.

9. Hotúrveve, Map 1:N, E. It is there shown somewhat upstream of Savet-tohe; at any rate it seems nearer the river.

10. She leaps far downstream to Ivθí-kwe-'akyulye, in the canyon below Mohave Valley and above Bill Williams Fork mouth, viz. Map 2:11, E, mentioned also in 8:159 and 11:44.

11. Amáţ-ehé'-kwaóóske, "white-earth kwaóoske," Map 2:25c, E, placed here, somewhat doubtfully, a bit below No. 24, the mouth of Williams Fork. There is a "have-white-earth" mentioned below in 22, much farther downriver.

12. Ho'au-nye-va-tše, "horse-flies' houses," Map 2:27, E. Tortoise, 19:38, speaks of it as a hill by the river a little way above Williams Fork mouth; but PS in 1953 specifically put it below the mouth.

13. On down to Ahmó-kutšeθílye, cf. 8:94, and Map 2:34, E, but it is there shown much too far downstream; PS in 1953 put it 1/4 m. above Moválya, Headgate Rock of the Reservation dam. This fits with 18:37, 38, where the two girls coming from the Gila country far SE go down Black Mt. Wash, Avi-soqwilye (Map 2:28, E)-hatai, and reach the river at Ahmó-kutseθilye.

14. Turning into an arrow, she flies S and lands at Amáţa-kwítše, Map 2:34c, E, which however does not appear in the 1953-1954 place name lists.

15a. To Aqwáqa-háve, Map 2:35, E, mentioned again in 3:32 and in 2:9, 8:94. In 1953 it was described as on Bouse Wash, 9 m. from Parker, near the eastern edge of the reservation.

15f. Nyohaiva carries her father's foot bone to Aví-itšorinyéne, Map 2:36a, E, and wins the contest. PS in 1953 translated it "tree-lizard rock" and put it at the E edge of the valley. The position on the map is probably about right, except for being too close to the stream.

16. On down to Moon Mt., Aví-haly'á, Map 2:39, E, and 2:7, 15:17.

17. On down to Avé-nye-vá, "rattlesnakes' house," Map 2:41, E; also mentioned in 8:90, near La Paz, in 1953 called Alapása.

18. On down to Qapotáq-iv'áu've, Map 2:42, E, also in 2:6, 8:90. In 1953 it was placed at the S end of the reservation, 2-3 m. below La Paz, 3 m. above Ehrenberg.

19. On to Aví-tuva'áuve, Map 2:43, E, also in 8:90.

20. On down to hill Ak'ulye-tšakapáve, "jackrabbit emerges," Map 2:48, E, and 8:89, also mentioned in 1953, as upstream from next.

21. On to Aví-tšítse, Map 2:49, E, also 8:89; given in 1953 as Aví-tšiétše, more or less across the river from Ahpe-hwélyve hill in the Palo Verde region, downstream of Blythe.

22. On to Ama'ṭ-ehé-"iδaúve, "take white paint," Map 2:51, E. Not otherwise mentioned, and possibly descriptive of the incident rather than a generally known placename.

23. On down to Avá-tšóhai, Map 2:52, E, and 8:89. Given in 1953 as Avá-tšúhaye, "15-20 m. SE of Cibola." If this is correct, the location would be considerably below 52 on Map 2, and definitely in Yuma territory.

This is Nyohaiva's farthest S, and from here her course is reversed to upstream.

25. Crosses river to California side and reaches Ahpe-hwely(e)ve, "where quarry metates," Map 2:1, W, described in 1953 as a sharp or double peak W of Palo Verde, at S end of Blythe Valley. This would place it farther off the river than I on Map 2, to the W or SW of Palo Verde town.

26. N up the W side to (Amáṭ-)táto'itše, Map 2:H, W. There seems to be no other mention of the spot, so the location of H on map is arbitrary, and, I would guess, considerably too far downstream.

27. Aqwa'qa-munyó, Map 2:G, W, but much misplaced on Map 2, because 1953 information puts the spot somewhere in Vidal Wash drainage N of Riverside Mts. and S of the "fish-tail" ridge which is an inland (W) outlier of the Whipple Mts. It must be more or less in the latitude of Parker, but off the river.

28. Mathá-tše-kwílyve, Map 2:F, W, not otherwise identified, but probably N of where it appears on Map 2. Not mentioned in 1953.

29. Onward (direction not mentioned) to Koθilye, at river, Map 2:E, W. In 1953, it was described as a wash entering the Colorado below the Riverside Mts. and again as a point c. 15 m. below them. This would put it not far from where E appears on Map 2.

Here they cross to the E side, which, by Map 2, would be somewhere in the vicinity of Avi-'itšorin-yene (Map 2:36a, E) where Nyohaiva had won the game in 15f. From here the route is upstream to Aqwáqe-háve on Bouse Wash, where the enemy are asleep.

32. At Aqwáqa-háve, Bouse Wash (see 3:15a), Otšouta is decapitated.

33. The victors go N to Ahá-δekupíδa, "owl water," Map 2:33, E, but position on Map 2 is merely by estimate. SW of 1953 makes it Ah'a-δokupit, "owl cottonwood" (not water), and puts it upriver from Bouse Wash but below Amaṭ-ya'ama.

And on to Sama'ókusa, where they dance. Map 2:30, E, but place on Map 2 is guessed; 1953 SE has it between Hanyora and Uh'ar-kuvasave.

35. Nyohaiva goes E "2 steps" and calls the place Amáṭ-ya'áma, Map 2:29, E; also mentioned in 8:94; said to be 1/4 m. from Avi-soqwilye of paragraph 36 below.

She throws Otšouta's head far S to Aví-melyekyéte, Map 2:L, W, a sharp rock or peak at Picacho on the river in Yuma territory, where the cut-off inland trail to Yuma begins.

36. She turns into a black rock as large as a house on which soqwílye hawks nest, on or at Aví-soqwílye, Black Mt., the conspicuous isolated peak ESE of Parker, Map 2:28, E. It is correctly shown by the contour line in Map 2.

GEOGRAPHY OF 4,
RAVEN

This narrative is without travel. The Raven-Crow brothers emerge from the ground, after Matavilya's house at Ha'avulypo has been burned down, from what was its NW corner (paragraph 1). In 26 they move to near the door, in 28 stand up outside the door, in 30-31 transform and fly off.

The only references to places are:

15. Successful war party returning from S will sleep at Hakutšyepa, mouth of B. Williams Fork.

17. From Amat-aθove in Chemehuevi Valley, near mouth of Chemehuevi Wash, on W side, they will send a messenger N announcing victory.

25. There will be a gathering, feast, and dance at Miakwa'orve playfield, Map 1:A, W.

ITINERARIES OF 5,
DEER

A. Route of the creators and killers,
Numeta and Hatekulye, carnivore gods

1. Power from Mastamho at Ha'avulypo. Sink into ground, travel north beneath it, emerge, above "Lizard Mt.," at Hatekulye-naka.

2. Sink in again, travel W (actually WSW) to "W of San Bernardino" city, perhaps Cajon Pass or the Sierra Madre, at any rate in Serrano territory. Four places are named here: Avi-kwi-nyehore, Avi-ku-tinyam (night or dark mountain), kwilykikipa, and Kwamalyukikwa. There they make two deer from clay.

3, 4. They institute bows, arrows, arrow poisons and "finish" the deer by means of wind and rain.

(5-22 deal wholly with Deer.)

23. Deer see the tracks of their creators in Amaṭ-ke-hoalye, the "yellow pine country," the Walapai Mts.

24. At Hoalye, east of the Walapai Mts. (more probably, on their E slope) the carnivore gods shoot the male deer.

25. At Blood-kutšinakwe-place and Blood-have-place, where the rocks are red, they kill the male Deer.

26. There they quarrel over division of the body and Jaguar (Numeta) goes off "North" to the Walapai Mts., and Hatekulye (Mountain Lion) to Ahta-kwat-menve, E of Kingman, "below" (downstream from) Hackberry. Both places are in Walapai territory, but the names are not known from the Walapai.

B. Route of the Two Deer

2. Created "at" the four places named in 2 in preceding list.

6. Go "E" to Hoalye-ke-sokyave, "yellow pine projecting horizontally," a railroad station in the "San Bernardino Mts.," probably Summit at the head of Cajon Pass. This pass "separates" Sierra Madre from the San Bernardino Range, and is known also from Mohave historic accounts as being on their travel route up Mohave River and down into the fertile southern California plain.

7. "E" (N and then NE) to Avi-kitšekilyke, N or W of Calico, near Barstow.

8. E to Ava-sa'ore, a mt. E or NE of Calico.

9. E to Aha-kwi-'ihore, "sandbar willow water," N of Blake.

10. To N, see Avi-waθa, New York Mts.

11. E to Hukθara-tš-huerve; E on to Apurui-ku-tokopa ("water jar holed"—a spring near the pass at Klinefelter, mentioned also in 19:26); farther E to Avi-kwi-nyamaθave, ("yellow? mts."—in a valley, N. of Ibis (Ibex), visible from it).

12. On E, See Avikwame; turn N to Avi-tšierqe ("Excrement Mt."—in a valley, perhaps Piute Valley), on to Kwanakwetšeθkyeve in Piute Valley SW of Avi-kwame peak (Mt. Newberry). Then on to Aha-mavara, to Amaṭ-qatšeqatše, and to Kwatulye-ha ("water-lizard?"), which appear to be parts of the Avikwame massif. Then on to Amaṭ-mehave-'auve and Hatom-kwiθike, described as a white area conspicuous on the S and E side of Avikwame. Here they say they are on Avikwame.

14. They turn S, passing by δokupita-toδompove, "owls regarding each other," and Ihore-kutšupetpa (whose ihore, sandbar willow, suggests they have come down to the river), to reach Avi-kutparve, just beyond where the river turns from W to flowing S—Map 1; B, W. Here they swim across to the Iδδ-kuva'ire cluster of village sites—Map 1; A, 1, 2, E.

15. Downriver on the W side, Map 1:3, 6, E, to Qara'êrve (Map 1:B, E).

16. On downriver to Selye'aya-kumitše, about a mile E of the site of Fort Mohave, where they see antelope, who have come from Mu'ulye-mat'are, "antelope playground," and who go off "westward" (sic for eastward) to Porepore-kutšeim—see p. 148, Map 2, J6, L3, below Yucca station, where the Black Mts. range ends at Sacramento Wash.

17. On downriver, S, to Kamahnulye, Map 1:G, E.

18. To Aqaq-nyi-va, raven's roost, Map 1:26, E. This is off the river, on a former channel, toward Spear Lake.

19. Still going generally downstream, but perhaps increasingly E from the river, they reach Nyiketate, Selye'aya-itšierqe (there are said to be two of this name), and the antelope playground mentioned in 16; and they see Avi-veskwi, Boundary Cone (which is NW of 26 on Map 1). All these places seem to be on the "mesa" sloping up E from Mohave Valley.

21. On to the foot of the mesa on which are Ikumnau-tšumi, Aha-kwi-nyamasave, and Hatoδike. Note 38, UC-AR 11:2, p. 44 gives descriptive localizations of these three places, but insufficient for their mapping. The second name recurs in 7:9, but for a different place.

22. Sleep and dream here; 4 great mts. mentioned: New York, Newberry, Walapai, and Kofa(?), omened by Deer's creators. They have passed the 2 first, the male will be killed in the third, the female will find refuge in the last.

23. They seem to veer more easterly from S and pass Maθkweha and Tšamokwilye-kw-iδauve, to reach Aha-kuvilye, "warm spring." This last might be an unnamed warm spring shown in Map 1 above the 2000-foot contour in the southern Black Mts. more or less due E of Map 1:26, E. The two other spots are unplaced, but Tšamokwilye-kw-iδauve may be a misbearing for Tšimokwily-avi (or Tšam-), Yucca on the railroad, at south foot of Black Mts.—see pp. 145, 148, Map 2; F9, J4.—The Deer are now definitely in Walapai territory, having edged out of Mohave Valley up the mesa and across the S end of Black Mts. range. They now turn definitely E up into Walapai (Hualpai) Mts. ahead, passing by unplaced Ahta-katarapa and Hanemo-nye-ha, both of which (cane, duck) suggest water holes. They reach the (crest of) the Walapai range.

From here, their remaining itinerary has been already given under A.

GEOGRAPHY OF 6, COYOTE

The geography of No. 6 is scattering, as expectable in tale elements told unsystematically or not too well known. Apart from a few mentions of identified places, such as θawêve, Avi-hamoka (in Coyote 6A), and Hukθara-ny-enyêve, Mukiampeve (in Coyote 6B), the longest Coyote story, 6A, revolves about Avi-kwa-'ahāθa, "a mountain beyond Phoenix." This is mentioned by Spier (1933:253) as Vi-kw-axás (Mohave θ is s in Maricopa), "greasy mountain," the Salt River Range, due S across the Salt River from Phoenix, between the Salt and the Gila, about 15 m. above their confluence.

An old man living here in 6A is Patak-sata, who appears in Spier (p. 392) as Patŭkcut in the long Halchidhoma-Maricopa Flute Lure tale, corresponding to Mohave No. 18, Satukhota. The hero who finally kills Patak-sata and the people of Avi-kwa-'ahāθa is Patša-karrawa, whom the 1903 narrator also called Coyote's younger brother in 6A, but in 1953 the Mohave told me the name meant "human being."

ITINERARY OF 7, MASTAMHO

In this narrative we have long stretches stationary at Avikwame (19-33, 42-80) interspersed with itineraries.

1. Matavilya dies at Ha'avulypo.
2. Coyote sent to Fire-mountain, Avi-'a'auva in W.
4. Coyote steals M's heart, runs SW to Amaṭa-hotave, not otherwise identified.
5. Coyote notifies mourner at Aksam-kusaveve, in N end of Mohave Valley, Map 1:6, W.
6. Mastamho at Kwaparvete.
9. He goes W to make spring Aha-kwi-nyamasave, "white water," for the Chemehuevi. (Cf. same name in 5:21, but on opposite side of river.)
10. N to Ha-tasaṭa where he makes the Colorado river with his staff (ataṭa, saṭa). The place is mythical. He also names Hivθi-kevutatše to the W of Ha-tasaṭa.
11-12. Mastamho leads the river to Ha'avulypo, Avikwame, Aqwaq-iove (Map 1: E, E) Mepuk-tsivauve (Map 1: L, W), and Ahwe-nye-va, "near Parker,"

but unidentified; the last name would mean "alien's house," perhaps an error for Map 2: 41, E; Ave-nye-va-(tše), "rattlesnake's house(s)," near La Paz, where the valley is indeed wide as called for by the text. But in that case "Parker" would have to be construed as "35 m. below Parker, at the S end of the (Parker) reservation."

14. M makes mts. W of river and Mohave Valley: Satulyku, "near Needles peaks"; Ohmo, "W of Needles City"; Mevukha, "S of Ibex (Ibis)"; Hatšaru-yove, "N of Java"; Avi-mota, "the same mountain range farther north"; Avi-kwi-nyamaθave, "The northernmost end of range."

15. W from Avikwame to Hukθara-tš-huerve and N to Avi-nyilyk-kwas-ekunyive, to plant seeds for the Chemehuevi.

16. On similar errand for the Walapai, he stops first at Avi-veskwi, Boundary Cone, overlooking Mohave Valley from the peneplain sloping up to the Black Mts. range, then does his work at Kitšehayare, "a small hill in a large valley, west of Kingman." This valley would be the upper wide part of Sacramento Wash.

17. For the Yavapai, he plans to work at Amaṭ-ko-'omeome and Amaṭ-ka-tšivekove, unidentified.

18. Actually he plants instead at Avi-ke-hasalye and at Ah'a-'iki-yareyare. The former is identified on p. 147 as the third night's camp of 8 made by a Mohave war party returning through Yavapai territory from an attack on the Maricopa. It is shown on Map 2 as E8 and I11, 20 m. WNW of Wickensburg and 15 SW of Congress Junction, and is placed also on pp. 145, 147, 148. For Ah'a-'iki-yareyare, where there are cottonwoods, see p. 147; it is NW of the other, perhaps on Date Cr.

19-33. At Avikwame.

34-35. Makes mat'are playfield at Miakwa'orve (Map 1: A, W) and a hill near by at Avi-kutaparve (Map 1: B, W).

36-37. Wild seeds planted at Av'a-θemulye, Amaṭ-kusaye, and Hatšioq-vaṭveve, viz., Map 1: 20, W; G, W; F, W.

39-41. Same at Avi-haly-kwa'ampa, Amaṭ-kaputšora, Amaṭ-kaputsor-ilyase, and Amaṭ-θono-hiδauve, viz., Map 1: H, W; 22, W; 22 bis, W; 23, W.

42-80. At Avikwame.

81-82. Mastamho walks backward S from Avikwame to Avi-kutaparve, Map 1: B, W. Begins to transform.

83. At Hôkusave, Map 1: E, W, he becomes Bald Eagle.

84. Flies S to sea.

85-92. Curve-billed Thrasher and Mockingbird instruct people about sex at Miakwa'orve, Map 1: A, W.

88. Quail comes to them from Hoatše-wameve and Amaṭ-ku-mat'are. The former is E of Avi-kwame, on or near the river, N21, E, in the list (above) for North of the settlements in Mohave Valley. It may have been below the present Davis Dam. See also 8:191. The second place of the couplet must have had a level playfield.

89. A bird comes from Avi-kunu'ulye, "tumescence mountain" which is N15, E in the same "North" list. Said to be 6 m. N. of Hoatše-wameve.—This visitor's actions conform to the name of his home.

91. Bittern (Blue Heron) arrives at Miakwa'orve from the S, passing Aksam-kusaveve, Map 1: 6, W, and then Hanemo-'ara, a "lake" or slough, Map 1: 5, W, where he decorates himself with a fish head-dress.

92. Dove has gone from Ha'avalypo to Otahve-k-hunuve, S of Ibis (Ibex), in Sacramento (Ohmo) Mt.; cf. 13:45. From there she goes to Oyatš-ukyulyuve and Ho-kusave on the river, Map 1: 16, W, and E, W, and then to Miakwa'orve.

93-97. Thrasher and Mockingbird lead their following to this same (83, 92) Ho-kusave on the river, Map 1: E, W, where they finish and transform the river and valley birds.

98-100. Those who will become mountain and desert birds they lead back first to Avi-kutaparve and Miakwa'orve, and then W across the Mohave desert to another play-field, Rattlesnake's, Haye-kwire-nye-mat'are, a playa or dry lake bed about 15 m. E of Mohave town and station. It has been called Mojave, Rogers, and now Muroc Lake.

101. They all fly off, as birds, to Avi-hamoka, Tehachapi Double Peak.

102. Only Hakutatkole, sick, is left at Rattle-snake-playfield, and goes S to Halyu-ilyve, then to Konyo-kuvilyo and Ha'tana, and then to the Gulf of California, because his illness comes from sea fog. There seem to be no other references to these 3 places, except the second, which, as Kwenyo-kuvilyo (Map 2: 71, E) is mentioned as E of the river, very far down, in Cocopa country, in the Epic, 8:83 (Kuenyo-kuvilyo), and in Yellak, 14:62.

ITINERARY OF 9,
ORIGINS

My version of the Mohave Origin myth is meager geographically, probably because it was the first narrative of any length that I recorded. I had not yet become aware of the minute localization to which the Mohave were addicted, so I did not press for it; whereas the informant would expect to make his myth more intelligible by not overloading it with geographic references that would be unfamiliar to me. I am confident that a full version would have been topographically particularized to the same extent as the Mastamho narrative, No. 7, which in content overlaps with the "creation."

However, I subjoin what there is, by the usual numbered paragraphs.

1. At Pi'in, far to the W across the ocean, Matavilya and the rest were born of Sky and Earth, who are still copulating there.

2. Matavilya and they move E to the middle of the earth, measuring with his arms. There he builds a house, at Ha'avulypo, "house-post water," in Eldorado Canyon, a normally waterless canyon affluent of the Colorado from the W, between Davis and Hoover dams.

5. Korokoro-pa or hiqo, who became White Man, goes off underground back to Pi'in.

9. Frog, having bewitched her father Matavilya, flees underground from Ha'avulypo, emerging four times: first, to the S, at Na'aikunyiloqa, which I cannot identify at all (even the recorded statement that it is a mountain west of the river, northerly from Needles, probably still south of the Nevada line, leaves me now at a loss and unconvinced); second, S or SE to Hanyiko-itš-qwampa, "frog's emergence," E of Needles and visible from it across the river as a depression below the top of the Black Mountains range (9:9, note 25); third, to another place of the same name, somewhere far to the S or SE; fourth, in the Gila region, to (H)Ikwe-nye-va, "clouds-their-home," discussed above in a separate section (Pt. II, B, 4). Chuhueche's son in 13:82 refers to the same four emergences, but calls the two first Hanyiko-'itš-kwampeve, does not name the third, and calls the final station "Frog mountain," Avi-hanye.

17-18. Mastamho goes N to make the Colorado River.

20. He carries the people N through the resulting flood to Akoke-humi, the SW end of the "Mojave Range," 5102 feet high, W of the river, opposite Chemehuevi Valley and the mouth of Chemehuevi Wash, S of "E2" on Map 2.

25-31. N to Avikwame, where he builds his house.

37. Sky-Rattlesnake summoned from S sea, Gulf of California.

39. He gives ritual name "My land Irīve" to a mt. W of Needles which is presumably Ohmo, Sacramento Mt(s).

50. Mastamho transforms into Bald Eagle; spot not stated.

SETTING OF 10,
THE FIRST ALYHA

Almost the whole of this ritual myth is localized
in Mastamho's house at Avikwame, or immediately
outside it—paralleling the restriction of No. 4 (Raven)
to the charred ruins of Matavilya's house at Ha'avulypo.

Only in paragraph 24 does Mastamho lead the new
transvestite and accompanying women and girls S to
the playfield at Miakwa'orve (Map 1: A, W).

ITINERARY OF 11,
TUMANPA

Tumanpa Short can be described as basically an
itinerary with incidents attached. Starting at Ha'avulypo
(in 1), it skirts Avikwame (2) to pass through later
Chemehuevi territory as far as the Providence Mts.
(4) and sand dunes beyond (7), to take an (impossible)
look at tribes farther to the W, returns to the Colorado River (8) and then follows the river step by step
from 9 to 54, leaving it only in 55 for a final leap or
flight E into the desert to petrify. The long sequence
from 9 to 54 is one of the best guides for the Mohave
toponymy along the river.

1. Ha'avulypo.

2. On way to Avikwame, to a mat'are; level
place, in northern Piute valley, at base, hipuk, of
Avikwame.

3. Aha-kuvilye, "stinking water," Piute Spring, S
and W of last.

4. Avi-kwa-havasu, Providence Mts. From there,
they "look" W to playing going on at Hayekwire-nye-
mat'are, Rattlesnake's playfield, namely Mojave or
Rogers or Muroc dry lake bed, which is 130 m.
distant.

7. "NE" (sic) from Providence Mts. to sand
dunes, Selye'aya-kwa-hawaye and -hatšāna; probably,
actually NW or W, to the sandy stretch between
Kelso and Baxter.

8-9. In unknown direction to Aha-kwoana (N7 of
"North" list), home of Numeta and Hatekulye, which
is unplaced, but evidently on the river and well
north. See also 12, n. 36.

10. S to Havirepoke (N9 of North list), at Cottonwood Island.

11. S to Ah'a-kwatθarve (N13 of North list).

12. S to Ham'ulye-tšieme, "Ashes come" (from
Matavilya's cremation).

13. S to Amaṭ-ku-vataqanye, a little sharp peak
across the river (W side) from Hardville, Map 1:

2, W. It is near Miakwa'orve, Map 1: A, W, here
called Mat'are-mai-muya.

14. On downstream to Avi-kwa-ahwaṭa, Map 1:
C, W.

17-18. Cross river to Map 1: 3 and 2, E, near
Iδδ-kuva'ire.

21. S to Amaṭa-kukyeta, Map 1: 9, E, near
Qara'erve.

22. At Qara'erve.

23. To Selye'aya-kumítše, E of Fort Mohave,
Map 1: C, E.

24. To Aqwaq-iova, Map 1: E, E, just S of Fort
Mohave.

25. S to Hanyo-kumasθeve, slough at foot of
mesa, Map 1: 14, E.

26. See Kwiyak-aqwāθa, Map 1: 15, E.

27. S to Kamahnuly-ve, Map 1: G, E.

28. S to Aha-ku-kwinve, Map 1: 27, E.

29. S to Nyahweye-ve, Map 1: 40, E.

30. S to Va'orve, Map 1: T, E.

31. S to Sampulye-kuvare, Map 1: X, E, and
Atšqāqa, Map 1: Y, E.

32. To 1910 bridge at Topock, at Kwaparvete,
Map 1: Z, E.

33. S "4 m." to Amaṭ-ehê-stutšive, Map 2: 1, E.

34. S to Hokiampeve, Map 2: 2, E, by the river
at foot of the Needles spires.

35. W a little to Avi-kwa-tšoh'ai, Map 2: 3, E,
one of the spires.

37. Downstream, S, to Selye'āya-mukyeta, Map
2: 4a, E.

38. S to Hatuṭva, Map 2: 5, E (Kwasukulyve
opposite).

39. S to Qampanyq-nyi-va, "Bats' houses," Map
2: 6, E.

40. S to Ammo-ny-unye, "Mountain sheep's road,"
Map 2: 7, E.

41. S to Tšimukwily-kwa-hakyê-ve and Humθavinye-
tšanaly-ve, Map 2: 8, 8a, E.

42. S to Avi-rrove-hiδauve, Map 2: 9, E.

43. S to Hamu-tšompa-kuya, Map 2: 10, E.

44. S to Ivθe-kwa-'akyulye, Map 2: 11, E.

45. S to Selye'āya-'ita, sand hills, Map 2: 12, E.

46. S to Nyaveδi-nye-vatše, "Ghosts their homes,"
Map 2: 13, E.

47. S to Hatše-kupilyke, Map 2: 14, E.

48. S to Avi-pa, "Person rock," Map 2: 15, E.

49. S to Tinyam-kosama, Map 2: 16, E; in Chemehuevi Valley.

50. S to Omaka, Map 2: 18, E.

51. S to Ahmo-kwe-'ataye, "big mortars," and
Akatu-'uvera, Map 2: 19, and 19a, E.

55. "SE" to Tšimu-sem-kutšoive or Sam-kutšoive, "Sister marry," near Aubrey, N of Bill Williams Fork, where they transform. This last stage is a long one—about 30 m.—almost due E, and may have been made by rising into the air.

ITINERARY OF 12, SALT

This is a longer itinerary in miles than Tumanpa, but with far fewer steps and some long jumps. The route is first away from the river E into the Arizona mountains and desert; then N and NW and across the river, N of the start; W or SW to Providence Mts. and Muroc dry lake, with a distant (impossible) view of tribes beyond to the NW; and then, in only 3 stages, ESE to somewhat short of the river in about the latitude of Parker.

1. Ha'avulypo, in Eldorado Canyon,
2. Others to Kwiltatpahve, on the W desert slope of N Mohave Valley.
3. Salt "E" to mt. Avi-kwa'me-ta, which sounds something like "great" or "real Avikwame," its summit; but this is due S from Eldorado Canyon. A mt. actually E of Eldorado would be in the Black Mts. of Arizona, or in the Cerbats, the second range.
4. E to Tu'kuva, a peak in the desert before reaching Hackberry from the W. The route seems not far from that of the Santa Fe R. R.
5. To Hoalye-puke, "yellow-pine butt," perhaps for butt or foot of the yellow-pine mts., which are the Walapai (Hualpai) Mts. The informant put Hoalye-puke at the far end of mts. stretching "E" from Kingman; but E of Kingman is flat desert, and the Walapai Mts. actually stretch S from a point some-what SE of Kingman. The statements and map do not agree. Moreover, in 4 the Salts are already approaching Hackberry from the W, in 6 they are N of it, but in 5 the reference is to Kingman, which they should have behind them in 4. Most Mohave references to Walapai places are hard to pin down, and the names often do not correspond with Walapai ones. Apparently the territory of the Southwestern Yavapai was better known to the Mohave.
6. To mt. Kwa'orve N of Hackberry.
7. "N to a desert valley." Actually, there is only high plateau N of Hackberry. If we read "NW," they would be going down Truxton Wash, ending in dry Red Lake (see note 14 to tale 12). But this would put them back in the valley where they were in 4, though then more southerly.

8-11. "Going on," that is, N or NW, toward Ati'-siara and Yava'awi, which are defined as in Walapai territory a day's walk from Peach Springs. This would put them close to the big southward swing of the Colorado during its westward course. If we disregard the reference to Peach Springs and have them going NW down Truxton Wash, they would be W of the S swing of the river and would hit this somewhere in the vicinity of Hualpai and Detrital Washes.

12, 13. Going N.

14. Going N, looking W, see Tobacco-place, A'u'vivave, "NW of Eldorado Canyon." The general area from which tobacco was traded was the vicinity of Las Vegas or beyond, NW of Eldorado.

15. They see, and in 16, reach, Owi-water-soqire, unplaced. Sleep there.

20. To Aha-kwoana, Hosive, Aqāq-tšuama, treated as one place, apparently on the Colorado, for the first of the 3 is mentioned in 11:8 as on the river. It may be in the northernmost part of the S-flowing stretch, below Hoover Dam.

20. They go W to Uqaliho, mentioned also in the Wilbur sketch of Long Tumanpa (see No. 11) as somewhere to the N of Ha'avulypo. If not on the river, it would be W of it.

21. W to the Providence Mts.

22. W to Muroc, Hayekwire-nye-mat'are, a long stage.

23. Backward, ESE, 160 m., still longer, to Haramaθeve-kutš-iava and -upaiva, SE of Amboy.

24. SE to Selye'aya-ku-vataye, sandhills S of Turtle and Riverside mts., stretching 20 m. ESE to within a few m. of the Colorado.

25. Transform at (Hi)me-kuvauve in this sandy region. It was said to be a day's walk from the Parker reservation, which would put it near the western end of the dunes. But the informant had previously said that [the beginning of ?] the sand-hills was "two deserts W of Parker."

ITINERARY OF 13, CHUHUECHE

The Chuhueche itinerary lingers long at Ha'avulypo (1-15), goes briefly to Avikwame, then proceeds on a many-stop journey W (19-40), then to an unclear, rapid return E to Sacramento Mts. (41-45). From there the route is southward to the river below Parker at Vidal Wash (46-57), crossing it there (58-63), and then S to (probably) Kofa Mt. (64-67). Here the younger brother becomes the superior, marries, transforms himself,

and his wife and son go off E and S to the sea (77-85).
The geography is incidental in the last section.

Origin.

 1-15. At Ha'avulypo.
 16-18. S to Avikwame.

Journey W.

 19. W to between (A) Miakwa'orve and Mat'are-
amai-muya playfields.
 20. W to Tšimuweve-samire; name Tšohotave
Mt. to N; both unidentified.
 21. A little on to W, name a mt. to SW.
 22. W to Avi-halykoyowa and Kunalya-kuvatatše,
unidentified.
 23, 24. W across a desert, which is the N-S
Piute Valley. The white streak Kwesoqĭrve is
abreast to the W of highway 95 where this crosses
from California into Nevada.
 27. W, nearly across Piute Valley, see mirage
to N.
 29. W to Aha-kuvilye, Piute Spring.
 30. NW to Kwikamtšotka, probably in Piute range.
 32. W 2-4 m. to Ohuere-imave.
 33. W to Aqāq-e'ara, perhaps in Lanfair Valley.
 35. W toward, and in 36 reach, New York Mts.,
Avi-waθa.
 37. "W," perhaps actually SW, to Analya-kaθa,
where there was mesquite, in the valley through
which the Union Pacific R.R. runs, perhaps near
Kelso. From here they see:
 (38), to the W, Haramaθeve-kwayumpa; cf. 12:23,
also:
 (39), a Like-Mohave village.
 40. Analye-kaθa is their most western stop (37);
they turn back, but SE, by a more southerly route
than they came.

Return E.

 41. To "Great-Sands," Selye'aya-ku-vataye. If it
is the same as 12:24, it lies some 70 m. SE of the
dunes of Haramaθeve of 38.
 42. To Oh'ara-'unuve, unplaced.
 43. "E again" to Mokwiθta's playfield, also unplaced.
 44. Farther E to Ground-squirrel's playfield,
locality unknown.
 45. On E to Otah-kunuve, "where they play dice,"
(cf. 7:92) in Sacramento Mt(s)., Ohmo, which lies
SW of Needles City; the highest peak, 3750 ft., is
at the N end of the curving range, 10-12 m. from

Needles. The spot may have been named after a
rock formation and have given rise to the narrative
episode of gambling; or vice versa.

S. in California

 46-47. S in the desert valley of Sacramento Mts.
to Screwbean Spring, Aha-kwa-'a'ise, near the S end
of the range, probably draining into Sacramento
Wash, and not to be confounded with a place of
similar name, Avi-'a'ise, E of the river, down
stream, and reached in 65 of the present story.
 51. "S" to Aqwāqa-munyo. There may be 2 places
of this name—see 13, note 75. One is misplaced on
UC-AR 11:2, Map 2 as G, W; it should be N of
Riverside Mts. instead of S of Big Maria Mts.
 53. From there they see Kuhu'inye, UC-AR 11:2,
Map 1, 33, W, and Sotulku, elsewhere Setulyku, a
peak in Chemehuevis Mt. (or NW end of the Mojave
range that crosses the river).
 54. On S to Ivθe-koskilye, 15 m. from river up
Chemehuevi Wash—apparently distinct from Koskilye
of 55. Ivθe is creosote bush, Larrea, popularly often
called greasewood.
 55. On S to Koskilye or Kwoskilye, at W end of
Whipple Mts. where the Needles-Parker trail (and
later wagon road) crossed the ridge. This was an
off-river cutoff S.
 56. S to Kwiya-selye'aya, unidentified.
 57. Aha-talompa, Ahatelomve, Hatalompa ("water
basin," or "drip fast"), on W side of river 1 m.
above Vidal Wash mouth, or 7 m. SW of Parker
Reservation school.

S in Arizona to Kofa Mt.

 58-62. Swim river here.
 63. Carried downstream 3 m., land on E bank at
Avi-ahmo, "mortar rocks"; see 13, note 91, above,
but it may be misplaced too far downstream there.
 64. SE, sidling off river to Aqwāqa-have, "deer
go through," on Bouse Wash; 9 m. from Parker, at
E edge of reservation.
 65. SE to Screwbean Spring, Avi-'a'ĭsa, a small
range running S from Bouse Wash. UC-AR 11:2,
Map 2, 38, W mistakenly has it on the river and
too far S.
 65. Here they see Avi-melyehwêke, Kofa Mt.
(4828 ft.) or possibly Castle Dome (3793 ft.) Peak,
respectively about 45 and 60 miles SSE. It is a
famous mt., associated with war.
 67. Reach Avi-melyehwêke.

Plot develops, geography becomes tenuous and spotty.

68. Far to the S, to Avi-tokwiyo, where the mythical Alakwisa are, who all died out simultaneously (Handbook, pp. 797-798). The mt. is unknown; the narrator considered it not as far S as Yuma, but far E of it. This would be in Western Yavapai territory, and Tokwiyo might well be Castle Dome.

69. Returns N toward Avi-melyehwêke, to Hoθampeve Mt. See 13, note 101.

72. Goes "E" (nearer NE) to Aha-kwa-hela, the Harquahala Mts., UC-AR 11:2, Map 2, H5, Western Yavapai.

73. Goes W across river to Amohta—"a day's travel upstream from Yuma."

Wife and Son.

77. After the younger brother's transformation, his wife goes E to Koaka-'amatša, Gila Bend, the historic home of the Kavelchaδom. See UC-AR 11:2, p. 146.

81. Her son goes E to Avilyha, unidentified.

82. On E to Avi-hanye, "Frog Mountain," where Frog transformed after fleeing for having bewitched Matavilya. It is described as "beyond Phoenix but before Tucson," which would put the mt. in Pima country. The same 4 emergences are referred to in 9:9, with somewhat different name attributions.

83, 84. "S" to ocean, transforms.

85. His mother also goes to Avilyha, and S, to ocean, and transforms.

GEOGRAPHY OF 14,
YELLAK: GOOSE

The first or full version, I, of Yellak is pretty consistently localized, and is followed by II, which is fuller on geography than on incident. The outline of II, above, is followed by a comparative list of content and by a list of geographical correspondences in the two riverine itineraries, as well as some of the more important spots mentioned in only one of the two versions. Also the Epic monograph (UC-AR 11:2) contains on pages 141-142 a list of placenames on the river below Mohave Valley, which includes the then identifiable ones mentioned in the Yellak I narrative—this list corresponding to UC-AR 11:2, Map 2. It would therefore be largely repetitive if a formal itinerary of Yellak were added here.

GEOGRAPHY OF 15,
ORIGIN OF WAR

1. All born at Avikwame (sic for Ha'avulypo).

4. Mastamho goes N to unnamed place, makes river with his cane.

5. He sows wild seeds in the W desert, at 4 places named but not geographically identifiable.

6. Back to Avikwame.

7. He sows wild seeds to the E at 5 Walapai localities also not identifiable.

13. Kwayu, a giant cannibal Mohave, settles at Mukiampeve, near Needles pinnacles—UC-AR 11:2, Map 2, 2, E, and p. 141. Kwayu is mentioned also in 6B (UC-AR 11:1, p. 48).

14. Halkutãṭa (Crayfish?) comes from S ocean, kills Kwayū.

15. Mastamho goes S to ocean, kills hiding Halkutãṭa there: the first warfare.

16. "Preaching" (orating) about war, Mastamho names four places connected with it: (1) Ava-tanêva to SE, Yavapai land; (2), Avi-qara-'δtata, a conspicuous erosion pillar, after which Monument Mts. (E part of Whipple mt. massif) are named; while the Halchidhoma still lived on the river, this marked their N boundary against the Mohave; (3), Matha-lye-vaδδma, which seems to mean "northern people, tribe" (viz. the Mohave as against the "Halchi-dhoma"?); (4), Tãha, a bell-shaped outlier peak of the Turtle Mts., perhaps marking the off-river boundary of the hostile Halchidhoma against the Mohave.

17. Continuing about war, Mastamho names four mts. formerly belonging to the Halchidhoma and approximately framing the present Colorado River (Parker) reservation: (1) Avĭ-h-elye'á, "Moon Mountain," UC-AR 11:2, Map 2, 39, E (cf. 2:7, 3:16 —UC-AR 11:1, pp. 25, 31); (2) Avĭ-vatáye, "Great Mountains," the Riverside Mts., UC-AR 11:2, Map 2, 32, (E), erroneously shown there as on E side (cf. 14:48, note 40); (3) Avĭ-sukwĭlye, "Hawk Mountain," UC-AR 11:2, Map 2, 28, E, dark, small mt. behind Parker (cf. 3:36, 14:45); (4) Avĭ-a'ĭse, "Screwbean(Mesquite) Mountain," UC-AR 11:2, Map 2, 38, E, but farther from river than there shown (mentioned also in 8:155, 158).

18, 19. Without placenames.

GEOGRAPHY OF 16,
FRAGMENTS

16A. Mountain Lion and Jaguar

Kuyak-úilta, on E bank of river, S of Eldorado
Canyon (Ha'avulypo), probably not far from Cottonwood Island.

Avi-θekwinye, mts. NE of last, perhaps in N.
Black mts., belonging to Walapai, not otherwise
specified.

Aví-kunyihore, far W, near San Bernardino, where
deer created. Cf. 5:2.

16B. Coyote and Moon

An unlocalized Coyote anecdote.

16C. Otur-kepaye

Avi-hakwahamve: unplaced; perhaps the form is
corrupt.

Tasilyke, in Mohave Valley, UC-AR 11:2, Map 1,
J, E, c. 6 m. upstream of Needles.

Hwatitotahuare, unplaced, probably a corrupted
form.

Ha-sôðape, UC-AR 11:2, Map 1, H, E, upriver
from Tasilyke.

Aha-pêna, downriver of last, and of next.

Qavkuaha, UC-AR 11:2, Map 1, I, E, 2 m. below
Ha-sôðape.

Sa'ontšive, UC-AR 11:2, Map 1, 24, E, 2 m.
below last.

The scene of the episode is on the east side of
Mohave Valley, between Needles and Fort Mohave,
more or less opposite the tracts fought over by the
birds in Yellak, 14:34, 70-72.

16D. Bittern and Dove

An unlocalized episode; given again in context but
somewhat differently in 7:86, 91 (UC-AR 11:1, pp. 64,
65), and localized there at the playfield Miakwa'orve,
UC-AR 11:2, Map 1, A, W, at the N end of Mohave
Valley. The episode occurs also in 16G, Sky Rattlesnake; see the section on Additional Shamanistic Data,
paragraph "d." In both 7 and 16G the woman is Kapeta,
Tortoise, instead of Dove; but in 7, Dove appears in
92, immediately following Bittern in 91.

16E. Vinimulye-patše II

Songs recorded from 3 localities in the itinerary.
(1). From beginning of narrative, at Gourd Mountain, Avi-ahnalye, far northwest in Nevada, in Cheme-
huevi-Paiute territory.

(2). From middle of song-cycle, at Avi-ly-kwa'ampa,
UC-AR 11:2, Map 1, H, W, above Needles—a crucial
spot in the events of Vinimulye-patše I.

(3). From end: four mountains far NW in Cheme-
huevi-Las Vegas Paiute territory: Avi-waθa (New York
Mts.), Kómota, Harákaráka, Savetpilye (Charleston Peak).

16F. Nyohaiva Song Repeats

No geography.

16G. Sky Rattlesnake

1. Matavilya at Ha'avulypo, in dark house.

3. [The personages of] Six singings are with him
as he dies there.

4, 5. Gopher sinks into ground to make from his
saliva the wood for burning Matavila's body, and
Amaṭ-kepisara wasp digs a trench for the cremation.

6, 7, 8. Mastamho sends Coyote W to Fire Mt.
(there seems to be no such actual mountain known to
the Mohave). Fly makes fire at Ha'avulypo, and
Aθ'i-maqáyere lights the pyre.

9, 10. Other tribes go off, the Mohave stay at
Ha'avulypo.

11. K-amáy-avé·-te, Sky Rattlesnake, goes S beyond
the Cocopa in delta to a lake—no ocean as yet.

12. Mastamho, to wash away the posts of Matavilya's
burned house, goes N to a four-named place—none of
the names seem to apply to actual places—plunges a
staff and makes the river flow, which follows him as
he walks ahead to (where it becomes) the ocean; then
he returns to Avikwame.

13-16. There he awaits the predicted flood, gathers
four tribes, holds them up out of the water, raises
Avikwame high, builds a house, and announces that he
will teach about curing (shamans).

17-20. He successively sends Quail woman, Quail,
Aθa-kwe'ataye, and Halyto·ṭa Spider to the ocean to
summon Kamayave·te to doctor Matavilya.

21-24. When Kamayave·te comes and puts his head
through the door in the Avikwame house, it is cut off.
The head rolls eastward into the river and in the ocean
transforms into a "snake with legs."

25-28. N of Avikwame, the blood, sweat, fat, glue
fluids of Kamayave·te, which will transform into Rattlesnake, Scorpion, Black-widow Spider, and Termite,
talk underground as "eggs," and Mastamho hears them
talk while he teaches the people to dance for certain
other sicknesses. (When the eggs hatch, they are
shamans and sit to the W of the Avikwame house.)

Here the formal myth about Sky Rattlesnake ends,
and what follows is additional shamanistic beliefs known
to certain kinds of shamans but not to the Mohave

generally. These dreamed episodes are indicated by
paragraphs lettered in order.

a. While Mastamho teaches the people at Avikwame
to dance and rattle with right leg and hand, the four
from Sky Rattlesnake's body grow and stand up as
shamans, who rattle and doctor with the left hand.

b. Mastamho leads the people from Avi-kutaparve
(UC-AR 11:2, Map 1, B, W) via Piute Spring (Aha-
kuvilye) and New York Mts. (in desert Chemehuevi
territory) to Double Peak (Avi-hamoka) in the Tehachapi Mts. far WNW. Sky Rattlesnake's offspring also
travel there, but separately, parallel with him.

c. At Double Peak, Mastamho makes a metate for
a woman, Desert Tortoise (Kapeta—men in narrative
19) to grind seeds for the Chemehuevi. "Therefore"
the Chemehuevi eat tortoise, as the Mohave do not.

d. American Bittern (Atsqeuqa) compliments her
looks, she smiles, and they are married (cf. also
16D and 7:91-92).

e. Rattlesnake paints up for war with cloud and
wind; Mastamho sets an enemy border at the Whipple
Mts. (Koskilye); Rattlesnake leads a foray, and returns
(to Tehachapi) with two scalps; but, if Avi-hamoka
Mountain assents, a person bitten by him dies, and
his shadow stays with Rattlesnake.

f, g. Buzzard takes one of the scalps; the insect
Kamay-hwekatš-hwunitšve and Rattlesnake transform
here; the scalps turn to rock and are kept at Avi-
hamoka.

h. Black-widow Spider may kill men only with
consent of a rattlesnake chief (sic) at Lyehuta, N of
Avikwame, an otherwise unidentified place. If Spider
tries to kill without permission, it is he himself that
dies and his shadow (soul) becomes a cloud ball that
makes rain.

i. Short Rattlesnake (Ave-hakθara) and Brave-Spider
(Halytoṭa-kwanamí) go off to one side, and have to do
with war, not shamanistic doings.

j. Scorpion, whose sting is not fatal, makes four
underground roads, but when he asks four rattlesnakes
to let him kill people, they remain silent. These four
are Two-Persons at Avi-haly-kwa'ampa (UC-AR 11:2,
Map 1, H, W); Blue-tooth at Kutšuvave (at W end of
"Chemehuevi Mts.," 10-12 m. W of the river—see 16G,
note 50); Ave-kwetšitšukyave in his home "house war
put" (Ava-axwai-tšivauk) at Koskilye in Whipple Mts.,
which mark a tribal boundary as above in e; and then
one in Riverside Mts. (Avi-vataye). So Scorpion returns
to Avi-hamoka.

k-l. Termite, the oldest of those sprung from Sky
Rattlesnake's body, lives in the heart of dead trees,
and also has underground roads. He attacks people with

his "night-body," his underground shadow or soul, which
enters a vein and passes to the heart. He can be prevented from killing by the shaman's blocking his road
with fine earth put on the patient's body.

As stated, paragraphs a-l are not formal narrative
but a mixture of origins, shamans' beliefs, and shamans'
practices.

ITINERARY OF 18, SATUKHOTA

Since this tale has been quite specifically analyzed
for its theme content in the comparison with the Halchidhoma and Diegueño versions, the itinerary here is
restricted as wholly to topography as intelligibility
allows.

A. Birth of Twins

1. Old woman S from Avikwame, stays in cave at
Tšesaha, in foot of Monument Mts. a little upriver
from the mouth of Bill Williams Fork. It is near Ahma-
va-'ahwêre on the river, and the pinnacles or natural
monuments called Avir-qorotat.

2. On the sand bar of the river apparently below
Tšesaha—place of her impregnation.

B. Eagle Pets

3, 5, 10. Twins go to (Avi-)Samakwiδike, mt. SW of
Parker, part or outlier of Riverside Mts., "across
from" Rice (i.e., not facing river). See 1953 Geographic
data, West side, Sumá-koθike.

14. On return come to Savat-kiale (not identified),
Savehê (half mile from Koskîlye, the natural pass inland
behind Whipple Mts.), Hoatše-wamveve ("hail-stones"),
close together. See 18, n. 51.

17. Return to Tšesaha.

C. Hunting and Cane

28-30. Twins go E to get cane for a flute.

31. Pima girls hear it at Aha-kupinye, "Warm Spring"
near Sacaton.

33. Start W (WNW).

37. Reach Black Mountain Wash behind Parker: Avi-
soqwilye hatai; 18, n. 99.

38. Reach Ahmo-ketceθilye, near Movalya, now
Parker Dam site and Headgate; 18, n. 101.

39. Twins come to Ahmo-ketmasava opposite
Moválya; 18, nn. 103, 104. Girls cross.

40. Girls come to Tšesaha.

41b. Girls go home in E.

E. Consequences

42. Twins vainly pursue a deer to Ahtcye-kuθuke
(or Utce-koθūke in 18, 44) W of Phoenix, return to
Tšesaha.

F. Twins Journey East and Die

43. Leave to go E to Pima girls at "Warm Spring."
44. Reach where they went in 18, 42, sleep there.
50, 51. Magically float to girls' house, join them.
52c. Girl's father gets Coyote, Raven, and Setkuwāka as allies, fly to attack the twins.
52e. Father gets Falcon, who kills twins.

G. Mother's Mourning and Departure

53b, 54. Satukhôta headdress turns into yellowhammer at Warm Spring, escapes to Tšesaha, and
mother knows of twins' fate.
63. Mother goes W from house at Tšesaha.
64. Going W, she passes through unidentified Oq'ôq
and Sahamkyêta tribes, reaches and enters ocean, and
lives there at Ocean's Middle.

H. Kuyahumare

65A. At "Warm Spring" younger Pima sister bears
a boy, Kuya-humare.
66a. With a rain flood, he kills everyone at "Warm
Spring" except his mother and her sister.
66b, 66c. He takes them both W to find his grandmother. At Williams Fork mouth, he goes upriver a
bit to opposite Amaṭa, there transforms both women
into Snipes; himself crosses to Amaṭa and Quail Run.
66d. Goes W past Tšesaha, through same tribes
and into ocean, joins her.

GEOGRAPHY OF 19,
TORTOISE

There is so little major action in this narrative
that its synopsis as already given is virtually an
itinerary and need not be repeated here, except to
summarize it briefly. The journey runs from Matavilya's death place at Ha'avúlypo west over Mohave
River to Tehachapi; then it returns, first with a SE
or ESE trend to Amboy in the low part of the Mohave
Desert, then northeastward by Providence Mts. to Mt.
Manchester (Aví-mota) on the confines of Mohave
Valley. Here the course changes to S, along the series
of mountains west of the Colorado River, apparently
to as far S as the pass between Whipple and Turtle
mts., from where it swings left (E) to the river at
Chemehuevi Valley, and then downriver to opposite
Bill Williams Fork mouth. Just above this, the Colo-
rado is crossed, and then the journey goes up Williams
Fork by eight or ten stages (mostly unnamed) to Cloud
Home or Ikwényevá mountain, where the final transformation takes place. The geographical identity of
this mountain is the subject of a separate section of
Part II, B, above.

The few places mentioned in the skeletonized version Tortoise II agree, except that this narrative begins
at Avikwame instead of Ha'avulypo. From there, Tortoise travels W into the desert. When he returned, it
was to part of Mt. Manchester, a saw-edge crest called
Tšarreyo. From there he traveled to "Dice-play,"
Hotah-kunuve, which is in the (Sacramento) mountains
W of Needles known also from Mastamho (Otahvek-
hunuve; 7:92) and Chuhueche (13:45) and which lies in
the vicinity of the places mentioned in 30 of Version
I. Thence E (and S) to Ikwé-nye-vá, which however in
version II was identified with the Gila drainage mountain of that name instead of the one on Bill Williams
Fork as in Version I.

APPENDIX I: SUMMARY FACTS ON THE MYTH CORPUS

For the reader's convenience of reference, in a large and somewhat shifting field, I append, in Table 9, a concise conspectus of all narratives presented in this volume, which may serve both as orientation and as a sort of index.

This table refers to the 19 main narratives collected, plus fragments or variants, indicated by the letters A, B, etc. or roman numeral II or repetitions of the title. The eleven columns respectively show the following:

1. Number assigned the narrative in print.

2. Its customary name.

3. Name of the narrator, with his clan affiliation (simulye) if known. All the informants are now dead. There was only one woman among them, and she, though old enough to know the stories, was confused; the Mohave men present at her telling protested that her stories were no way to dream. Of the major informants, Blue Bird and Eagle Sell were the youngest, and they had entered middle age. Perhaps the oldest and certainly the frailest was blind Inyókuta-vére—Vanished-pursue, it would mean in English, I was told—who was dead on my return a year later.

4. The interpreters: JJ for Jack Jones, clan Owitš, one of whose native names was Kwatníalk, which denotes one of the racer snakes; LW, Leslie Wilbur, clan Malyihka, who had been to Indian school; and RM, Robert Martin at Parker, also once a schoolboy and in 1953-1954 busdriver for the school below Parker. He was the only half-breed in both lists, a fact he volunteered to me, though I should have taken him for a full-blood (See plate 8,c).

5. The year of dictation.

6. The place of dictation. N denotes Needles or vicinity; FM, Fort Mohave; P, Parker; SF, San Francisco, where (at the Affiliated Colleges, now University Medical Center) the University's Museum of Anthropology was situated from 1903 to 1931, and where we had facilities for visiting Indians to stay.

7. Number of "stations" mentioned by the narrator in his tale, each station usually marked by a group of songs on one theme. Usually also each such group is assigned to a named locality, but sometimes several groups on several related themes are sung at the same spot. At the beginning and end of a song cycle or recital, there may be passages of narrative unassociated with songs; but even these the narrator usually marked

as "stations" by making a pause. In the text, stations are indicated by numbered paragraphs.

8. The total number of songs specified by the narrator. The total was reached by adding up the numbers mentioned by him at the end of each paragraph-station. Mostly he did not know what total he had reached at any point, or at the end.

9. The protagonist, hero or heroes, or personage whom the tale is about. It will be seen that in fully half the formal narratives of length, there are two brothers who are cooperative throughout, or become rivals, or war from the beginning of the narrative. The younger is usually superior. If the brothers are destroyed, it is the younger who leaves a hero son. There is one narrative about brother and sister, which ends in incest—though this is very unobtrusively presented. In addition to the avenging son in Cane, Chuhueche, and Satukhota, we have two instances of slow dying and of a successor: Matavilya followed by the great Mastamho, and Goose by Grebe. (There is a latent connection between the two pairs in the unsuccessful denial and revolt from Mastamho by Grebe and in Yellak II by Goose.) Another possible line-up however is of Matavilya-Mastamho with the prevalent elder-younger brother heroes, if we construe Mastamho as younger brother instead of son of Matavilya, for which there is warrant in most origin myths of other Yuman tribes, even though Mastamho bears an unrelated name there. It is possible that the Father-Son relation of the pair is a confused adaptation to rumbles of Christianity that had reached the Mohave. Sixty years ago they equated Mastamho with Christ, and it was God who had died, when they spoke English.

It is curious that I do not recall having ever heard any of the paired Mohave heroes spoken of as twins, though twins enjoyed a special and favored position in native life.

Apart from the pallid sister in Tumanpa, there is only one woman protagonist, Nyóhaiva, and she as an inciter of war and victory celebrator!

Animal personages are throughout viewed as human during the narratives. They transform only at the end, often after indecision, trial and error, and effort.

10. Place of beginning of each story. This is most often at Ha'avulypo or Avikwame—Eldorado Canyon and Newberry Mountain, both just west of the river and

TABLE 9

Conspectus and Index of Narratives

(1) No.	(2) Name	(3) Narrator (Clan)	(4) Interpr.	(5) Time	(6) Place	(7) Stations	(8) Songs	(9) Protagonists	(10) Begin at:	(11) End at:
1	Cane (cf. 17)	Bluebird (Hipa)	JJ	1904	N	104	182	2 rival brs, 1 son	Avikwame	Mekoaṭa, river rock
2	Vinimulye-patše	Black Anus (Maha)	JJ	1904	FM	29	200	Warring brs	Mohave Vall.	Providence Mts.
3	Nyôhaiva	Eagle Sell (Nyo'iltše)	JJ	1905	SF	36	110	f. warrior (insect)	Mohave Vall.	Below Parker
4	Raven	Pamitš (Nyo'iltše)	JJ	1903	N	32	186	2 brs	Ha'avulypo	Ha'avulypo
5	Deer	Yellow Thigh (Kaṭa)	JJ	1903	N	26	90	2 brs	Hatekulye-nyikuya	Walapai land
6A	"Coyote"	f. Mahtšitnyumêve (Maha)	JJ	1903	N	?	?	Patša-karrawa	Grease Mt., Gila	Tehachapi
6B	"Coyote"	f. Mahtšitnyumêve (Maha)	JJ	1903	N	?	?	Kwayú, Crayfish	Needles Peaks	Sea to S
C-H	"Coyote"	f. Mahtšitnyumêve, and JJ	JJ	1903	N	....	....	Coyote	Unlocalized	
7	Mastamhô	Baby Head (Hoálya)	JJ	1903	SF	(102)	....	Mastamhó	Ha'avulypo	Avikw., Hokusave
8	"Epic"	Inyôkutavére (Nyo'iltše)	JJ	1902	opp. N	(197+)	....	Hipáhipa	Mohave V to desert	N. of Moh. V?—unfinish.
9	Origins	NYavarúp	JJ	1902	N	(50)	....	Matav., Mast.	Ha'avulypo	not recorded
10	First Berdache	NYavarúp	JJ	1902	N	?	in rite	Mastamhô	Avikwame	Avikwame
11	Tumanpa Short	Falcon Grazes (Nyo'iltše)	JJ	1908	SF	55	123	Br, Sis	Ha'avulypo	"Sister marry," Ariz.
	Tumanpa Vanyumé	Wm. Mellen (Musa)	LW	1908	N	....	....	2 brs (ex 4)	Ha'avulypo	Boundary Cone, Moh. V
12	Salt	Falcon Grazes	JJ	1908	SF	25	117		Ha'avulypo	Salt desert opp. Parker
13	Chuhueche	Falcon Grazes	JJ	1908	SF	85	169	2 brs, 1 son (insects)	Ha'avulypo	Kofa Mt., S Ariz.
14	Yellak: Goose	Eagle Sell	JJ	1905	SF	82(65)	427	Goose, Grebe	Source of river, N	Hokusave in Moh. V
	Yellak II	Hakwe (Owitš)	LW	1908	N	89(85)	4-500	Goose	Eggs, far N	Hokusave in Moh. V (?)
15	War	Musk Melon	Jim	1903	N	unfin.	....	Mastamhô	"Avikwame"	
16A	Mt. Lion, Jaguar	NYavarúp	JJ	1902	N	....	....	2 brs	Hatekulye-nyikuyá	San Bernardino
B	Coyote and Moon	NYavarúp	JJ	1902	N	....	....	Coyote trickster	Unlocalized	
C	Otúr-kepáye	Baby Head	JJ	1908	SF	....	....	4 birds	In Mohave V	Unfinished
D	Bittern and Doves	Robert Martin	RM	1954	P	....	....	Bittern	Unlocalized	
E	Vinimulye II (cf. 2)	Kutene (Nyo'iltše)	LW	1908	N	....	....	Warring brs	Gourd Mt., Nevada	NY Mts., Charleston Pk
F	Nyôhaiva song repet.	Eagle Sell	LW	1908	N	....	....	as in 3	as in 3	
G	Sky Rattlesnake	Falcon Grazes	JJ	1908	SF	....	....	Sky Rattlesnake	Ha'avulypo	Avikwame: sea to S
17	Cane, repet. of 1	Blue Bird	LW	1908	N	86	....	as in 1	as in 1	
18	Satukhóta	Rattlesnake Dead (Nyo'iltše)	RM	1953	P	78	152	2 brs, 1 son	Parker Dam	Sacaton; W ocean
19	Tortoise	Perry Dean (Moha)	RM	1954	P	76	316	(2) brs, Tortoise	Ha'avulypo	Cloud Home Mt., B W Fk
	Tortoise II	Doctor's Sack (Vimaka)	LW	1908	N	....	....	1 Tortoise	"Avikwame"	Cloud Home Mt., Gila

north of Mohave Valley. If the story is to be connected with ultimate origins, it is usually taken back to Ha'a-vulypo and at least alludes to Matavilya's death. Beginnings at Avikwame occur in the instituting ritual myths 10 and 15, Alyha and Warfare, in the romantic, plot-interested Cane, and perhaps when a narrator was careless. Avikwame visually dominated Mohave Valley, Ha'avulypo is much farther north and lies hidden—and unimpressive—in a small side canyon; by 1900-1910 even most old informants had perhaps never seen it, at any rate did not describe it as if they had. Still farther up, probably not far below Hoover Dam, was Hatekulye-nyikuya, Wolf-Jaguar's Cave, of nos. 5, 16A, and tangential mention in 8, the Epic. Both this and Ha'avulypo were beyond territory settled by the Mohave or habitable to them. Farthest upstream of all is the wholly legendary and unknown source of the river, the "Wet-lying" at which Mastamho plunged his staff, or eggs hatched, in the two versions of 14, Yellak. This is the only narrative that attempts to follow the whole course of the river, from source to sea, and that never strays from the river.

11. Place of ending of story. With few exceptions, this is outside Mohave Valley. The exceptions are: in 7, (9?), 14, 14 II, where Mastamho first transforms the birds and then himself into Bald Eagle at Hokusave, "nose-piercing place," in Mohave Valley some miles north of Needles; and in Vanyumé Tumanpa, 11 II, at Boundary Cone near Oatman within the drainage of Mohave Valley, but well above its habitable portion. There are a few other termination transformations on or near the river, though south of Mohave Valley: in 1, Cane; 3, Nyóhaiva; 12, Salt. But prevalently places of ending lie well outside Mohave land, often at a distance of from 100 to 200 miles. In sunwise circuit from the west, they run thus: San Bernardino, in narrative 16A; Tehachapi, 6A; Providence Mts., 2; New York Mts., 16E; Ha'avulypo, 4; Walapai land, 5; Bill Williams Fork region, 11; "Cloud Home Mt." Artillery Mts. in same region, 19; "Cloud Home Mt." in Gila Region, 19 II; Sacaton 18; Kofa Mt., S. W. Arizona, 13; ocean to S, 6B, 16G; ocean to W, 18.

It is evident why geography cannot be omitted from Mohave myth or dreamed narrative or cycled song without obliterating one of its very dimensions.

APPENDIX II: MOHAVE TEXTS AND SONGS RECORDED

Between 1903 and 1910 I recorded at Needles or in San Francisco, or had recorded for me, on Edison or Columbia paraffin phonograph cylinders, 25 parts of 7 Mohave myths, and some 470 Mohave songs from 20 song cycles, which were stored in the University's Museum of Anthropology.

This would have been a valuable collection if it had not been for deterioration of the cylinders with time. This deterioration ranged from total (by breakage, etc.) to much to considerable. At best there is always an increase of what is now called "surface noise" beyond what went into the original recording.

Of the narrative texts about half could still be transcribed with some profit onto magnetic tapes by Jim Hatch in 1957. About half of these in turn I had written by hand into notebooks from dictation, mostly

by interpreter Jack Jones listening—phrase by phrase —to the phonograph recordings when they were still fresh, in 1908-1910. Unfortunately, the interlinear English is too crude a translation to be satisfactory for grammatical analysis.

Probably a hundred or more of the Mohave songs were transcribed for me by ear into musical notation by a professional musician, W. F. Kretschmer, who with experience became adept at this difficult and wearing task. These notational transcripts are in my possession, and I have analyzed part of them for structure, variation, scale, and the like. Many song series were still known and sung among the Mohave in 1953 and 1954, and presumably survive in 1960.

I list here the basic phonograph cylinders: first narrative texts, then songs.

Narratives: Portions of Myths

Cylinder	Date	Narrator	Myth
*14- 56- 63	1903	Jo Nelson (Baby Head)	Mastamho Myth—57, 58, 59, 60 in notebook 55, pp. 3-35, 47-51, book 62, pp. 57-61
68	1903	Jo Nelson (Baby Head)	Satukhóta Myth fragment
136- 138	1905	Eagle-Sell	Yellak Myth
227- 228	1905	Eagle-Sell	Nyohaiva Myth, end and beginning.—227, 228 in notebook 62, pp. 54-56, 68-70
910- 911	1908	Blue Bird	Cane Myth, end
1554-1555	1910	Achyora Hanyava	Tumanpa Short, beginning and end
1574-1581	1910	Achyora Hanyava	Chuhueche Myth, end

Transcribed also into Writing

Cylinder 57;	notebook 5503-17
58;	5523-35
59;	5547-51
60;	6257-61
227;	6254-56
228;	6268-70

Cylinder	Date	Narrator	Songs
14- 64	1903	Jo Nelson (Baby Head)	Four rattle beats of singings
65	1903	Jo Nelson (Baby Head)	Hacha
66	1903	Jo Nelson (Baby Head)	Chutāha
68	1903	Jo Nelson (Baby Head)	Satukhóta song and fragm. myth, Nyohaiva song
69- 71	1903	Jo Nelson (Baby Head)	Alysha
72- 73	1903	Jo Nelson (Baby Head)	Vinimulye-pache
74	1903	Jo Nelson (Baby Head)	Tumanpa
75- 135	1903	Jo Nelson (Baby Head)	[†]Raven, 61 songs, in sequence
139- 225	1905	Eagle-Sell	Yellak, 87 songs in sequence
226	1905	Eagle-Sell	Yellak as sung by Hakwe—cf. 959-974
228- 269	1905	Eagle-Sell	Nyohaiva, 42 songs in sequence (230 same as 68)
769- 909	1908	Blue Bird	Cane, 141 songs in sequence
912- 923	1908	Guy Howard	Chiyere (Birds), selections
924- 933	1908	Bill Mellen	Tumanpa Vauyumé, selections
934- 945	1908	Doctor Sack	Tortoise, selections
946- 958	1908	Kuteve	Vinimulye-pache, selections
959- 974	1908	Hakwe	Yellak, selections—cf. 226
975- 991	1908	Eagle-Sell	[‡]Yellak, 16 songs, repeats of specific songs in 228-269
994	1908	Guy Howard	On flageolet, courting tune at night
**1126-1137	1908	Doctor Sack's half-brother	Salt, selection—cf. 1558-61
**1138-1149	1908	Atsyeq	Frog, selections
**1150-1161	1908	Kunalye(-a'auve)	Deer, selections
**1162-1173	1908	Kupahwai, died 1910	Ohwere, selections
**1174-1185	1908	Kunalye(-a'auve)	Alysha, selections (cf. 70-71)
**1186-1197	1908	Achyora Hanyava	Chuhueche selections (three are same as 1562/65/71)
**1198-1209	1908	Achyora Hanyava	Tumanpa Short selection
1542-1553	1910	Achyora Hanyava	Tumanpa Short selection
1556-1557	1910	Achyora Hanyava	Shaman's curing songs for Rattlesnake and Spider
1558-1561	1910	Achyora Hanyava	Salt, selection—cf. 1126-37
1562-1573	1910	Achyora Hanyava	Chuhueche, selection

*Prefix 14- denotes phonograph cylinders.
[†]Raven songs by Jo Nelson, printed Raven tale 4:1-32 by Pa-mitš.
[‡]986-991 repeats of 230, 231, 245, 259, 261, 263.
**Recorded by Leslie Wilbur at Needles; all others by Kroeber.

APPENDIX III: MOHAVE DIRECTIONAL CIRCUITS

In 1948 (UC-AR 11:1, p. 69), I discussed Mohave directional circuits as they appeared in formal narrative. I then cited nine cases from tales 1-7; these are repeated in the following tabulation (Table 10) along with fifteen further instances from tales 9-18. The conclusions reached in 1948 are confirmed by the additional material. Four is the significant number in the culture, and naturally is frequently associated with cardinal directions. The directions are also most often named in a continuous circuit. When a noncircuit order is followed, if this shows pairing into N-S and E-W, it is probably owing to American influence on the interpreter while speaking English. But when one such pair occupies middle position among four directions, the sequence is neither typically American nor typically Mohave, and can be accepted at face value as illustrating Mohave lack of rigor in these matters.

There are about as many cases of sunwise as of counter-sunwise circuit: 11 as against 13. Every cardinal direction, and most in-between ones, begins and again ends circuits. If there is a preference for ending a circuit on south, so that final action most often is southward, that is not for any mystic reason or symbolic preference, but because Mohave actual life was oriented that way: houses had doors opening to the south, most itineraries move downriver, first origins were in the north but souls went south, and so on. Two of the 24 circuits are semicircles only; five of the 24 cases deal wholly with intermediates like NW instead of primary directions. Four colors are mentioned four times, but the hues are different and their order is different each time; once there are no directions mentioned, once the colors are only implied by blood, saliva, etc. It is clear that the Mohave are not ritualists, certainly not rigorous ones. They keep within the confines of a pattern, but freely improvise _ad hoc_ combinations and omissions within it.

Here, as a sample, is the count of frequency of full circuit ending:

S 8; SW 2; W 5; NW 1; N 3; NE 0; E 2; SE 1.

TABLE 10

Directional Circuits

Tale	Cit.	Note	Direction	Begin	End	Reference and Association
Cane	1:81	71	Counter	N	E	Dives to change appearance
Nyohaiva	3:34	65	Counter	S	W	Creates wand magically
Raven	4:4	10	Sunwise	W	S	Creates gourd
Raven	4:30	27	Counter	E	S	Walk before transforming
Deer	5:5	13	Counter	W	N	Look about
Deer	5:22	39	Sunwise	W	S	4 actual mountains
Mastamho	7:37	58	Sunwise	SW	SE	4 kinds of seeds planted
Mastamho	7:75	105	Counter	N	S	Half circuit, withdrawal
Mastamho	7:85	127	Sunwise	N	W	Dancers' lines face
Origins	9:3	17	Counter	E	S	Matavilya sick, lies. —E pain, N blood, W saliva froth, S sweat
Origins	9:42	87	Counter	SW	(NW)	Corners of pyre lit
Origins	9:45	90	Sunwise	NW	SE	Half circuit, desert tribes sent off
Origins	9:47	.....	Sunwise	W	S	Planning to plant
Origins	9:47	93	Sunwise	NW	SW	Men given planted food
Origins	9:50	111	Sunwise	W	S	Lies down to transform
Alyhá	10:1-3	1,4	Counter	SE	SW	Order of mention of 4 women
Salt	12:10	21	Counter	E	S	Tears > salt: red, black, white, earthy
Salt	12:14	27	Counter	N	E	Worms on tobacco: whitish, blue, black, yellow
Chuhueche	13:9	12	Counter	S	W	Throws soil
Chuhueche	13:15	22	....	...	...	Mt. sheep colors: black, yellow, white, domestic
Yellak	14:66	3	Counter	W	N	4 steps in direction
War	15:3	5	Sunwise	N	W	Lift Matavilya's body
Sky Rattl.	16G:5	33	Sunwise	W	S	Wasp throws out soil
Sky Rattl.	16G:10	37	Counter	W	N	Starts to go off
Satukhota	18:61	181	Sunwise	N	W	Mother starts to leave

REFERENCES

Boas, Frans.
    1916.   Tsimshian Mythology. BAE-R 31.
    1935.   Kwakiutl Culture as Reflected in Mythology.
            AFLS-Mem. 28.
Castetter, Edward F., and W. H. Bell.
    1951.   Yuman Indian Agriculture. Albuquerque,
            Univ. N. Mex. Press.
Cushing, F. H.
    1936.   Outlines of Zuni Creation Myths. BAE-R 13.
Devereux, Georges
    1948.   Mohave Coyote Tales. JAFL 61:233-255.
Du Bois, Constance Goddard.
    1904.   The Story of the Chaup: a Myth of the
            Diegueños. JAFL 17:217-242.
Kelly, Isabel T.
    1934a.   Southern Paiute Bands. AA 36:548-560.
    1934b.   MS., cited in Kroeber, 1959, p. 308.
Kniffen, F., et al.
    1935.   Walapai Ethnography. AAA-Mem. 42
            (A. L. Kroeber, ed.).
Kroeber, A. L.
    1906.   Two Myths of the Mission Indians. JAFL
            19:309-321.
    1907.   Shoshonean Dialects of California. UC-PAAE
            4:(no. 3):65-105.
    1908.   Origin Tradition of the Chemehuevi. JAFL
            21:240-242.

    1925.   Handbook of the Indians of California.
            BAE-Bull. 78 (pp. i-xviii, 1-995, of which
            ch. 50, 51, pp. 726-780, deal with the
            Mohave). A replica edition with identical
            paging and illustrations was issued in 1953
            at Berkeley by the California Book Co.
    1943.   Classification of the Yuman Languages.
            UC-P Linguistics, 1:21-40.
    1948.   Seven Mohave Myths. UC-AR 11:(no. 1): 1-70.
    1951a.   A Mohave Historical Epic. UC-AR 11:(no.2):
            71-176
    1951b.   Olive Oatman's Return. Pp. 1-18 of Kroeber
            Anthropological Society, no. 4.
    1957.   Ethnographic Interpretations 7-11. UC-PAAE
            47:2, pp. 191-234; 47:3, pp. 235-310.
Möllhausen, B.
    1861.   Reisen in die Felsengebirge Nord-Amerikas.
            2 vols. Leipzig.
Spier, Leslie.
    1933.   Yuman Tribes of the Gila River. Chicago.
    1946.   Comparative Vocabularies and Parallel
            Texts in Two Yuman Languages of Arizona.
            Univ. N. Mex. Publ. in Anthr. no. 2.
Von Valkenburgh, R. F., and M. Farmer
    1934.   MS., cited in Kroeber, 1959, p. 309.

PLATES

PLATE 1

a. Avikwame, Newberry (or Dead) Mt., Nevada, north of Mohave Valley, as seen from Davis Dam. It is the pivotal point in Mohave dream and myth.

b. Avikwame, Newberry Mt., as it dominates Mohave Valley on the north. The view is from Arizona, opposite Needles.

c. Boundary Cone, Arizona, northeast of Needles.

d. Mouth of Eldorado Canyon into Colorado River, between Davis and Hoover dams, in Nevada.

e. Ha'avulypo, "housepost water," where the first god Matavilya sickened and died, in Eldorado Canyon. The erosion pinnacles are the houseposts that remained after the first house was burned and washed out. In the background is the Black Mountains range across the Colorado.

a

b

c

d

e

PLATE 2

a. The cremation pyre has just been lit for a kinsman.

b. Mohave women wailing around a dying kinsman on his cremation bier. Several of the outer shawls or capes are of the 4-bandanas type.

c, d. Mexican style houses of wattle and mud in the outskirts of Needles, probably about 1900-1905. The shade porches and windbreaks are old Mohave. The litter and disorder are typical of the period, but probably greater than in native times, through accumulation of white man's utensils and castoffs. Costumes of both men and women are characteristic of the period.

a

b

c

d

PLATE 3

a-c. Three interior views of a Mohave house, showing two center posts, rafters, low side walls (sitting height only), arrow-weed thatch and walls (covered by a heavy layer of sand), soft sand floor, and absence of furniture (a, apparently photographed from the east wall looking southwest; b, photographed from southwest corner; c, photographed from southeast corner).

a

b

c

PLATE 4

Mohave Indians from a lithographed drawing by R. H. Kern. The woman carries a Chemehuevi-made basket on her head—the usual mode of transport. The men are finger-painted in white cross stripes. One carries a bundle of tule rushes; the other stands with one foot against his other knee, leaning on his bow.

PLATE 5

a. All dressed up—hair washed, face painted, a hundred feet of white Venetian beads around throat, shoulder cape of blue and white bead lacework and fringe, holding bead necklaces for sale to tourists. Both the skirt and the ground-length cape are of calico with appliqué. The latter might also be made of four identical bandanas sewn together. Women's highly stylized face paint designs are shown in Handbook, figs, 61, 62.

b. Ready for Sunday afternoon shinny game. Studio portrait.

c. Typical young Mohave in Sunday best, about 1900-1905—arm garters, silk kerchief-tie, vest, and bandage-belt low on hips. Studio portrait.

a

b

c

PLATE 6

a. Mohave girl, unmarried, clan Musa. Typical hair style and chin tattooing. 1908.

b. An aged Mohave couple, about 1900-1905. She has laid on her head a small baby-carrier, perhaps made to sell to tourists. The pottery bowl and metate behind her are old-style Mohave; so is the windbreak of arrow-weeds. Courtesy of Jeanne E. Wier.

a

b

PLATE 7

a. "Space" or Aspasaham, "Eagle-sell," dreamer, singer, and narrator of myths 3 (Nyóhaiva) and 14 (Yellak: Goose). Intelligent, sensitive, a clear expositor, he spoke little English and was completely Mohave inside, but supported his family by working steadily for the Santa Fe Railroad in the locomotive roundhouse or ice plant at Needles. Studio photograph, probably shortly before 1905.

b. Mother of Jack Jones, a typical Mohave crone.

c. Jack Jones, first interpreter, showing his casual, humorous attitude and temperament. A close-up of his face appears in the frontispiece of UC-AR 11:1. He lived relaxedly in both American and Mohave cultures: had helped kill a witch-shaman, lost three wives in one day, did not receive schooling, but as an adult learned his letters by listening in from the rear of a first-grade classroom.

a

b

c

PLATE 8

a. Aspam, half Chemehuevi, half Mohave. 1908.

b. Leslie Wilbur, interpreter of myths Yellak II, Cane II, and collector of phonograph records. He had had schooling at Fort Mohave. 1908.

c. Robert Martin, interpreter in 1953-1954.

d. Ave-puya, "Dead Rattlesnake," narrator of Satukhota in 1953.

e. Perry Dean, narrator of myth 19 on Tortoise.

a

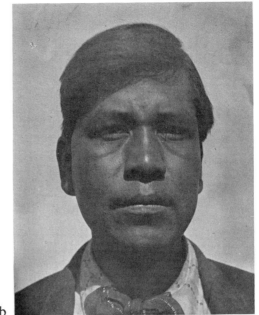

b

c

d

e

PLATE 9

a. Robert Martin, Kroeber, and Ave-puya. 1953.
b. Robert Martin, Kroeber, and Perry Dean. 1957.

a

b